The Drama of Dissent

The Drama of Dissent

THE RADICAL POETICS OF NONCONFORMITY, 1380–1590

RITCHIE D. KENDALL

THE UNIVERSITY OF NORTH CAROLINA PRESS

CHAPEL HILL AND LONDON

© 1986 The University of North Carolina Press

Manufactured in the United States of America

Library of Congress Cataloging-in-Publication Data

Kendall, Ritchie D.

  The drama of dissent.

  (Studies in religion)

  Bibliography: p.

  Includes index.

  1. English literature—Puritan authors—History and
criticism. 2. Puritans—England. 3. Lollards.
4. English literature—Early modern, 1500–1700—History
and criticism. 5. English literature—Middle English,
1100–1500—History and criticism. 6. Radicalism in
literature. 7. Dissenters, Religious—England.
I. Title. II. Series: Studies in religion (Chapel Hill,
N.C.)

PR120.P87K46   1986   822'.2'09   86-1289
ISBN 0-8078-1700-7

For Mary

Contents

Acknowledgments   ix

Prologue   3

1. The Lollards: The Unmasking of Mystery   14

2. The Lollards: Displaced Drama   50

3. John Bale: The Cloistered Imagination   90

4. Thomas Cartwright: The Drama of Disputation   132

5. Martin Marprelate: Syllogistic Laughter   173

Epilogue   213

Notes   217

Bibliography   263

Index   275

Acknowledgments

With a book as long in the making as this one, the list of creditors is necessarily long as well. At Harvard, Alan Heimert first taught me to respect the intellectual and spiritual complexity of the Puritans. Enthusiastic teachers and loyal friends, David Staines and Larry Benson encouraged my early work in medieval studies; Morton Bloomfield freely shared his great learning and kindness in guiding the first versions of my study of the Lollards. Special thanks belong to Herschel Baker. For six years, by precept and example, he demonstrated that rigorous scholarship and a graceful style are not incompatible. Whatever success I have achieved on either score is surely owed to him. My gratitude also extends to Andrew Delbanco whose good humor and passion for ideas sustained me through my graduate days.

While at Chapel Hill, I have been particularly fortunate to be surrounded by energetic and generous colleagues who have given me more than my fair share of support. Darryl Gless, Peter Kaufman, and Alan Dessen have been careful readers of more than one draft of this book, and James Thompson was a patient listener and an even more patient instructor in the mysteries of word processing.

This project has taken me to a number of libraries to whose staffs I am indebted. They include the Houghton Library, the Folger Shakespeare Library, the Bodleian Library, the British Library, and Dr. Williams's Library. The last three libraries have graciously permitted me to reproduce here a number of passages from manuscripts in their collections.

My most forgiving creditor is acknowledged in the dedication.

The Drama of Dissent

Prologue

This is a study of the aesthetic convictions of a diverse group of religious dissenters active in England between 1380 and 1590. Interest in the complex commerce between theological belief and literary practice in the late Middle Ages and Renaissance has burgeoned in recent years. Among its most accomplished products has been the series of complementary books beginning with Barbara K. Lewalski's *Protestant Poetics and the Seventeenth-Century Lyric* and quickly followed by John N. King's *English Reformation Literature: The Tudor Origins of the Protestant Tradition* and Janel Mueller's *The Native Tongue and the Word: Developments in English Prose Style, 1380–1580.*[1] Each of these works noticeably distances itself from earlier attempts to plot the intersection of spirituality and aesthetics by eschewing the time-honored practice of unearthing discrete religious meanings buried beneath and utterly contrary to apparently profane textual surfaces. While still insisting on a significant theological component in the production of secular as well as sacred literature, they do so by tracing with care nativist and continental literary ideas born of the Protestant devotion to scripture. At the outset of their undertakings, each argues for the existence of a consensus among Protestant and what might be called proto-Protestant thinkers sufficient to speak of *a* Protestant poetics.[2]

The argument for a consensus among reformers is itself grounded in Patrick Collinson's continuing reexamination of the rancorous ecclesiastical contentions that plagued Tudor England.[3] The efforts to establish a phylogeny and taxonomy of religious belief in this period have proved almost as divisive as the theological conflicts that they help document. In the last decade that controversy has increasingly centered on ascertaining the extent of divergence within the English Protestant movement in the closing decades of the sixteenth century. Under the revisionist assault of Patrick Collinson and his followers, the rigid distinctions once made by John F. H. New and others between establishment Anglicanism and opposition Puritanism have collapsed.[4] The Anglican has virtually lost that name which a later age invented for him and has become instead the Protestant. The Puritan, once ecumenically defined as anyone who sought "to rid life, or some phase of it, of the evils that have enwrapped it" has seen his territory diminished and his title reduced to lowercase.[5] Witness Peter Lake's emphatic act of demotion: *Moderate puritans and the Elizabethan Church*.[6] Observing the derogatory origins of the term "Puritan," the revisionists have encouraged the use of that party's own favored epithet, "the godly."[7]

The work of Collinson and others has purged us of a host of theological and historical absurdities (not least of which is the conviction that Puritans were Calvinists and their Protestant adversaries not).[8] His approach almost without exception has positively shaped critical inquiry into the theological roots of Renaissance aesthetics. Nonetheless, its ready adoption by literary scholars presents its own potential dangers. Neither Collinson nor Lake in rejecting the existence of "a rigidly defined, party-based conflict" seeks to supplant it with a "conflict-free consensus." Lake in particular continues to argue for the Puritan's distinctive worldview predicated on "the insistence on the transformative effect of the word on the attitudes and behavior of all true believers" and manifested in "a constant struggle to externalize his sense of his own election through a campaign of works against Antichrist, the flesh, sin and the world."[9]

Confronted, however, with audiences unaccustomed or unwilling to crack their brains on difficult points of religious disputation, the literary scholar may well be tempted under the aegis of consensus to push theological affinities into identities and dissolve the wars of truth into an unrefined mass of interchangeable positions supposedly testifying to a monolithic Protestant point of view. Perhaps more insidiously the uncritical blurring of distinctions within the Protestant camp encourages the continued privileging by literary scholars of canonical works whose "moderation" makes them readily conformable to contemporary predilections and tastes. Most investigations of cultural change during the English Reformation persist in clustering about the same defining works, which remain appealing precisely because even their spirituality may be construed as being sophisticated—i.e., disinterested and nondoctrinaire. Pursued to excess, the argument for consensus may ultimately prove self-destructive, unwittingly encouraging audiences hostile to theological argument to dismiss the understanding of a diluted "Protestant context" as exterior and extraneous to the period's literature.

To deny the presence among English Protestants of a body of mutually held aesthetic assumptions dependent upon shared doctrinal convictions would be fruitless. Nonetheless, I would suggest that it is both plausible and important to discern within that common inheritance a strain of distinctly radical formulations—the product not only of divergent theological allegiances but of particular psychological, economic, and social pressures as well. To acknowledge and delineate a poetics of dissent is to enhance our appreciation of the wide range of literary issues debated in the period and the tensions inherent in any artist's approach to the problem of valuing and exploiting imaginative experience.

The dissenting tradition here explored is broadly conceived: from itinerant Lollard preachers to Edwardian gospelers to moderate Puritans. The lack of an encompassing label for this assembled company is perhaps daunting but not surprising given that these men and women are not ordinarily recognized as a corporate body. Whether in fact we can speak of an aesthetic common among them all is the burden of this book as a whole. If that burden is not met, if the characteristics ascribed to them do not convincingly define a species, the author might plead that Adam himself would be hard pressed to invent a name for so elusive a beast. As it would be hopelessly awkward to title a book (let alone write it) without a name for this aggregate, I have opted for the nomenclature "nonconformist." The term is not altogether satisfactory. It is laden with highly specific, legal connotations, as, for example, when one speaks of those deprived of their ministries for refusing to wear the garments prescribed by Elizabeth's bishops. What is more, its suggestion of noncompliance sits uncomfortably with the institutional preferments enjoyed by men such as John Bale and John Foxe. Lastly, the term may appear either idiosyncratic or regressive in the light of revisionist history.

Alternative nomenclature is, however, equally deficient. Collinson's "godly" is useful only within the more limited time frame of Tudor history; one may also question whether anything is to be gained by trading a term of ridicule for one of self-approbation. Despite its drawbacks, "nonconformist" does convey some sense of the kind of religious party I describe here. All of these men and women self-consciously viewed themselves as opposition figures—even on those occasions when they unexpectedly found themselves in establishment roles. Nevertheless, they also regarded their dissent as a means of reforming existing institutions, not of ignoring or replacing them. More important, as I hope to show, the element of negation in the term nonconformist is itself suggestive of the complex process of self-definition that characterizes this movement, its pursuit of identity through a ritual combat with an ambivalently regarded nemesis.

If nonconformists did indeed define themselves by negation, the obvious starting point for an examination of their aesthetic principles is the drama. The portrait of the Puritan and his ideological ancestors as implacable enemies of the drama has survived the rewriting of English cultural history with astonishing tenacity. The rehabilitation of the intellectual and spiritual reputation of the Puritan, begun by Perry Miller and furthered by both disciples and critics,[10] has shattered the stereotypical image of the dour Puritan but has left intact our perception of his unrelenting hostility to the theater. Since Elbert N. S. Thompson first documented the development of the Puritan animus toward the stage,[11] the conviction that nonconformity and drama, like oil and water, do not mix has remained largely unchallenged. Even as recent and as sensitive a critic of the literary temper of the English Puritans as Lawrence Sasek merely echoes the judgments of his predecessors when he flatly declares, "Whatever the complexities, ambiguities, and differences of opinion among the puritans with regard to other literary matters, their condemnation of the stage was unequivocal and almost univocal."[12]

The near unanimity of critical opinion is not difficult to fathom once the documents in the case have been assembled. Witnesses for the prosecution (in the stage controversy the nonconformist is invariably arraigned as a criminal) include a series of antitheatrical tracts beginning with John Northbrooke's *Treatise Against Dicing, Dancing, Plays, and Interludes* (c. 1577) and ending with William Prynne's *Histriomastix* (1635). Add to these the testimony to a family history of animosity toward the stage—the fifteenth-century Wycliffite treatise against miracle playing—and the smoking pistol—the closing of the theaters in 1642 by a Puritan-controlled parliament—and a guilty verdict is assured.[13]

That the creations of the stage aroused deep anxieties among the reformers would appear an inescapable conclusion. But if nonconformists, to borrow Stephen Greenblatt's term, "self-fashioned" themselves by battling an ambivalent enemy, where is the contrary strain of attraction amid all this shrilly voiced revulsion?[14] Studies of dissident attitudes to the drama have been consistently weakened by their failure to move beyond the narrow confines of the overtly antitheatrical broadside. The tracts themselves, as William Ringler has persuasively demonstrated, are largely responses to the social institution of the permanent London stage.[15] Virtually silent on the plays performed there, they have little to offer on the nature of theatrical experience itself. The credentials of these witnesses are also dubious. Anne Hudson has challenged the Wycliffite pedigree of the medieval broadside.[16] As for the Tudor and Stuart polemicists, although they are undeniably Puritan in their ethical outlooks, are they Puritan in their theological allegiances? These are for the most part one-issue authors who failed to distinguish themselves in other areas of religious discourse; their status as "experts" ironically disqualifies them as reliable spokesmen for an entire movement's response to the theater.

Even were the defense forbidden to present its own evidence, compelled instead to argue solely from the hostile testimony already marshaled, the case for ambivalence might still be made. Consider the generic shape of the antitheatrical tracts. If these men and women were "unequivocal and almost univocal" in their condemnation of the stage, how is it that each of the antitheatrical treatises is itself dramatic in form? The arguments of *A Tretise of Miraclis Pleyinge* climax in a debate between the author and an imagined detractor.[17] Northbrooke's nineteenth-century editor noted quizzically that "it is singular that, while condemning every thing like plays, he conveys his arguments in a dramatic form—a dialogue between Youth and Age."[18] Phillip Stubbes's *Anatomy of Abuses* is also "made Dialoguewise," and Stephen Gosson assails the theater in "five actions." William Prynne's *Histriomastix* similarly mimics the genre it ridicules.

Those critics who have conceded the dramatic shape of the tracts have responded with either perplexity or indifference. David Leverenz, the most perceptive student of the stage controversy, finds in Prynne's theatricality "no more conscious motive than to beard the lion in its den."[19]

Such not implausible explanations—that the Puritan with both malice and mischief contrived to hoist the theater with its own petard—lose credence when the scholar moves beyond the antitheatrical broadside into the main body of nonconformist written expression. There, in the doctrinal, disputational, pastoral, and literary documents of the movement, the radical reformer reveals himself not as a single-minded enemy of the drama but as its troubled lover. Although the reformers tended to excoriate representational drama, they nonetheless labored tirelessly to transform their own world of letters into a theater of the soul. Repeatedly in the nonconformist canon, the reader encounters the products of an inherently theatrical imagination. Dialogues, dramatic satires, saints' lives, animadversions, and fictionalized records of prelatical examinations—all are attempts to dramatize the soul's awakening to its idealized self through a ritualistic encounter with its spiritual adversaries.[20] For all its theatricality, however, the agon between the sanctified mind and the reprobate multitude rarely leads to the generation of pure drama. The works of the nonconformist spirit almost invariably stop short of the stage, each failing to make the final leap from the merely dramatic to the drama itself. The drama is instead at once diluted and displaced.

The drama was more than an isolated source of agitation to the radical reformer, more than a persistently annoying burr. Drama touched the raw nerve of nonconformity. As the quintessential embodiment of the freedom of the creative imagination, it confronted the reformer with both an emblem of the debased aesthetic of orthodoxy and a dark, threatening mirror of the dangers of his own. His sharply divided responses to the stage helped crystallize his attitudes toward aesthetic experience as a whole. The poetics of radical dissent are steeped in ambivalent theatricality. Although the drama is both my point of departure and my continuing touchstone, this book is not, strictly speaking, either a history of the nonconformist assault on the theater or an extended appreciation of nonconformist plays. It is rather an attempt to understand the genesis, articulation, and practice of a poetics grounded in ritual patterns of self-dramatization. At times the nonconformist theater of the soul does wear the more familiar faces of the English stage: the drama born of the liturgy and festivals of the medieval church, the drama engendered in the rhetorical methods of the schools, the drama adapted from classical and Renaissance Italy. Yet in the bulk of its manifestations, it is as self-consciously other in form as it is in origin and rationale.[21]

To complete my own rite of self-definition by negation, I would like to position this work vis-à-vis several areas of current scholarly inquiry that intersect with my own concerns and views. The first of these might best be represented by Jonas Barish's *The Antitheatrical Prejudice* and two works that to a degree share its perspective: Russell Fraser's *The War against Poetry* and Richard Lanham's *The Motives of Eloquence*.[22] Barish's and Fraser's books are overtly preoccupied with exploring the Puritan animus to the theater in particular and to the imagination in general. Lanham's work implicitly does the same. All three employ remarkably similar strategies: they conquer by dividing, each critic herding mankind into two warring camps. For Lanham there are serious men and rhetorical men; Fraser deploys proponents of "Naked Truth" and guardians of "Poetic Ambiguity"; and Barish matches "Syndrome A" against "Syndrome B," Stoic-Christian ideals of constancy clashing with the protean playfulness of Italian humanism.

Whatever banners they may affix to these opposing factions, all three, of course, are playing variations of the Plato-Aristotle game and are frank in admitting so. Barish, Fraser, and Lanham are equally candid in declaring their allegiances. Without exception, each endorses the vision of fluidity and vilifies that of fixity. And the game is unusually well played, I think, particularly by Barish and Lanham, who produce that sense of clarity and distinction that illuminates and thrills the mind. Yet all three works are troubling—troubling because they ultimately embody the very spirit they arraign. They are works of the Puritan mind, at least as they themselves define it. Puritan in that they divide the world into sheep and goats (Fraser with no apparent irony labels his enemies "the great simplifiers");[23]

Puritan in that they seek to define man in his essence rather than his particularity; Puritan in that they are "serious," indeed obsessive, in their attempts to declare and fix a knowable truth.

Paradoxically these works are Puritan in a deeper, psychological sense as well. The Puritans and their ancestors attacked in the drama those things which they feared and loathed within themselves. The assault on a well-defined, external enemy was, for the nonconformist, a rite of self-exorcism. In assailing the Puritan, each critic is likewise defining and ultimately idealizing himself through public combat.[24] The Puritan becomes the receptacle for all that the critic tends to deprecate within himself: fastidiousness, rigidity, naïve idealism, dull earnestness, the inability or unwillingness to negotiate quotidian and mundane obstacles. The caricature of the professor is disturbingly close in line and shadow to that of the maligned Puritan. The scholar then needs the Puritan in much the same way that the Puritan needed the drama. And, as with the Puritan, the exorcist's charm requires exaggeration. To say so is not to vitiate the considerable achievements of Fraser, Lanham, and Barish but to qualify some of their insights and to warn the reader of the attitudes and circumstances that nurture them. To say so may also incidentally explain why the stereotype of the drama-hating Puritan has so successfully resisted modification.

References to the displacement of ambivalence and to the institutional determinants of scholarship betray certain Freudian and Marxist colorings in my work as well as my debt to at least two significant students (one recent and one perennial) of the Puritan ethos, David Leverenz and Christopher Hill. Leverenz's splendid *The Language of Puritan Feeling* was published just as I was completing the dissertation from which this study grew.[25] As my notes will make clear, we share much in our views of the Puritans. While I have no quarrel with Leverenz's satisfying examination of the Puritan consciousness, I find it difficult to endorse his attribution of its features to certain distinctly historical and regional patterns of child-rearing in sixteenth- and seventeenth-century England and America. If such is the case, why do we find a similar psychology of aesthetics among fourteenth-century Lollards? The same doubts tend to qualify my considerable admiration for the Marxist analyses of historians such as

Christopher Hill and Michael Walzer.[26] In their attempts to trace Puritan and Lollard thought to newly emerging modes of capitalist production, they are forced to invent an ever-receding horizon of preindustrial revolutions, banishing their precapital, feudal paradise further and further into the misty past.

A study that blends unequal parts of Renaissance and medieval ingredients with the mixture weighted more heavily toward the former, invariably signals the author's proportionate loyalties and expertise. Although it will perhaps be a weak palliative to medievalists who have justly grown impatient with cultural histories forever stigmatizing their subject matter as mere prolegomenon to better things, I should point out that this study began in a seminar in Middle English readings and takes its primary direction from those readings. Scholarly ontogeny aside, forging links between early and late materials often invokes the less laudatory meanings of "to forge." One feels a strong temptation to play the Malvolian critic and "to crush this a little," to force a conjunction between Lollard and Puritan ideologies. The specter of the martyrologist John Foxe haunts all such efforts, reminding us how great knowledge and exertion accompanied by even greater partisan zeal can lead to both the conscious and unconscious misuse of sources.[27] Although I have attempted to be always cognizant of that dangerous impulse, and have perhaps overreacted with paroxysms of citation and qualification, distortions remain in my treatment of the Lollards—both in terms of the perceived unity within the party itself and between that party and later reformers. As in all such broadly based studies, the author can only hope that his reader deems that the rewards outweigh the occasional transgression.

Having chosen to make my argument from a group of representative men, it remains to justify those specifically singled out for study. As in so much medieval literature, Lollard writings produce few names or distinct personalities. Although an earlier generation of antiquarians attributed the bulk of Lollard prose in English to John Wyclif, more recent scholarship typically discredits the association, assigning these works instead to various university-trained disciples or less educated itinerant preachers. Necessarily then, the first two chapters constitute a group portrait. The materials discussed were selected in large part because of their accessibility: the full range of Lollard vernacular prose and poetry available in printed sources and a select body of manuscript material in the Bodleian and British Libraries. The latter choices were limited by the duration of an NEH grant and often guided by the bibliographic work of Anne Hudson. The investigation of Lollard thought was also narrowed by a decision to restrict the study to vernacular works. The Lollard spirit is in great measure defined by its quest not only for a vernacular Bible but also for a universal debate of religious issues. The translation of that debate from the Latin of the university scholar to the native tongue of the artisan marks the beginning of the long nonconformist assault on the barriers between "lerned" and "lewed."

The selection of John Bale as a spokesman for the radical reformers of the early Tudor period is problematical. William Tyndale was the more original and influential theologian; John Foxe was the more accomplished propagandist; but Bale remains a fascinating and suggestive figure.[28] His life spanned the reigns of all five Tudor monarchs, and his historical interests led him to explore the connections of doctrine and temperament between the reformers of his own day and those of the Lollard period. As a writer, his efforts are multifarious, encompassing everything from biblical commentary to abusive, doggerel verse. Above all, his willingness to write for the stage, while harboring much the same doubts about dramatic representation found among other medieval and Renaissance nonconformists, marks him as an attractive subject for a study of radical poetics. To compensate for Bale's relative obscurity, I have attempted to trace, both in the text and the notes, some of Bale's debts to the theology of Tyndale and the literary and historiographical legacy he bequeathed to Foxe.

The choice of Thomas Cartwright and Martin Marprelate as representative voices of Elizabethan Puritan sentiment is more conventional. Cartwright has always been regarded as the most respected and prominent of the late Tudor reformers. As for Martin Marprelate, twentieth-century critics have now added to his long-standing notoriety the title of the greatest of Puritan artists before Milton and Bunyan. Neither achievement nor fame, however, fully accounts for the place these two reformers must occupy in a study of radical poetics. Although to a modern reader nothing may seem less similar than the turgid disputational prose of Cartwright and the madcap satire of Marprelate, Elizabethan contemporaries regularly linked their work. The tense and unhappy relationship between these two disparate personalities will, in fact, prove crucial to an understanding of the complexity and contradiction that distinguish the dissident aesthetic—and of the uneasy balance it attempts to strike between the playful and the serious, the gamesome and the earnest, the dramatic and the nondramatic.

CHAPTER ONE

The Lollards

THE UNMASKING

OF MYSTERY

In the same year, near the close of the fourteenth century, the life histories of two Lollard worthies abruptly end. William Swinderby had once been a hermit and before that a self-proclaimed scourge of feminine wantonness; now, in 1391, he was an itinerant preacher of Wycliffite heresy and in trouble with the bishop of Hereford. Weighing the uncertainties of exile against the glories of martyrdom, he chose the former and fled to the Welsh hinterland never to be heard from again.[1] Sir John Clanvowe's exit was more emphatic. Courtier, poet, and acquaintance of Chaucer, Clanvowe died as a Crusader, on campaign against the Infidel near Constantinople.[2] It is difficult to imagine two more unlikely comrades in spiritual arms than Swinderby and Clanvowe. The geographical distance separating their fates was surely no wider than the gulf of class, education, and doctrine that lay between them. Contemporary chroniclers, nonetheless, arraigned both as Lollards. Smelling a Lollard in the wind was not always a precise art, even when practiced by inquisitors more experienced than Harry Bailly; religious eccentricity of almost any breed was liable to incur that generic term of disapprobation. In the cases of Swinderby and Clanvowe, however, modern scholars have not been inclined to quarrel with the judgment of the past; the theological kinship of hermit and knight has been reaffirmed, a kinship that underscores the wide range of religious experience and doctrine that can legitimately be called Lollard.

As a system of belief Lollardy achieved neither the stability nor the consistency of later dissenting platforms. Even at its fountainhead, the thought of John Wyclif, the channel never ran entirely straight. Wyclif's revolt against Oxford skepticism and his subsequent conversion to an extreme brand of realism prompted an impressive outpouring of tracts and treatises, but few if any of its students would grant the resulting corpus the status of a summa. Wyclif's decisive break with church orthodoxy came in 1380, with his disturbing teachings on the sacrament of the altar. The vehement rejection of transubstantiation cost him his Austin allies at Oxford and eventually his place at the university. Yet it has been argued that even on this momentous matter of the Eucharist, Wyclif never produced a satisfactory formulation.[3]

Placed in the hands of followers, Wycliffite theology was subjected not to refinement but rather to simplification and often distortion.[4] The blame for the gradual degeneration of Wyclif's ideas must rest in part with the master himself. Tact and flexibility were apparently not among Wyclif's natural endowments. Their absence, which had earlier aborted a career in diplomatic service, undermined his position at Oxford and threatened the integrity and survival of his ideology. Undoubtedly aided by Wyclif's intransigence, Archbishop Courtenay completed his triumphant purge of Lollardy from the university in 1382. Once cut loose from its academic moorings, the reform movement was doomed to drift. In an age characterized by burgeoning anti-intellectualism, the preempting of an educated ministry conspired with stirring calls to individual biblical study to produce a multitude of hybrid beliefs.[5] The last cruel blow to the movement's doctrinal coherence was dealt by Sir John Oldcastle's badly bungled uprising of 1414. Having irrevocably linked Lollardy to sedition by his attempt to topple royal as well as papal power, Oldcastle condemned Lollardy to an underground existence.[6] Beyond the debacle of St. Giles Fields, only glimpses of Lollard life and thought may be caught and only then when reigning bishops inclined by temperament or outside pressure drove the dissenters from their secret conventicles into the light of the ecclesiastical courts.[7]

Despite Lollardy's subsidence toward the idiosyncratic and the ill-defined, there is a unity behind its diversity. Anne Hudson, who has done so much to make a critical examination of Lollard literature feasible, has said that its readers will always find "a community of ideas and assumptions between texts of very different types."[8] Investigating bishops sought to define that community systematically by assembling inventories of aberrant positions upon which suspects might be examined.[9] But with the notable exception of Reginald Pecock, whose curiosity proved so unfortunate, the bishops were not interested in understanding Lollardy: they were concerned with eradicating it.[10] To fathom Lollardy's unity we need to progress beyond articles of condemnation and toward an appreciation of the shared conception of the religious life. From its beginnings, nonconformity has been preoccupied with patterns of ethical and spiritual conduct. How must the "known man" live and how is such a man known by the shape of his life?[11] Although they might differ widely on the finer points of predestination or the benefits of sacramental worship, the Lollards did hold a common image of what constituted a life acceptable to the deity. It is in this murky, half-lit world of religious sensibility, rather than in the clear light of doctrinal declarations, that we must search for the complex relations between Lollardy and drama. The Lollards made few direct statements about the drama; as an art form it did not yet present the same conscious, gnawing problem that it would to late Elizabethan and Stuart Puritans.[12] The issues addressed by *A Tretise of Miraclis Pleyinge*, the sole extant Lollard treatment of the stage, are of concern but not central concern.[13] What is central is the degree to which the Lollard sensibility was compatible with the aesthetic and religious principles of contemporary drama and the extent to which the Lollard felt compelled to generate his own theatrical conventions in order to give voice to the drama of his spiritual life. This chapter will be devoted to an exploration of the Lollard way; the next to the aesthetic that emerged from it.

FROM EUCHARIST TO BIBLE

The holi prophete Dauid seith, a Lollard defense of the vernacular Bible, concludes with a rousing call to the study of "the fruit and veri sentence of al the lawe of God." The appeal to the lay reader is couched in a revealing metaphor: "[A]s Crist strecchid forth hise armes and hise hondes to be nailid on the cros, and hise leggis and hise feet also, and bowide doun the heed to schewe what lowe [love] he hadde to mankynde, so alle cristene peple schulde strechyn forth here armes and hondis and alle here menbris to enbrace to hem silf the lawe of God thourg veri bileue and trewe obedience therto, and trewe mayntenaunce therof to here lyues ende."[14] The recreation of Christ's sacrifice in the celebration of the Eucharist had been the most potent ritual of Christian devotion for fourteen hundred years.[15] Although our author, in common with many Lollards, was no scoffer at the Eucharist and its companion sacraments, his language suggests the displacement of one idea of sacrifice with another, the substitution of one way of reconstituting the mystical body of Christ for another.[16] Reading, studying, preaching, and living the Bible was to become, for the early Lollards and succeeding generations of nonconformists, the ritual cornerstone of a reformed church.[17] The suffering of Christ in his passion, the godhead's painful dying to the flesh of this world, elicited from his followers a reciprocal gesture. They, too, were called upon to "strechyn forth here armes and hondis and alle here menbris," to make recalcitrant flesh embrace in understanding, will, and affection the transcendent truth of Christ as embodied in Holy Writ. By participating in the sacrament of the Bible, the Lollard reaffirmed his participation in Christ's true church.

Scripture had long enjoyed an exalted status; the Lollard was to elevate it still further.[18] Once reserved for the privileged scholarship of the church doctor, the Bible was to be placed in open circulation. There it was to become the fulcrum upon which the devotional life of all Christians was to pivot. In sermon, treatise, and courtroom confession, the Lollards testified to the primacy of scripture. "[H]it is al on," claims a Wycliffite preacher, "to loue God and to louen his word." Intones another: "It mai be þat pope Innocent lieþ. It mai be þat alle þe foure ordris of freris lien wiþ munkis and chanouns. Also it mai be þat al þe vniuersite of oxford lieþ and oþer also. It mai be þat aggregat persone þat haþ his see in the chirche lieþ. But in no wise mai it be þat truþe þat is god lieþ. And þer for euery man schuld hard cleue to crist and his lawe."[19]

The novelty of the Lollard platform is nowhere more evident than in the fear and loathing it occasioned among the orthodox. The popularization of the Bible would invite chaos, they predicted. Poaching upon the estates of learning bred men contemptuous of social fences as well as spiritual ones. The defenders of church tradition countered with injunctions reminding the potential rebels of their appointed stations and the knowledge appropriate to them: "[Knights] shuld sett her besines abowte þe good gouernaunce in þe temperalltee in þe tyme of pees and also abowte diuers poyntes of armes in þe tyme of werre [war]. . . . Prestes shuld principally entermet [undertake] to lern þe lawe of Criste and lawfully to teche itt. And lower men shuld hold hem contente with þe questions and þe sotelte of þer own labour."²⁰ For Hoccleve, a Bible-reading public promised a world turned upside down. Knights grew effeminate, bailiffs and reeves neglected their crafts to "dote or raue" upon "Crystes lawes," and women gossiped over the precious truths of scripture:

> Some wommen eeke, thogh hir wit be thynne,
> Wele argumentes make in holy writ!
> Lewde calates [foolish women]! sittith down and spynne,
> And kakele of sumwhat elles, for your wit
> Is al to feeble to despute of it!²¹

Hoccleve looked longingly back to a shadowy past where the priest spoke in imperatives and the congregation murmured "Amen." Now, it seemed, the only sounds audible in the church were the contentious interrogatives of religious malcontents:

> Our fadres olde & modres lyued wel,
> And taghte hir children / as hem self taght were
> Of holy chirche / & axid nat a del
> "Why stant this word heere?" / and "why this word there?"
> "Why spake god thus / and seith thus elles where?"
> "Why dide he this wyse / and mighte han do thus?"²²

Although we may smile at Hoccleve's exaggerated terror at the prospect of scripture-spouting shrews, his vision of a new Babel—a cacophony of clashing voices shouting words they cannot fathom—is not fantastical. How could the open Bible produce the harmony its advocates anticipated among choristers drawn from a largely illiterate society?[23] The elevation of the Bible demanded a reevaluation of its intrinsic nature and the ways in which its truth was transmitted and made accessible. At the core of Wyclif's own scripturalism was an insistence upon the inward consistency and outward sufficiency of God's word, views repeatedly endorsed by his followers. For one Wycliffite preacher, the apparent contradictions of the Bible dissolve in the face of its principal lesson, the love of God: "Wordis of God ben monye by dyuersite of resoun, but alle þei rennen togydre in o myddyl poynte; and so þei ben alle Godis word, þat is hymself."[24] The sufficiency of scripture as the complete guide to holy living was attested to by the inexhaustibility of its teachings. Let "no man drawe ony treuþe fro goddis wordis, for þei enclosen alle nedeful treuþe & profitable for mannys soule."[25] Like the magical wine vessels of mythology, no matter how often the thirsty Christian came to drink, there was always more of Christ's elixir to be found. Furthermore, no matter what gifts of experience and learning the reader brought to the study of scripture, there were always new meanings that remained hidden. The ever-receding horizon of scriptural truth, argued the Lollard, was at once testimony to its divine nature and an inducement to the believer to devote all his energies to its elucidation. "Lord, siþ goddis lawe is so myche & so hard to vndirstonde, as austyn & oþere seyntis techen, þat þouȝ eche man hadde neuere so gret witt & myȝtte lyue hool & sond in bodi & wittis til þe day of dome, he schulde euere haue ynowȝ to lerne and ocupie him þerine at þe fulle,"[26] why then should we bother ourselves, we who are "of lesse wittis & schortere tyme & feblere of complexion"[27] than our ancestors, with means of enlightenment less rich and certain?

As the Wycliffite metaphor of crucifixion implies, the process of scriptural devotion was riddled with tension and an almost muscular straining.[28] All of the believer's resources were to be summoned to confront the exhausting task; all his attention was to focus undeviatingly on the love and understanding of God's word. To be lax meant risking the "scatering of [his] love."[29] The Bible offered infinite wisdom, but its offer was extended only to those willing to do battle with its intentional difficulties. In this combative sense of religious truth and its discovery, we find the awakening of that ethos of struggle which marks all later nonconformist thinking. Nothing is revealed to those who do not wrestle for the truth, to those who shun the Christian warfare.

The efficacy of God's law manifested itself in its accessibility as well as its inexhaustibility. To all believers God granted enlightenment from the perusal of his words: directly if they were literate; indirectly, through a preacher or reader, if not. More important, the active believer was promised an ever-increasing capacity for understanding. By confronting the text "goode man ben exercisid, either [or] ocupied, and that in expounnynge hooly scripture thei haue a newe grace, diuerse fro the first autouris."[30] Reading or hearing the Bible read was itself perceived as the cause of that grace that enabled a man to read with still greater understanding: "Sett þin herte in holi studie & purswe aftir wiþ al þi strengþe & þou schalt fynde it in schort while more swetter þan þe honycombe. . . . Haue þou þi þouȝt in Goddis heestis . . . & he schal graunt an hert to þee & lust of wisdam schal be ȝouun [given] to þee."[31]

The momentous shift in the nature of Christian devotion occasioned by the Lollard attempt to substitute the ritual of biblical exegesis for that of the Eucharist cannot be overstressed; yet that shift is often masked by the deceptive sense of continuity between the devotional literature of the Wycliffites and their adversaries. The Lollard remodeling of Archbishop Thoresby's "Instruction for the People," for example, tacks antimendicant invective onto the prelate's unimpeachably orthodox manual without noticeably shaking the foundation of the work.[32] In much the same vein, literary historians investigating the spate of social, economic, and religious criticism in the later Middle Ages have underscored the conventionality of Lollard polemic. Gerald Owst's study of sermon literature and John Yunck's treatment of venality satire suggest that Wycliffite attacks on ecclesiastical abuses are often indistinguishable from their more orthodox counterparts.[33] We must not, however, be blind to the revolutionary wolf lurking in woolly conventions. In its early stages Lollardy was forced, like primitive Christianity, to draw much of its theoretical and practical machinery from the work of its enemies. Never allowed to reach its full maturity, Lollardy failed to outgrow its early dependence on the language and instruments of orthodox Christian worship. It would remain the task of later Puritanism to explore fully the ramifications of the shift from Eucharist to Bible and to implement a devotional program in accordance with those implications. The Lollards had begun the work, however, and it is possible to trace in their writings their new sense of the nature, generation, and expression of Christian belief.

The preeminence of the Bible in Lollard devotion inevitably led to a devaluation of the sacerdotal element of Christianity. The priest's claim to spiritual authority had always rested on his unique status as a mediator between the sacred and the profane: "[Þ]er is none erþly poure egall to þe powre of prestehod."[34] It was by virtue of his divinely sanctioned role in the Mass that remembrance became recreation and divine eternity and human temporality merged.[35] For the Lollard, priestly efficacy came increasingly to depend not upon office but upon conduct, judged as for all Christians by the example of the Bible. The priest, in effect, became simply another medieval craftsman whose credentials were established by the production of his masterpiece—an exemplary holy life.[36] As with the craftsman, shoddy work precipitated a loss of clientele. Although in principle they might acknowledge the benefits of sacraments administered by priests in sin, in practice the Lollards sought their spiritual wares from more trustworthy peddlers. The common Puritan practice of "shopping" for a suitable ghostly mentor, much as one might shop for a reliable carpenter, had already begun in the late Middle Ages. The priest's eucharistic role was diminished not only by the new criterion by which his competence was evaluated but by a change in the work itself. The power to enact the miracle of the consecration of the elements reverted to the deity. No longer perceived as a divine magician transforming bread and wine into the body and blood of Christ, the priest became a master of ceremonies, reduced to commenting on actions performed by another.

The priesthood's loss was God's gain. Everywhere in their writings we find the Lollards reinvesting God's grandeur, surrendering to his direct control offices that the clerical class had appropriated to itself since the earliest days of the church.[37] The loss of the church's Christ-like intercessor measurably widened the gap between the human and the divine. The complementary portraits of a deity, unfathomable and omnipotent, and man, ignorant and powerless to do good to himself and others, began to emerge clearly from the literature of the fourteenth-century reformers. Firmly fixed in his heaven, the Lollard God was more distant and severe than his orthodox counterpart who graciously condescended to reenact his bloody sacrifice for the comfort of his followers. The Lollard tendency to deny Christ's physical presence in the elements of the altar was symptomatic of their sense of God's ultimate inaccessibility.[38] The elaborate expositions of God's friendship with man, which permeate popular sermon literature of the period, are noticeably absent in the writings of the Lollards. Friendship implied a common ground of interest, ability, and understanding. What could man offer God that was not tainted with his wretchedness? Lollard tracts overflowed with testimonies to man's meager capacities; Lollard wills vied with each other in their expressions of revulsion at man's unworthiness.[39]

The priest was not the only mediating element of Christian worship expunged by the reformers. The church had long labored to construct about the altar where time and eternity intersected in the priest's hand, a sacred middle ground. Within the precincts of a physical world sanctified by the holy church and demarcated by the relics of her saints, salvation was to be found.[40] The Lollard tolerated no such halfway houses; between the hovel of the simple believer and the new Jerusalem of the redeemed lay a void, which man-made bridges could not gap. Even in its earliest phases, Lollardy moved inexorably away from the stone nave and its sacred space and toward Milton's temple of "th' upright heart and pure": "[S]oþely in þe olde lawe was salomons temple a figure of þe chirche in þe newe lawe, but not þat the chirche shulde be siche, but fre & large vndir þe cope of heuene, & stonde in vertues of mannus soule; but antichrist wole close it nou in coolde stones þat moten perisshe."[41]

Lollards under examination were fond of proclaiming the open field a worthy rival to the church as a place of worship. In their actual assemblies, however, they evidently favored local households. With the advent of systematic persecution heralded by Arundel's *De Heretico Comburendo*, the statute of 1401 that made death by fire the penalty for heresy, the retreat from public places to private dwellings became a matter of necessity as well as preference. Testimony to the widespread existence of religious meetings held in the relative safety of the Lollard home is recorded in many diocesan registers. The confession of Hawisa Moone of Loddon is typical in its description of Lollard conventicles. Listing her accomplices, Hawisa admits that they "haue ofte tymes kept, holde, and continued scoles of heresie yn prive chambres and prive places of oures, yn the whyche scoles Y have herd, conceyved, lerned and reported the errours and heresies which be writen and contened in these indenturis."[42] In such "scoles of heresie," usually consisting of the immediate family, its servants, and local neighbors harboring similar convictions, a new kind of church was emerging, centered on the hearth rather than the altar and ritually united in Christ through the spiritual consumption of his word rather than his body.

The Lollard's church resembled a one-room schoolhouse. In it gathered Christians of varying levels of spiritual progress whose sole source of instruction was a text whose capacity to be all things to all people made it the foundation of all community. Having abandoned the gaudy and devalued miracles of a suspect church, the Lollard turned to the homely but more reliable miracle of God's written word: "For bileue is insensible & more trewe þan siche signes; as þis treuþe is insensible þat two & þre maken fyue, & ȝit it is more certeyn þan ony sensible þing here. Þus bileue of hooly writ passiþ alle þes clepid myraclis."[43] If bridges were to span the void between man and God, they would be made not of things like the engineering wonders of Sin and Death in *Paradise Lost* but of words. Perhaps the failure of Lollardy stemmed not from the power of its enemies or the miscalculations of its leaders but from its premature vision of a Gutenburg galaxy, its worship of the written word in an age of handwritten texts and massive illiteracy. The simultaneous flourishing of nonconformity and pamphleteering in the sixteenth and seventeenth centuries was no mere coincidence.

THE LOLLARD WAY

The Lollard emphasis on reading subtly altered the shape of the Christian's experience. The intensity of his spirituality was to be measured by the ever-increasing perspicacity with which he deci-

phered the Holy Book. The ecstatic rejuvenation experienced in ceremonial worship yielded to a progressive and incremental acquisition
of spiritual learning.

> And þus hit falluþ now vnto men to knowen rudly furst a þing
> and generally, as philosophres spekon, and after schulde þei
> knowe more sotylly þe same þing. And þus Crist by his man-
> heede teelde furst mysty wordys, and siþ God by his fingur
> schewode sutilte of hem. And ʒet þis Hooly Goost schal haue
> ordre of his lore, for furst he schal meue mennys erys in sensi-
> ble voyces, and siþ he schal be slydon in and teche mennys
> þowtis in al þat Crist haþ spoke byfore, in general wordys; ne
> þei schal not cese anoon to lerne more sutylly, but euere in þis
> lyʒf þei wexen more rype til þat þei comen to heuene, and þere
> knowe al fully.[44]

There is no rigid separation here between seeing darkly on earth
and face to face in heaven. The saint in bliss will indeed see clearly,
but the clarity of his vision will be the outgrowth of his earthly education, not a refutation of it. Among the living there are no leaps in
spiritual apprehension, only the slow and painful process of winning
truths from a document that yields them grudgingly. The Lollard
always argued that religious experience as a whole was not disrup-
tive. God's influence permeated earthly existence like a continuous
misty rain; it never inundated the land at one moment or left it
parched and barren at the next; it was not hoarded in one place but
equally distributed: "And þenne shulde grace come to men, as hevene scateriþ reyn; but now castiþ Antecrist to hepe hise disciplis, so
þat ilche may strengþe oþer in her malice; as ʒif hevene of oon
cloude send gushyng of watir, and overflowede som erþe, and some
wer left drye. Þus Crist sente hise apostlis, when þei weren rype, to
diverse londis, to sowe wateris of wisdom, and closede hem not in
cloysteris as Antecrist doiþ."[45]

The life of the Lollard saint is ideally deliberate and controlled,
uninterrrupted by pivotal, epiphanic moments: "Loke furst þat he be
grownded in stable bygynnyng, and siþ þat he procede in graciows
mene, and siþ þat he ende in fulnesse of charite, and þanne his lyʒfe
is sawmpled aftur þe Trinite."[46] Perhaps for this reason pilgrimage,

with its connotations of slow but steady progress, exerted such a persistent hold on the nonconformist imagination from *Pierce the Ploughman's Crede* to *Pilgrim's Progress*. In characteristic fashion, the Lollard author of *The Lanterne of Liȝt* translates pilgrimage into a metaphor for the lifelong study and dissemination of biblical truth: "[P]restis ben pilgrimes þat studien holi writ til þei haue plente in her mynde of þis heuenli wisdam and þanne þei hiȝen hem fast aboute in al þe brood world to dele þis goostli tresour among þis witles peple . . ."[47]

In contrast, the images of holy living to be culled from popular orthodoxy suggest a very different ideal. Vernacular sermons of the day dwell lovingly on miraculous conversions, on momentous shifts in spiritual orientation that overshadow all prior and subsequent experience. Typical is the tale from the *Legenda Aurea* of the conversion of a loose woman. Lured by the promise of wealth, the woman addresses five Ave Marias to an image of the Mother and Child. Suddenly the image comes to life and offers the sinner salvation if she will confess her crimes to a priest. Struck by the miracle, the woman hurries to the priest, acknowledges her sins, dies, and is snatched away by the angels. The quality of the convert's life preceding her rebirth is of no interest to the preacher or his audience; we know merely that she was sinful. The activities that might follow such a transformation are similarly insignificant; she dies because her spiritual development is instantaneously made complete. Popular orthodoxy tended to dwell on the moment of redemption, popular Lollardy on the life of redemption.[48]

Miracles of the Host, a favorite species of the tale of conversion, are also instructive in understanding popular conceptions of spirituality. One of the most frequently repeated was the tale of the dog who demonstrates his superiority to a Jew by instinctively treating the Host with reverence while the unbeliever willfully desecrates it. The lesson typically inculcated by the tale is unquestioning obedience: "So be þis meracle þou may be stered to beleue þer-on in þat, þat an vnresonable beeste so dud, þat neuer had techynge of holy churche."[49] When this preacher turns to the significance of the physical appearance of the Host, he notes that one side is engraved with "þe articles of þe feyȝþ, with þe wiche clerkes shuld melle [undertake] hem for to dispute hem. Þe pleyn side is to þe þat arte a lewd man, in token þat þou shalt not melle þe no farþur but to beleue as holychurche techeþ þe pleynly."[50] The blank side of ceremony had little appeal for the Lollard; his concern was with the rational apprehension of truth imbedded in words. The religious questioning that was so crucial to his way of faith, was, in the orthodox mind, reserved for the learned.[51] Among the masses, disputation was a sign of disobedience and spiritual confusion. Warns the orthodox preacher: "[Þ]e more þat þou disputes þer-of, þe farþur þou shall be þer-fro."[52] Such a call for obedient silence ran counter to the Lollard's thirst for intellectual awakening. The holy child and the holy ancient—whose sanctity is predicated on the absence or decay of intellection and justified by Christ's injunction that each man "receive the kingdom of God as a little child"—are common heroes of the orthodox imagination. They are noticeably absent in Wycliffite hagiography. Militant anti-intellectualism never defined the main current of Lollard thinking, although the gradual loss of an educated ministry inevitably invited its presence.

The assault on holy ignorance was matched by the attack against its allied religious affection—wonder. Wonder represents a short-circuiting of the intellect in the face of an event that defies the laws governing routine existence. Custance's ability in "The Man of Laws' Tale" to hurl overboard a sturdy man ought not to arouse curiosity as to the effects of excess adrenaline on physical strength. Awe and wonder at a God who periodically oversteps the bounds of earthly expectations is the proper response. Wonder is the reaction demanded by miracles, and the Lollard sought to dilute and domesticate the miraculous, to translate momentous wonder into the wonderful moments of quotidian virtue.

In place of wonder the Lollard offered dread: "And right as a nail smiten in holdith two thingis togidere, so drede smiten to Godward holdith and susteineth oure bileve to hym."[53] This was not that "servyle drede" with which God punished man's sins but a more difficultly defined emotion, "love-drede."[54] Unlike English Calvinism, Lollardy offered no systematic doctrine of assurance; the final disposition of the human soul was forbidden knowledge. "[N]o man woot [knows] of himsilf without special reuelacioun of God . . . , whethir he be of the noumbre of hem that shulen be sauid, of the noumbre of which noon mai pershe . . ."[55] Although assurance was beyond man's reach, Wyclif and his followers counseled the believer to make the hope of salvation operative in this life: "And þis kunne not we knowe ful certeyne, but han glymeryng & supposyng, & þus we moten lyue here in beleue & in hope to crist, þat riȝt entent & goode werkis grounde vs in hope, þat crist wole saue vs."[56] "Love-drede" was the emotion suited to this spiritual state of mind. The very duality of the term suggests the state of hyperanimated antici-pation characteristic of the Lollard believer. He hoped for and acted upon the assumption of his spiritual health, but was continually checked by the fear of debilitating illness. Each believer by necessity became a physician to his own soul, seeking with the aid of the Spirit, to identify the symptoms of malaise or well-being: "Al ȝif suche þingus ben pryuye and passen worldly wit of men, neþeles þe Hooly Gost telluþ men somme of suche signes, and makiþ hem more certeyne þan men can iuge of bodyly helþe."[57] "Love-drede" thus fostered both intellection and self-examination, prodding the be-liever to survey past and present for that "glymeryng and suppos-yng," that illusive solid ground on which to build the edifice of a Christian life.

The idea of "grounding" spiritual experience was pervasive in fourteenth- and fifteenth-century reformist thinking. The word as-sumed an almost talismanic quality; linked with "in Goddis lawe" it acted like an exorcist's charm, assuring the hearer that the doctrine that followed was thoroughly purged of the "dremys and fantasies" of the unbelievers.[58] The need to shackle the human personality, perceived as forever straining to slip its bonds to the mundane and hurl itself into a transcendent world of wonder, betrays the deep and abiding Lollard distrust of mystical experience. The world of wonder is rife with dangers to the fragile human soul. Longing to glimpse the beyond, the untutored man is easily seduced by spectacles that seem to satisfy his ghostly yearnings but which are, in fact, blind alleys, spiritual cul-de-sacs. His eye is captured by a pageant or the entourage of a nobleman, and the wonder and delight reserved for man's clear apprehension of God in heaven is bestowed upon a lesser object: "And siþ a man haþ delyȝt to see a pley here in erþe, or a lord, or þing of wonder, and þerwiþ feediþ his soule, myche more þis clere syȝt of God and alle hise creatures schulden fully feedon þe blissyde sowle, and þeraftur blesse þe body."[59]

Nowhere was the rejection of ungrounded mystical experience more vehemently voiced than in the Lollard denunciation of contemporary church music. The late Middle Ages had witnessed the rise of a new kind of music, the intricate polyphonic song of the *ars nova*.[60] For Wyclif's followers, such church music epitomized the ill-disciplined religious exercise. Engineered to lift the soul on complex and interweaving lines, the new music "distract[ed] þe syngere fro deuocion and lett[ed] [hindered] men fro consceiuynge of þe sentence."[61] Emotion and imagination were liberated from the business of enlivening the understanding, free now to fasten on any pleasure, no matter how transitory, no matter how base. Convinced that a soul so stimulated would ordinarily settle upon lesser objects of devotion, Lollards and later nonconformists joined in associating polyphonic music with lechery: "[Þ]is stiriþ men to pride & iolite & lecherie & oþere synnys, & so vnableþ hem many gatis [ways] to vnderstonde & kepe holy writt þat techeþ mekenesses, mornynge for oure synnys & oþere mennus, & stable lif & charite."[62] For those few who attempted not only to soar with the music but decode the words, the exercise was doomed to failure as well: the strain of such contrary tasks prompted the "akying of hedis [headaches]." Beyond these pitfalls lay others. To the orthodox defense of church music as a legitimate imitation of the angelic choirs of heaven, the Lollard polemicist replies: "& ȝif þei seyne þat angelis heryen [praise] god bi song in heuene; seie þat we kunnen [know] not þat song, but þei ben in ful victorie of here enemys & we ben in perilous bataile, & in þe valeye of wepynge & mornyge; & oure song lettiþ [hinders] vs fro betre occupacion & stiriþ vs to many grete synnes & to forȝete vs self."[63]

True religious ecstasy is finally beyond the range of human activity, reserved for those translated by death. Only after the battle for truth and holy living is fought and won is man entitled to a mystical self-annihilation. To anticipate the joys of heaven, to permit ourselves to bask in the pleasures of our own imaginations, is to abandon our duly appointed "occupacion." Confrontation with the enemy within, with our adversaries without, and with the misapprehension that clouds our understanding of God's word—this, not transcendence, must be the instrument by which man shapes his religious identity: "Ffor iche mon schulde be a kny3t, and ryde here in worldly travel [labor]; ffor by þis travel schulde a mon make blis to his soule and gete to hit þo joye of heven, for mede of his travel."[64] The untimely and unauthorized assumption of that bliss in moments of devotional frenzy can lead only to the loss of identity: we can only "forþet vs self." In the end, the Lollard preferred the unvoiced harmonies of a life dedicated to enacting biblical truth to the sounds of an earthly choir echoing in a stone nave: "Þerfore synge we in hert by holy desire, seyyng psalmus by clene werkis and heryyngus [praises] and ympnus [hymns] to God for his large 3iftus of mercy, wiþ brennynge charite in studyynge understondynge and techynge holy writte . . ."[65]

The same fear of the distracting counterpoint of the *ars nova* haunted the Lollards in their approach to the Bible. In the "General Prologue" to the second Wycliffite translation of the Bible, the author weighs the relative pedagogical worth of the various books of the Old Testament. The books of Solomon are to be avoided by the neophyte. Ecclesiastes and Canticles, he argues, are too difficult for most readers because their author speaks in a variety of personae, some of which seem to endorse immoral activity. There is no sole voice of intent to guide the immature reader; meaning emerges only from the play of voice against voice.[66] On the other hand, the author enthusiastically endorses the Psalms of David, a "book of solitarie speches." In his soliloquies and prayers, the author finds an ideal of clarity and accessibility missing amid the complex interlacing of positions and personalities in the books of Solomon. This Lollard predilection for the monophonic was shared by later nonconformists and helped determine their response to the drama.

The Lollard might sidestep the problem of complexity of meaning in one book of the Bible by directing the novice to another less difficult. He could not long evade, however, the issue of multiple levels of meaning within the Bible as a whole. Since Origen, the church had traditionally acknowledged different levels of meaning in scripture, later conceived as being four in number: the literal or historical, the tropological or moral, the allegorical, and the anagogical. The

Lollards in principle concurred; the author of the "General Prologue" expounds upon the four levels at some length.[67] Nevertheless, in practice the Lollard was instinctively drawn to the literal meaning of the text. Citing Augustine, the biblical translator notes that the "literal vndirstonding is ground and foundament of thre goostly vndirstondingis." More important for the disputatious Lollard, "oonly bi the literal vndirstonding a man may argue aȝens an aduersarie."[68]

Although Augustine's *De Doctrina Christiana* is the guiding force behind the exegetical system championed in the "General Prologue," crude borrowing turns a sophisticated instrument into a rather blunt tool. The author fastens eagerly upon Augustine's rule for distinguishing literal from figurative speech in the Bible, but ignores the call for a preliminary education in natural sciences, languages, history, and philosophy:

> Such a reule schal be kept in figuratif spechis, that so longe it be turned in mynde bi diligent consideracoun, til the expownyng either [or] vndirstonding be brouȝt to the rewme of charite; if eny speche of scripture sounneth [tends toward] propirly charite, it owith not to be gessid a figuratijf speche; and forbeedith wickidnesse, either comaundith profyt either good doynge, it is no figuratyf speche; if it seemith to comaunde cruelte, either wickidnesse, either to forbede prophit, either good doinge, it is figuratijf speche.[69]

Ignoring Augustine's distinction between conduct that is absolutely evil and historical customs that may be acceptable in one age and not in another,[70] the author's formula becomes a means of devaluing those spiritual meanings beyond the reader's grasp. The rule becomes in effect this: if the text is readily comprehensible, it is probably literal and therefore wholesome; if the text is unduly difficult, it is probably figurative. Since all the wisdom scripture veils may be found openly elsewhere, the reader may safely ignore the difficult text until he is better equipped to discern its meaning: "If we undirstonden not þe witt, graunte we þe forme of þe wordis, and confesse we þe truþe of hem, al if [even if] we witen [know] not which it is."[71]

The Lollard tendency to downgrade the "mysty" meaning was undoubtedly fueled by the specter of its abuse. The friars in particular were singled out by the Lollards for their crimes of willful and self-serving misinterpretation. Divorcing the spiritual meaning from the literal, the mendicant preacher (so the charge went) transported his auditory into that world of unsanctified imagination in which all the signposts to truth, the literal meaning of God's words, had been deviously removed. Friars like Chaucer's who spoke their sermons after their own "symple wit, / Nat al after the text of hooly writ," offered idiosyncratic error rather than universal truth. It is one of the continuing ironies of the conflict between Lollard and friar that the mendicants were pioneers in transmitting scripture to the layman and early champions of the Bible's literal sense. But then the annals of history are filled with tales of reformers reforming the reformation and entrepreneurs scrambling for the loyalty of the same clientele.

THE VOICE OF THE PROPHET

Near the conclusion of his "General Prologue" to the second Wycliffite translation of the Bible, the author issues a challenge to the university world, now becoming increasingly hostile to the Lollard reformer: "But wite ȝe, worldly clerkis and feyned relygiouse, that God both can and may, if it lykith hym, speede [help] symple men out of the vniuersitee, as myche to kunne [know] hooly writ, as maistris in the vniuersite."[72] The warning that God may ignore the scholar struggling to understand the Bible and instead bestow his gift of enlightenment on the simple, unlearned man seems to violate both the distrust of miraculous intervention and the yearning for intellectual confrontation we have been tracing in Lollard thought. Far from being an anomaly, this invocation of inspired perception is characteristic of Lollardy—testimony to another side of a religious spirit often too narrowly conceived as either rationalistic or commonsensical in bias.[73]

The radically opposed constituencies of Lollardy may be glimpsed in the prepatory steps to biblical study outlined in *The holi prophete Dauid seith*. They are six in number. The prospective reader must first pray for understanding. He must "meke hem silf to God in doynge penaunce" in order "that God opene to hem the trewe vndirstondyng of his lawe, as he openede witt to hise apostolis to vndirstonde hooli scripture." He must surrender his will to God, remembering that "he herith the desire of pore men that knowen verili that thei haue no good but of God." He must beseech from "wel-willid men and weel lyuynge, the trewe vndirstondyng of hooli writ." He must seek out the holy example of the apostles who learned their lessons from the Holy Ghost, the "spesial techere of wel willid men." Lastly, he ought to study the work of the doctors.[74] Not unexpectedly, the Lollard author omits Augustine's insistence on an exhaustive education as a prerequisite to any scriptural foray: the author knows the resources of his audience. The predominance of prayer over even modest scholarship is nonetheless significant. What is offered here is a largely passive experience for which the believer readies himself to receive an infusion of understanding once meditation has breached the mental and spiritual obstructions to truth. Reminiscent of exercises in self-examination preceding communion, the program is an apt reminder that for the Lollard the study of the Bible was a ritual activity, an act of devotion in which the Real Presence might be as or more authentically perceived than in the Eucharist itself. When the Lollard confronted the Bible, he confronted not only a text but the deity himself. Hence his attitude toward scripture was inherently divided as was his sense of the transmission of its truth.[75]

Ample evidence of the Lollard reliance upon inspiration as well as reason in their reading of scripture appears throughout the writings of the reformers. In a sermon on Galatians 4:1, the preacher couples his call for "traveling in holi writ" with an invocation to the Holy Ghost to grant the gift of understanding without which our reason labors in vain. Noting the extreme difficulty of Paul's words, the preacher concedes: "But wel I woot þat God grauntiþ to fewe men to knowe hem here; but ӡet we schulden trowe þes wordis and worschipe hem, and traueyle on hem to wyte what þes wordis menen, as men schullen wyte aftur in heuene. And for to haue mynde of þis seynt þat men passe not fro þis wyt, somme men wolon go nyӡ hise wordis bi vndurstondyng þat God ӡyueþ hem; for ellis myӡten alle hise wordis be alyenyd [taken away], and al his wyt by anticrist."[76]

Though "traveling" itself does not produce ghostly understanding, it is seen as a necessary prelude. The act of struggling to understand God's word summons inspiration. Understanding becomes not an outcome of ratiocination but a divine reward for it, not the instrument of knowing, merely its ordinary and expected concomitant. The diligent application of will and intellect to the holy text ritually invokes and authenticates inspiration. In typical nonconformist fashion, the gift of enlightenment is seen as being reserved for a precious few, a "saving remnant" set aside by God to keep his truth alive and efficacious. These men are privy to God's most secret communications: "If God rowne [whisper] in þin eere, and bid þe feght in his cause, as God taght by prophetis in þe Olde Testament, feght fast in Gods cause, as he hymself biddes þe . . ."[77] The power of divine inspiration to drive error from the earth—once the gospel is given a free course—is described in a lyrical passage whose metaphoric language echoes its near mystical theme. "And þenne wyndis of treuþis shulden blowe awey þe heresyes, and cler þe eyr of holi Chirche, þat is now ful troble. Þenne shulde lyf of grace come doun fro God, and lyʒte ilche man aftir þat he wer worþi."[78] Significantly, the first heresy to be blown away is the doctrine that God's grace must be mediated by a prelatical church.

The concept of unmediated inspiration was dangerous. How was the believer to distinguish between true and false inspiration? The orthodox enemies of the Lollards were only too willing to set their minds at rest; the source of the wind that filled them was pinpointed with unwelcome specificity:

Wandrynge wedercokkes wiþ euery wynd waginge;
Þe spiritis of þe deuel makyn ʒoure tokenys—
Þourʒ quenching of torches in ʒour taylende ʒe resseyue ʒour
     wisdom.[79]

For centuries, the church by virtue of its longevity and its claims of the continuity of the Apostolic Succession had stood as a warrant for the authenticity of its devotional rites. In the eyes of the reformers, however, the church was a discredited institution; its lapsed credibility could no longer pretend to sanctify the means of salvation it offered. Having cut themselves off from the sacred authority of the Roman church, the Lollards found themselves in the center of that transcendent world of wonder they so loathed and feared. Their repeated insistence that their imaginative apprehension was grounded in the indisputable truth of God's word was at best a limited palliative. The Bible might well be the authentic word of God, but rarely was its meaning immediately obvious. As we have seen, for all their struggling and wrestling with the meaning of words, in the end it was inspiration, not ratiocination, that brought understanding and assurance. Their claims to objectivity always came to rest on subjective evidence.

The Lollard partly assuaged his misgivings by providing himself with an Old Testament role model. In the example of the Jewish prophets, men chosen by God to speak his truth to an erring generation, the Lollard found a biblical precedent for what was, to the outsider, mere eccentricity or madness. The prophets, too, had held no place in the ecclesiastical institutions of their day; they, too, had drawn their truth and calling directly from the deity. And they, too, had often assumed their mantles of prophecy with reluctance: "And herefore þe holy prophete ysaie crieþ þat woo is to hym, for þat he was stille and dwelte among synful peple, & telle hem not here synnes, siþ þis is offis of a prophete."[80] The task of telling the sinful people of their sins fell to every true believer. In a defense of the vernacular Bible, the Lollard author enjoins all Christians to "profecie," i.e., to preach and teach. In a treatise on the seven deadly sins, it is argued that since all men will be divines in heaven, each man must begin learning his destined office on earth: "And so iche mon here mot nede con divinite, somme more and somme lesse, if he wil be saved. Ffor in þo state of blis schal iche mon be a divyne, better þen any mon is here, for þerin stondes his blis. And so, if men traveilen wel here in þis service, þei ben more disposid to con hit in hevene."[81] The priesthood of all believers is a hallmark of the Lollard movement.[82]

The Lollard fear of spiritual dislocation was further allayed by a New Testament exemplar. Increasingly, there was a tendency among the reformers to seize upon the simple, godly life, modeled after the conduct of Christ and the apostles, as a sign of salvation. Epithets such as "the simple godly," "poor and simple men," and "the well-willed man" became near semantic equivalents of the Puritan term "saint."[83] Sir John Clanvowe's description of these "saints" in his devotional treatise, *The Two Ways*, demonstrates how even a knight of Richard's court came to see humility, simplicity, and patient suffering as the customary marks of the chosen:

> And also swiche folke þat wolden fayne lyuen meekeliche in þis world and ben out offe swich forseid riot, noise, and stryf, and lyuen symplely, and vsen to eten and drynken in mesure, and to clooþen hem meekely, and suffren paciently wroonges þat ooþere folke doon and seyn to hem, and hoolden hem apayed with lytel good of þis world, and desiren noo greet naame of þis world, ne no pris ther of, swiche folke þe world scoorneth and hooldeþ hem lolleris and loselis [Lollards and rascals], foolis and schameful wrecches. But, sikerly, God holdeth hem moost wise and most worsshipful, and he wole worsshipen hem in heuene for evere whan þat þoo þat þe world worsshipeþ shuln bee shaamed and pyned for euere in hell . . .[84]

Throughout Clanvowe's exercise there is a persistent sense that the number of souls preordained for bliss is very small. As Gordon Leff has pointed out, Wyclif's realist metaphysic had already led him to denigrate the visible church for its failures to mirror the archetypal reality of the ideal church.[85] The true church consisted of the elect; their election, however, was not made known to the world. The metamorphosis of Lollardy into the code of a small, persecuted minority inclined to trust in its ultimate salvation, while firmly convinced of the damnation of its opponents, heightened Wyclif's extremism. God's truth resided not in cathedral churches but in the hearts and minds of a scattered company of the faithful. The visible church of popes and prelates, as the persecutors of these "poor and simple men," came inevitably to be associated with Antichrist: "[I]n þe court of Rome is þe heed of anticrist. And in archebischopis & bischopis is þe bodi of anticrist. But in þise cloutid sectis as mounkis chanouns & freris is þe venymous taile of anticrist."[86] The Lollard was thus called upon to denounce the beast—to cry with the prophets of Israel and bear witness with the apostles to a world fallen victim to the enemies of God.

Yet, for all this comforting division of humanity into warring factions marching under the contrary banners of Christ and Antichrist, the Lollard was not all that comfortable.[87] Neither his enthusiastic assumption of the mantle of prophecy nor his embrace of the simple life of the Gospels fully masked the Lollard's anxieties. The Bible echoed with warnings against false prophets whose lonely cries in the wilderness were barely distinguishable from the lamentations of God's own.[88] In Lollard tracts the same language, with only slight variation, serves to describe religious activities worlds apart. The true prophet stirs men to worship God; the false "prophete, either [or] a feynere of dreamys," will "styre men" to idolatry. The Lollards' confusion was the inevitable outcome of a religion that harbored at its core a seemingly irreconcilable contradiction—a religion that championed objectitivity, intellection, and reason and yet was fueled by the passionate subjectivity of private inspiration.

THE LANGUAGE OF REFORM

The uneasy alliance of reason and inspiration at the center of Lollard thought determined the reformers' gingerly approach to the problem of symbolism and language itself. As is so often the case with an opposition party, the Lollards were clearer about what they disliked than what they liked. Their disapproval of the friar's habit is indicative of their quarrel with religious symbolism. The mendicant costume had always been invested with symbolic significance. Questioned about the meaning of his habit, an apologist for the Dominicans replies that the "grete coope þat is so wijd signefieþ charite," the hood "shapun as a sheeld" indicates "suffraunce in aduersitee," and the scapular "bitokeneþ boxumnesse dewe vnto our prelatis."[89] In the popular imagination, the garments assumed a holiness in and of themselves, as evidenced by the practice of burying the dead in a friar's habit. The gesture effectively transformed the habit from a sign of sanctity into an object of sanctity. In the conflation of the literal and spiritual both elements suffered denigration. The sign was stripped of its reality as a physical object and the spiritual truth it signified was demeaned by the carnal cloak it was forced to wear. And the confused Christian was left to drift aimlessly in the discredited middle ground of orthodox spirituality. Again we can see the influence of Wyclif's extremist brand of realism at work.[90] Wyclif argued strenuously that all being was indestructible. Objects possessed of temporal being could not be destroyed without in turn destroying their corresponding archetypes or ideas that resided in the mind of God. This, however, was impossible. For the Lollard, man-made symbols were dangerous precisely because they tempted men to think that such acts of annihilation might occur; that the object meant to suggest a higher reality might be construed as being that reality and therefore cease to be itself. The problem lay less in the symbol than in man's fallen perception and his penchant for ungrounded, transcendent experience.[91]

Behind Lollard misgivings about devotional symbols lay the Wycliffite assault on the scholastic interpretation of the Eucharist. Transubstantiation, argued the Lollard, confused the physical reality of the consumption of the bread and wine with the spiritual reality of man's participation in the mystical body of Christ to the detriment of both. To think of the ruler of the universe physically confined in a wafer was abhorrent; at the same time, the suggestion that the bread ceased to exist in the act of consecration was absurd. For the Lollards, talk of the accidents of bread and wine accompanying the substance of God merely obscured the fact that the Eucharist possessed a double nature: it was bread and wine in its earthly aspect and Christ in its divine aspect. One was perceived with the physical eye, the other with the spiritual. Rational comprehension and intuitive perception were to be held apart at arm's length, coexistent but not coextensive: "And þis þing þat he saw wiþ his eyȝe was a dowue [dove], and þis þing þat he saw wiþ his soule was God."[92]

In Lollard writing, apprehension about the conflation of the physical and the spiritual manifested itself in a wary attitude toward metaphor. Metaphor is, after all, a species of linguistic transubstantiation.[93] In the act of creating a new set of referents for an object, the metaphor projects the reader from a world of familiar coordinates into one of alien dimension. In the fusion of vehicle and tenor, the former is lost in the latter, and the reader's grasp on the known is loosed. The simile, on the other hand, offered the Lollard a more palatable alternative. The conjunctive "like" or "as" keeps vehicle and tenor at a safe distance from each other. The tenor orbits about its vehicle like an electron cloud about its nucleus—there is no fusion and hence no dreaded explosion. The integrity of the literal and figurative universes is maintained while their unity is clearly suggested. On the observer's side, the all-important sense of anticipation is nurtured. We glance from vehicle to tenor and back again, always waiting for an epiphanic moment of union in which total intuitive understanding is granted, but always aware that it is a consummation only to be wished for.

One of the more interesting manifestations of Lollard simile is a stylistic form that might be called embryonic or nascent allegory. A representative example is found in *Þe Grete Sentence of Curs Expouned*:

> As whoso were, up peyne of hangyng and drawyng, to fede many lege men of oure kynge, and toke þerfore wagis ynowe, and wastide hem, and suffride þe kingis lege men die for hunger, or ȝelde þe castel and hemself to þe kyngis enemys,—he were a cruel traitour and sleere of all þes men; and ȝit more traitour, ȝif he lettide [prevented] oþere knyȝttis of oure kyng to vitele þes men asegid, and rescowe hem of here enemyes. So it is of þis worldly prelatis and curatis, þat taken cure of soulis and tiþes and offryngis to teche hem Goddis lawe, and purge hem of synnes þoruȝ preier and prechyng and good ensaumple, last þe devel þat evere ensegiþ mannus soule cumbre hem in synne and brynge hem to helle.[94]

What we have here is a potential allegory of a very familiar kind—the castle of the soul besieged by sin—canonized in such works as *Sawles Warde* and *The Castle of Perseverance*. The distinctive feature of this short piece is its deliberately arrested development. It is not so much an allegory as an image frozen at the point of becoming an allegory. The literal level (what is happening as opposed to what it means) is highly developed, accounting for more than half of the substance of the passage. Only once the independent reality of this aspect of the story is given full expression, does the writer summon up his connective "so it is" and proceed on the figurative level we have all been expecting. Even then, however, nearly half of the symbolic reading is preoccupied with a catalogue of clerical abuses. Only in the final sentence is the traditional castle-soul equation verbalized and then in a manner that barely acknowledges the symbolic content of the passage.

The heavy emphasis on the historical meaning of the anecdote further diverts the reader's attention from the allegorical dimension of the siege. Were this a pure allegory, we would simply view the knights as emblems of the warfaring Christian. In the nascent allegory of the Lollard writer, however, they are real knights as well, the anticipated instruments of the coming spiritual revolution. To English knighthood, the Lollard addressed exhortations to action and warnings against the plots of the prelates.[95] This allegory joins their number. The writer's hesitancy at embracing symbolic meaning thus enriches the literal meaning of the tale at the expense of the figurative. When, at last, the reader reaches the figurative level, he finds not a vision of a higher truth but the barest of glimpses. This rather awkward embryonic allegory—"scarce half made up"—seemed at once to satisfy the Lollard need for a sense of the transcendent while assuaging his fears about spiritual disorientation in the face of ungrounded religious experience.

Other such allegories appear elsewhere in the works of the reformers.[96] Perhaps the most interesting, because it demonstrates how closely Lollard literary practice was dependent on the reformers' approach to biblical exegesis, comes from the "General Prologue" to the second Wycliffite Bible. The nascent allegory arises in a summary of Nehemiah 4:16, which describes the rebuilding of the walls of Jerusalem: "Thanne half the part of ȝunge men made the werk, and half the part was redy to bateyle; with oon hond thei maden the werk, and with the other thei helden the swerd; and eche of hem that bildide was gird with his swerd."[97] The language of this brief passage shifts rapidly within its limited confines. The first sentence is a literal paraphrase of the scriptural passages. The second sentence seems ready to burst into the figurative interpretation for which the passage obviously calls. The language becomes taut and artfully balanced—the builders on the one hand, the defenders on the other; the tool in one hand, the sword in the other. Surely we are about to have a paean to the true Christian who secures the good and wards off the evil. But our expectations are stymied. The language reverts to bare fact, although "gird with his swerd" may hint at the Pauline figure capable of transforming the text into allegory. The author once again returns to rather mundane paraphrasing. Only after numerous recapitulations of the story does he finally acknowledge the metaphor lurking in the text: "This proces of Esdras and of Neemye schulde styre vs to be bisy to biylde vertues in oure soule, aftir turnyng aȝen fro caitifte [captivity] of synne, and to fiȝte aȝens temptaciouns, and byilde faste vertues, as thei fouȝten with oon hond aȝens enemyes, and biyldeden with the tothir hond."[98] It is as if he were insisting that the reader imitate the double action of the builders of Jerusalem, one eye fixed on the literal truth of the action, the other glancing toward the spiritual reading beyond. Only by keeping both views in prospect simultaneously can the believer avoid the Scylla and Charybdis of pure carnal sight and pure imaginative vision.

The Wycliffite distrusted the fixed stare of both those who saw the physical world as opaque and those who saw it as transparent. Contemporary religious symbolism was seen as encouraging this rigidity. Attacking the misuse of the mendicants' habits, he argued that the symbol of holiness was deceptive: it implied a constancy of holy purpose that no friar might claim; it declared a fixity of purpose reserved for another world: "Cristis religion telliþ lityl bi siche sensible habitis, but now takiþ oon & now an oþer, as dide crist on good fryday. for þise habitis crien to þe folc holyness & stablenesse, þat god wole haue hid to hym, & þus þei ben ofte false signes & garnementis of ypocritis, as crist clepiþ ofte pharisees."[99] Even Christ in his tenure on earth, the Lollard claimed, deliberately changed his garments to prevent his followers from trying to diminish his godhead by confining it to any single symbol. Instead, he provided a sequence of symbols that kept mind and eye in movement preventing the inevitable falsification that comes when the mind fastens on a single sign and is seduced from continuing its search for the unknowable deity.[100] Only God could see the one in the many: "Lord, who cowthe undirstonde þat a sparke of fire, turnede aboute in derke nyȝte, semes to make cercul, but mennus siȝt holdes prent of þinge bifore seen for a littyl schort while, til alle þe fire be turnede? And so þe greet siʒt of God holdus togedur alle þinges þat han ben and all þat schal be."[101]

The Lollards sought to imitate Christ's accommodating ways. They would create symbols in process, words moving toward metaphor and allegory but stopping short, arrested images that tantalized the mind, drawing it forever onward and upward.[102] Language, like life, was to be a pilgrimage. Ornate and elaborate images that transfixed the mind were to be put aside. By their very richness such symbols tempted the devotee to gaze in wonder, to rest in a human image of bliss. Lollard imagery is sparse and crude. Even when the Lollard writer spoke in metaphor, his language was stripped of ornamentation. Like the simple wooden crosses he reluctantly offered as an alternative to jewel-encrusted crucifixes, his metaphors were drawn from the rustic and domestic.[103] As Peggy Ann Knapp has noted in her study of the language of the English Wycliffite sermons, their author's success lay "in creating homely and idiomatic English expressions for theological and exegetical abstractions."[104] Although it is perhaps unwise to read seventeenth-century literary practices into fourteenth-century writing, it seems clear that an ideal of plain style was beginning to emerge from the Lollard distrust of the overwrought symbol.[105]

THE RITUAL OF STRUGGLE

While the Lollard trope is characterized by plainness and abortive development, its contextual field, Lollard discourse, is distinguished by contentiousness. All species of Christian belief are combative by nature. In positing the locus of his real existence not in this world but the next, the Christian declared his enmity toward the life and values that took their sustenance from the earth. The Lollard who warned his auditory that "no man mai putte from him, þat ne schulde be chosen of God, to fiʒte wiþ her goostli enemyes, and bi victorie to gete blisse," might have repeated those words before an examining bishop without fear of contradiction. Yet for all its conventionality, Lollardy's embrace of Christian warfaring was something new—new in the intensity with which it was voiced and new in the purposes for which it was consciously and unconsciously employed. That the Lollard donned "the breastplate of faith" with such avidity must in part be attributed to the larger pull exerted by that illusive holy grail of all nonconformity, the primitive church. To the Lollard the primitive church offered an idealized image of a life lived in close proximity to the purity of Christ's actions and words. So too, that church, in its precarious yet persistent survival amidst overwhelming hostility and systematic harassment, sanctioned the minority status of the beleaguered Lollards. Identification extended beyond the mere fact of persecution to the heightened spirituality and communality such persecution promised.

The Lollard thirst for struggle, for an environment teeming with enemies eager for contention, however, is more than an act of accommodation to the inevitable fate of an opposition party. Lollardy as a theological outlook demanded the ritual of ideological combat. A religion of divisive extremes, Lollardy attempted to resolve the struggle of its internal contradictions by projecting that struggle outward into the public arena. By playing out their subjective dilemma in the field of objective action, by attacking in their enemies those elements of dogma and practice which they feared in themselves, they managed to maintain a delicate inward balance. Thus the barrage of assaults on the ungrounded spirituality of orthodox devotion was more than an attack on a series of ecclesiastical abuses; it was an attempt to placate Lollard doubts about the validity of their own intuitive approach to religious truth. The dynamics of such exorcism were most pronounced and, therefore, perhaps most effective when the opponent closely resembled the Lollard. The proof of the principle is the special animosity that the Lollard reserved for the friar. Had the mendicant orders not existed, the Lollard would have had to invent them. As they did exist, they constituted the perfect dark mirror of the Lollard mind, a nemesis whose failings enacted the most terrible of Lollard nightmares.[106]

The friars did not start out this way. Until he savaged the church's teachings on the Eucharist, Wyclif could count many a friar, particularly the Austins, among his allies. From its beginnings, Lollardy fell into a reforming role prepared for it in part by earlier mendicant movements. Lollard affinities with such radical opponents of the *ecclesia carnalis* as the Spiritual Franciscans have long been noted; and even after the decisive split with the mendicants, abstract praise for the rule of St. Francis, if not for its present, degenerate incarnation, is a commonplace of Lollard polemic.[107] A life of voluntary poverty in emulation of the apostles, advocacy of lay education, vernacular preaching, and the defense of the Bible's literal truth—all these platforms had been espoused and practiced by mendicants of diverse orders. Undoubtedly, by offering much the same wares as those of the itinerant peddler of Lollardy, the friar presented himself as an unwelcome competitor, the experienced salesman of the old, established firm.[108] But it was because the friar, in his alleged iniquities, gave corporeal form to the chimeras and demons haunting the Lollard consciousness that the mendicant earned his privileged place at the right hand of Antichrist. The Bible, venerated as the fixed foundation of devotional piety and forensic reasoning, suddenly loomed in the glosses of the friar as the proverbial nose of wax, subject to the manipulative whims of every reader. As for the church of the elect, its transcendent universality was translated into idiosyncratic sham by the arbitrary rules and orders of the mendicants. In every step of his pilgrimage, the Lollard saw in the friar the wrong turn.

By excoriating the erring ways of the friar, the Lollard denied his own. If the unsteady ground of private religion tumbled the mendicant into the slough of spiritual madness, the Lollards' allegiance to "þe comoun sect of god" (exquisite oxymoron) guided him safely along the path of Christ's truth. So essential did the orders become to the psychodrama of nonconformity that their ghostly presence continued to be invoked long after their enforced retreat from England. Well into the seventeenth century, radical Protestants such as Milton were still ritually slaughtering the scapegoat of the orders to appease their troubled spirits. Only if we recognize in the orders the externalized anxieties of the nonconformist mind, can we adequately account for the persistence and vehemence of such loathing as well as the recklessness with which it was indulged.

Consider the case of Margery Baxter whose minor escapades in the wars of truth are recorded in the court-book of Bishop Alnwick. An apparent fulfillment of Hoccleve's prophecy of the Lollard virago,

Margery seems to have delighted in friar-baiting: "Et illa Margeria respondebat quod ipsa communicavit cum dicto fratre, increpans eum quia sic mendicabat et quod non fuit elemosina facere nec dare sibi bonum nisi voluerit dimittere habitum suum et ire ad aratrum, et sic quod ille placeret magis Deo quam sequendo vitam aliquorum aliorum fratrum."[109] Margery's bold assault all but invited an accusation of heresy, one that her Carmelite adversary was only too happy to provide—that is until Margery threatened to accuse him of attempted rape. Other than revealing a rather unscrupulous brand of resourcefulness, the fictitious charge is suggestive of the curious way in which the Lollard viewed the friar: as seducer and as enemy, as lover and as assailant.

Although the friar's threats were forestalled, Margery was brought to trial; significantly, her accuser was a neighbor to whom she had boasted of her encounter. The need not only to fight the good fight but to publicize it as well is characteristic of the nonconformist temperament as we will discover. Memory of Margery's blow for God's law must have quickly faded, preserved as it was in a hostile legal document, but recollections of similar incidents were to achieve a minor immortality in fictional works such as the twin poems "The Layman's Complaint" and "The Friar's Answer."[110] These poems provide an interesting commentary on the atmosphere of debate and controversy that Lollardy provoked and indeed demanded for its survival. Portrayed in them is a weary friar who visits humble cottages in his district seeking contributions for his order. Instead of alms, however, he receives abuse. At every door, budding exegetes revile him, citing biblical injunctions against mendicancy. The poems are, perhaps, a reformer's idyll. How many friars might reasonably expect such an embarrassment of Lollard riches in their limiting districts? How many friars would fear the snatches of memorized scripture and polemic the rank-and-file Lollard might summon up against their superior learning? As a dream vision, though, the poems reveal much about the world the Lollards wished for, if not the one they actually inhabited. In that world, acquiesence to truth could not be imposed; it had to be earned. And the appropriate process by which it was earned was debate.

The debate is the natural mode of Lollard discourse and of all subsequent nonconformist writing as well.[111] Inevitably, when the Lollard composes—whether in sermon, tract, history, or poem—he creates an adversary against whom he may define the nature of his convictions. Here is an itinerant preacher doing battle with the hypothetical objections of his auditory, imagined not merely in their substance but in the tone, phraseology, and even the context in which they might be broached:

> And of þis it wole sue [follow] ferþermore þat þou hast foul mysgouerned þee in þi wordis ny3 þe bigynnyng of þi sermon: where þou menedist as I haue vndirstondun þat þe sectis whos signes þou blamest þus weren not plantid yn bi þe fadir of heuene / Sire as for þese euydencis þat þee semeþ goen a3ens me þou shalt vndirstonde here þat þese mounkis of þe oold lawe of þe which seynt jerom spekiþ: hadden neþer founder ne rule saue oonli god & his rule / and among oþer þingis of profeccioun: þei hadden uttirli forsake worldli lordship.[112]

As the sun begins to fade, the preacher reluctantly attempts to bring his sermon to a conclusion. "I mai tarie þou no lenger & I haue no tyme to make now a recapitulacoun of my sermon."[113] Indeed, he makes a number of premature valedictions, unable to surrender his pulpit. He yearns for a debate of the issues that can never fully end—a Lollard Valhalla where combatants wield their verbal swords in eternal conflict:

> [A]nd of an oþir þing I beseche 3ou here. þat if ony aduersarie of myn replie a3ens ony conclusioun þat I haue shewid to 3ou at þis tyme: reportiþ redili his euydencis, & nameli if he take ony euydence or colour of hooli scripture / and if almi3ti god wole vouche saaf to graunte me grace or leiser to declare mysilf in þese poyntis þat I haue moued in þis sermoun, I shal þoru3 þe help of him in whom is al help declare me, so þat he shal holde him answered. But I presume not þis upon my kunnyng saue oonli upon þe truþe of god þat is my3ti to defend it silf.[114]

In Margery Baxter and this anonymous itinerant preacher, we confront both a layperson and a clergyman in quest of worthy opponents, men and women who might try their doctrine, confirm their faith, and translate the nonconformist psychomachy into objectified action. Although neighbors, wandering mendicants, and obstreperous sermon-goers made, no doubt, adequate adversaries, the Lollard ultimately found his most satisfying opponents in the courts of the examining bishops. That the instrument chosen by the established church to eradicate religious dissent became the vehicle of preserving, refining, and glorifying that dissent is one of the governing ironies of the history of nonconformity. The degree to which the prelatical examination became the focal point of the spiritual lives of the reformers, both among those who suffered its hardships directly and those who experienced them vicariously, can be gauged in part by the increasing range of reference to the event in Lollard literature. In the controversial tract *De Blasphema, Contra Fratres*, the Wycliffite author abruptly invokes the inquisitorial dynamics of heresy proceedings in order to clarify his views on the nature of the Eucharist: "And so, if prelates opposed me, what were þe sacrament of þo auter in his kynde,—I wolde sey þat hit were bred, þo same þat was byfore; ffor þus teches þo gospel þat we shulden bileve. And if þou ask forþer, wheþer hit be substaunse of material bred, nouþer wolde I graunte hit, ne doute hit, ne denye hit, byfore audytorie þat I trowed schulde be harmed þerby, bot sith þat I supposid or reputid þat hit is so."[115]

The passage shifts rapidly from doctrinal declaration to counsel, instructing the prospective examinate on how to parry the questions of the bishops and their circle. Prelates, he warns, are always anxious to "wrynge oute anoþer absolute answere,"[116] but the believer must not satisfy them. The practice of equivocation, evident in both the studied vagaries of nonconformist responses and the exasperation of fulminating examiners, begins early and lasts long. Although examinates undoubtedly resorted to such tactics to evade the consequences of their heresies and goad their tormentors, the prevalence of equivocal response is testimony to an instinct for the limits of knowledge as well as a bent for self-preservation or sadistic delight. The author of *De Blasphema* does not blame the absolutist bishops for entrapment; instead he claims they "faylen bothe in logik and divinyte, and schewen hom unable to examyne of heresye." They fail because they are unwilling to suspend judgment where direct evidence from the Bible is lacking; they fail because they are unwilling to thrust their principles into the refining fire of religious debate. Snatching at a divine certitude beyond human grasp, they fall into the errors of Antichrist. The very format of the protestation demanded of the examinate, argues one Lollard tractarian, betrays the heretical nature of the prelate's insistence on an "absolute answere."[117]

The counseling offered in *De Blasphema* is only an interlude in a larger polemical work. Other Lollard writings, however, pursue more systematically the task of readying the potential examinate for his court performance. *The Sixteen Points* discusses at length the questions that bishops ordinarily put to suspected Lollards. Its author also advocates circumspection: "Trewe cristen men schulden answere here aviseliche, trewliche, and mekeliche to þe poyntis and articlis þat ben put aȝens hem: aviseliche þat þei speike not vnkonnyngliche, trwliche þat þei speike not falseliche, and mekeliche þat þei speike not prowdeliche in her answere . . ."[118]

For the author of *The Sixteen Points*, prelatical examination finally holds more than the promise of doctrinal clarification: it offers the believer an instrument of faith and a system of consolation.[119] In the heat and anxiety of questioning, in the exchange of challenge and response, "þan schall be grace in þer speiking or answering be [by] þe helpe of Crist." William Thorpe, recounting his own examination before Arundel, more explicitly asserts that under the pressure of questioning the godly cease to speak their own minds, giving voice instead to the truths of the Holy Ghost: "And for þe feruent desir & þe greet loue þat þe men & wymmen hau to stonden hem silf in truþe, & to witnessen it, þouȝ þei ben sodeynli & vnwarned brouȝt forþ to ben apposid of aduersaries þe holi goost þat ruliþ hem & moueþ hem þrouȝ his charite, wole in þe our [hour] of her answeringe, speke in him, & schewe sich wisdam whiche all her enemyes schulen neiþer aȝen seie [gainsay] neiþer aȝen stonde lawfulli."[120] As described by Thorpe, as well as other reformers, the experience of trial was simply a heightened version of the believer's daily quest for biblical truth. In the arduous search for true meaning, the saint was granted an inspired revelation of that meaning.

The bishop's examination, like the study of the Bible or the confrontation with hostile neighbors or friars, was at once a spiritual ritual and an intellectual exercise. The true Christian must never rashly seek transcendent visions of the life to come. He must instead turn toward and do battle with his earthly adversaries, Bible in hand. And in that struggle, it may happen that God will visit him with his comfort and understanding; and that in the feeling of God's grace, he will come to a more stable assurance of his communion with the rest of God's saints. Here was a solution of the Lollard's doubts about the validity of his inspirational experience—a solution not voiced in theory but achieved in action. By grounding his life in the continuing war against the visible enemies of biblical truth, the Lollard secured a degree of certainty in the invisible world of inspiration. The prelatical examination and kindred rituals of truth-testing were the true Eucharists of the Lollards. Both were Christian mysteries, rites in which God miraculously manifested his presence in the created world. They were mysteries, too, in the sense that their enactment reconstituted spiritual community and reaffirmed the believer's participation in it. At the same time, examination, Bible reading, and peripatetic disputation were rituals governed by the exercise of reason. They were, in short, rational mysteries, and their performance appropriately invoked logical miracles.

The magical and wondrous miracles of the Host were displaced in Lollard lore by miracles more consonant with the religious rituals from which they emerged and to which in turn they testified. Instead of tales of bleeding bread and reverent dogs, which they dismissed as "bodli myraclis," the Lollards celebrated the "gostli" or common miracles of everyday life:[121] the miracle of patience in withstanding the backbiting and wicked counsel of one's neighbors; the miracle of ethics in "the working of virtues, departing from iniquity, and obeying the commandments of God";[122] the miracle of forensics in disputing with the learned doctors of Antichrist's church. The Lollard explained his curiously unmiraculous miracles in characteristic fashion. The author of *Whiche ben trew myraclis & whiche ben false* argues that "forsoþe bodili myraclis þe morie glorie þat han here & þe more þei ben shewid heer to men þe lasse meryit shuln þei haue in heuen / but gostli myraclis þe lasse þei be seyen here of men / in so muche þei shulen haue þe more ioȝe in heuen."[123] A fellow controversialist insists that the bodily miracles that once accompanied the death of the true church's martyrs are now inappropriate. The enemies of Christ are so entrenched in their sins that God "wol not schewe him seche euydens to repent him self of his tyrauntrize." The key point, though, is that such miracles have been devalued by their familiarity; their effect is soporific rather than enlivening: "þe feiþ schuld wax dulle þorʒ [through] custome of miraclis bi þe wiche it was first quekened / ffor and [if] myraclis were þat ryue and custumable þan were þei no myraclis."[124]

The Lollard conceived the religious life to be a pilgrimage in which religious enlightenment emerged from a continuous and unmediated intellectual struggle with the enemies of God's law. They had emphasized the rational element of Christian devotion, partly in response to what they regarded as the failure of church-sanctioned worship and partly to mask and balance their own dangerous reliance on personal inspiration. The result was an image of life not as fulfillment but as readiness, a life in which the contrary elements of their devotional practices lay suspended, held in balance by an unending war with the adversary.

The Lollards

The little attention Lollard aesthetics has hitherto attracted among literary historians has been directed almost exclusively to the supposed Lollard animus toward the stage. In Jonas Barish's recent *The Antitheatrical Prejudice*, the Lollard once again plays a disconcertingly inept interlude between more polished but similarily misguided acts of iconoclasm, Plato and the Puritans. That this discussion rests upon a single, minor broadside, *A Tretise of Miraclis Pleyinge*, highlights what has become a habitual and narrowly conceived dismissal of nonconformist aesthetic thought.[1] And yet neither Barish nor Russell Fraser before him is fundamentally wrong, it seems to me, in fastening upon the ethos of the theater as central to the nonconformist dilemma. What finally limits their approaches is a preoccupation with overt assaults on the stage and an unwillingness to explore how both fear of and attraction toward self-transforming theatricality constitute part of a larger and more complex response to aesthetic experience as a whole. Vociferous, public displays of hatred may speak eloquently of the repressed, unvoiced tensions within an ideological system. In a party defined politically, psychologically, and doctrinally by the consciousness of its opposition status, that observation becomes all the more pertinent. If the Lollard way is brought into focus by its charged rivalry with mendicancy, its poetics can be similarly illuminated by its curiously ambivalent response to the drama.[2]

The medieval dramatist and the itinerant Lollard preacher vied for the loyalties of much the same audience, one created by the rise of the pious layman and his hunger for new and more engaging modes of devotion.[3] While the Eucharist remained central to orthodox worship, its use had long been aliened by the priesthood.[4] As the immediacy of the experience became gradually lost to the commoner, alternative means of reaffirming spiritual community arose: Lollardy, with its rational mystery of truth tried, offered a radical substitution, the medieval cycles, a more orthodox one. *The Plaie called Corpus Christi*, as its name implies, presents a direct dramatic analogue to eucharistic worship.[5] As in the sacrament of the altar, spectators were drawn into a ritual recreation of Christ's original sacrifice, their participation assured by surrounding Christ's passion with vivid human approximations and perversions of that divine act. Abel, Noah, Joseph, the shepherds, and others performed their own domesticated deeds of sacrificial love, while Cain, the tyrants, and the instruments of Roman and Jewish oppression played their dark counteraction of selfish blindness. Emotional identification with the figures of accommodation encouraged the spectator to cast his own life and actions in the events of biblical history. To choose the good meant to experience vicariously the supreme good of Christ crucified and the benefits he promised.

The convergence of Lollard devotion and cyclical drama extended beyond eucharistic parallelism. The mysteries, too, offered a program of biblical instruction: a series of dramatic, vernacular sermons drawn from scripture, often with expositors carefully policing the interpretative response of the spectator.[6] The shared characteristics of cycle and sermon, however, could only have exacerbated for the Lollard the sense of the more fundamental differences that separated them: obvious differences in the religious creeds they canonized and, more significantly, in the theological assumptions behind their pedagogy.

That the cycles gave voice, eloquent voice, to a vision of the Christian life alien to Lollardy is undeniable. Throughout the cycles, for example, the commerce between human and divine is consistently mediated. Angelic middlemen enact the rites of a holy priesthood. The angel of the shepherds' plays conducts a service in holy song before directing the herdsmen to the Christ child. The divinely ordained sacrifice of Isaac is officiated by an angel who will later substitute a sheep for the child; in traditional typological fashion, both the sacrifice of Christ and the priest's subsequent recreations of that sacrifice at the altar are heralded. In the Joseph and Mary plays the angel assumes the role of priestly confessor who by prodding and consoling successfully resolves the marital woes of a troubled husband.

On those rare occasions when mediation is eschewed, as in the Towneley *Processus Noe cum filiis*, divinity proves amiable and accommodating. To a people whose God remained fixed in heaven, immanent only through his word, the language of divine friendship offered in the cycles is utterly foreign. If the anthropomorphism of the Towneley father violates the tenor of Lollard belief, so too does the posture of his human servant. Noah like so many of the heroes of the cycle witnesses his obedience with a good-natured, bumbling ignorance. This spirit of devotion which happily dismisses intellectual enlightenment achieves its highest expression in the shepherds' plays, dramas exploring the first laymen's responses to the incarnation. There the shepherds demonstrate their right motivation through an awkward mimicry of divine harmony:

> What songe was this, saye yee,
> that he sange to us all three?
> Expounded shall yt bee
> erre wee hethen passe;
> for I am eldest of degree
> and alsoe best, as seemes mee;
> hit was "grorus glorus" with a "glee."[7]

The shepherds' stumblings over the unfamiliar Latin of the *Gloria in excelsis* are ludicrous, but the intent behind them is not. The ceremony is valid precisely because their deficiencies in learning proclaim all the more stridently their stance of total submission. Comedy and pathos are subtly blended in this episode to produce a mixed tonality and emotional complexity endearing to modern critics but undoubtedly troubling to reformers who preferred plainsong to polyphony and the solitary voice of the Psalmist to the bewildering array of Solomon's personae.[8]

Lollard objections to the thematic content of the cycles must finally be extrapolated: we have no record of a direct assault on the plays' image of the holy life. What little the Lollards did have to say about the mysteries is preoccupied more with methodology than subject matter. And here the Lollards consistently link the plays to the failures of orthodox devotion as a whole. The plays, too, are perceived as arrogant attempts to create human analogues for the divine, to fuse through mortal devices a fallen world and a risen one—encouraging their spectators to forget the former and debase the latter. "On the Minorites" is one of the cruder efforts of Lollard propaganda, its arguments rarely rising above frenzied imprecation. Yet when the poet does try to explain his quarrel with stage-struck friars, it is to the question of blurred distinction that he repeatedly returns. Recalling the descent of an angel in one play, he is angered that the divine being more resembles a dispenser of pork than of grace: "Þer comes one out of þe skye in a grey goun, / As it were an hog-hyerd hyand to toun."[9] Viewing a series of scenes from the life of St. Francis,[10] he insists on unmasking the theatrical illusion by recounting the action not in terms of the fictional characters but of the local grey friars who play them. A work as naïve as "On the Minorites" is an unlikely source of dramatic theory, but it is important to note that even rudimentary Lollard thought regards the wedding of the real and the imagined with trepidation. Artists who seek to body forth the spiritual in the physical succeed only in compromising both.

In his attack on the cycles, the author of *A Tretise of Miraclis Pleyinge* warns that anglicizing the eternal landscapes of the Bible will undermine the audience's conviction of their reality. Men will cease to believe in the integrity of a spiritual world once it has been mapped in familiar coordinates: "And therfore many men wenen that ther is no helle of everelastinge peine, but that God doth but thretith us, and not to do it in dede, as ben pleyinge of miraclis in signe and not in dede."[11] At the same time, the Lollard feared that audiences would abandon their responsibilities in this world by repeatedly surrendering themselves to the imaginative creations of another. When a Wycliffite writer derides the actor playing Herod for titillating his female audience with his stage gesturing, the seduction that troubles him is more than sexual.[12] He is worried about the ways in which men and women are readily seduced into abandoning their hold on the real. Forgoing the only secure path to the spiritual, the Bible, they recklessly grasp symbols constructed out of the erring imaginations of their fellow mortals. They enter a world of fiction in which signs have no assured capacity to lead men to truth. Kolve has suggested that the Lollard attack on the drama was fueled by an inability to understand the difference between the fictionalized world of play and the workaday world of earnestness.[13] In fact, the Lollards understood the play world all too well. They agreed that man's efforts to devise a middle ground between the sacred and profane, whether in images of saints, paintings of biblical scenes, or acting of mystery plays, could provide means of religious enlightenment. But what dangerous means. It was so easy for the pilgrim to enter the artist's world and never exit; so easy for the signs that seemed transparent and permeable to become opaque and impenetrable; so easy for the fictional to be mistaken for the historical. In this world, man is all too likely "to forȝet [him]self."

The more elaborately the Christian artist embellished his creation, the more alluringly he blended the miraculous with the familiar, the more successfully he fashioned worlds in which the spiritual imagination might be tempted to make its home, the more dangerous and deadly became his creation.[14] The mystery plays presented just such a world. Their greatest achievement, their undeniable power to transport their audience out of the present and into a timeless universe of the artist's creation, was, in the eyes of the Lollard, their most demonic element. For the Lollard refused to concede that the universe of the artist faithfully mirrored God's; indeed, he believed that more commonly the artist's world slyly usurped it: "[T]hey ben ginnys of the devuel to cacchen men to byleve of Antichrist, as wordis of love withoute verrey dede ben ginnys of the lecchour to cacchen felawchipe to fulfillinge of his leccherie."[15]

Even if it happened that the artist on the stage and the priest at the altar did manage to lead their audiences heavenward, why, asked the Lollard, take their danger-fraught path? God himself had provided man with the properly sanctified bridge to his true home. He had given man signs and symbols enough in his book of truth. What is more, he had crafted that truth in images as seductive as those of the human artist. The language he spoke was at once familiar and foreign, commonplace and miraculous. The open passages of the Bible summoned the reader or auditor with a voice as recognizable as his neighbor's tongue; the misty sections beckoned him further into a world of transcendent knowledge. Simply by committing his heart to an understanding of God's words, he was assured of finding his way to the deity, not with unreliable human escorts but with the Holy Ghost himself as his guide. The universe was a place too easy to become lost in, and the price exacted for losing one's way too great, to accept any other guide.

SAINTS AND EXAMINERS

The doubts and fears of reformers commenting directly upon the drama tend to cluster about the experience of the cycle plays: the transfixion of the spiritual imagination in a realm of unsanctified symbols; the obstruction of the elemental confrontation between the anxious believer and his unfathomable lord; and the substitution of the stasis of awestruck wonder for the dynamics of "love-drede." Lollard misgivings about the cycles manifest a distrust of all forms of religious devotion dependent upon man's fiction-making capacity. Committed to a discovery of scriptural truth that began with reason but ended in the promptings of the Holy Ghost, the Lollards understandably regarded other competitive varieties of intuitive apprehension as suspect. Yet did anxiety over compromising the authenticity of his spiritual vision prevent the Lollard from exercising his artistic vision?

The need to reenact publicly events of spiritual signficance in order to revitalize the mystical community first engendered by those events lies behind the rituals and art of all religions. Although Lollardy had devalued the central rite of orthodoxy, the Eucharist, the movement was not without its own ceremonies of regeneration. The investiture of scriptural devotion with sacramental significance is evident from the way in which its proper performance was seen as recreating the pivotal events in Christ's life. In *The holi prophete Dauid seith*, biblical study "remembers" the Crucifixion;[16] in the Wycliffite sermon for Palm Sunday the eventual triumph of such study recollects the Resurrection: "[Þ]ei dreedon hem þat Godis lawe schal qwikon aftur þis, and herfore þei make statutes stable as a stoon;

and geton graunt of knytis to confermen hem, and þese þei marken
wel wiþ witnesse of lordis, leste þat trewþe of Godis lawe hid in þe
sepulchre, berste owt to knowyng of comun puple. O Crist! þi lawe
is hyd ȝeet; whanne wolt þow sende þin aungel to remeue þis stoon
and schewe þi trewþe to þi folc?"[17] The Lollards had devalued the
Eucharist and presumably those contemporary dramatic modes that
gave it representational shape. Around their own rationalistic mystery, however, a number of the reformers began to create a new
celebratory art—one that embraced the ethos of drama if not its
form.

The Lollard conception of life was itself agonistic. Scriptural devotion demanded a ceaseless combat between reader and text periodically climaxing in new levels of spiritual understanding and self-
transformation. Beyond the private drama of exegetical enlightenment was the public drama of truth tried. In protracted debate with
his enemies, the believer strengthened his newly won insights into
God's word and the saintly identity such insight conferred. As popular Lollardy emerged in the fifteenth century, prelatical examination
came increasingly to embody in its most vivid form the sacramental
trial of truth. Lollard after Lollard was summoned to appear before
the alleged limbs of Antichrist and defend his religious beliefs. The
utmost vigilance was demanded of those who hoped to escape the
bishop's sophistical snares. Coaching prospective examinates, one
Lollard warns, "Þerfor witte welle þis þat, wane a coupulatif is
madde, þouȝ þer be many trewþes, if it afferme a falshed it schal be
denyed altogidur: falsenes is so venemus."[18] Faced with cunning,
educated opponents, the Lollard was called upon to exert his intellect and fortify his faith. The event became a rite of belief whose
stichomythic play of question and response, of charge and counter-
charge, became indelibly printed upon Lollard consciousness and
Lollard discourse. The reformers' reproduction of courtroom testimony enabled those never examined to partake communally in the
experience.[19] Noting that evidence of later Lollard thought comes
almost exclusively from diocesan records of such heresy trials, John
Thomson and, more recently, Anne Hudson have argued that the
formulaic quality of the questioning lends an appearance of systematization to Lollardy that may never have existed.[20] The Lollard

mind, however, was deeply and genuinely not merely superficially unified in the experience of examination. The heresy trial became at once a devotional mode and a metaphor for the Christian life. Persecution emerged again as essential to the life of the faithful, as it had once been in the primitive church: "We must nede breke þe nutt, if we wole haue þe kirnel; we must nedis suffre traueile, if we desiren rest. So must we nede suffre peyne, if we wole cum to bliss."[21]

By summoning the Lollards into their courts and eventually burning them at the stake, the bishops provided the reformers with their own recurrent drama of redemptive sacrifice. Obligingly, the prelates assumed the roles of Herod, Pilate, Caiaphas, Annas, and the Pharisees and offered to their victims the roles of Christ and the apostles. Evidence that the reformers began to regard reports of prelatical examination as a species of tyrant play emerges early. The Latin poem "On the Council of London" recounts the so-called Earthquake Council held in 1382 at Blackfriars.[22] In the exchanges between Nicholas Hereford and Philip Repingdon and their adversaries, memories of Christ's trials before Caiaphas, Herod, and Pilate are invoked. Drawing from Luke, the poet observes that just as the common enemy, Christ, temporarily reconciled old rivals, the high priest and the governor, so now the persecution of the Lollards unites monk and friar: "Thus did Herod and Pilate become friends."[23] The poet, however, seems to be thinking of mystery play accounts as well as biblical descriptions of these events. The influence of the cycles is particularly evident in the portrait of the mad examiners. The stormy John Welles speaks "with winds and tempests," while his fellow inquisitor, Peter Stokes, is "with all things angry and too puffed up."[24] Matthew and Mark alone among the Gospels provide the precedent for the angry tyrant; both describe Caiaphas as rending his robes when confronted by Christ's claim to godhead. It is the cycles that drew elaborately detailed portraits of the madness of the evil inquisitor extending Caiaphas's self-destructive rage to Herod, Pilate, and Annas.[25] The richness of this Lollard's account of the behavior of Stokes and Welles is suggestive of the poet's debt to the cycles and perhaps an unconscious acknowledgment of his attempt to fashion his own tyrant play, one never meant to grace a stage.

All of the members of this acting troupe were amateurs. Systematic persecution had never been a religious tradition in England. The bishops, as McFarlane and others have so judiciously pointed out, were at best reluctant inquisitors, anxious to avoid inflicting the final punishment on members of their flock.[26] The Lollards were equally inept at playing the martyr. Annals of early Lollardy are filled with embarrassing recantations by prominent advocates of the cause.[27] Philip Repingdon went so far as to change roles, trading his martyr's robe for that of a church inquisitor.[28] In time both parties learned to play their parts with a grim determination—the bishops to burn men to defend their faith, the Lollards to be burned to witness theirs.

THE TRIAL OF WILLIAM THORPE

The emergence among Lollard writers of "displaced drama," literary and quasi-literary works that gingerly approach but never quite adopt dramatic form, can be seen in *The Examination of Master William Thorpe*. An autobiographical account of one Lollard's appearance before Archbishop Arundel in August 1407, the *Examination* enjoyed considerable popularity in the fifteenth and sixteenth centuries.[29] Possession of or familiarity with the text appears to have been one of the certain signs by which the "known man" was betrayed to church authorities.[30] Circulated first in manuscript, the work was later printed in Antwerp in 1530. Three early Protestant luminaries—William Tyndale, John Bale, and John Foxe—all participated in either editing, translating, or printing Thorpe's narrative. It was anthologized by Bale along with several recorded examinations that together constitute the beginnings of nonconformist hagiography. Bale, who himself would assume the task of "purifying" the popish mystery cycles, was quick to recognize that, as a species of spiritual discourse, the examination bore distinct affinities to church drama in general and the tyrant play in particular. Observing in his marginal commentary on the examinations of Anne Askew the conduct of the interrogating bishops, he writes: "Aforetime hath not been seen such frantic outrage as is now; the judges, without all sober discretion, running to the rack, tugging, hauling, and pulling thereat, like tormentors in a play."[31]

If we look closely at Thorpe's *Examination*, the fraternity Bale instinctively perceived between the examination and the theater of the guilds should become more evident. Having briefly set the scene (the examination occurs in a closeted room off the great chamber of the archbishop) and having introduced his dramatis personae (Thorpe, Arundel, a parson of St. Dunstan's, and two clerks of the canon law),[32] Thorpe embarks on his primary task of rendering in dialogue a trial of truth. The plot of Thorpe's displaced drama is again that of Christ's examination. Thorpe plays Christ, Arundel plays Caiaphas, and his clerks play the tyrant's minions.[33] Thorpe, like his master, displays complete self-possession, his answers alternating between enigmatic evasion and brazen defiance. Arundel's initial calm soon collapses into the frantic behavior of the tyrants of the mystery cycles. Cursing and threatening, he apes the high priest's barely restrained impulse to trade forensics for fisticuffs: "And þe archbischop as if he hadde not quyetid wiþ my seiynge, turnede him aweiward & ȝede hidir & þidir, & seide, bi god I schal sette vpon þi schynes a peire of pillers, þat þou schalt be gladde to chaunge þi vois."[34]

In his anger, Arundel abuses Thorpe in asides to his clerks: "[H]erde ȝe euer losel speke þus. [C]ertis þis is þe lore of hem all, þat where euer þei come if þei mowen be suffridde, þei enforsen hem to enpunge þe freedam of holi chirche."[35] The sycophants, in response, voice impatience and counsel their master to bring the trial to a speedy end: "[S]er it is forþ daies & ȝe haue ferre for to ride to nyȝt. þerfore sere make an ende wiþ him, for he wol noon make, but þe moore sere þat ȝe bisien ȝou for to drawe towardis ȝou, þe more contumax [contumacious] is maade, & þe ferþer fro ȝou."[36] The action climaxes as Arundel breaks into physical violence, "smytyng wiþ his fist fersli upon a copbord [and speaking] to me wiþ a grete spirit, seiynge, bi [Jesus] but if þou leeue suche addiciouns, obeiynge þee now here wiþouten ony accepcioun to myn ordinaunce, or þat I go out of þis place I schal make yee as sikir as any þeef þat is in kent . . ."[37] Shaking with anger and unable to proceed with the investigation, he leaves the task to his followers.

The inherent theatricality of Thorpe's *Examination* emerges perhaps most clearly in its consistent presentation in dialogue of a complete

action—one in which the central character, prompted by an alter-
ation in fortune, reevaluates himself and his role. As so often occurs
in radical discourse, the nonconformist first learns what he is by
recognizing what he is not. And Thorpe is not Arundel. The violence
of the archbishop's language becomes at once the hallmark of unregenerate speech and, in its sputtering incoherence, an emblem of the
impotence of evil in the face of godliness. Awareness of Arundel's
false witnessing and its ultimate powerlessness forces Thorpe to consider more closely the nature and sources of his own responses. Fear
of misspeaking gradually fades as under the pressure of the prelate's
"aposynge" he begins to recognize that holy "answeringe" is divine
speech, borrowed not invented, received not imagined: "And [in]
myn herte I was noþing . . . a gast wiþ þis manassynge [menacing]
of þe archebischop. But more her þoruȝ myn herte was confortid &
stablischid in þe drede & loue of god. . . . [And] I preiede god for his
goodnesse to ȝeue me þanne & alwei grace, to speke wiþ a meke &
an esy spirit, and what euer þing þat I schulde speke, þat I miȝte
haue þerto trewe autorite of scripture or open resoun."[38]

The pivotal moment comes when, unable to summon the inward
resources to answer Arundel's pressing question on the doctrine of
Chrysostom, Thorpe surrenders to a trust in God. The Holy Ghost
will bestow the answers he himself cannot conceive: "I hadde not
bisyed me to stodie aboute þe witt þer of. But liftynge up my mynde
to god, I preied him of grace, & anoon I þouȝte how crist seide to
hise disciplis, whanne for my name ȝe shulen be brouȝt before jugis,
I schal ȝeue to ȝou mouþ & wisedom, þat all ȝoure aduersaries
schulen not aȝen seie [gainsay] & tristing feiþfulli to þe word of crist
I seide . . ."[39]

This is the comfort that Thorpe had promised to the readers of his
work who, like him, might face further questioning, whether before
hostile bishops or doubting neighbors: "And for þe feruent desir &
þe greet loue þat þese men & wymmen hau to stonden hem silf in
truþe, & to witnessen it, þouȝ þei ben sodeynli & vnwarned brouȝt
forþ to ben apposid of aduersaries þe holi goost þat ruliþ hem &
moueþ hem þoruȝ his charite, wole in þe our [hour] of her answeringe speke in him."[40] In his struggle against his learned opponents,
the simple believer will be empowered by the inspiration of the Holy

Ghost to offer true responses. He will "play" Christ by an *imitatio* not only of his actions but of his words as well. Understanding will come from no gifts of his own other than a will to fight for God's law. Here again is the basic formula of enlightenment that we have already seen in Lollard theories regarding the study of the Bible.[41]

Upon this moment of anagnorisis arising from the agon of good and evil, Thorpe's displaced drama turns. As if to demonstrate that we have reached the peripeteia, roles are suddenly reversed and Thorpe, for a time, examines the archbishop. Arundel explodes with his cupboard-slamming gesture signaling the overthrow of the forces of the Antichrist and the conclusion of the trial. Thorpe's private victory, like Christ's, elicits public abuse at the hands of the nonbeliever: "[A]nd þanne I was rebukid & scorned & manassid on ech side. And ȝit aftir þis dyuerse persoones crieden vpon me, to knele doun to submytte me, but I stood stille & spak no word."[42] The play quickly shifts scene. Thorpe sits alone in prison; the crowds have departed, and suddenly a calming silence envelops the sufferer and his audience:

> I was þanne gretli confortid in all my wittis not oonly forþi þat I was þan delyuered for a tyme fro þe siȝt, fro þe heeringe, fro þe presence, fro þe scornynge & fro þe manassinge of myn enemyes, but myche more I gladid in þe lord, forþi þoruȝ his grace he kepte me so boþe amonge þe flateryngis specialli, also amonge þe manassingis of my aduersaries, wiþ outen heuynesse, & a grippinge of my conscience I passid awei fro hem. For as a tree leyde vpon a noþer tree ouer thwert on crosse wyse, so weren þe archebischop & hise þree clerkis alwei contrerie to me & I to hem.[43]

The stability of Thorpe's faith and its utter contrariety to the language and logic of Antichrist engender a living icon, a cross not built of wood or emblazoned with precious metals and stones, but one made of spiritual sinews and embellished with the glory of a life spent in suffering for the truth of God's word. Man must neither bear crosses nor kneel to them; he must himself become the animated symbol of Christ's passion by laying his soul athwart the evil of the world. Nearly a generation later, Margery Baxter would challenge an erring neighbor with the same image of the persecuted believer as the only legitimate representation of the spirit of the cross:

> Dicens in lingua materna, "lewed wrightes of stokkes hewe and fourme suche crosses and ymages, and after that lewed peyntors glorye thaym with colours, et si vos affectatis videre veram crucem Christi ego volo monstrare eam tibi hic in domo tua propia." Et ista iurata asseruit se libenter videre velle veram crucem Christi. Et prefata Margeria dixit, "vide," et tunc extendebat brachia sua in longum, dicens isti iurate, "hic est vera crux Christi, et istam crucem tu debes et potes videre et adorare omni die hic in domo tua propria, et adeo tu vanum laboras quando vadis ad ecclesias ad adorandas sive orandas aliquas ymagines vel cruces mortuas."[44]

Thorpe's drama ends with such a Lollard adoration of the true cross. It is a cathartic moment, both for Thorpe who has found relief and an assurance of his godly nature and for the reader who experiences a release from the pain of his own vicarious persecution. In this sacramental art, reader and author become linked in a shared sense of escape from agony and doubt, "oonyed [made one] in trewe feiþ, in stidefast hope and in parfiȝt charite."[45]

Thorpe's triumphant icon of righteous suffering conveniently emblematizes an act of aesthetic as well as moral choice. In that choice the nonconformist's ambivalent response to fictionality—and its most autonomous manifestation, the drama—stands revealed. The history of nonconformity is an attack on the fixed and solidified image, whether carved in stone, voiced in metaphor, or enacted upon a stage. In the fusion of a transcendent truth to its temporal signifier, the artist seduced his audience into loving the human over the divine. As Thorpe's living cross suggests, however, dissenters actively sought to shape both in the raw materials of their lives and in their records of those lives human images of the divine. These creations offered glimpses not of unity but of congruence, of likeness not identity. As an event and as a written story, Thorpe's examination possesses literal and historical truth. Yet in its ritual reenactment of the events of Christ's life, it boldly advertises its figural meanings.[46]

There is no extant orthodox record of Thorpe's trial; its accuracy is, therefore, impossible to assess.[47] Even a casual reading of the *Examination* suggests, however, that Thorpe has a preconception of the form and meaning this confrontation will assume; and he does everything in his moral and literary power to ensure that the pattern of Christ's experience shows through his own. In this sense both his life and his work are a fiction, an imagined representation of the divine rendered first in deeds and then in words describing those deeds. As the author of *A Tretise of Miraclis Pleyinge* had warned, "wordis . . . withoute verrey dede . . . ben ginnys of the devuel." Within the account of his trial, Thorpe's anxiety to make visible the timeless truths lurking behind quotidian experience demands imaginative elaboration and distortion. There is an artistic consciousness behind this work shaping its readers' responses. Consider Thorpe's use of flashbacks, in a manner reminiscent of a drama's subplots, to highlight the archetypal design of his encounter. Three times in the course of his trial, Thorpe summons dialogues from his past to explain his present conduct. In the first episode the scene is domestic: the reformer's parents vainly threaten and plead with their son to embark on a career in the priesthood (one wonders whether Thorpe's parents might not have sympathized with Arundel's frustration). A troubled Thorpe wanders off to discuss his vocational crisis with a group of wise men, i.e., Wycliffites. Here he discovers a true sense of calling and willingly casts his lot with the poor priests. The action of the subplot mirrors, with some variation, the action of the main plot: a series of confrontations leading to the believer's newfound assurance of his proper role in God's providential plan. Rather than Christ's appearance before the high priest, Thorpe is here invoking an earlier biblical episode, Christ's debate with the doctors of the temple. That expedition, too, marked an awakening to the higher responsibilities of a divinely appointed mission.

The other two episodes offered by Thorpe also witness in dialogue the trying of truth. In the first, we glimpse Thorpe haranguing an auditory who foolishly prefer the sacrament to God's word. At the sound of the sacring bell, they run to Communion, leaving the apostle alone but more deeply convinced of the superiority of hearing over seeing: "[G]oode men ʒou were better to stooden here stille, & to heere goodis word. ffor certis þe vertu & þe mede of þe moost holi sacrament of þe auter stondiþ myche moore in þe bileue þereof þat ȝe owen to haue in ȝoure soulis, þan it doiþ in þe outward siȝt þer of. & þerfore ȝou were better to stonde stille quyetefulli & to heeren goddis worde, siþ þoruȝ heeringe þerof men comen to veri bileue."[48] The last interlude, prophetically, is set in prison. There an agent of the ecclesiastical court, by feigning loyalty to Lollard principles, dupes Thorpe into confessing his heretical views on tithes. Although Thorpe succumbs to his enemy's wiles, the ruse once exposed merely confirms his sense of righteousness. Now Thorpe has his Judas. All of Thorpe's flashbacks in their mirroring encourage the audience to read the universal patterns couched in a variety of particular events.[49]

The fashioning of an animated iconography that moves uneasily between the real and the imagined, the literal and the figural, the historical and the fictional is complemented by the creation of a similarly internalized and divided drama. *The Examination of Master William Thorpe* flirts with the world of the drama, never fully embracing either its defining elements or its ethos. Although dialogue predominates, narrative intrusions restrict the free interplay between action and audience, discouraging the spectator's total immersion in a fictive universe. Thorpe's depiction of the sudden joy of the archbishop upon receiving a petition from Shrewsbury urging stern action against Lollardy demonstrates the author's characteristic bracketing of primary dialogue with narrative exposition. "And as if þis askinge hadde plesid þe archebischop, he seide þanne þere bi my þrifte þis herti preier & feruent request schal be þouȝt on."[50] The single line of dialogue more than adequately captures the intonations of the self-satisfied man. Yet Thorpe will not let Arundel's words speak for themselves nor will he trust his reader's apprehension of them; instead he uses his editorial remarks to direct, ground, and finally control the reader's perception to a degree not possible either in pure dialogue or in the still more open commerce of theatrical experience. It is as if we were privy to the director's heavily annotated prompt-book in which all thoughts about the staging of the play are recorded alongside the dialogue. The act of interpretation is restricted and imaginative freedom repressed.

What matters perhaps more, however, is that the crucial ingredient of impersonation is never fully realized.[51] Thorpe may suggest the similitude between his own experience and that of Christ—may even speak his "lines"—but he does not play Christ in the manner of either the priest at the altar or the actor on the pageant cart. The surrender of the actor's own identity proves abortive. Even when in the climactic moment of his interrogation he submits to the Spirit, there is no real sacrifice of identity; his personality remains intact though the Spirit dwells within him. Thorpe as Thorpe and Thorpe as Christ vibrate side by side much as the physical elements of the Host coexist with the spiritual presence of the Son. If we may speak of his playing a role, it is only in the sense of playing an idealized self, of putting on an elect image of his fallen self. Thorpe stops short of drama: as Wyclif stopped short of seeing the sacrament as a spiritual annihilation of the physical reality of the bread, as the itinerant Lollard preacher stopped short of creating an allegory in which a literal event was consumed by its figurative meaning, as Margery Baxter stopped short of fashioning a material crucifix.

At one point in his narrative, Thorpe gives us a rare glimpse into his own understanding of the function of his art. Charged with preaching against pilgrimages, Thorpe explains his position by differentiating between those who superstitiously visit the sites of reputed miracles and those whose whole lives are a "trauelynge to ward þe blis of heuene." These latter pilgrims are also men and women in search of miraculous deeds; they, however, seek them not in shrines but in the lives of the saints:

[Þ]ese blessid pilgrymes of god, whan þei heeren of seyntis, or of vertuouse men or wymmen, þei bisien hem to knowe þe lyuynge of seyntis & of vertues men & wymmen: how þei forsoken wilfulli þe prosperite of þis lyf; how þei wiþstoden þe sugestiouns of þe fend & how þei restreyneden her fleischli lustis; how discreet þei weren in alle her aduersitees; how prudent þei weren in conselynge of men & of wymmen mouynge hem to haten euere al synne & to fle it, & to schame euere greetli þerof, & to loue alle vertues & to drawe to hem ymagynynge, how mekeli crist & his sueris [followers] bi ensaumple suffrynge scornes & sclaundris & how pacientli þei aboden &

token þe wraþful manassynges of tirauntis, how homely þei
weren & seruysable to pore men, for to relevue hem & confort
hem bodili aftir her kunnynge & her power. & how deuoute þei
weren in preieris, how feruent in heuenli desiris & how þei
absentid hem fro spectaclis & fro veyn siȝtis, and heeringe &
how stable of contenaunce þei weren. how herteli þei weileden
and sorewiden for synne, how bisili þei weren to lette & to
distroie alle vicis; & how laborouse & ioieful þei weren to sowe
& to plante vertues.[52]

What we have in this twisted bit of prose is an intricate set of
nested boxes. At the center is the tale of the archetypal saint, Jesus
Christ, whose suffering at the hands of menacing tyrants defines
saintly conduct. Around his deeds are clustered the analogous experiences of his followers who are inspired, "bi ensaumple," to imitate the pattern of his life. The "ymagynynge" of the pattern of
Christ's suffering and that of the apostles becomes, in turn, the instrument for the "conselynge of men & of wymmen" by "seyntis or
. . . vertuouse men or wymmen." Finally, the recorded lives of these
saintly teachers become the devotional vehicles that enable Thorpe's
"blessid pilgrymes" to mount the "step noumbrid of god toward him
in to heuene." The piling up of the dependent clauses, each beginning with "how" and each describing acts of the saintly life, obscures
the identity of the subject of the clauses. Are these clauses referring
to Christ, his followers, the counseled men and women, their in-
structors, or the pilgrims? The question is irrelevant as the historical
and imaginative narratives of each group collapse into those of the
others and finally come to rest on the bedrock of Christ's exemplary
life. All Christian existence radiates from and is justified by the way
in which Christ lived while on earth. Flourishing his logical acumen,
one Lollard preacher warns his adversaries that a responsible clerk
will not offer a "short" argument as a proof of right conduct, i.e., a
holy man did thus and therefore so may or should we. Such conclusions can only be drawn from Christ's deeds. "[Þ]erfore you most
argue þus, petir seide or dide þus & in þis he suede [followed] þe lijf
or þe loore of jesus crist: þerfore petir in þis dide or seide wel & in
þis it is hoolsum to sue petir."[53] Christian art is, for Thorpe, not

"spectaclis & . . . veyn siȝtis and heeringe" but forensic biography: the "aposynge and answeringe" of persecuted saints in conflict with corrupt authority. Thorpe's own autobiographical saint's life, its theatricality displaced from the stage to the soul and finally to the text, is an example of this Christian art.

THE APPEAL OF SATIRE

Thorpe's *Examination* stands alone in the fifteenth century as a consciously artful recreation of a historical act of "aposynge and answeringe." Surviving records of heresy trials are almost always official in nature. It would be over a century before similar autobiographical works appeared and then under the supervision of compilers such as John Bale and John Foxe. By Foxe's time it is possible to speak of these accounts as a distinctive genre, albeit one closely related to the Puritan saint's life and the spiritual autobiography. The Lollards did, nonetheless, find other modes of artistic expression capable of dramatizing scriptural debate without stirring the "dremys and fantasies" of the unsanctified imagination. Their dominant vehicle in literary enterprises was satiric dialogue. Explorations of this quasi-dramatic form would eventually contribute to the emergence of the animadversions of Bale and his Puritan descendants as well as the incomparable dramatic satire of Martin Marprelate.

As we have seen, dialogue was the characteristic configuration of nonconformist discourse. The choice of satire was also a natural one for the reformers. Verse attacks on clerical abuses had been a staple of medieval life for centuries. As Yunck has shown, by the end of the twelfth century the conventions of such venality satire had already become stereotyped.[54] By grafting their own writing onto a long-standing tradition of anticlerical satire, the Lollards were able to lay the foundation for establishing the historical continuity of the true church, a problem that was to occupy ecclesiastical reformers well into the sixteenth century.[55] Both Bale and Foxe would respond with a Protestant hagiography documenting the survival of a church of true believers independent of a fallen Rome.[56] The Lollards, some one hundred and fifty years earlier, had already begun to formulate a theory of church history based on the prophecies of the reign of Antichrist to bolster their similar claims. The traditions of the apostolic church, the Wycliffites argued, were maintained in a more or less pristine form for some thousand years after the death of Christ. Pope Sylvester I's acceptance of temporal dominion from the Emperor Constantine plunged the church into corruption. The institution's growing subjugation to Antichrist climaxed in the emergence of mendicancy and the promulgation of the doctrine of transubstantiation under Innocent III.[57] Association with the satirists of the church's postmillennial decline did more than ease Lollard doubts about the pedigree of their movement; it enabled them to hawk their revolutionary wares in a way that appeared to belie the radical nature of their beliefs. The need for expediency and a borrowed respectability was served.[58]

Satire proved congenial to the Lollard sensibility in other ways as well. The Lollard's sense of election, we observed, was predicated on his struggle with an erring adversary. True identity and doctrine emerged from the delineation of reversed, falsified images of themselves. This dependence in reformed thinking on definition by negation should not be mistaken for theological immaturity. If this were the case we might expect a diminution of the contentiousness of nonconformity as the movement regained its university foothold in the Tudor period. No such mollification occurred. Even in the writings of its most highly regarded thinker, Thomas Cartwright, Elizabethan Puritanism was marked by a preponderance of polemical over purely theoretical or doctrinal literature. Attacks on perversions of the norm outweighed formulations of that norm.[59] To such a mental outlook, satire was well suited. The lion's share of any satire is denunciatory. The normative vision against which corruption is judged is often barely stated, the mere hint of something better waiting in the wings.

For the Lollard troubled by misgivings over the idiosyncratic nature of his belief, satire again proved convenient and congenial. The enemy in satire is the deviant personality, individuals or groups deemed to be in violation of society's true but often hidden or compromised values. The struggle between the satirist and the object of his scorn is a struggle between health and disease, sanity and madness. At stake is the survival of the social organism which, the satirist counsels, must reject those cancerous elements that threaten its existence. It is the task of the satirist to expose and exorcise society's enemies by convincingly demonstrating their antipathy to that society's essential principles. In the process, roles are reversed: the enemy is transformed from an entrenched majority into a subversive minority, the satirist from isolated critic into public defender. By repeatedly casting his rivals in the role of threatening deviant, the Lollard satirist reaffirmed his own sense of sanity, well-being, and importance.

The ideal victim of the Lollard satirist's self-exorcism was the friar. From the crude vituperation of "On the Minorites" to the doctrinally oriented *Jack Upland*, the mendicant plays the villain. And an easy target he was: his embrace of a private order of religion immediately marked him as a religious anomaly;[60] his immunity from the jurisdiction of the ecclesiastical hierarchy emphasized his position as an alien within English society—more loyal to pope than king.[61] Jack Upland reports with particular horror how the limiting districts of the mendicants seem to deny the native boundaries that separate manorial estates: "Whi sette ȝe al þe kyngis lond to ferme to ȝoure lymytouris as ȝe weren lordis of alle mennes goodis, & ȝe wole not suffre o frere to begge in anoþeres lymytacioun vnpunyschid?"[62] The upward mobility of the friars, their skill in climbing the social ladder, subverted social boundaries as well. The author of *Pierce the Ploughman's Crede* complains:

> Now mot iche soutere [cobbler] his sone * setten to schole,
> And ich a beggers brol [brat] * on þe booke lerne,
> And worþ [become] to a writere * & wiþ a lorde dwell,
> Oþer falsly to a frere * þe fend for to seruen!
> So of þat beggers brol * a bychop schal worþen
> Among þe peres of þe lond * prese [press] to sitten,
> And lordes sones lowly * to þo losells aloute [bow down].[63]

That the charges leveled against the friars were precisely the same as those brought against the reformers should come as no surprise.

Lollard satire was an act of self-purification. By projecting onto the friars those crimes of which he himself was accused, the Lollard proclaimed his innocence.[64]

Satire's last claim upon the Lollard imagination was the attractive personae it offered the reformers. The most common was the rude but righteous laborer.[65] His immediate literary source was Piers Plowman. It is a Lollard version of Langland's pilgrim who voices the reformers' party line in *Pierce the Ploughman's Crede*. The saintly plowman from Chaucer's *Canterbury Tales* is recruited to relate a debate between proponents of the Lollard and orthodox platforms in *The Plowman's Tale*. Finally, there is Jack Upland, literally, Jack the Countryman. A clear descendant of Piers, his rude soothsaying elicits caustic mimicry from his Dominican opponent, Friar Daw:

> But Iak þou3 þi questions semen to þee wyse,
> 3it li3tly a lewid man maye leyen hem a water [overthrow
>   them];
> For summe ben lewid, summe ben shrewid, summe falsly
>   supposid,
> And þerfore shal no maistir ne no man of scole
> Be vexid wiþ þy maters but a lewid frere
> Þat men callen Frere Daw Topias, as lewid as a leke.[66]

The frequent use of the simple commoner as spokesman in Lollard satire suggests the extent to which anti-intellectualism was coming to dominate Lollardy in its later phases. The apotheosis of the ignorant but well-living plowman is testimony to the triumph of a conception of godliness that emphasized simple, moral living at the expense of education and training. To live and feel God's truth was more valued than laboring to understand it through the exercise of reason. In Lollard satire the balanced play of reason and inspiration found among the immediate popularizers of Wyclif's doctrine can be seen breaking down.

If Piers Plowman was the immediate source of the Lollard uplander, his distant ancestor was the Hebrew prophet. The enemy of evil in high places and the defender of the imperiled believer, the prophet was, for the Lollard, the Old Testament type of the examined Christ. Hauled before kings and priests to be questioned, tortured, and killed for the truth he preached, he was the original of a pattern of behavior sanctified by Christ and enacted by the Lollard. The caustic denunciation of social and spiritual evil, the jeremiad, offered the Lollard satirist a literary model that carried an indisputable biblical sanction. It was above all the example of the prophets that enabled the Lollard to justify vitriolic speech and to distinguish it from its heinous cousin, backbiting. To the charges of the orthodox preacher—"þei will com to þe churche and knokke hem-selfe vn þe breste and turne þe eyen owteward as þei wold goy to heven all hote, but ȝitt þe [they] will bacbite here euen -cristen and make wrouth and debate where-as loue was a-fore"[67]—the Wycliffite preacher recalled Elijah's mocking words to the priests of Baal: "For Hely þe prophete bad preestis of Baal þat þei schulden crye strongly, leste þer god slepte, or spak wiþ oþre men, þat he myhte not heren hem. And þus scorneþ Powle spekyng to Corynþios, 'where I dide lasse to ȝow þan oþre apostles diden? But þat I took not of ȝow, forȝyue ȝe me þis wronge!' And so often in Godis lawe is scornyng wel ment, as ȝif hit were leueful doon on good maner."[68]

Satire pleased the Lollard. Indeed it became the dominant belletristic exercise among English nonconformists well into the Elizabethan age. Martin Marprelate's brilliant satiric forays answered the same spiritual needs met by the less accomplished efforts of a Jack Upland. Yet satire pleased more than for its sanctified vituperation or its appealing authorial voices. It pleased because, when cast into dialogue, it was capable of yielding the same kind of quasi-dramatic experience as Thorpe's *Examination*. Like Thorpe's work, satiric dialogue could replay the essential drama of "aposyinge and answeringe" without ever ascending the all too dangerous stage; it could give artistic form to the Lollard sacrament of truth found and truth tried. How this task was accomplished will be the subject of the remainder of this chapter.

SATIRIC DIALOGUE

The Lollard psychodrama of apposing and answering finds its simplest expression in the companion poems "The Layman's

Complaint" and "The Friar's Answer."[69] These satires appear in the flyleaf of a fourteenth-century manuscript written in the same fifteenth-century hand. Both poems seem to be the work of Lollards. In the first, the author assumes the voice of a Lollard bibleman denouncing the simoniacal practices of the mendicants. The second poem is written in the voice of a friar lamenting the collapse of his lucrative trade of begging because of Lollard teachings. As he goes from door to door, instead of donations he receives scriptural lessons:

> Allas! what schul we freris do,
>   Now lewed men kun holy writ?
> Alle abowte wherre I go
>   Þei aposen me of it.[70]

The friar finds himself an unwilling participant in a debate with a shopkeeper over voluntary poverty. From indirect speech the poem turns to direct dialogue:

> Þan þei loken on my nabete [habit],
>   & sein, "forsoþe, withoutton oþes,
> Wheþer it be russet, black, or white,
>   It is worþe all oure werynge cloþes."
>
> I saye, "I, not for me,
>   bot for them þat haue none."
> Þei seyne, "þou hauist to or þre;
>   ȝeuen hem þat nedith þerof oone."[71]

It is uncertain whether these two poems were written as a single unit, yet clearly their fifteenth-century recorder regarded them as companion pieces. The poems do complement each other in striking ways. "The Friar's Answer" offers an imagined confrontation between a defender of Christ's law and one of its enemies. "The Layman's Complaint" provides a representative greeting of the sort our friar has been encountering: "Þou þat sellest þe worde of god, / Be þou berfot, be þou schod, / Cum neuere here."[72] Together the poems constitute a small-scale dramatic debate about the nature of the religious life. Although it is the Lollard's adversary who is "apose[d]," we have already seen in Thorpe's *Examination* that the direction of the questioning in nonconformist displaced drama can and does change. The confrontation remains a trial of truth whether the believer challenges his opponent or is challenged by him. The debate ends with the friar's prophecy of mendicant defeat, which unites the Lollard audience with their poet by encouraging a conspiratorial jest at the friar's expense:

> If it goo forþe in þis maner,
>   It wole done vs myche gyle;
> Men schul fynde vnneþe [scarcely] a frere
>   In englonde wiþin a whille.[73]

"The Friar's Answer" is interesting for a number of reasons. First, the poem suggests that at least some Lollards were willing, within limits, to the play the role of another—to don the mask and voice of their opponents in order to enact the drama of the soul's enlightenment. The Lollards attacked the mystery cycles for their vivid impersonations of evil, yet we see here a Lollard masquerading as an agent of Antichrist. It would appear that the absence of stage representation and the reader's clear perception of the separation between the play figure and the real author (the humor of the poem obviously rests on this perception) overcame any qualms the writer might have had about creating a distracting fiction. Second, the poem demands our attention because it again highlights the almost compulsive need of the Lollard for an opposition against which to define himself. Thorpe had his adversary ready-made in Archbishop Arundel; this Lollard poet had to invent his examiners to declare his views.

Pierce the Ploughman's Crede is the most accomplished of the surviving Lollard dramatic satires; it is also the only one to use the pilgrimage to structure its narrative, invoking Langland's work and anticipating Bunyan's. The poem concerns the search of an unlettered man for the spiritual knowledge necessary to salvation:

> A and all myn A.b.c. * after haue y lerned,
> And [patred] in my pater-noster * iche poynt after oþer,
> And after all, myn Aue-marie * almost to þe ende;
> But all my kare is to comen * for y can noh3t my Crede.[74]

The knowledge the pilgrim seeks is orthodox enough: every parishioner was expected to learn his Paternoster, his Ave Maria, and his Creed, as well as the seven sacraments, the Ten Commandments, the seven vices and their corresponding virtues, and the gospel precepts of Christ. Although the Creed remains the prime object of his quest, the shape and implication of his education are heterodox.[75] *Pierce the Ploughman's Crede* enacts a distinctly Lollard pilgrimage. The journey is less physical than psychological, a series of formalized confrontations with opponents of God's law ending in enlightenment under the guidance of a just and holy man. At the conclusion of the enterprise there is no shrine, only a poor man; along the way there are no merry interludes, only harsh disputation. The life of the soul is continuous movement in the face of persistent obstruction.[76]

The poem falls with a clean symmetry into two equal parts of about four hundred twenty long lines of verse each. The first half of the poem is an agon, captured in dialogue, between the pilgrim and representatives of the four mendicant orders. As he encounters each friar, the pilgrim presents him with the same dilemma:

"Sire, for grete godes loue * þe graiþ [plain truth] þou me telle,
Of what myddelerde man * my3te y best lerne
My Crede? For I can it nou3t * my kare is þe more."[77]

On each occasion, the pilgrim's inquiries into the virtues of a rival order provoke the friar into a denunciation of the principles and practices of his competitor and a panegyric on his own.[78] The pilgrim concludes by dismissing the claims of both. The second half of the poem consists of Pierce the Ploughman's long-winded sermon on true belief and its enmity toward the teachings of the corrupted church. The structure of the poem as a whole, with its movement from negative to positive formulation, thus mirrors the internal dynamics of the individual confrontations between the friars and the pilgrim. At all levels, the poem reproduces the Lollard pattern of thrust and parry, of conflict promoting self-discovery. Despite its crudities, the Crede is devoid of neither intelligence nor style.

The pilgrim first encounters a Friar Minor. Might a Carmelite be helpful in teaching him his Creed? asks the pilgrim. Scornful laughter is the reply. The Carmelites are lecherous, lazy, and avaricious, purveyors of false miracles and deceptive stage plays. Their order is ungrounded either in tradition or in scripture; it would appear that "þe foles foundeden hem-self."[79] The friar is voicing the greatest of Lollard fears, that of spiritual solipsism. To drift in free fall through a self-created, imagined world is the Lollard version of hell. By having each order attack its fellow in a round-robin of self-destruction, the satirist graphically demonstrates the fundamental Lollard conviction that an erroneous argument must eventually collapse under the weight of its own falsehood.[80] In contrast, the more closely the godly argument is questioned, the stronger and more obvious it becomes. Hence the same conflict that strengthens the true church, asserts *The Lanterne of Liȝt*, destroys the false: "Þis chirche whanne it is beten, it wexiþ þe hardir; whanne it is blamed, it wexiþ þe dullidar; whanne it is tauȝt it is þe lewidar; whanne it is done wel to, it is þe schrewidar; and þanne it falliþ doun & comeþ to noȝt, whanne it semeþ in mannes iȝe, moost strongli to stonde."[81]

The Minorite's glorification of his own Franciscan brethren rapidly slips into an unconscious act of self-condemnation. Having denounced the Carmelites for their violated vows of poverty, the Minorite solicits funds for the building of a convent. A generous contribution from the pilgrim will assure him of immortality, for his face will appear in a stained glass window in the new chapel:

"And myȝtestou amenden vs * wiþ money of þyn owne,
Þou chuldest cnely [kneel] bifore Crist * in compas of gold
In þe wide windowe westwarde * wel niȝe in the myddell,
And seynt Fraunces him-self * schall folden the in his cope,
And presente the to the trynitie * and praie for thy synnes."[82]

The conflation of an eternal and a historical landscape in a man-made creation was the same outrage that troubled the Lollard in his response to the church drama. By conjoining a present day yeoman with a thirteenth-century saint in a window depicting the trinity, the orthodox artist duplicated the wedding of eternity and time that for the Lollard was God's prerogative alone. Lollard art, like Thorpe's *Examination*, only suggested the congruity and contingency of the here and the beyond without daring to bind the two together.

The pilgrim's first, favorable response to the lecture of the friar is short-lived. The uncharitable backbiting of the Minorite prompts the pilgrim to reexamine his words. Applying common sense and scripture (the author blithely ignores the discrepancy between the pilgrim's fluency in the Bible and his ignorance of the Creed), he slowly dismantles the friar's arguments:

"And also y sey coueitise * catel to fongen [goods to receive],
Þat Crist haþ clerliche forboden * & clenliche destruede,
And saide to his sueres [followers] * forsoþe on þis wise,
'Nouȝt þi neiȝbours good * couet yn no tyme.'
But charite & chastete * ben chased out clene,
But Crist seide, 'by her fruyt * men shall hem ful knowen.' "[83]

Having apposed the friar's falsehood, the pilgrim is granted his first glimmerings of truth and with them a new determination to try men's spirits: "Þanne þouȝt y to frayne [question] þe first * of þis four ordirs, / And presede to þe prechoures * to proven here wille."[84] His path takes him to a Dominican convent.

Nowhere in the poem is the artistry of the satirist more in evidence than in his depiction of the elaborate, fantastical home of the preaching friars. For over sixty lines the pilgrim describes with awestruck wonder the richness of their dwelling. The passage announces its kinship with the late medieval dream vision in which protagonists wander down empty corridors in palaces of the imagination. The fastidious care that this usually austere poet lavishes on architectural details specifically recalls Chaucer's portrait of the exterior of the House of Fame:

Wiþ arches on eueriche half * & belliche y-corven,
Wiþ crochetes on corners * wiþ knottes of golde,
Wyde wyndowes y-wrouȝt * y-written full þikke,
Schynen wiþ schapen scheldes * to schewen aboute,
Wiþ merkes of marchauntes * y-medled bytwene,
Mo þan twenty and two * twyes y-noumbred.[85]

Again and again, the poet returns to the pilgrim's bewilderment in the face of such overwrought art: "And whan y cam to þat court * y gaped about."[86] As the reader follows the pilgrim through the convent, he too becomes lost in this artful world, captured and transfixed by the seductive ornamentation of the verse. Our journey toward plainspoken truth has been halted; pilgrim and reader are adrift in that limbo between physical and spiritual reality so dreaded by the nonconformist mind.[87]

The Lollard artist does not, however, permit us to remain lost for very long. Having demonstrated the danger of the fixed and ornamented icon and the wonder it inspires, he slowly brings us back to solid ground. Four times the pilgrim jostles us and himself into awareness by remarking on that most mundane of realities, money. How much did this splendor cost? The first note of fiscal reality is dimly sounded: "Þe pris of a plouȝ-lond * of penyes so rounde / To aparaile þat pyler [column] * were pure lytel."[88] By the end of the tour, it is a trumpet clarion.[89] Under the weight of taxes, plowland, and harvest yield, the dream vision collapses. Instead of gaping in wonder, the pilgrim now critically examines the setting: "Þanne turned y aȝen * whan y hadde all y-toted [spied out], / And fond in a freitour [dining room] * a frere on a benche."[90]

In each of his subsequent debates, the pilgrim becomes more assertive and more confident in the strength of his godly discourse. He interrupts the boastful Dominican to lecture him on humility and angrily interrogates the Austins and Carmelites. As in Thorpe's *Examination*, the spiritual growth of the protagonist is highlighted by the progressive degeneration of his adversaries. The madness Thorpe found in Arundel's frustrated evil, surfaces in the increasing vehemence of the friars' abuse of their rivals. The Austin declares himself almost " 'madde in mynde, / To sen houȝ þis Minoures * many men bygyleth!' "[91] The first half of the poem ends with a somber pilgrim reflecting upon "þe falshede of þis folk."

As the wayfarer contemplates his experiences with the mendicants, he comes upon a man of another sort, a plowman clothed in tatters. In contrast to the Dominican castle of air, the earth itself is Pierce's native element; he is literally grounded in the life of the soil: "Þis whit waselede [this man bemired himself] in þe [fen] * almost to þe ancle."[92] Alongside him labors his wife while their three young children sit by the side of the field—a silent rebuke of the sterility of the orders. That the physical journey leads to a poor man rather than a shrine reveals again the poet's attempt to give artistic life to the

Lollard concept of pilgrimage. Richard Knobbyng was confessing to a commonplace of Lollard thought when he declared at his heresy trial that "Y have holde, beleved and afermed . . . that noon pilgrimage owith to be doo to ony places or seyntes, be oonly to the pore peple."[93] Yet the scene is not idyllic: the fearsome poverty that had recalled the pilgrim to reality in the Dominican convent is graphically evident here. There is no polyphony in the plowman's field, only the plainsong of hunger: "And alle þey songen o songe * þat sorwe was to heren; / Þey crieden alle o cry * a carefull note."[94] Life on earth, the Lollard preachers argued, is neither laughter nor singing but the weeping of sin: "And so, ȝif we þenken of weiling of oure owne synne, and mournyng of oure neiȝboris synne þat we dwellen wiþ, and tariyng of oure blisse þat we shal have in hevene, we have litil mater for to lauȝhe, but raþer for to morene."[95] Nevertheless, in the midst of this sorrow there is warmth and charity. The friars' scornful laughter for the penniless seeker of truth is itself mocked in Pierce's generous offer of food for the body and the soul.

There follows a lengthy discourse by the plowman instructing the wayfarer in some of the basic principles of Lollard thought. As is so often the case in the writing of the reformers, positive doctrine emerges from the refutation of false doctrine. There is no cause to reproduce Pierce's arguments; they are the commonplaces of Lollard polemic. What needs to be noted is the way in which Pierce's sermon functions within the pilgrim's spiritual education. In his encounters with the friars, the wayfarer glimpsed the evils of false religion. Pierce's diatribe now places those individual complaints against mendicancy in the context of the larger struggle of the forces of Christ and Antichrist, transforming the wayfarer's fragmented vision into a clear and whole understanding of Christian existence. Like most sinners moving toward faith, the pilgrim is alternately docile—" 'A! Peres,' quaþ y þo * 'y pray þe, þou me telle / More of þise tryfllers * hou trechurly þei libbeþ [live]?' "—and rebellious—"It semeþ þat þise sely men * han somwhat þe greved / . . . & þerfore þou wilnest / To schenden [ruin] . . . hem * wiþ þi sharpe speche."[96] For every few steps forward, there is one backward. Yet the pilgrim endures (as the modern reader may not) Pierce's lengthy philippic, and his reward is the holy grail he has sought—the conning of the Creed.

Throughout his lecture, Pierce provides the wayfarer with clues to interpret his recent experience (and the reader with testimony to a level of authorial sophistication he may hitherto have been unwilling to concede). Consider the plowman's description of the effect of the friars' ornate palaces on the humble Christian's mind:

"For þouȝ a man in her mynster * a masse wolde heren,
His siȝt schal so be set * on syndrye werkes,
Þe penounes & þe pomils [banners and pommels] * & poyntes
of scheldes
Wiþ-drawen his deuocion * & dusken his herte;
I likne it to a lym-ȝerde * to drawen men to hell,
And to worchipe of þe fend * to wraþþen [anger] þe soules."[97]

Everywhere one finds that the second half of the poem is a key to reading the first. Perhaps the most significant of these interpretative interludes for our purposes is Pierce's discussion of the examination of the evil man:

"Proue hem in proces * & pynch at her ordre,
And deme hem after þat þey don * & dredles, y leue
Þei willn wexen pure wroþ * wonderliche sone,
And schewen þe a scharp will * in a schort tyme,
To wilne [desire] wilfully wraþþe * & werche þerafter.
Wytnesse on Wycliff * þat warned hem wiþ trewþe."[98]

Try the truth of the evil man, says Pierce, and he will grow violent. The true man, on the other hand, grows calm and self-possessed when he is examined, ever more confident in the strength of his convictions. The recollections of Wyclif's persecution suggest again that the "frayning" or questioning of the evil man is simply an inverted form of the examination of the saint; the two events go hand in hand forming the basis of nonconformist art. This lesson of Pierce's is important enough for a restatement, one that demonstrates that behind the Lollard trial of good and evil lay the collective memory of Christ's appearance before the bishops and its dramatization in the tyrant plays of the mystery cycles:

"Lakke [blame] hem a litil wiȝt * & here lijf blame,
But he lepe vp on heiȝ * in hardynesse of herte,
And nemne þe anon nouȝt [call you a thing of naught] * & þi
   name lakke
Wiþ proude wordes apert [openly] * þat passeth his rule,
Boþe wiþ 'þou leyest, & þou lext [lie]' * in heynesse of sowle,
And turne as a tyrant * þat turmente him-selue,
Loke nowe, leue man * beþ nouȝt þise i-lyke
Fully to þe Farisense [Pharisees] * in fele of þise poyntes?"99

Pierce the Ploughman's Crede moves consistently from experience to understanding, from an event to its meaning, from the letter to the spirit behind it. The first half of the poem, like the literal base of the embryonic allegory of the Lollard, has its own integrity that is amplified, not usurped, by the spiritual meaning of the poem's second half. As a work of art, the satire faithfully reenacts the central Lollard ritual of the soul's awakening through its intellectual debate with the false logic of evil. Just as important, the *Crede* invites the reader to participate in the same process of true religious enlightenment—moving from incident to explanation—that the pilgrim himself undergoes. By the end of the poem, protagonist, teacher, author, Christ, and reader are inextricably linked in a holy family whose union is both created and celebrated in this ceremonial art of the Lollard faith.

The anonymous author of the *Crede* apparently took at least one more turn at the plow. *The Plowman's Tale* begins:

"Of freres I have told before
In making of a 'Crede,'
And yet I coud tell worse and more,
But men wold werien it to rede!"100

Awareness of the limitations of an audience's endurance unfortunately does not guarantee a lively poem. If indeed the poets of the *Tale* and the *Crede* are one, and this authorial claim is more than a conventional bid for borrowed credentials,101 there has been a distinct falling off here. The latter work is marked by an uncharacteristic timidity. Its narrator is a religious neuter who feebly attempts to defuse the obviously heretical content of the poem by masquerading as a Canterbury pilgrim with pretenses to Chaucerian disinterestedness:

> Wyteth [blame] the Pellican, and not me,
> For herof I nil not avowe,
> In hy ne in low, ne in no degre,
> But as a fable take it ye mowe.
> To holy churche I will me bowe;
> Ech man to amende him, Christ send space!
> And for my wryting me alowe
> He that is almighty, for his grace.[102]

The echo of Chaucer's delightfully nondoctrinaire "Nun's Priest's Tale" is unmistakable.

Although cast in the form of the medieval debate—the contestants are a reform-minded Pelican and an orthodox Griffin—the *Tale* lacks the vigorous battle of ideologies that redeems the *Crede*. The Griffin's perfunctory performance of the role of ritual adversary encourages repetitious tirades more than religious self-discovery. Only in the last third of the poem does the author allow his opponent a significant place in the proceedings. Once the Griffin finds his argument, and the poet a willingness to test the tenets of his faith, a genuine debate of religious principles ensues. The vague threats of the Griffin mount, gradually crystallizing into the palpable instruments of prelatical oppression. The twin punishments for heresy and treason are now conjured up by a Griffin firmly cast as examining bishop:

> "Thou shalt be brent in balefull fyre;
> And all thy secte I shall distrye,
> Ye shal be hanged by the swyre [neck]!"[103]

By the close of the poem, like the mad inquisitors of cycle play and heresy trial account, the Griffin rages out of control, "grinn[ing] as he were wood / . . . [and swearing] by cockes herte blood / . . . thee all to-race [tear to pieces]; / And make thy flesh to rote and moule."[104] The displaced drama reaches its customary moment of recognition as the Pelican awakens to the necessary convergence of persecution and redemption in the Christian life.

The Plowman's Tale is a minor work weakened by a confusion of purpose and a persistent clumsiness in execution. The climactic play of evil and good, instead of providing a rousing conclusion, merely reminds us of what has been missing from the opening two-thirds of the work. The poem does sport the same dualism as the *Crede*, that is, debate and exposition, only in the *Tale* the components are reversed, with lecture preceding conflict. If we do have the work of a single writer, it is tempting to speculate that he was experimenting with the placement of his structural elements, perhaps in an effort to achieve a more decisive ending. In any case, the poem falters whereas the *Crede* proceeds with a modicum of zest and propriety. *The Plowman's Tale* does, however, have its moments of eloquence. Significantly, they are only elicited when the Griffin's antiphonal voice is allowed to be heard, underscoring again the Lollard's compulsive need for authentic adversaries as a precondition of spiritual enlightenment. For example, in an interlude that recalls the heterodox destination of the *Crede*'s pilgrimage, the author argues that devotion is properly bestowed not on shrines but on the true monuments of Christ, poor men.[105] As he pleads for a fully realized Christian charity, the poet achieves a simple elegance in his versifying:

> "To men and woman that ben pore,
> That ben in Christes own lykenesse,
> Men shullen offre at hir dore
> That suffren honger and distresse;
> And to suche images offre lesse,
> That mow not fele thurst ne cold;
> The pore in spirit gan Christ blesse,
> Therfore offreth to feble and old."[106]

The passage hints at a Christian poetry that eschews the ornate without sacrificing beauty or feeling. There is here and elsewhere in the poem evidence of a genuine attempt to reanimate a religion grown cold and institutionalized in its devotion and art. That a poetry so cut off from the sophisticated mainstream of fourteenth-century literature could, at times, satisfy the spiritual needs of those disenchanted with customary devotional forms is an achievement.

The Plowman poems provide no cause to proclaim the discovery of a new, brilliant, but "strangely neglected" genre in medieval art. It is, however, important for literary critics nurtured on the ambiguity, complexity, and philosophical disinterestedness of "the canon" to acknowledge the imaginative works of people who burned with a different though no less intense religious fire than a *Pearl*-poet—and who, like him, tried to find an artistic medium to express that zeal.

The hesitancy threatening both the doctrinal and aesthetic clarity of *The Plowman's Tale* is evident in the Jack Upland series as well, where the readiness to embrace dramatic fiction is even more seriously reduced. The three Upland satires, *Jack Upland*, *Friar Daw's Reply*, and *Upland's Rejoinder*, have not fared well even among those scholars who have devoted some energy to their study. Their last editor, P. L. Heyworth, viewed his textual labors as a variety of euthanasia: "They have earned their neglect. If I tidy them away to an honest grave it is not with any claim to 'definitiveness,' but because there is no good reason why they should ever be disinterred again."[107] At the risk of appearing ghoulish, it is my intention to summon up the dead. Such conjuring is not meant to bestow upon Jack Upland and his opponent literary immortality. No one possesses that much magic. Rather, I hope to show that *Jack Upland*, like the Plowman poems, is experimental; it is an effort to create out of borrowings from orthodox literary forms a Lollard art that is dramatic without being drama.

The first satire, *Jack Upland*, begins conventionally enough—with a denunciation of society of the sort so common in the sermon literature of the period.[108] The nature of Lollard discontent might be heretical, but discontent itself was very much in vogue. Society has been turned upside-down, says Jack, and in this topsy-turvy world Antichrist reigns supreme. Priests, no longer satisfied with their ordained tasks—preaching the Gospel, studying God's law, and administering the sacraments—have taken upon themselves temporal employment. While priests overstep their proper domains, monks retreat from theirs, having "closid hem as from þe world in wallis of ston, cloistris & sellis."[109] Commoners have abandoned the tilling of the earth and have become the nowhere men of late medieval society—lawyers and merchants. Perception becomes clouded as "uertues [are] transposid to vicis" and "Goddis lawe & loue amonge nei3boris" are destroyed.[110] The real problem, however, is yet to be described. Having rehearsed the list of his nation's ills, Upland turns his wrath upon the friars: "Thes ben þe flateringe freris of al þe fyue ordris, falsli founden in oure feiþ & first schulen be distried. Þes ben cockers in counentis [brawlers in convents] and coueitous in markettis, marrers of matrymonye & Caymes castel-makers, Pharesies fagynge [flattering] þe folk & profetis fals, vnsikir soudiouris [soldiers] sette al bifore, vayne men & voide in Antecristis vowarde— God scheeld vs from þis capteyne and his oost."[111]

Upland's sputtering, angry alliterative imprecation proves incantatory: like a demon rising from a trapdoor in a stage, an adversarial friar suddenly appears ready to partake in the ritual of "aposynge and answeringe." But he is never a fully conceived literary character, rather a phantom whose presence is attested to solely by Jack's incessant questioning: "Frere, hou many ordris ben in erþe, & whiche is most perfi3t ordre? Frere, of what ordre art þou and who made þin ordre? What ben þi rulis & who made þi cloutid rulis, siþ Crist made hem not ne noon oþer a þoursende 3eere aftir þat Crist sti3e [ascended] into heuene?"[112] Even when Jack not only interrogates the shadowy friar but imagines his responses as well—"& 3if 3e seie, Iacke nay oure relegioun is not in oure abite, frere, whi art þou prisoned and clepid apostata for leuynge þin ordre & weringe a blewe gowne & a reede hood?"[113]—the result is dumb show albeit in the broad contours of the heresy trial.

By the end of the work, the satirist himself seems to grow tired of this ventriloquist's act and issues a call for a real opponent to challenge his spiritual convictions: "Go now forþ frere & fraiste [examine] 3oure clerkis, & grounde 3ou in Goddis lawe, & 3eue Iacke an answere, & whanne 3e asoilen [answer] þat I haue seide sadli in truþe, I schal asoile [release] þee of þin ordre & saue þee to heuene."[114] The preceding exercise, it turns out, is preparatory, an effort to stimulate the soul's adrenaline in anticipation of a more significant episode of Christian warfare. The dummy is in fact a fly, bait to catch a contentious, real-life friar. There is, then, a species of the "growth of the believer's mind" story lurking behind the rather dull, flat surface of *Jack Upland*. The satire depicts a Christian training his spiritual perception by gradually subjecting his beliefs to increasingly more serious challenges from his enemies. Truth, suggests the satirist, is no more to be found in self-contained fictions than in walled-up cloisters. Only in the head-to-head encounter between the Christian and the unregenerate world that surrounds him is truth to be discovered and maintained. Upland's call for a debate beyond the precincts of his work, then, resembles the Lollard preacher's call for an ongoing disputation outside the limits of his sermon. Both constitute a form of Lollard palinode, a final rejection of the artist's private world in favor of a public one.

Upland's prayer for a redeeming adversary was answered. *Friar Daw's Reply* is a point-by-point refutation in verse of Upland's Lollard heresies. Probably the work of a Dominican friar, the satire is everything that *Jack Upland* is not. It is above all a playful poem. Friar Daw opens on an elevated note with a literary self-consciousness and pretension that mocks Upland's homespun prose:

> Who shal graunten to myn eyen a strong streme of teres
> To wailen & to wepyn þe sorwyng of synne,
> For charite is chasid & flemed out of londe
> And euery state stakerth [staggers] vnstable in him silf.[115]

Daw's displays of rhetorical skill, however, are no more than a stalking horse for the coarse and vituperative satire that follows. The friar claims the ability to defeat his opponent on any level, but Upland's rusticity demands an answer in kind. Shedding his eloquence, Daw slips into the ragtag intonations of the rude soothsayer, "Frere Daw Topias, as lewid as a leke."

Despite the pretense to plainness, there will be more than one stylistic shift for Daw in the course of the poem: sheer pleasure in the game dictates his mercurial strategies. Lies and evasions, imprecations and insults are all summoned forth along with learned refutation. Monstrously ingenious allegorical readings of the Bible of the sort that so rankled the Lollards proliferate. But Daw is well aware of his sins. He mocks his own clever reading of Revelation all the while insisting on the accuracy of its spirit if not of its letter:

> Iak, þus to dubby [meddle] with scripture me þinkiþ grete
>   folie,
> For as lewid am I as þou, God wote þe soþe;
> I know not an a from þe wynd mylne
> Ne a b from a bole foot, I trowe ne þi silf noþir.
> And ȝit, for al my lewidhed, I can wel vndirstonde,
> Þat þis priuy processe perteneþ to ȝour secte.[116]

Daw is undoubtedly a clown, but he is not a fool. His insights into
the workings of his opponent's mind are often telling. In particular
he seems attuned to the unlikely wedding of debased scholastic
logic with inspired declamation that marks Upland's argumentative method. Daw is merciless in his ridicule of Upland's prophetic
stance, dismissing the satirist's claim to an authentic vision as the
ravings of a possessed soul. Lollard inspiration is unkindly viewed
first as the winds of fashion and then as broken wind. Even as he
castigates the Wycliffites for their idiosyncratic mysticism, however,
Daw lashes out at their embrace of the scholastic's reasoning tools:

> Iak, þou shewist sikirli what schole þou hast ben inne,
> Of sutiltee of arguyng me þinkiþ þi brayne ful þinne:
> Go grees a sheep vndir þe taile, þat semeþ þee beter,
> Þan with sotil sillogismes to perbrake [break to pieces] þi
>   witt.[117]

Daw is here reacting directly to the contradictory strains that run
through Upland's work; emotional prophecies of the "greete ab-
homynacioun of Antecrist" mingle uneasily with dry, mechanistic
reasoning. The same conjunction (indeed, near-conflation) of logic
and inspiration may be found in the work of the itinerant preachers:

> And of þis processe we most suppose here þat þis holi peple so
> ful of þe holigost . . . hadden sum maner of speche & logic
> wherbi þei communed in worde & spake of þis sacrament; þe
> wiche logic was oon among hem alle printid in her hert bi þe
> plente of þe holigost that mai not contrarie crist. . . . And it is
> not lefful to douȝt here but þat þis logic was oon among hem
> alle, ffor ellis þei schuld haue diuided into diuerse logikis in her

communyng & so haue had mater of dissension & striff as men han nou3.[118]

For Daw such extremes of the languages of objectivity and subjectivity are symptoms of a diseased mind. For Upland such balancing of antipathies testifies to a religious outlook grounded in reason, common sense, and the Bible's literal truth, but liberated and justified by the direct operation of the Holy Spirit on the godly man. The conflicting elements remain unfused, held in an inward tension by the outward struggle with the nonbeliever. Only dramatic dialogue can sustain the uneasy blend.

Daw's coltish enthusiasm contrasts vividly with the plodding earnestness of Jack Upland. Daw seems to epitomize the Lollard conception of the reprobate: he is a dancer, a juggler, and a player rather than a pilgrim. His language is a reflection of his reprobation: ornate, convoluted, and deceptive. When a second Lollard satirist, some fifty years later, takes up Upland's name and cause to attack Daw, he can only repeat again and again that all the friar speaks is ungrounded.[119] The author of *Upland's Rejoinder* uses the term like an exorcist's charm to banish the demons from Daw's playful language.

The author of *Jack Upland* is more leery than the *Crede*-poet of fictional enterprises. Although the bulk of the *Crede* consists of unembellished didactic religious verse, the poet does create around the dogmatic dialogue at the core of his work an imaginative world filled with ornate cloisters, seedy taverns, and muddy fields. Careful to warn his reader that fiction ungrounded in scripture and quotidian reality can deceive, the poet nonetheless sees his own brand of fabling as a safe devotional tool. He lavishes attention upon the depiction of his rude soothsayer, Pierce:

[I] sei3 a sely man me by * opon þe plow hongen.
His cote was of a cloute * þat cary [a coarse material] was y-
    called,
His hod was full of holes * & his heer oute,
Wiþ his knopped schon [shoes full of knobs] * clouted
    [patched] full þykke;
His ton toteden out [peeped out] * as he þe londe treddede.[120]

The painstaking inventory of each ragged garment that hangs from the body of his rustic saint seems a conscious mockery of the *descriptio* of the dream-vision youth as typified by the portrait of Mirth in *The Romance of the Rose*. Fashion, not poverty, dictates that Mirth's garments are "al toslytered for queyntise / In many a place, lowe and hie."[121] Pierce's garments declare his allegiance to the mud-bespattered world of reality; Mirth's proclaim his total alienation from that world. The *Crede*-poet's attack on the values of the dream vision, here and in the cloister scene, suggest a rejection of a variety of fiction-making but not of fiction-making itself. The *Crede*-poet is an artist working in a tradition of poetic expression. Although he may turn the tradition on its head by rejecting the principles it upholds, he is, nonetheless, still operating within the confines of its conventions. In some sense our poet has merely traded heroes. Mirth has become the villain. His analogues in the *Crede* are the fashionably dressed friars who pass their days in the pursuit of pleasure. Danger, the rude, unkempt watchdog of the Rose, is the hero. His analogue is Pierce who guards his deity's inviolable truth. The relative worth with which the different landscapes in the dream vision are invested are also reversed in the *Crede*. The walled garden, represented by the Dominican cloister, is rejected as the overwrought creation of an ungodly imagination; the terrible world banished beyond the confines of the garden is the true world of magic, represented by Pierce's fen of suffering and enlightenment.

The author of *Jack Upland* is of a wholly different orientation. Christening his protagonist Jack Upland and thereby announcing his persona's poetic kinship with Pierce, he nonetheless refuses to exploit the literary resources placed at his disposal. There is no attempt to characterize Jack, either by speech or dress. He is the mere shadow of a fictional character. His opponent is even less fully realized, a shadow of a shadow. The whole work toys with the idea of fiction and in the end abandons even that dalliance. Public combat outside the poem's private fiction is preferable.

The contrast between these authors points to a diversity of response among the reformers to the creations of the imagination. In histories of canonical literature, we seem always to trace a course of literary development that is organic and progressive. Early works are simple and dogmatic while later works are complex and open. Such, for example, is the pattern charted by Joel Altman in his description of the emergence of Elizabethan drama from the disputational exercises of the schools.[122] Whether such "evolutionary" histories are accurate accounts of literary events or the fulfillment of our own ideological and aesthetic preconceptions, the story clearly does not hold for nonconformist art. If such patterning were the case, we would expect an art form—like the one documented by Altman—that "outgrows" its fear of fictionality in general and the stage in particular. With each new author and era, nonconformity would move inexorably closer to the Globe. Or conversely, nonconformity would "degenerate," gradually succumbing to its latent and lamentable antipathy to the imagination. In fact, nonconformist art moves in many directions propelled by individual psychology, tensions in doctrinal agenda, and shifts in historical pressures. There are nonconformist dramas (in the most technical sense of the term) and nonconformist works that are dramatic in a much broader, ritualistic, and psychological sense. Their "drama quotient" neither declines nor rises according to any simple, chronological scheme. Ultimately these works are best understood not by marking (and implicitly condemning) their deviation from a canonical norm but by recognizing their autonomous integrity and unity as forms of a spiritual, internalized theater that on rare occasions may converge with mainstream literature. The complexities of heterodox versus orthodox art and of drama versus displaced drama may be explored more copiously in the varied work of John Bale.

CHAPTER THREE

John Bale

John Bale is a taxonomist's nightmare: his doctrinal allegiances defy simple categorization. A lack of intellectual discrimination hobbled his own efforts to inventory the lives and views of his fellow reformers. Religious personalities as diverse as Martin Luther and Sir John Oldcastle faded into indistinction when subjected to his uncritical praise.[1] To their divergent theological outlooks, temperaments, and qualities of mind, Bale was oblivious. Perhaps Bale's blurred vision explains in part his ability to survive a period unrivaled in English history for the frequency and violence of its shifts in religious loyalties. Bale lived to see all five Tudor monarchs—and their conflicting visions of the English church—enthroned. Henry VII was still in power when the young Bale was placed in a Carmelite convent in Norwich. Here, steeped in the lore of his order's heroes, he became an avid defender of Roman orthodoxy. His tenure as a mendicant hagiographer extended well into the reign of England's first Reformation king, Henry VIII; but by the early 1530s, Bale had been converted to the "new learning," and the vigor once reserved for trumpeting the virtue of Rome now served the gospel of reform.[2] His predilection for partisan vitriol quickly brought him to the attention of Thomas Cromwell who enlisted him in a growing company of Protestant propagandists. To their work Bale contributed those allegorical and scriptural plays that have earned him his literary footnote.[3] When Cromwell lost favor in 1540, his fall precipitated a host of lesser falls, Bale's among them. The Continent beckoned—as it would to future generations of unheeded prophets—and Bale answered the call. Safely harbored in northern Europe, he continued his interrupted task, churning out pamphlets vilifying the enemies of reformation and canonizing its advocates.

The accession of Edward VI in 1547 meant a new swing of the pendulum and a subsequent rise in Bale's fortunes. From the earliest days of his conversion, Bale had courted the role of beleaguered saint. As a stipendiary priest at Thorndon in Suffolk, he had reveled in the taunts of hostile parishioners; in the heart of Yorkshire orthodoxy, he had willingly done battle with one of its champions, Thomas Kirkby.[4] Whether by chance or the political cunning of Edward's advisors, Bale in 1553 was recruited to a post certain to feed his appetite for affliction: the bishopric of Ossory in Ireland. The animosity of his charges must, though, have exceeded even Bale's sanguine hopes. Upon news of the accession of the Catholic Mary, what had been vocal opposition to the new bishop turned violent. His servants were attacked, a number of them murdered, and his own life threatened. Once again Bale fled to the Continent, undoubtedly expecting further evidence for his conviction that "in exile are the powers thereof most earnestly proved of them that have faith."[5]

The nature of the exile's life had altered dramatically, however, between the 1540s and the 1550s. Mary's retreat toward Rome had forced a wide range of reformers to migrate.[6] The English company rapidly divided into opposing camps, some rallying about the second Edwardian *Book of Common Prayer* (1552), others urging a more complete reformation modeled on John Calvin's Geneva. In the so-called "Troubles at Frankfort," which foreshadowed the long struggle between Anglican and Puritan, Bale sided with the more moderate reformers.[7] Although the tenor of his previous life bears the earmarks of a Puritan mentality, by the mid-1550s Bale was a tired man. Never blessed with a finely tuned mind, Bale had little patience with the exacting distinctions now being made within the body of reformed thought. He was a man driven by the idea of dissent more than by any of its individual tenets. Nothing could induce him to join men whose radical agitation threatened to splinter a spiritual opposition whose homogeneity Bale had spent his life documenting. By the time Bale returned to an England made safe by Elizabeth, he had apparently lost his taste for combat. Pleading ill health, he refused the arduous task of once again disciplining his Irish flock and opted instead for the calmer life of a prebendary of Canterbury Cathedral. His death in 1563 marked the end of a stormy career played out against a still stormier historical backdrop. With a resignation appropriate to his future trials, a younger John Bale had urged the godly to accept their share of hardship in an unsettled age: "Let the faithful believer therefore, considering the mischief of this time, wherein nothing is like to be certain and sure in land, shire, city, town, no, nor yet house, appoint himself to persecution, loss of goods, exile, prison, sorrow, and death of body for the truth's sake, thinking that his portion is in the land of the living."[8]

AN IMAGE OF BOTH DRAMAS

Behind the sometimes bewildering vagaries of his religious and political loyalties, there is a deeply imprinted unity in Bale's thought. Throughout, his portrait of human nature and history is consistent—invariably drawn in bold primary colors. Intermediary shades denoted moral confusion to him, not depth or subtlety of vision. He began his literary career heralding the Carmelite monopoly on sanctity.[9] When he abruptly transferred his affections to the new learning, he acquired neither caution nor moderation. Where a more sensitive man's enthusiasm for neatly segregating his neighbors into sheep and goats might have been tempered by so radical a shift in perspective, Bale's was intensified. The objects of his youthful worship quickly became the victims of his mature scorn; *The Actes of the Englyshe Votaryes* preempted the lives of the Carmelite saints. Part chronicle, part gossip column, the work documented the scurrility of England's religious orders.[10] Once-ridiculed reformers, among them Wyclif, became the new luminaries, and their suffering for righteousness' sake the stuff of sacred history.[11]

As a historian, Bale urged his fellow Christians to exploit the past. Recollection of their former bondage to Catholic sin was to goad the faithful into completing the regeneration of the church begun by Luther. Self-definition for the nonconformist had always demanded the externalization of inward misgivings.[12] Such a strategy Bale adopted—with a single-minded violence frightening to behold. Crimes of the Catholic past were to be led, like captured prisoners, in triumph before the multitudes. Gazing on this pageant of sin, the believer was invited to reckon those battles lately won and those yet to be fought. As the title of Bale's most ambitious theological work, *The Image of bothe churches*, intimates, the task of the nonconformist historian was to assemble two complementary chronicles, one documenting the perseverance of the true church of Christ, the other the machinations of its enemy, the church of the Roman Antichrist. The veracity of the one could never be recognized without a clear sight of the falsehood of its demonic other.[13] Like twin stars, one dark and one bright, these two churches were destined to revolve about each other until God decreed the cessation of all human endeavor.

> And as for our partes, we are not so ignoraunt of the rules of Christes relygyon, but we knowe that hys flocke of true beleuers, hath had alwaies their wolues Math x. their blasphemers, persecuters, and slaunderers, that they myght bryng fourth godly frutes in pacyent sufferaunce for loke what the threshyng flaile doth to the corne (S. Gregory saith) the fyery fornace to the golde, and the polishynge fyle to the yron, the same doth aduersyte to the ryghtous man, for it maketh hym perfyght. Wicked persons are in all places to be tollerate of priuate men (I say not maye) because there canne be no Abel, unles he be vexed of some maliciouse Cain.[14]

In the light of such doctrine, persecution and affliction became the ordinary concomitants of divine election. Hatred of our adversaries is "a most manifest signe of saluacion" and "the trewe churche of Christ knowne . . . but by persecucyon for ryghtousnesse sake. For hys churche ys euermore as he was, hated, blasphemed, vexed, trobled, scorned, dysdayned, accused, lyed vpon, and cruellye afflicted vnto deathe, els is it not of hys marke."[15]

What distinguishes Bale's thinking from similar Lollard formulations was his insistence that the enemy by which man measured his sanctity was an internal as well as an external demon. The individual soul, like the church, had to battle its own negative self, the dark self, which ruled in the absence of God's grace and which even after conversion struggled to reassert its primacy. Former sin was never to be repressed; instead it was to be hauled into the light of day where it might shame the soul into greater exertions. So Bale responded to his own dark days of thralldom among the mendicants. When ridiculed by his Suffolk congregation for his Carmelite past, Bale made no apology. "And wher as in yor vnadveysed furye ye haue called me fryr, I am nother dyscontented nor ashamed of yt, no more than saynt powle was, whan he reported hymself sumtyme to be a pharyse and a persecutor of ye cristen sort. But wher as ye curse me, I schall with saynt powle blesse yow."[16] The blackness of his youth merely served to illuminate his present godliness. Thus not only did every Abel require his Cain, but every Paul had to harbor his pharisaical self. In his concern with this internal struggle between a man's unredeemed past and his sanctified future, Bale was a harbinger of the seventeenth-century Puritan preoccupation with the conflict between the so-called old and new creatures.[17]

Despite a deep concern for the individual, Bale's principal interest centered upon the soul of his nation. It is no coincidence that his finest play, *King Johan*, is ultimately more concerned with the trials of the allegorical England than with those of the historical John.[18] As a chronicler of England's persecution and eventual redemption, Bale anticipated Foxe's celebration of England as an elect nation.[19] Blessed with true gospel preaching and a dedication to the life of the spirit, England was the last nation of God, according to Bale, to succumb to the foreign corruptions emanating from the unholy church of Rome.[20] The beautiful anecdote of Pope Gregory's paternal concern for the English soul, born of his chance meeting with two blond slaves from that island, became in Bale's "revisionist" chronicle a tale of unnatural affection. The sight of the two boys, sneered Bale, aroused Gregory's appetite for sodomy not sanctity. The arrival of Augustine and his missionaries in the sixth century was no longer viewed as the Christianization of a pagan island but celibate Rome's contamination of an innocent world still charged with the holiness of the apostolic vision.[21] With each succeeding wave of Continental influence, that vision was further threatened. The Norman conquest, the spread of mendicancy: each submerged the gospel truth under a new flood of Catholic falsehood. And yet in the face of this onslaught, England never fully lost its dedication to scriptural principles. The advent of Wyclif and his Lollard disciples briefly reanimated the nation. Not until Henry's heroic break with Rome, however, was Christian liberty restored to an England once again the undisputed favorite of the Lord.

John Bale has never engendered affection among Renaissance scholars. One senses the reluctance with which the historian of the stage approaches the awkward plays of the 1530s, and the relief with which the theologian hurriedly passes over Bale's scurrilous tales of papal indiscretion. Yet for all the celebrated unpleasantness of "bilious Bale," there is something compelling in his work when viewed as a whole. Even as we acknowledge his penchant for coarse expression, parochial gossip, and strident jingoism, it is possible to see a serious and not ungifted mind wrestling with what can only be called a grand obsession—the public examination and exposure of the dark side of the religious mind. It is, above all, Bale's confrontation with the cloistered imagination and his exploration of its impact on religious devotion that entitles him to more than polite dismissal. His investigative field was admittedly limited: he confined his studies almost exclusively to the religious orders. These were, for Bale, the principal breeding grounds of religious deviancy. They were also the world he knew. Bale's hasty marriage upon abandoning the orders combined with his vehement attacks on celibacy speak eloquently of his unsuitability for the life of the convent. Whether a sense of public spirit prompted him to expose the sexual crimes of the orders or a more selfish need to hide a private confession of sin beneath the objectivity of history is not a penetrable mystery. The reliability of Bale's evidence, in any case, is of less interest than the quality of the speculations it prompted.[22]

Bale's quarrel with the religious orders was centered on the admissability of the vow. The willful assumption of obligations never prescribed in God's word struck him (as it had the Lollards) as presumptuous. God himself had plotted in scripture the course by which lost innocence might be retrieved. By vowing to abide by his own rival set of rules, the votary declared his disallegiance to God and a faith in his own ability to fulfill tasks that only God could empower him to perform. This claim of self-sufficiency was abhorrent to the Lollards;

to Bale, a follower of Luther and Tyndale, it was an utter impossibility. Cut off from divine truth, the votary was condemned to a self-made prison. Bale's analysis of the vow moved beyond Lollard theorizing, not merely because of his advocacy of justification by faith but also because of his concern with the nature and consequences of sexual repression. The impulse toward procreation was natural and insurmountable. "[W]ho can vowe," asked Bale, "that hys hear [hair] shall not growe, nor his nayles increase, and fulfyll it in effecte? Nomore can they do to lyue chaste, onlesse the Lorde geue it, whyche he neuer doeth in causes unnecessary."[23] Instead of channeling the sexual appetite into its God-ordained path, marriage, the votary futilely attempted to block its course. Denied egress, the carnal appetite turned back on itself, engendering an array of unnatural longings. In the mind thus cloistered away, fantasies and dreams of illicit activity bred corruption and unrest in every aspect of the life of the soul. "For in a cruciate or fearfully vexed conscience can never dwell true repentance. So unquietous always is the foolish desperate mind, as is the troubled raging sea."[24]

The Catholic faith in voluntary chastity was viewed by Bale as a dangerous form of spiritual regression, a doomed effort to return to the safety of a presexual infancy. Bale shared with the Lollards a deep mistrust for the apotheosis of the holy child. In *The Apology of Johan Bale againste a ranke Papyst*, Bale derided a religion which privileged the devotion of young boys. "The more chast those hartes be (say they) from whens the vowes come, the more acceptable are these vowes to God. Wherfor the vowes of yong boyes are better in value, than the vowes of their eldars."[25] Redemption, argued Bale, was not to be sought in an impossible dream of infantile purity. Innocence was regained by the continuous struggle of a mature believer to understand God's truth as recorded in scripture and to defend that truth against its enemies. Man's holiness was incumbent upon an acceptance of spiritual growth, development, and change. We will find in all of Bale's plays heroes whose goodness is childish naïveté. Only after the trial of affliction will they achieve a sanctity sufficient to confront the moral and spiritual dilemmas that lie beyond the cloistered walls of childhood and the monastery. In contrast, Bale's typical stage villain is a satanic Peter Pan, a creature damned by his obstinate refusal to grow up.

Among his countrymen, especially those dwelling in the insularity of the English hinterlands, Bale discerned many recalcitrant souls whose nostalgia for the devotional life of their youth—comforting in its familiarity and maternalism—threatened to impede the Tudor Reformation. As preacher, prelate, and propagandist, Bale waged war against "foolish northmen" and stubborn west countrymen, the inhabitants of the "dark corners" of England.[26] Lost in superstition, and prone to insurrection, they became Bale's symbol of the unsanctified mind itself: rude, dark, and endlessly wavering, a raging sea incapable of achieving the tranquillity of an ordered religious vision. As a class they were epitomized by the fantasy-ridden hag. "An infynyte swarme beholde we of olde dottynge bawdes and beastes, that with conscyences loaden with synne . . . taketh euery paynted stocke & stone for their God, besydes the small beades that their lecherouse chaplaynes hath blowen vpon."[27] Their love of ceremony and icons signaled their kinship with the Israelites. The Jews, claimed Bale, were "flexible and prone to ydolatry" not because they were evil, but because as believers they were mere infants. Incapable of comprehending a religion of spirit, they were granted a religion of objects. God coaxed the Jews with the toys and games of ceremonial pageantry until their "tendre infauncy" gave way to "more years of discression."[28] The birth of Christ marked the advent of spiritual maturation. Nonetheless, the Catholic regressively sought shelter in a world of ceremonial play, ignoring the more laborious worship God now demanded.

The language of the Catholic imagination necessarily reflected the infirmities of its adherents. Bale's villains are always gamesters. Addicted to the pursuit of play, they exult in impersonation, disguise, and deception. Success for them is measured in finely turned jests and well-executed practical jokes. Their language exhibits the same gamesome spirit. As with children, sound takes precedence over sense. Congruence of thought and expression yields to correspondences of vowels and consonants. Alliteration and rhyme were the ligatures of Catholic argumentation. The Vices of Bale's plays speak in nonce words and non sequiturs as reason becomes a slave to the ear's fondness for similarities of tone. The heroic Natural Law speaks directly: "I am the law of Nature." His adversary, Infidelity, wanders in verbal mazes:

> I thought so! by your stature,
> And by your ancient gature,
> Ye were of such a rature
> When I first heard ye speak.[29]

When Bale attacked Ponce Pantolabus's verse pamphlet on the genealogy of the Protestant heresy, he found in its "mangye mangled meters" and lame rhymes both the symptom and the cause of the author's corrupt theology. Pantolabus's fondness for the superficial felicities of expression spoke of a devotion to the accoutrements of true religion rather than its substance. Bale compares him and those of like persuasion to the ornaments of a Gothic cathedral: they believe themselves part of its foundation when in fact they are its gargoyles, spewing forth spurious doctrine.[30]

Bale saves the vilest of his scatalogical abuses to mock the immaturity of Catholic discourse. "He cutteth his crotchettes as short as chyldes dyrt / that they shulde ronne rounde on his tonge."[31] The speech of orthodoxy, like the orthodox mentality itself, made no intellectual progress; its alliterative orgies produced a spiritual stutter. "Than mustred they in their myters / they sayled in their sylkes / they glyttred in their goldes / ruffled in ther rochettes / flickered in their furres / and ratled in ther rynges."[32] The words here are Bale's own. But Bale is consistent in reserving the circularity of alliteration for the characterization of evil; the extended alliterative passage is Bale's attempt to imagine his enemies in their own tongue.

The language of orthodoxy was deficient not only in its dependence on a kind of aural logic but in its curious disjunction as well. Bale mimicked its failure to connect in his Catholic "checklists," haphazard inventories of devotional practices. All of the Vices of Bale's dramas participate in this exercise in random association; in his nondramatic writings Bale produced in his own voice catalogues emblematic of the disordered sensibility: "Following his ways therefore, they have always for lucre's sake gloriously garnished their holy mother, the madam of mischief and proud synagogue of Satan, with gold, silver, pearl, precious stone, velvets, silks, mitres, copes, crosses, cruets, ceremonies, censings, blessings, babblings, brawlings, processions, puppets, and such other mad masteries . . . to provoke the carnal idiots to her whoredom in the spirit."[33] Like the child who proudly rehearses his accumulated wisdom without weighing the relative worth of its parts, the orthodox mind embraces accretion without organization. Groaning under the weight of such unprofitable practices, the soul must suffocate. "Innumerable are the cumbrous and unprofitable burdens of their fantasies and dreams, wherewith they noy men's consciences, drown their small faith, and overload their souls."[34]

As a corrective, Bale offered the plain-speaking of the nonconformist. The self-intoxicating elegance of rhetorical flowers, the dangerous singularity of "inkhorne terms"—all were to be eschewed for a simple, common speech. "He that doth speake the thynge that is true and certayne / & without false colours of cauteles doth vtter it in wordes playne / is moche better occupyed . . ."[35] The clever seductions of human speech—"Though the mermaydes songe be swete / yet ys yt full of poyson (as are also your honyed rhetoryckes) and leadeth them vnto deathe which geueth them therof the hearinge"[36] —were to be replaced with the common attractions of scriptural language: "Not only in this revelation, but also in all other books of the scriptures, doth the Holy Ghost at his appointment allure us to his kingdom by the examples and parables of such things as we have in daily custom."[37] In contrast to the verbal idiosyncrasies of the defenders of orthodoxy, nonconformist discourse was to be accessible to all levels of intellectual comprehension as was the unadorned truth of scripture itself.

Yet even a casual glance at Bale's own prose seems to belie his endorsement of a plain style of writing and preaching. Bale's writing is not so much plain as it is crude and brutal. Like many of his contemporary polemicists, Bale equated plainness and perspicuity with coarseness and violence.[38] His idea of simplicity is better understood as a certain bluntness of manner (often associated with the unsweetened words of the Old Testament prophet) than as a complete disavowal of verbal ingenuity. It is Martin Marprelate's sense of calling "a spade a spade" that defines the Tudor polemicist's plain style, not an austerity of expression. At the same time, visibly emerging in the work of Bale and other Tudor nonconformists is an ideal of precision in prose that would not be fully articulated until the seventeenth century. Without quite abandoning the playfulness of language—its ability to suggest multiple meanings and unexpected correspondences—Bale's prose does aim toward a more controlled and unambiguous use of words. As in the pronouncements of the Royal Society, one finds in Bale an attempt to limit the degree of play permitted between a word and the object it describes.[39]

The language of both Marprelate and Bale was meant to be corrosive. It is blunt, coarse, and anatomical because it sought to dissolve the incrustations of Catholic tradition. Only abrasive speech could peel away the centuries of corrupted theology beneath which the gospel's truth lay buried. To overcome a millennium of rote response to Christian worship, each word of nonconformity had to jolt and disturb the reader as well as guide and educate him. It is perhaps for this reason that Bale perceived such affinities between his own work and that of the Lollard satirists. His accounts of papal and mendicant iniquity are often punctuated with verses from the early poets of reformation. Bale concludes his treatment of the trials of Oldcastle, for example, with a stanza from a medieval Latin satire on the church. Although he finds the poetry "gross and imperfect according to the time then, wherein all fresh literature was clearly extinguished," he admires its crude liveliness, "even in the zeal of Elias and Phinehas for rebuke of sin."[40]

The whole thrust and purpose of Bale's religious writing was the documentation of the ineluctable conflict between the world of grace and the world of demonic self-sufficiency. Every treatise or pamphlet Bale ever wrote had as its ultimate subject this violent yet necessary clash of the sanctified company with its tireless adversaries. Such warfare was the means ordained by God to assure the godly of their election and to gather them to himself. It is this same agon of good and evil that is at the center of the plays written by Bale during the late 1530s. Throughout the first two chapters, I have suggested that behind the nonconformist objections to the social institution of the drama was a deep ambivalence toward the idea of drama. On the one hand, the nonconformist looked upon the world of play as a barrier between the believer and his God. On the other hand, the nonconformist saw his own life as a form of internalized theater whose reproduction in satires, saints' lives, and courtroom scenes was essential to the communal worship of the brethren. In the plays of John Bale, we will find the same ambivalence. Here was a nonconformist who overcame his party's reluctance to write stage plays and yet, within his plays, demonstrated the same anxieties about the dangers of theatrical representation felt by his comrades.

THE PLAYS OF JOHN BALE

John Bale's *A Comedy concernynge thre lawes* is typical of the nonconformist dramas that the renegade friar provided for his benefactor, Thomas Cromwell. As announced in the prologue, the play's theme offers few surprises: the conflict of good and evil, here witnessed in the struggle between the laws of Nature, Moses, and Christ (the embodiment of God's contractual relationship with man) and their common nemesis, Infidelity. Each of the laws enters firm in his innocence but quickly succumbs to the blandishments of Infidelity's minions. Having suffered pollution and defeat, all three are eventually restored to their former glory by Christian Faith. The play thus recapitulates what was, for Bale, the basic pattern of Christian history: purity, decline, and renewal.[41]

The drama proper opens with a cautious reworking of the familiar salutatory speech of the God of the cycle plays. Instead of establishing his divine credentials, Bale's deity warns his audience against a carnal understanding of his nature.

> I am Deus Pater, a substance invisible,
> All one with the Son, and Holy Ghost in essence.
> To angel and man I am incomprehensible;
> A strength infinite, a righteousness, a prudence,
> A mercy, a goodness, a truth, a life, a sapience.[42]

By underscoring the purely abstract quality of his deity, Bale forces a perceptible wedge between the actor and the God he represents.

The fear that in the heat of performance an audience might mistake an imagined world for the spiritual world it figured forth had haunted the nonconformist mind since the beginnings of Lollardy. Bale deemed himself guilty of encouraging just such a delusion in his early efforts as a dramatist. Summoned before Bishop Stokesley at London in 1536, Bale used the examination as a forum to renounce all iconic art that tempted the believer to conceive of divine truth in gross or carnal terms. Responding to a charge that he had discredited the harrowing of hell, Bale replied:

> As concernyng ye second artycle. I neuer denyed, descendit ad inferna, to be an artycle of ye crede, but desyred ye peple reuerentlye so to receue yt. . . . I requyred them also to be very cyrcumspect in receyuyng the seyd artycle. And not to beleue yt as yei se yt sett forth in peynted clothes, or in glasse wyndowes, or lyke as my self had befor tyme sett yt forth in ye cuntre yer in a serten playe. for thowgh ye sowle of crist soch tyme as hys corse laye in ye graue, ded vysytt hell, yet can we not iustlye suppose yt he fawgt vyolentlye with ye deuyls, for ye sowles of ye faythfull sort, . . .[43]

The opening words of God the Father in *Thre lawes* suggest Bale's continuing reservations about the propriety of theatrical representation; indeed, the fear of playing was to be a major factor in determining the character of Bale's dramatic art.

Nowhere is the formative influence of Bale's "stage fright" more apparent than in the playwright's rigidly divided approach to the characterization of his Vices and Virtues. The first of the play's three agons begins with an encounter between Natural Law and Infidelity. Like most of Bale's heroes, Natural Law is a cardboard figure, a mouthpiece for the author's doctrinal pronouncements. His adversary stands in vivid contrast. He is the quintessential nonconformist villain—a carefree, reckless gamester who regards sincerity and perspicacity as annoying infringements upon his pursuit of linguistic pleasure. His initial speech—built from snatches of peddlers' songs—is a jarring exercise in free association, as the sight of a potential gull turns his thoughts abruptly from the selling of brooms to the merchandising of devotional aids.

Broom, broom, broom, broom, broom! Buy broom, buy, buy,
  buy;
Brooms for shoes and pouchrings;
Boots and buskins for new brooms;
Broom, broom, broom!
Marry! God give you good even;
And the holy man Saint Steven
Send ye a good new year.
I would have brought ye the pax,
Or else an image of wax
If I had known ye here.[44]

The response of Natural Law to this madcap discourse is literal-minded and plodding. Infidelity's lament that his strenuous singing threatens his health elicits a painfully earnest sympathy: "That might have done ye smart."

Around so simple a being Infidelity runs semantic circles, mixing superstitious platitudes with arrogant mockery. His language moves with the caprice of a drunk whose lurching gait shuns the straight path as if it were cluttered with obstacles invisible to the sober eye. The felicities of rhyme, puns, and clever insults easily divert the speaker from the business of making sense. Infidelity is a victim of the cloistered imagination, the inhabitant of a private verbal universe whose map he alone possesses. Although Natural Law cannot navigate the perils of Infidelity's unsanctified speech, he does perceive its utter lawlessness:

Ye are disposed to dally,
To leap and oversail
The compass of your wit?
I counsel ye yet, in season,
Somewhat to follow reason,
And gnaw upon the bit.[45]

This preliminary confrontation evolves into a formal debate on the nature of nature. Infidelity argues that nature is inherently evil, given to outbreaks of disease and flood, pestilence and animal violence. Such apparent discord, counters Natural Law, is in fact God's orderly use of the natural elements to chastise the disobedience of man.

The Vice's position is a direct challenge to his opponent's very being, for in such a world as Infidelity describes natural law is a contradiction in terms. The Vices in Bale's plays always conspire not only to blur the identity of the heroes but to undermine the concept of stable identity itself. The Vices' contempt for fixed identity emerges only after the departure of Natural Law's inhibiting presence. Once his guardian has vacated the stage, Infidelity gives free reign to his disorderly impulses. Summoning his cohorts, Idolatry and Sodomy, he plots the overthrow of his saintly foe. The world of the three conspirators—descendants of the morality Vices and the mystery tyrant's minions—is one of pure child's play. Natural Law's sincerity had dictated that character, appearance, and name were one. In this misguided domain, identity is fluid. Although Infidelity himself conjures up Sodomy and Idolatry, commanding them "to appear / Like two knaves as ye be,"[46] he fails to recognize them. Sodomy first speaks offstage, claiming the common name of the Vice, Ambo. When he does enter, he appears as a monk. Idolatry follows closely behind disguised in the garments of the necromancer. Confused by their costumes, Infidelity wonders, "Such two I never saw!"[47] His confusion eventually focuses on Idolatry: this character, it appears, has altered not only costume but gender as well. "What?" cries Infidelity in bewilderment, "sometime thou wert a he!" "Yea," says Idolatry, "but now Ich am a she, / And a good mid-wife, perde!"[48] Even sexual identity is unstable in this delirious world where the joy of playing precludes stability of character. Both Idolatry and Sodomy speak the same slippery language as their ringleader. While reserving the stately cadences of rhyme royal for Natural Law, Bale employs a sing-song, eight-line stanza containing two triple rhymes to characterize the speech of his villains. The jangling verse is a fit container for the haphazard medley of incantations, quack cures, and cynical merriment rehearsed by the three conspirators.

> If ye cannot sleep, but slumber,
> Give oats unto Saint Uncumber;
> And beans in a certain number

> Unto Saint Blaise and Saint Blithe.
> Give onions to Saint Cutlake,
> And garlic to Saint Cyriac
> If ye will shun the headache—
> Ye shall have them at Queenhithe.[49]

Villainy in Bale's play is rural and lower-class. Infidelity, we remember, enters singing a refrain from a peddler's song. Idolatry is an old peasant woman lost in thoughts of superstition, homegrown remedies, and kitchen vices. This is the world that the mystery plays had celebrated: the world of the foolish but kindly shepherds feasting on imaginary food and tending flocks of imaginary prized sheep; the world of Noah's shrewish wife, ready to die for the pleasure of gossiping with her companions. The Lollards as well, particularly those who had learned their doctrine outside the university circle, found Christian good residing in the breast of the common man whom they canonized in the figure of the plowman. For Bale, the commoner holds no such immediate attraction.[50] He is the ignorant backwoods man clinging to pagan and Catholic superstition and daring to make war on England's saintly king of reform. The Vices of the morality plays often spoke in dialect, but Bale must have taken special delight in characterizing his villains as non-Midland speakers.

> Nor I, son, by my troth!
> Cha caught a courage of sloth,
> And such a cumbrous coth,
> Ich wot not what to do.[51]

Over these demonic bumpkins presides Infidelity: guardian spirit of the "dark corner" and champion of its cloistered fantasies:

> Spare none abomination,
> Nor detestable fashion,
> That man's imagination
> By wit may comprehend.[52]

Natural Law's reappearance at the close of the first act is calculated to shock. Utterly transformed from his former glory through the black magic of Infidelity's evil, he enters as a leper. His disease is the consequence of man's attempt to accommodate divine truth to his own conceits. In his first appearance Natural Law wore no disguise; his very flatness as a character signaled his purity. Now his deformity conceals and denies his God-given identity just as the costumes of Sodomy and Idolatry had obscured theirs. The play world of the Vices has broken loose from its confines and spread its unholy disorder through the world at large. Yet this second encounter does not end on a wholly pessimistic note. Natural Law turns in his agony to the Christian rulers of the world and urges them to correct the ecclesiastical abuses that cripple true religion. He then looks to the deity from whose grace he seeks an even greater restoration.

Bale viewed human history as a story of fallen reformers. Each arose in a world of corruption, shone briefly in his Christian purity, and then was obscured by the age's superstition and repression. Yet as each faded from view, he bequeathed a portion of his brilliance to another who in turn would shine with still greater glory. Only in his own time, which he persistently identified with the Apocalypse, did Bale envision a complete triumph of the reformed way of life. Bale's plays reflect this ebb and flow of Christian history. His heroes are rarely seen in isolation but rather as participants in the larger triumph of history itself. Each contributes to a vast movement whose end is an earthly reformation in which all time is redeemed. The triumph of Henry's purified English Church provides Bale with the saintly perspective that enables him to become its faithful chronicler, restoring to credit reformers once scorned but now revealed as pillars of the true church.

Bale's vision of history dictates the highly schematic and repetitive quality of his plays. As soon as Natural Law has disappeared, the next contestant approaches, ready to reenact with only slight variation the dramatic encounter that preceded it. Moses' Law enters, preaches the commandments, is challenged by the ever-playful Infidelity, suffers from the plots of the master Vice and his two companions, Avarice and Ambition, and is corrupted. Christ's Gospel similarly falls victim to Infidelity, False Doctrine, and Hypocrisy. The cycle is only broken in the concluding act when Infidelity is overthrown by God's Vengeance and the three Laws are redeemed and reunited. Bale's fondness for such formulaic structure may have its roots in his pedagogy as well as his historiography. During Edward's reign, Bale published young Princess Elizabeth's translation of the meditations of Marguerite d'Angoulême, queen of Navarre. In his epilogue to the work, Bale provided a scriptural rationale for the repetition of conceits in religious literature.

> If the ofte repetynge of some one sentence, engendereth a tedy-
> ouse werynesse to the reader, lete hym wele peruse the holy
> workes of S. Johan the Evangelyst, & I doubt it not but he shall
> fynde there the same maner of writynge. And hys occasyon is
> (as all the chefe writers afferme) the necessary markynge of the
> preceptes of helthe, or of matter chefely concernyng the sowles
> saluacyon. For a thynge twyse or thryse spoken entereth moche
> more depely the remembraunce than that is uttered but ones.[53]

Despite its repetitious quality, *Thre lawes* does have a sense of dra-matic movement and variation. Each tableau, while conforming to the basic pattern of purity, corruption, and promised renewal, exhib-its a slightly different deployment of its dramatic elements. In addi-tion, the characters of both the heroes and villains (despite the ef-forts of the latter to abort the process) are brought into clearer focus as the play unfolds. Infidelity was introduced in the first agon as a purveyor of the obsolete accoutrements of Catholic devotion. In the second agon, as he laments the passing of the good old days when priests filled their auditors' ears with ribald tales and stories of mirac-ulous conversions, he comes to embody England's nostalgia for the Catholic pulpit. "It was a good world when we had such wholesome stories / Preached in our church, on Sundays and other feries [holi-days]."[54] When huddled with his fellow conspirators, the Vice is quick to fasten upon scriptural preaching as their common enemy. The law of God is to be kept from the masses who will now be forced to read their religion in symbols created by men. "Yea, never spare them, but evermore play the biter, / Expressing always the tropes and types of thy mitre."[55]

As the particularity of these events fades into the universality of their meaning, they gradually assume the colorations of their deter-mining ritual, prelatical examination. In the fourth act, Evangelium is persecuted for his pulpit oratory. The Vices will treat Evangelium as they once treated Christ himself, culling from his sermons the heretical beliefs upon which he will be examined. "As He preached here, we followed from place to place, / To trap Him in snare, and His doctrine to deface."[56] Recollecting the Wycliffite simile that likened the papal suppression of the gospel to the burying of Christ in the sepulcher, the conspirators vow to place four "knights" on guard against true preaching: prelates, lawyers, ignorant lords, and corrupt judges. It is no coincidence that these were the men whom the brethren might expect to face in their own courtroom encounters. The dialogue between Evangelium and his tormentor, Pseudodoctrina, similarly invokes the experience of examination:

> P: Show me, brother mine, who did thee hither send.
> E: The Father of Heaven, of His mere benevolence:
>   I desire, therefore, to have free audience.
> P: Ye mind then to preach afore this company?
> E: In the laws of God would I instruct them gladly.
> P: Preach here thou shalt not, without the authority
>   Of pope or bishop, or of some of their affinity.
> E: God's word never taketh his authority of man.[57]

Once Evangelium has been condemned, the action, for Infidelity, seems to have reached its logical and satisfactory end. "My business all is now at a good conclusion, / That I have here brought these three laws to confusion."[58] The portrayal of Infidelity as a dramatist in his own right, only hinted at earlier, becomes emphatic in this act as Infidelity declares his dedication to the stage:

> Now will I contrive the drift of another play;
> I must work such ways Christ's law may not continue.
> In a while am I like to have none else of my retinue:
> Companions I want to begin this tragedy.[59]

In the Vices' eyes he has crafted a tragedy depicting the overthrow of divine order. Although the bulk of the play's events would seem to bear out his contention, the audience is always aware of the larger drama to which Infidelity's plot is merely subsidiary. This drama, "compyled" by John Bale but ordained by God Himself, is a comedy.[60] The outlines of its dramatic shape and the assurance that its downward motion will be arrested and reversed have been made known to us in both the prologue and the opening scene. The events of the final act will confirm the triumph of God's drama over the drama of the Vices.

There are then two plays being performed here, and Bale exploits the distinction to demonstrate the opposition between godly stagecraft and Catholic playing. In the process Bale resolves his own ambivalent attitude toward the rectitude of his vocation. All the negativity that Bale as a nonconformist found in the dramatic arts is concentrated in the demonic play of the Vices. The sense of the play as an escape from contingency and law, of its tendency to confuse rather than clarify spiritual identity, of its establishment of a world that rivals God's universe—all these aspects of the drama are found in Infidelity's play within a play. As practiced by Infidelity, drama represents the most demonic product of the cloistered imagination. His tools are the discredited instruments of Catholic devotion, his audience the same that continued to demonstrate its fondness for the mystery cycles.[61]

The demonic interludes of *Thre lawes* share the cycles' disdain for the boundaries between real and stage worlds. When Infidelity enters singing snatches of a popular ditty, he presents to the audience a mirror in which they may view themselves. The subsequent bouts of singing, dancing, jesting, and plotting also provide moments of readily recognizable human behavior calculated to reach out beyond the stage world. Yet for Bale all this activity is suspect. The fear that the play world of the imagination will escape its confines, that game will usurp earnest, stands foremost in Bale's mind. Infidelity's boast that his conquest of divine law has made the world safe for his playing strikes at Bale's deepest anxieties about the potentially satanic nature of play.

An alternative to this dark stagecraft is offered by the emblems of nonconformist virtue. Their dramatic domain frames the play with the first and last acts and, within the central body of *Thre lawes*, their appearances surround each act's core of demonic playing. Thus at all times Bale's purified drama is seen as surrounding and controlling the polluted drama of the Vices. The nature of the Virtues' sanctified drama is utterly opposed to its demonic counterpart. The Virtues are deliberately two-dimensional in nature. Bale wished his audience to contemplate them with critical detachment rather than embrace them with emotional spontaneity. For the same reason their language is stripped clean of the cadences and diction of colloquial speech. Their dialogue is formal and stilted, circumscribed by the rhyme royal stanza. Their interaction is similarly divorced from the all-too-human play of warm fellowship and angry contention that marks the behavior of the Vices.[62] The Virtues speak to each other in a prescribed formula that pays deference to God's ordered creation and their places within it. This is a true holy family with God the Father presiding, an image of the community of saints. In contrast, Infidelity presides haphazardly over his sons; quarreling and dissent define this reprobate rabble.

> I must fetch ye in—there is no remedy.
> A naughty whoresons—have I brought ye up hitherto?
> And know not your father? ye shall drink both ere I go.[63]

The true play world of *Thre lawes* is cold and conceptual, a world of game that is played in deadly earnest. Purged of the verisimilitude that threatens to blur the distinction between artistic illusion and reality, this world is above all safe. The highly stylized conception of its characters restrains without crushing the audience's impulse toward identification. The abstract figures of the Laws do have a limited human dimension, and they play a familiar role. Defenders of the Bible's holy truth, they are made to suffer for their convictions; but in their struggle with the forces of unbelief their election (i.e., restoration) is made manifest. Bale's play beseeches its audience to identify with these martyrs but not in the heedless way in which the unwary soul responds to Infidelity. The potential saint is asked to discern the pattern of sanctification visible in the conduct of the three Laws and then is invited to discover the same in his own life. This process is not devoid of emotion, but the spectator's enthusiastic recognition of his fraternity with Bale's saints is predicated upon the exercise of his intellect. The spectator must survey the life of the play's hero and then examine his own before he can inwardly declare that a state of analogy exists between the two. As in so much of nonconformist art, this process of identification stops short of ecstatic self-annihilation. The spectator does not become Natural Law so much as he gradually learns to see that he is like Natural Law.[64] As always, the simile supplants the metaphor, and the dynamics of iconic worship are eschewed.

John Bale's divided drama, with its carefully demarcated zones of holy and demonic play, is emblematic of the ambivalence behind the nonconformist response to the stage. *Thre lawes* is a play that attacks playing or, more accurately, one that exposes the dangers of commonly held conceptions of drama while offering a safe alternative. Although the play affords scant delight to a modern reader, it is, judged on its own terms, a remarkable achievement. Here is a play that satisfies the need of its nonconformist author to reenact publicly the dramatic ritual of the sanctified soul turning toward God, and yet, at the same time, it routs the demons of dramatic representation from their lairs. Bale accomplished this feat without employing any conventions that cannot be traced to the stagecraft of either the mystery cycles or the morality plays. Like the author of *Pierce the Ploughman's Crede*, Bale generated a new art form from wholly conventional elements.

The debt of *Thre lawes* to the morality is substantial. The confessional speeches, the playful Vices, and the tale of the corruption and eventual restoration of a representative Christian soul (the three Laws, we may recall, are different aspects of a single entity) all betray the play's roots in the morality tradition. Unlike the mystery cycles, which were compromised by their liturgical parentage, the moralities presented little threat to the nonconformist sensibility.[65] Their potency sprang not from the recreation of a eucharistic event but rather from a depiction of spiritual warfare. Often that warfare assumed the form of a series of debates or confrontations between a doubting soul and its tempters. Catholic excrescences—the miraculous death-bed conversion, the emphasis on priestly confession, the role of angelic messengers—could easily be purged by a reform-minded playwright. The reliance of the morality on conceptual rather than naturalistic representation may also have enhanced its appeal to radical Protestants.[66] As has been noted, Bale associated verisimilitude in drama with the false playing of the Vices. A drama tending toward abstraction, on the other hand, could underscore that distinction between art and life without abandoning a necessary concern with events and characters of human dimension.[67]

Bale was, nevertheless, attracted to certain elements within the mystery cycles as well, particularly to their vast historical perspective. To a man determined to rewrite all human history from the vantage point of reformed theology, the mysteries, like the popish chronicles, were instruments of Catholic devotion imploring to be converted to the service of Christ's religion. W. T. Davies's listing of Bale's lost plays suggests that the author did, in fact, plan such a project.[68] Only two of these plays—*Johan Baptystes preachynge in the wyldernesse* and *The Temptacyon of our lorde*—survive. We will look closely at the former.

Johan Baptystes preachynge, unlike the mystery play versions of the Baptist's life, is a drama about the vocational basis of Christian identity. The mystery accounts of John's mission concentrate almost exclusively on his baptism of Christ, and modern texts, in acknowledgment of this focus, often refer to the play as "The Baptism of Jesus." Bale's title is a reminder of the Protestant playwright's preoccupation with John's role as a preacher of the new dispensation. His play falls symmetrically into three sections, each highlighting John's evangelical office. In the first section, John preaches to and converts the sinful masses represented by Common Crowd, Publican, and Soldier; in the second, he debates the nature of religious devotion with the Vice-like figures of Pharisee and Sadducee; and in the final part, he confronts his master Christ and awakens to the full scope of his spiritual vocation. Although preaching is the subject of the play, religious disputation is its method. John's battle with the misconceptions of his converts, his defense of Christian truth against the Jewish establishment, and his troubled questioning of Christ as to his own worthiness all testify to the nonconformist preference for contested rather than received truth. The conversion of his auditory requires no carnal miracles, nor is it dependent on their well-intentioned ignorance. The rational appreciation of John's arguments—pursued through an earnest process of logical inquiry and authenticated by the gift of understanding—replaces the mystery play formula of ceremonial mimicry. Significantly, the confessions of John's converts center upon vocational sins. The commoner places his trust in superstition rather than labor; the soldier supplements his sparse income with booty got by violence; and the publican oppresses the poor with his collection of taxes. John, however, urges them not to abandon their offices. As the Lollards had preached and as William Perkins would codify, so Bale's John teaches: Christian identity must be sought not in extraordinary callings but rather in man's gracious performance of the task set before him.[69] To the soldier, John preaches:

> Of war ye have laws—use them with right always;
> Do not spoil nor rape, take no unlawful preys;
> The office ye have for the public unity,
> Mind to exercise to the land's tranquility—
> Ye may thus please God, in doing your feat right well.[70]

Bale reserves a contemporary gloss of John's warning for his epilogue. "Hear neither Francis, Benedict, nor Bruno, / Albert, nor Dominic, for they new rulers invent."[71]

The lessons John has only preached in the first episode must now be experienced in his conflict with the Pharisees and Sadducees. These men claim spiritual preeminence solely on a perfunctory performance of their callings, yet fail to achieve the holiness of even the lowliest commoner laboring in faith. Like the Vices of *Thre lawes*, these villains are purveyors of a debased theatricality, "painted hypocrites" who "play most wicked parts." They are also thinly disguised representatives of prelatical oppression. Just as Arundel's agent examined Thorpe by posing as a sympathetic convert, so Pharisee and Sadducee feign friendship in order to expose John's heresies. "Let us dissemble," proposes the former, "to understand his meaning." His fellow conspirator agrees: "Well pleased I am that we examine his doings; / His doctrine, paraventure, might hinder else our livings."[72] Once convinced of John's heterodoxy, they threaten imprisonment.

The arrival of Christ adds a new dimension to Bale's exploration of Christian office. The rendition of the scene is not innovative; much the same treatment can be found in the cycles. The previous discussions of calling, however, alter our approach to the event. John's own spiritual growth is suddenly brought into focus. The preacher who had exhorted others to accept their ordained missions must now master his own painful lesson. John's insistence on his inability to baptize his lord is patiently refuted by a higher teacher. God's grace, says Christ, will make him sufficient for his labors. "The man which have faith lacketh no sanctification / Necessary and meet for his health and salvation— / Thine office, therefore, now execute thou on me."[73]

In Bale's version of the baptism of Jesus, then, the tale is one of John's awakening to the necessity of seeking identity in the faithful execution of a divinely appointed vocation. The pattern of John's religious education proves typically Balean in its reproduction of the intellectual and spiritual dynamics of examination. John teaches pure doctrine, is challenged by institutionally sanctioned falsehood, and is then restored to an even deeper sense of truth by God's intercession. Bale has here transformed a Catholic play into a ritual drama of nonconformist enlightenment. Bale undertook the same task in *The Temptacyon of our lorde* where again he appears to have been attracted to the possibility of staging another trial of truth. The contest in this play concerns rival systems of scriptural exegesis and conflicting valuations of biblical wisdom. Its climax marks the triumph of Christ's Protestant biblicism over Satan's Catholic glossing, the victory of a living text over its moribund shadow.[74] The curious tonality of this hermeneutical agon will similarly inform Milton's great displaced drama *Paradise Regained*.

Bale's *King Johan*, alone among his extant plays, deals with nonbiblical subject matter: the early thirteenth-century struggle between Pope Innocent III and King John over the relative powers of church and state. The shift from sacred to profane history is less radical than has sometimes been suggested.[75] Bale's early plays, despite their largely biblical landscapes, dramatize contemporary religious controversies. John the Baptist's attire may be first-century Jerusalem, but his doctrine and bearing are sixteenth-century London. Bale's chronicle of the unhappy reign of John similarly blends recent English history with biblical reminiscence. Sedition, the chief Vice, is a historical personage, Stephen Langton, but evokes memories of the biblical tormentors. John himself is both a medieval king and Christ betrayed by "a false Iudas kysse." For Bale, it was the historian's duty to underscore the congruence between the sacred and the profane, the events of the Bible being the sole glass through which the meaning of secular history might be read. When Bale turned to biblical exegesis following his first exile from England, he found in the visions of St. John the master narrative of all human activity. No faithful chronicle, he argued, could be written without Revelation as a guide to uncovering God's intentions hidden in the activities of saints and sinners. This prophecy gave "full clearance to all the chronicles and most notable histories which hath been wrote since Christ's ascension, opening the true natures of their ages, times, and seasons." Although Bale cautioned that the holy text is "a light to the chronicles, and not the chronicles to the text,"[76] his own work repeatedly employs each as aids to the reading of the other.

Some ten years after the composition of the polemical *King Johan*, Bale formally defended the use of historical narrative in religious argumentation. The issue had arisen in a debate with a "ranke Papyst" on the lawfulness of vows. Mocking his adversary's citation of a light fable as a "story of authoryte," Bale denounced the use of *fictio* in a serious religious exercise. It was acceptable to enliven a sermon or tract with occasional moments of light-hearted invention, but such inventions should not be construed as substantive contributions to religious debate. Only history and scripture could perform that office. The "merry tale of a nunne whych would be marryed," recorded by Augustine and pressed into service by Bale's opponent, might elevate an audience's spirits but not their understanding.[77] Had Augustine wished his auditors to accept his tale as an integral part of his theological argument, "the party had bene named, and also the place of her dwelling." Its historical veracity once confirmed, the story might then be considered "grounded matter" and hence "of credite."

King Johan is an exercise in theological disputation; and its author was anxious to ensure that his pronouncements would carry authority. He therefore provided a sufficient quantity of "grounded matter": historical events in which the parties and their places of residence were named and biblical allusions that bore the imprint of the Holy Ghost. To this mixture of scripture and chronicle, Bale, as in his other plays, added a third element: allegory. Purely fictive, the allegory deliberately clashes with the historical narrative, its abstraction defusing the potentially dangerous naturalism of the play's

events while underscoring their universality. By balancing imaginative invention with the authority of chronicles "cleared" by scripture,
Bale produced a work of religious art amenable to his nonconformist
sensibilities.

In its broad strokes *King Johan* conforms to the highly schematic
designs of the earlier plays. The opening section of the drama cele-
brates King John's native excellence and the growth of his spiritual
awareness in the face of papal oppression. The large middle section
of the play chronicles the triumph of the forces of corruption. The
last section, although it necessarily documents John's eventual destruction, does suggest renewal: first, by restoring John's good name,
so tarnished in orthodox chronicles; and second, by projecting the
play forward to King Henry's successful completion of King John's
abortive rebellion. The achievement of the play, then, does not rest
in Bale's discovery of a new dramatic formula but rather in the richness with which he embellished his old one.

Perhaps the most interesting development in Bale's dramatic art is
the new and telling light brought to bear on the demonic play world
of his villains. The evil play within a play, only hinted at in the
conspiracies of Infidelity and his minions, emerges fully mounted in
King Johan. The most important of the villains, Sedition, makes his
entrance in the opening scene where he comes upon John and England conferring on the conduct of the clergy. In Sedition's unsanctified vision, the wedded interests of king and country constitute
"bycherye." Of course it is Sedition himself who will prove the adul-
terer when he attempts to woo England from her rightful lord: Bale's
ironies are not remarkably subtle. John immediately recognizes the
reprobate voice of an adversary, yet he is careful to qualify his attack
on Sedition's unruly playfulness, making no outright rejection of
game in the interests of earnest. The two, John suggests, are not
incompatible: "Thow canst with thy myrth in no wysse dyscontent
me, / So that thow powder yt with wysdom and honeste."[78] From
the beginning of his drama, Bale distinguishes, as he had done in
Thre lawes, between holy and demonic playing. The stolid monarch
who acts out an internalized drama of God's making is contrasted
with the protean Sedition whose play is externalized and self-
generated.

It is corrupt language that first betrays Sedition's true nature. The godly, John had suggested, speak words powdered with the wisdom of biblical citations; Sedition's are seasoned instead with gross obscenities, witty wordplay, and nonsensical alliteration.[79] Unfixed in the verities of God's word, the Vice's speech proves as unreliable as his loyalties. "I haue a great mynd to be a lecherovs man— / A wengonce take yt! I wold saye, a relygyovs man."[80] Like the clergy whom John vigorously attacks, he and his fellows reside in the dark corners of the repressed Catholic mind. "Lyke backes [bats], in þe darke ye always take yowr flyght, / Flylteryng in fanseys, and euer abhorre the lyght."[81] Above all, Sedition is the consummate player:

> In euery estate of þe clargye I playe a part:
> Sumtyme I can be a monke in a long syd cowle,
> Sumtyme I can be a none and loke lyke an owle,
> Sumtyme a channon in a syrples fayer and whyght,
> A chapterhowse monke sumtym I apere in syght,
> I am ower syre Iohn sumtyme, with a new shauen crowne,
> Sumtym þe person and swepe þe stretes with a syd gowne,
> Sumtyme þe bysshoppe with a myter and a cope,
> A graye fryer sumtyme, with cutt shoes and a rope;
> Sumtyme I can playe þe whyght monke, sumtyme þe fryer,
> The purgatory prist and euery mans wyffe desyer.
> This cumpany hath provyded for me morttmayne,
> For þat I myght euer among ther sort remayne.
> Yea, to go farder, sumtyme I am a cardynall;
> Yea, sumtyme a pope, and than am I lord ouer all,
> Bothe in hevyn and erthe and also in purgatory,
> And do weare iij crownes whan I am in my glorye.[82]

There is an intoxicating quality to this litany of unholy religious occupations. Climbing slowly up the ecclesiastical ladder from the humble rungs of the village priest to the glorious heights of the pope and his master Antichrist, Sedition envisions a universe in which all of the inhabitants are projections of his own imagination.[83]

His oratory as such represents a debased imitation of Bale's own lawful activities as a playwright. The artist of nonconformity is not a willful creator but an obedient compiler.[84] Although the saints' lives he dramatizes are enactments of his own spiritual dilemmas and triumphs, his art is neither subjective nor solipsistic. The lives of the brethren are one life, its configurations scripted in the Bible and reaffirmed in the promptings of the Holy Spirit. At least so Bale believed. In Sedition's encomium on play, the stratagem of self-exorcism that we have traced back to the Lollards resurfaces. Fears about the verity of the holy artist's visions are placated by attributing falsehood and instability to the mental creations of his orthodox counterparts. Sedition is an alluring speaker; his soliloquy has passion and eloquence—all the passion and eloquence Bale himself could muster. Here is a potent emblem of the volatile union of fear and attraction with which the nonconformist approached the idea of play and impersonation. Bale fashions a lively paean to the dramatic impulse and its power to transform identity, and then places it in the mouth of a devil. Can we expect less from a man who bitterly renounced his Carmelite association, but not the vocational desires it fostered? who traded one brand of hagiography for its near mirror image? It is a perilously illusive boundary that separates the old Bale from the new and the art of damnation from the art of salvation.

The opening scene of *King Johan* provides the first intimation that the conflict between John and Innocent is a collision of two kinds of plays: the first play concerning John's exchange of an earthly crown for a heavenly one, the second the conspiracy of the papal agents to secure a downfall which turns out to be their own. In the next scene, placed by Bale at the very seat of the cloistered imagination, Rome, the nature of the second drama is more closely investigated. In the safety of the papal court, Sedition along with Dissimulation, Usurped Power, and Private Wealth plot the play that will catch the soul of a conscientious king. As with the Vices in *Thre lawes*, this acting troupe is riddled with envy, mistrust, and rancor.[85] Although they are cousins, Sedition and Dissimulation fail to recognize each other when they first meet. Community and the ritual art that sustains it inevitably collapse among men whose restless, idiosyncratic wills are permitted to determine their identities and values.

The center of the scene—and indeed the conspiracy itself—is the mounting of a pageant of the genealogy of evil (i.e., of the conspirators themselves). Private Wealth first proposes the task, suggesting the order in which the procession should appear so as to illustrate that "of me, Privat Welth, cam fyrst Vsurpyd Powr." A dispute erupts, however, over the proper staging of the play, with Sedition attempting to impose his own interpretation of the papal corruption of religion. He orders Usurped Power or the pope:

> To bare me on þi backe and bryng me in also,
> That yt maye be sayde þat fyrst Dyssymulacyon
> Browght in Privat Welth to every Cristen nacyon,
> And that Privat Welth browght in Vsurpid Powr,
> And he Sedycyon, in cytye, towne and tower,
> Þat sum man may know þe feche of all owr sorte.[86]

Dissimulation's scenario, in which Usurped Power rides upon the shoulders of his three cohorts, is enacted in the end. This proliferation of blocking proposals—which a modern audience might find evocative of the open-endedness of the stage—reveals for Bale a devotion to form at the expense of meaning. One reading is no better than the next because all are ultimately arbitrary, the inventions of ungrounded fancy rather than the compilation of a sanctified imagination. In contrast to Bale's own work, whose emphasis on rational disputation promises "your inward stomach [to] cheer,"[87] the Vices' play offers only pleasure for the eye. They are creating a visual symbol, an icon, whose terrible fiction they intend to realize in the court of the godly King John. Like Infidelity and company, these Vices are addicted to play for its own sake; to turn all the world into an unbounded playground is their dearest hope: "I wold euer dwell here to haue such mery sporte."[88]

Heading back to England to make that island safe for their antics, the Vices assume historical roles: Sedition becomes Stephen Langton, the monks' candidate for the archbishopric of Canterbury; Private Wealth becomes Pandulphus, the papal legate; and Dissimulation assumes the role of John's alleged murderer, the Cistercian monk Simon of Swynsett.[89] These fluctuations in identity reenforce our awareness of the Vices as demonic actors; they also underscore Bale's sense of the archetypal patterns of behavior underlying human history, patterns that only the Bible enables man to discern. The conspiracy to unseat King John proceeds with a feeling of inevitability born of Bale's vision of history as a tale of the corruption of holy innocence. The playlike atmosphere that surrounded the Vices in their Roman games seems to pollute at once the clear air of England. Replacing the earnest discourse of John and England is the numbing performance of the ritual of excommunication, another dumb show of Catholic devotion in Bale's eyes. Replacing the living community of Christ's body composed of king, country, and the three estates is a religion of death shorn up with the fragments of its ruin:

> Here ys fyrst a bone of the blyssyd trynete,
> A dram of þe tord of swete seynt Barnabe;
> Here ys a feddere of good seynt Myhelles wyng,
> A toth of seynt Twyde, a pece of Davyds harp stryng,
> Þe good blood of Haylys and owr blyssyd ladys mylke,
> A lowse of seynt Fraunces in this same crymsen sylke.[90]

Against this world of spiritual dissolution struggles the lonely King John. More than any of his other protagonists, Bale's King John resembles the isolated heroes of Lollard tradition: scorned, abused, and examined for their heretical beliefs.[91] Like Thorpe, he learns to see his life as a reenactment of Christianity's primal drama—the trial and execution of the son of God for his challenge to the corrupted institutions of contemporary religion. Dying at the hands of his own Judas, Dissimulation, he discovers the strength to pardon his enemies and the comfort promised to believers persevering to the end.

The true nature of John's martyrdom emerges from its contrariety to the bogus sainthood of Dissimulation, whose dream of canonization is a fit conclusion to the play he has scripted, a gross parody of the joys of the saintly martyr:

> To sende me to heauen goo rynge the holye belle
> And synge for my sowle a masse of *Scala Celi*,
> That I maye clyme vp aloft with Enoch and Heli.
> I do not doubte it but I shall be a saynt;
> Prouyde a gyldar, myne Image for to paynt.
> I dye for the church with Thomas of Canterberye;
> Ye shall fast my vigyll and vpon my daye be merye.

> No doubt but I shall do myracles in a whyle,
> And therfor lete me be shryned in the north yle.[92]

It is characteristic of Bale's devotion both to the word and history that John's sainthood is confirmed by his enshrinement in a text—the purified chronicles of England—rather than in the gaudy confines of an earthly tomb. The king himself achieves a new level of self-awareness by recognizing both the historical and spiritual dimensions of his inherited role. He is indeed his father's son:

> A lyke dysplesure in my fatheres tyme ded fall
> Forty yeres ago for ponnyshment of a clarke.
> No cunsell myght them to reformacyon call—
> In ther openyon they wer so stordy and starke—
> But ageynst ther prynce to þe pope they dyd so barke
> That here in Ynglond, in euery cyte and towne,
> Excomminycacyons as thonder boltes cam downe.[93]

In a similar self-authenticating gesture, Bale interrupted his documentation of religious persecution in England, *The Actes of the Englyshe Votaryes*, to find his own tale of woe among the stories of its victims.[94]

King Johan concludes by saluting the victory of the new learning in Bale's own rescue of John's besmirched reputation. In her role as the mourning Mary, England proclaims: "Report what they wyll in their most furyouse madnesse, / Of thys noble kynge much was the godlynesse."[95] Verity, often identified as the Reformation but also here a guardian of true history, provides the saint's obituary. The arrival of the last great spirit of reform, Imperial Majesty or Henry VIII, marks the final regeneration of England's holy community and the recovery of its status as an elect nation. Nonetheless, in the closing lines of the play, the forces of evil make one last entrance. It is appropriately Sedition, the Vice whose quarrel with John had set the drama's tragic events in motion, who appears. His gamesome mood, however, abruptly dissipates once he recognizes that his theater of demonic play no longer exists. "What myschiefe ayle ye that ye are so blunte to me?"[96] Crestfallen, he resembles nothing so much as the wayward child who suddenly discovers that his parents have come home and that punishment is imminent. In an expertly conceived episode, the Virtues verbally constrain the trickster until, like the Proteus he so closely resembles, he is obliged to confess the truth of his identity and history. The scene dramatizes the efforts of the godly playwright to make play and symbolism safe by forcing signs to conform to the things they signify. Sedition is constrained into a form that betrays his true nature; he must abandon the reckless, ungrounded dissimulations that breed distrust, rebellion, and spiritual blindness. The conspirators of Rome had sought to make England a suitable setting for their unholy drama; now Bale exacts his revenge by making England a stage fit for the presentation of the sacred drama of nonconformity. Bale has reformed the theater as his liege has reformed the kingdom. We have moved, Bale claims, "from ceremonyes dead to the lyuynge wurde of þe lorde."[97]

THE DRAMATIST IN EXILE

Bale's career as a dramatist halted as abruptly (if not as violently) as did the life of his patron Thomas Cromwell. Bale's interest in the drama, however, was not so easily terminated. Although there were no new plays, there were new performances.[98] Bale himself recounts the staging of three of his works at Kilkenny in the last year of his Irish appointment. "The yonge men, in the forenone, played a tragedye of Gods Promyses in the olde lawe, at the Market Crosse, with organe, plainges, and songes very aptely. In the afternone agayne they played a commedie of Sanct Johan Baptistes preachinges, of Christes baptisynge, and of his temptacion in the wildernesse, to the small contentacion of the prestes and other papistes there."[99] The staging of Bale's nonconformist plays coincided with the pageantry marking the coronation of Mary. The symbolism of the occasion was not lost on Bale. The two contrasting events formed for him "an image of both dramas": on the one hand, the edification of a reasoned dramatic discourse; on the other, the fantasies of a dumb show.

Bale may also have encouraged the private reading of his plays when public performances were no longer feasible. In a pamphlet from the same period, he praises a young servant castigated by a local priest for studying *Thre lawes*.[100] Bale's spirited defense of his play as a source of edification as accessible in the study as on the stage is suggestive of the nonconformist's fluid conception of what constitutes dramatic discourse. The curriculum of the modern university consistently undermines our understanding of that conception—not only in its broad division into departments, but also in its compartmentalization within disciplines. The common separation of Renaissance studies into dramatic and nondramatic literature necessarily obstructs the appreciation of an aesthetic that recognized no such boundaries, either between dramatic and nondramatic or between belletristic and nonbelletristic. For a brief moment in the turmoil of the Tudor period, circumstances conspired to allow a writer of Bale's temperament to produce a highly politicized drama for the stage. When those circumstances changed, Bale did not alter his course. He continued to feed his instincts for ritualized drama just as his Wycliffite ancestors had—by internalizing them in a literature that might produce a theatrical experience outside a theatrical environment.

In his editing of Thorpe's *Examination*, Bale had already recognized the dramatic potential of the heresy trial. He joined to his compilation of Thorpe's narrative, accounts of the examinations of two other reformers: Sir John Oldcastle, the Lollard heretic and traitor, and Anne Askew, an early Tudor Protestant.[101] The extent of Bale's intrusions in the two documents varies markedly. Askew herself had recorded her experiences—a practice inaugurated by Thorpe and imitated by subsequent generations of nonconformist martyrs. Bale's efforts here are confined to appreciative commentary. Since Oldcastle bequeathed no such account, Bale was left with the task of gathering evidence from a number of often hostile sources, as well as with a welcome opportunity to obscure the more idiosyncratic of the knight's beliefs.[102] However different the saints themselves and the manner in which their trials were preserved, the results are virtually indistinguishable.

As in Thorpe's *Examination*, we are once again encouraged to see the events as Caiaphas plays. " 'No ground have ye in all the scriptures,'" Oldcastle lectures his interrogators, "'so lordly to take it upon ye, but in Annas and Caiaphas, which sat thus upon Christ and upon his apostles after his ascension.'"[103] The judges are raging tyrants, their victims patient apostles. Like those stubborn children, Iniquity and Sedition, the inquisitors are quickly angered when the world fails to conform to their wishes and imagination. "Then, because I did add unto it 'the catholic church,'" recounts Askew, "he flung into his chamber in a great fury."[104] In their frustration, the prelates deny their proper vocation as judges and instead debase themselves by assuming the dress and calling of the executioner. Bale comments:

> Mark here an example most wonderful, and see how madly in their raging furies men forget themselves and lose their right wits now-a-days. A king's high counsellor, a judge over life and death, yea, a lord chancellor of a most noble realm, is now become a most vile slave for antichrist, and a most cruel tormentor. Without all discretion, honesty, or manhood, he casteth off his gown and taketh here upon him the most vile office of an hangman, and pulleth at the rack most villainously.[105]

Bale regarded the testimonies of Thorpe, Oldcastle, and Askew as the beginning of a reformed martyrology, a record of the disputations between the opponents of a corrupt ecclesiastical hierarchy and their adversaries. Instead of immortalizing the bogus miracles of the Roman saints, this new chronicle would celebrate true miracles: godly reasoning and unwavering faith. "Of his own chosen martyrs," declares Bale, "Christ looketh for none other miracle but that only they persevere faithful to the end, Matt. x., and never deny his verity afore men, Luke xii."[106] Such a chronicle would supply, in its lively representations of exemplary lives, guides to holy conduct and reaffirmations of communal faith all bound up within the safe confines of displaced drama.

Bale was never to complete his mission as martyrologist. Like the reformers portrayed in his plays, he was obliged to pass the gospel torch on to one younger and more capable. In John Foxe's *Acts and Monuments*, the nonconformist drama of examination (with its final act shifted to the martyr's stake) becomes at once more rigorously historical and yet more obviously devotional in nature. When Bale undertook to dramatize Anne Askew's examinations, he himself played a dominant role, fragmenting Askew's account and then overlaying it with his own strident commentary. Foxe's approach is antithetical. Askew is granted centerstage throughout. Only once does Foxe intervene and then to document the forging of Askew's recantation in the prelatical registers. The Foxe of legend is a ghoulish artist specializing in the rendition of burning flesh; the real Foxe may be partisan, but he is surprisingly detached in his observations of the legal trials of the early Protestants. It is finally the sheer weight of the accumulated evidence combined with the dispassionate accounts of intense pain and cruelty that animates Foxe's work.

In Foxe's records we can see the examination of faith—whether before a ruthless bishop, a conscientious father, or a stern minister—continuing to enjoy the sacramental status it had already earned among the Lollards.[107] Language usually reserved for the sacrament of the altar is enlisted by both Foxe and his troupe to recount the ecclesiastical trial and its fiery conclusion. One martyr ascends the scaffold, chanting "Introibo ad altare Dei." Another dubs his bloody sacrifice the "seal" of Christ's doctrine. A third expects by bearing the cross of his persecution "to communicate with our Sweet Saviour Christ."[108] And communicate he does. The experience of prelatical interrogation, he later confides to his cellmate, is akin to a eucharistic feeding. "Furthermore, he that did lie with him afterwards in prison, in the same bed, reported that he heard him say, that even in the time of his examination, he was wonderfully comforted; insomuch as not only in spirit, but also in body, he received a certain taste of that holy communion of saints, whilst a most pleasant refreshing did issue from every part and member of the body unto the seat and place of the heart, and from thence did ebb and flow to and fro unto all the parts again."[109]

In the early Middle Ages allegorical interpretations of the mass had encouraged communicants to see the ceremony as a divine drama.[110] Bale's and Foxe's examinates similarly seem attuned to the inherent theatricality of their communal ritual and the sacramental art it spawned. Consider, for example, Ridley's remarkable dress rehearsal for his impending confrontation with the ecclesiastical authorities. Inventing a fictional inquisitor, one "Antonian; meaning, by that name, some popish persecutor—as Winchester," Ridley proceeds to examine himself. First he anticipates Antonian's questions, then he formulates a response, and finally he sends both to Latimer for the elder man's comments. Question, response, and sympathetic commentary: such is the pattern Bale imposes on Askew's examination and many of his discursive pamphlets as well. Typical, too, is the element of fictionalization, the blending of the imagined and the historical having been practiced as far back as Thorpe. As in the examination it forecasts, Ridley's exercise is marked by a climactic moment of realization. Having exhaustively argued the key tenets of his faith against his imagined foe, Ridley suddenly halts like a child caught unawares in his pantomimed play.

> "Good father, . . . here, me thinketh, I see you suddenly lifting up your head towards heaven, after your manner, and then looking upon me with your prophetical countenance, and speaking unto me, with these or like words: 'Trust not, my son, . . . to these word-weapons; for the kingdom of God is not in words but in power. And remember always the words of the Lord, "Do not imagine aforehand, what and how you will speak: for it shall be given you even in that same hour what ye shall speak; For it is not ye that speak, but the Spirit of your Father which speaketh in you." ' "[111]

Ridley recognizes both the necessity for and worth of his disputational efforts. He is also aware, however, that at the critical moment of trial the straining of human reason must submit to the quietude of an unearthly inspiration. He knows that the ritual he is about to enact can only partially be rehearsed; ultimately a genuine performance is an extemporaneous performance. Both the anticipation and the recollection of examination may be human art, but the event itself is divine art. As in Bale, compilation takes precedence over creation.

The self-consciousness with which the Tudor examinate approached the role-playing of the courtroom was acute. In the face of the antagonism of the reprobate, Tyndale had urged those saints impelled by the Spirit "to play Paul" and chastise the fallen.[112] It is just such a performance that John Rogers enacts when confronted by the scornful Stephen Gardiner. "And in Athens, the wise men of this world, and such as gave their endeavour to wisdom, said by St. Paul, 'Quid vult spermologus hic dicere?' What will this prater (as my lord chancellor said to me, Shall we suffer this fellow to prate,—when I would fain have said that thing that I have here written), trifler, news-carrier, or bringer that telleth whatsoever men will have him for gain or advantage?"[113] This convoluted sentence with its heavily impacted parenthetic interlude is deliberately distorted, forcing the reader to collapse the personalities and situations of Rogers and Paul. The Tudor saint dissolves into the biblical hero and yet, as in all nonconformist acting, the player is never totally subsumed by his persona. Even as the distinction between actor and role fades, the examinate retreats in a paroxysm of reassuring similitudes: " 'We make not ourselves like unto them, in the singular virtues and gifts of God given unto them; as of doing miracles, and of many other things.' The similitude and likeness of them and us consisteth not in all things, but only in this; that is, that we be like them in doctrine, and in the suffering of persecution and infamy for the same."[114]

Foxe himself, much like his elder companion in exile Bale, carefully distinguishes between holy and demonic playing. The trials of the saints are "lamentable and bloody tragedies" that instruct men in the art of holy living and dying. In contrast, the antics of the papists are "comical spectacles" or merry "pageants" that offer only laughter and refreshment.[115] One such incident concerns "a false fearful imagination of fire." Assembled at St. Mary's Church in Oxford for the recantation of one Master Malary, church dignitaries, college officials, and students are put to rout by a rumor of fire in the building. Foxe recalls with glee the panic and mayhem, the hasty surrender of social dignity, the blind and ignoble pursuit of self-preservation.[116] The episode is a rhetorical triumph precisely because Foxe allows its emblematic dimension to develop covertly. Driven by invisible demons into a passionate frenzy, these persecutors embody the unruly orthodox mind. While their victims through faith transcend the agony of a real fire, they through false imagination suffer the torments of an illusory flame. This is an embryonic allegory in the manner of the Lollards, hovering between the historical and the symbolic. One player abandons all for the sake of himself; the other sacrifices himself for the sake of all. Ironically the participant in the orthodox spectacle ultimately loses himself in delusion; the actor in the holy tragedy finds himself in the assurance of his election.

Bale may have lacked Foxe's subtlety and historical rigor, but he had, like his stage hero John Baptist, pointed the way. The saint's life, whether cast as prelatical examination, autobiography, or eulogy, would become standard Puritan fare for generations to come.[117] For Bale, however, the genre proved less attractive than the disputational pamphlet. Here, too, Bale was a pioneer, reveling in this hybrid literary form which blended satire, drama, and theological argumentation. Typically these pamphlets appropriate some orthodox work, reprint fragments of its author's argument, and then furnish lengthy and caustic refutations. A representative effort is *Yet a course at the Romyshe foxe*. Edmund Bonner, bishop of London, is the adversary.[118] A victim of Bale's addiction to the stereotype, his face appears regularly in the author's pageants of unholy churchmen, a Catholic bogeyman only tenuously connected to his historical counterpart.

The governing metaphor for this first confrontation is the examination. The bishop's tract that Bale endeavors to refute is itself an account of the aftermath of a prelatical trial, the recent recantation of William Tolwyn at Paul's Cross. Anxious over the impact of Tolwyn's confession—Bale after all had expended much of his literary energy recording the exemplary steadfastness of the Protestant saints—the reformer seeks to minimize the damage done. He accomplishes this by turning his pamphlet into an examination of the examiner, himself providing that unwavering defiance which Tolwyn in his weakness of faith had failed to offer.[119] The text is a dramatic dialogue, a trial enacted before an audience summoned to jury duty. "And therfor lete him stande forth here hardelye, and tell hys owne tale. I thynke by that time ye haue throughlye harde it hauynge always recourse to the scriptures, ye will saie in this matter as I do."[120] The outcome of this agon is never really in doubt. What the audience is to witness is the strengthening of faith through a ritualistic challenge of belief. As in the case of the stage plays, the pamphlet is meant to fortify those members of the audience who can see their own lives figured in the protagonist's struggle.[121]

The language and tone of Bale's pamphlet are much like those of the plays, a combination of satiric jesting and earnest declamation. The reckless, demonic playing with which Bale had characterized the Catholic Vices of the dramas is here attributed to Bonner. In the hour of questioning, the nonconformist affirmed, the examined saint would "play" the Holy Ghost by speaking his words. In providing Tolwyn with the words of his recantation—"For though the voyce be Tolwyns, the wordes of the voyce are my lordes"[122]—Bonner perverts the promised holy drama. He fills his victim not with divine wisdom but with his own superstition, the signature of the unsanctified artist.

Bale himself, the pamphlet's hero, is far more playful in his speech than the wooden Virtues of the Cromwellian plays. His language, usually blunt and earnest, sometimes falls into the clever jesting of the Vices, those masters of the pun and the slip of the tongue. "Styll ys my lorde busye with thys bagge or sachell, declarynge the contentes therof to the great confusyon of Tolwyn, I had almost sayd of hymselfe but that I stopped yt in tyme."[123] This is precisely the kind of gaming that Bale had eyed so warily when practiced by Sedition in *King Johan*. It would seem the absence of a stage mitigates Bale's fear of playing. Tricks of speech are, nevertheless, employed cautiously, Bale evidently preferring that caustic speech which carried scriptural sanction.

The Apology of Johan Bale againste a ranke Papyst, written during the halcyon days of Edward VI's reign, shows Bale again employing the satiric pamphlet as an alternative to the stage play. More than any other of his short works, the pamphlet demonstrates the author's self-conscious application of his stagecraft to prose disputation. Bale's "Letter to the Reader" rehearses again the horrors of the dramaturgy of the priesthood. As actors at the altar, as actors in life, they are false players: "To nothing might the priests of the priesthood, be more aptly compared, than to daunsing apes, whose natural property is, to counterfet al thinges that they se done afore them, and yet are they neuer that they seem to resemble."[124] As an antidote to this world of shadows, Bale offers a brightly lit arena in which the drama consists of two men, one of the Spirit and one not, debating the meaning of a scriptural text. The chapter under consideration is Numbers 30, and the issue at stake is the propriety of the vow. What we have is another version of *The Temptacyon of our lorde*, whose central event is the debate between Christ and Satan over the correct reading of Psalms 91:11–13. Bale sets the stage with a few words. Recently the author had been invited to discuss the religious vow at the supper table of a friend, "the captayne of thys playe." Perplexed by some of Bale's views, the host submitted them to the examination of an orthodox chaplain who promptly penned a refutation. Bale now defends his arguments, printing all of the parts of the disputation: his original comments (*censura*), the chaplain's refutations (*obiectio*), and his own defenses (*responsio*). Together the various arguments form a drawing-room drama. The pamphlet is typically Balean —a moment of conflict recollected in extreme agitation. The saint's final victory is at once martial and intellectual as he successfully wields the sword of the Spirit in a final inspired reading of the biblical chapter.

Bale's pamphlet dramas are all of a piece. The object of controversy may be varied, but the shape of the conflict between good and evil, between true and false play, is rarely changed. *A Mysterye of Inyquyte*, written during Bale's first exile, casts Ponce Pantolabus's genealogy of heresy as the villain, much of the debate centering on the establishment of a pure language of religious controversy. *An Expostulation or complaynte agaynste the blasphemyes of a franticke papyst of Hampshyre* pits Bale against a clergyman resistant to reform. The pamphlet demonstrates Bale's desperate need for adversaries against whom he might play out the drama of his redemption. The origin of this long-winded diatribe is ludicrously trivial: the offending priest had once spat upon and reviled its author. *An Answere to a papystycall exhortacyon*[125] is a verse agon between Papyste and Chrystiane and merely proves that Bale's doggerel is no better than Pantolabus's.

Of more interest is Bale's *A Dialoge or Communycacyon to be had at a table betwene two chyldren.*[126] The work is, in a sense, a child's portion of the godly victuals served up by Bale in his supper conversation in the *Apology*. An important document in the history of the religious attitude toward children, the dialogue reminds us of the nonconformist aversion to the holy innocent whose sanctity rests in an un-tutored embrace of Catholic devotion.[127] Bale instead offers his children an intellectual exercise; they are to reenact at the supper table a duel of wits between one versed in biblical wisdom (the elder son) and a yet uninstructed soul (the younger son). The debate will end in mutual spiritual growth witnessed in the conversion of the latter and the reaffirmation of the faith of the former. The dialogue, which differs from Bale's other pamphlets only in the relative simplicity of its discussion, reminds us how easily these other dialogues may be conceived of as playbooks, recorded debates meant to be read aloud for the edification of actors and audience.[128]

More than any other writer of his time, Bale exhibits the complexity of the nonconformist response to the stage. A study of his work reveals a man obsessed with the idea of drama. In the brief period of Cromwell's ascendancy, when the theater was accessible to men of radical temperament, Bale wrote plays dedicated to the advancement of the new learning. When exiled from the stage, he channeled his dramatic instincts into alternative forms of propaganda: saints' lives, autobiography, examinations, and disputational pamphlets. In all of them, Bale sought to recreate in dialogue the agonistic encounter between the true believer and those who sought to undermine his faith. At the same time, a contrary spirit drove him to deny his impulse toward the dramatic, to condemn the cloistered imagination whose unlicensed play produced an unholy theater of deceit and delusion. A man who lived in a universe of stark antimonies, Bale resolved his problem by parting the waters of drama like some Old Testament saint. All that he feared in the stage, he sequestered among his enemies and their creations; all that he could safely love, he appropriated as his own. The result is a severely limited art. There is nothing in Bale's drama, displaced or otherwise, that can match the human passion to be found in the mystery cycles that the reformer sought to purify. Bale paid the price when he made drama safe for the saints. Nonetheless, when we read a play like *King Johan*, there is a human dilemma to which we can respond—the dilemma of its author, a man who hated and loved drama with the same breath and yet somehow managed to fashion an artistic creation to house his divided soul.

Thomas Cartwright

T H E   D R A M A   O F   D I S P U T A T I O N

John Bale's exercises in pamphlet warfare helped determine the literary strategies of the reformers for the remainder of the
sixteenth century. His renderings of the ritualistic encounter of saint
and sinner fit the combative mood of the Marian exiles who flocked
home from Calvinist Europe to find a queen determined to forestall
any radical reformation of her church. Bale's heady brew of earnest
invective and gamesome satire was served up again in similar fashion by such polemicists as Anthony Gilby and the authors of the
great Puritan register.[1] They too blended satiric jest, dialogue, and
meager fictional embellishments of scene and character to recreate
the essential drama of nonconformist spirituality: the elect soul forging its identity in forensic encounter.

The sense of literary community born amid the privations of exile
continued to flourish back in England. The returning zealots proclaimed their artistic lineage at every opportunity. To establish a
precedent for his *Pleasaunt Dialogue Between a Souldior of Barwicke,
and an English Chaplaine* (1581), Gilby turned instinctively to the
"Romyshe foxe" satires of "that olde Doctor Turner (reuerende in
other nations abroad for his great learning, and amongste the Godly
at home, for his great zeale . . .) [who] did almost thirtie yeares ago
espie, and bewray unto the worlde, the crafte of Satan."[2] A similar
literary self-consciousness had emerged among the Lollard propagandists. John Bale's cultural archaeology joined these two literary
circles, separated by time and circumstance yet unified in aims and
practice.[3] With the printing of the Martin Marprelate tracts in the
closing decades of the century, the satirical-dramatic tradition of the
reformers both climaxed and expired. Marprelate's explosive trea-

tises awoke the full wrath of the ecclesiastical establishment; by the 1590s, Archbishop Whitgift and his supporters had effectively silenced their Presbyterian foes.[4] Not until the stirrings of revolution later in the next century would Puritan literature again explore the theatrical possibilities of polemic. In the interlude, Puritan writers, led by the example of William Perkins, would channel their instincts for dramatic dialogue into the sermon and other forms of pastoral theology.[5]

The tenor of Puritan discourse in the last three decades of Elizabeth's reign is dictated in large part by Thomas Cartwright. To the modern student, Cartwright's contemporary status as theological luminary is somewhat difficult to fathom; nonetheless testimonies to his erudition and acknowledgments of his preeminence as a spiritual leader came freely from both sides of the religious spectrum. No less an authority than Calvin's heir, Theodore Beza, had pronounced him a nonpareil in learning: "Here is now with us your Countrey-man, Thomas Cartwright, then [than] whom I think the Sun doth not see a more Learned Man."[6] If the eulogies of Cartwright's first biographer, Samuel Clarke, can be credited, pulpit eloquence had much to do with his renown. "At that time he was so famous for his Ministry, that when his turn came to preach at Saint Maries, the Sexstone was fain to take down the Windows by reason of the multitudes that came to heare him."[7] Cartwright's only extant vernacular sermon sequence—*A Commentary upon the Epistle of Saint Paule written to the Colossians*, preached during his ministry among the English merchants based in the Low Countries—may offer little evidence of an extraordinary oratorical talent, but it does showcase Cartwright's skill in applying his materials and style to the particular nature of his auditory. Conventional admonishments against spiritual lassitude are made strangely new when immersed in the language of the mercantile venture. "Againe, as the riche man taketh all paines and neuer rests: so wee are to labour with diligence for the treasure of the word: for nothing cometh by idlenesse. And hence it is that because we are not treasured with the Word, & haue it not in store, wee are driuen to such distresses in time of affliction and trouble: and therefore wee are to labour to haue the word richly dwelling in vs, that so we may draw out of our store-houses in time of need."[8]

Cartwright himself was to argue in the *Replies* that only a minister attuned to the hopes and anxieties of his parishioners could preach affectively.[9] That pastoral gift for immediacy surfaces vividly in the reformer's epistolary advice to his sister-in-law.[10] The wife of radical activist John Stubbe, Mistress Anne Stubbe had rejected the more moderate stance of the Presbyterians and had instead embraced the tenets of Separation. Tempering firmness with compassion, Cartwright urged his wayward relative to abandon her purist theology, which ignored the frailty of mankind. Even the godly can neither know nor practice all of Christ's teachings, he wrote, "but rather suffer themselves to be ouerreached by the crookednes of theire affeccons."[11]

Pastoral solicitude is an admirable thing, but it is not the stuff of which heroes are ordinarily made—George Herbert and Richard Baxter notwithstanding. Yet Cartwright was hailed by members of his party as a hero. The designation seems all the more unlikely when his life is measured against those models of Christian courage idolized by a previous generation of martyrologists. He can claim few of their virtues. Gleanings from both private and public writings suggest an often querulous man preoccupied with the ill state of his health. His petitions to Lord Burghley are laced with complaints about "the infeebled and weak estate of my body."[12] Cartwright's inordinate fondness for metaphors concerning sickness, proper diet, and the offices of the physician has its roots, no doubt, in the venerable image of the good doctor; however, the conviction that this is a man whose obsessive anxieties about his physical well-being repeatedly trespass into the realm of spiritual concerns seems inescapable. In his preface to the 1574 translation of *Ecclesiasticae Disciplinae*, Cartwright's lamentations over the sickness of the English Church seem curiously displaced by the author's fears for his own personal health. "In these so many, so great, so old, and as it vvere hard houldinge diseases, althoughe I bee almost ouercome bothe vvith despeire off recouering the former health, and feare of losinge that vvhich vve haue: yet ceasse I not novv and then to lift vp my minde so throvven dovvne, and to aduance it to the hope off a better estate of thinges."[13]

The robust aggressiveness of most nonconformist dissent is notice-ably absent in Cartwright. Although his writings feature the obliga-tory endorsements of the Christian warfare, it is indicative of Cart-wright's temperament that his favorite metaphors for the soul's combat are drawn not from the battlefield but from the playing field. The Pauline figures of wrestling and racing consistently attract him. "[Paul] proceedeth here in the similitude of the wrestlers . . . declar-ing that as they did endeuour the mastering of the mates with whom they wrestled by strokes of the body: so he went about in wrestling to master the body of sin that was within him by beating and wound-ing it through abstinence from those things which it naturally de-sired."[14] Although he portrays the soul's combat with all the athletic straining associated with Puritan self-discipline, Cartwright instinc-tively domesticates its violence. Thus in the sermons on Colossians, Paul's "great strife and agony" are translated into "a similitude taken from the custome of the Country, where at certaine times there was a great meeting to wrestle & run for mastery."[15] Bale's holy wars yield to Cartwright's holy games.

The mystique of martyrdom similarly held no appeal for Cart-wright. For many Puritans persecution was a sacramental rite—whether experienced personally in the courts of the prelates or vi-cariously in the pages of Foxe. Cartwright, in contrast, found the benefits of persecution problematical. While conceding that the spirit "is often times sharpened / and quickened by persequution," on the whole he deemed peace the greater "aide to godlie increase / and confirmacion off the church."

And althowghe the persequution shoulde giue some advance-ment to knowledge that waies: yet it hindreth more other waies / in that it letteth the often meetinges to heare the vvorde of God / wherby knowledge is bredd: in that also pouertie (wher-with it is continually yoked) draweth many cares for this pres-ent life / for them / and theirs. Likewise continuall feare they be in / even duringe the time of their meetinges for the vvorde off God (enemie vnto the vunderstanding & puttinge to flighte the powres of the mind / vvherwith knowledge is gotten) and also the often / and soudein shiftinges from place to place: must needes be a lett to thattainment off knowledge in the vvord of God.[16]

Behind the reformer's obvious effort to accommodate the noncon-formist ethos to a world in which its adversaries belonged to the true church and possessed at least the outward marks of godliness, there is evidence of a mind shrinking from the discomforts of strife and contention. There is a symbolic aptness in the fact that Cartwright occupied the mastership of the Warwick hospital for the last seven-teen years of his life, administering to the less than challenging spiri-tual needs of twelve indigent men. Extended but largely untroubled exiles figure prominently in his biography. He spent some sixteen years on the Continent and several more in the safety of the Channel Islands.

Many of Cartwright's admirers came to tax him for spiritual cow-ardice, for his unwillingness to fight the good fight, yet his reputa-tion as the bold champion of Puritanism remained largely intact.[17] In 1596 Job Throckmorton prefaced his edition of Cartwright's *Briefe Apologie against Mr. Sutcliffe* with a rousing call to the faithful, urging them to imitate the reformer's courage in the face of slander and persecution.[18] Throckmorton casts the conflict between saint and ac-cuser into the old mold of the prelatical examination:

> For as long as the Lord giueth Satan leaue to buffet & assaile his church, so long thou maiest be assured there will neuer want a Rabshakeh, a Shimei, or a Senecherib to play their partes. Neu-erthelesse, heerein thou maiest comfort thy selfe, if thou marke how and in what sorte this reviling generation is curbed, as it were, snaffled and restrained by the powerful and righteous hand of God, that in the middest of their forwardnesse and boldnesse to blunder out what they list without blushing, they can hardly for their liues blunder out a truth, as if the Lord in his secrete judgement had purposely and apparauntly blasted their penne with a lying and distempered spirit.[19]

Throckmorton's energetic preface, however, is hopelessly at odds with Cartwright's hesitant pleas of innocence voiced in the pages that follow.[20] Cartwright is not the hero that Throckmorton yearns for him to be.

Why then did Cartwright remain for the Puritans their acknowledged champion? Martin Marprelate for one had no doubts.[21] The "holy T. C." had earned the undying admiration of the reform party by conquering that defender of Anglican depravity, John Whitgift, in the battle of wits known as the Admonition controversy.[22] In this single episode of scholarly disputation, Cartwright had given Puritanism legitimacy. Nor was Martin alone in his judgment. Although later scholars of the controversy have been divided over its outcome, Tudor Puritans spoke with unanimity when they declared their man victorious: in both learning and argumentative skill, Cartwright had undoubtedly bested his rival. Officially the hostilities did not commence until 1572, but the battle had been brewing for some time. Cartwright and Whitgift were old antagonists. For a period the two men had followed parallel careers at Cambridge (both were awarded baccalaureates in the last year of Mary's reign); by the late 1560s, however, their paths had radically diverged. As Lady Margaret Professor of Divinity, Cartwright began preaching the gospel of Presbyterian reform. Whitgift in turn mounted the pulpit to defend the existing episcopal system. While Whitgift garnered preferment for his loyalty, Cartwright's rebellious stance earned him the enmity of Archbishop Grindal. In 1570 he was successfully barred from taking a doctoral degree, a severe blow to the status-conscious professor. Cartwright's sneering appellation of Whitgift as "Master Doctor" in the *Second Replie* hints unpleasantly at jealous frustration.[23] With the elevation of his once and future adversary to the vice-chancellorship of the university, Cartwright's woes multiplied. Prior to his departure to Geneva in 1571, he was deprived of his professorship by Whitgift; and, upon his return to England in the spring of 1572, he was similarly stripped of his Trinity fellowship.

Against this backdrop of personal and professional rivalry, a more significant clash of theological outlooks was developing. Only months after Cartwright's return to England, two Puritan advocates, John Field and Thomas Wilcox, issued an anonymous pamphlet, *An Admonition to the Parliament*, upbraiding England for its failure to institute a church government sanctioned by scriptural decree and apostolic practice—such a one as already existed in Calvin's Geneva.[24] God's word, the pamphleteers insisted, provided express prescriptions not only for the salvation of the individual but for the organization of the visible church as well. The English Church might possess valid doctrine, preaching, and sacraments, but it lacked the necessary element of church discipline—"an order left by God unto his church, wherby men learne to frame their wylles and doyngs accordyng to the law of God, by instructing and admonishing one another, yea and by correcting and punishing all wylfull persones, and contemners of the same."[25]

The first *Admonition* was soon followed by a second, which explored the glories of pastors, doctors, elders, deacons, and widows at greater length and with heightened acerbity. By this time the Anglican hierarchy had gathered its own forces, and an answer to the Puritan party platform had been formulated. Whitgift's *Answere to a certen Libel* is a well-crafted and well-reasoned defense of contemporary Anglican practice. In a relatively calm manner, he undermines the Puritan claim for the existence of a pure, primitive church whose model men are compelled to imitate through all time. The tyranny of scripture established by the Puritans is likewise assailed. Though God has decreed the exact nature of the process of salvation, he argues, all other matters concerning the ordering of church ceremony and rule are left to man's discretion. The only condition that God imposes on this freedom is the injunction that no church practice so devised be contrary to scripture. In the spring of 1573, Cartwright printed his *Replye to an answere*. Reproducing brief passages from his opponent's work, Cartwright urged a submission to scripture that went beyond Whitgift's formulation of a double negative of compliance. A true and healthy church must be more than "not contrary to" scripture; it must draw its very life and soul from scripture.[26]

Whitgift replied to these assertions with the same air of reason and patience that distinguished his first effort. Chastising Cartwright for his distortive editing of the *Answere*, Whitgift now included the complete texts of all previous tracts when he published his *Defense of the Aunswere* in the winter of 1574. By this time Cartwright had retreated to the Continent, put to flight not by Anglican logic but by a warrant for his arrest. Nonetheless, he continued the battle, finishing the first part of the *Second Replie* in 1575 and the second in 1577. Whitgift did not respond. Apparently he felt no obligation to satisfy the inexhaustible thirst of his adversary for the contention of issues that he himself considered safely laid to rest. His refusal to proceed further was interpreted less generously by the Puritans, who saw in the Anglican's silence an admission of defeat. Martin Marprelate gloated: "It is a shame for your Grace, John of Cant. that Cartwright's books have been now a dozen years almost, unanswered. You first provoked him to write, and you first have received the foil. If you can answer those books, why do you suffer the Puritans to insult [exult] and rejoice at your silence? If you cannot, why are you an Archbishop?"[27]

For both the selective reader and his less fortunate companion, the comprehensive reader, the documents of the Admonition controversy provide a flimsy basis for Marprelate's intimations of Puritan glory. It is hard to evade the pronouncements of the foremost student of the controversy, Donald J. McGinn, who has unhesitatingly awarded victory to John Whitgift. Cartwright's writing is "turbid, tiresome, and crude"; his reasoning is "bewildered, . . . confused as it is by a mystical yearning for perfection." The dark and muddled quality of his work convinces the reader of the "hopelessness of trying to reason with this Puritan fanatic and his followers, for Whitgift's 'lucid and impressive' defense . . . brought from Cartwright's successors, both in his own time and later, nothing but abuse and ridicule." In its totality the debate represents the overwhelming triumph of Whitgift's "common sense" over Cartwright's "sentimentalism."[28]

The problem with McGinn's assessment is that it is inescapably Anglican in perspective—as are the majority of the pronouncements made by literary historians and critics. Whatever our religious loyalties, we are all Anglicans to the extent that we perceive correct judgment to be the outcome of a process in which institutionally entrenched specialists guided by the voices of the past carefully weigh and balance evidence and rival claims to truth. From this vantage point, Whitgift, with his judicious reasoning, his healthy but by no means obsequious regard for the wisdom of his predecessors, his sweet air of accommodation, and his sparing use of inflammatory rhetoric, is immediately perceived as an ally. He is one of us. Cartwright's efforts, when observed in the same light, seem misguided. What can a reader make of a man whose supposedly reasoned discourse moves erratically between extremes of dry, logic-chopping argumentation and metaphoric reverie? If he possesses an Anglican eye, he will agree with McGinn that here is mere bewilderment— reason "confused . . . by a mystical yearning for perfection." If he can train himself to see like a Puritan, however, what he perceives will be radically different.

Cartwright had no intention of confining himself to reason when he debated with his foe, any more than did Jack Upland when he wrestled with his imaginary "frere" or John Bale with his demonic Bonner. His controversy with Whitgift is more than a clash between "two divergent and apparently irreconcilable ideals" of ecclesiology; it is a conflict between two antithetical attitudes toward the nature of godly discourse. Both the methodology of debate and the objects of debate are at issue. Although neither his capacity for fiction-making nor his interest in the belletristic is immediately apparent, Thomas Cartwright is a Puritan artist and his battle with John Whitgift a nonconformist displaced drama. His audience, as in virtually all nonconformist art, consists of the faithful. As Cartwright himself informs his opponent, "I will never weary my pen to confute those whom their own consciences are too strong for, and confuteth every night when they go to bed; for that were nothing else but to reason with the belly that hath no ears to hear, or with the back that hath no eyes to see."[29] Cartwright's spectator may be afflicted: with the pain of God's desertion, the numbness of spiritual lassitude, the doubt of eternal election. His understanding may require prodding, his religious affections arousal. But he is not in need of conversion. He is already a member of the "church within a Church."[30] To answer his needs, Cartwright plots a dramatic agon between a representative sinner and a representative saint, the cathartic conclusion of which will be a mystical enlightenment sparked by the conflict of reason. By observing or, as Bale says, by "weigh[ing] such matters . . . that shall your inward stomach cheer,"[31] the godly spectator will awaken to his confraternity with the mystical body of true believers.

John Whitgift is, in this ritual of sanctification, as much a fiction as Thorpe's Arundel. Cast as false reason in a battle with godly learning, he exists only to validate and authenticate the subjectivity of a personal vision by providing the necessary prolegomenon of objective struggle. Martin Marprelate's cry of triumph is the applause of a Puritan spectator at the close of a ritual act of edification. His response is prejudiced only in the sense that all Puritan thought is ultimately subjective and self-interested. For Marprelate and other reformers, the calm reasoning of the future archbishop—the object of McGinn's high praise—is background not foreground. Whitgift's meritorious labors are in the end ancillary to the drama of spiritual regeneration being played out beyond and above him. To comprehend fully the nature of Cartwright's displaced drama, we must first examine his particular brand of nonconformity. Only by understanding Cartwright's diagnosis of spiritual disorder, and his prescription of its most apt remedies, can we perceive why the reformer found turgid disputation so congenial.

"ASLEEP IN OUR SECURITY"

Early in his response to Cartwright's *Replye to an answere*, Whitgift vents his frustration over his opponent's unmannerly style of debate. Cartwright, he charges, is subject to fits, his interludes of hot, emotional declamation continually subverting the rational basis of their exchange. "Touching the falsification and untruth you charge me with, I think you be not in good earnest; it is but because you could no longer temper your heat: for you make many of these outcries; but I suppose you use them only as means to cast up your melancholy, which you call 'zeal.' "[32] Unlike modern commentators who insist upon seeing Cartwright as a failed Anglican disputant rather than as a successful Puritan propagandist, Whitgift was quick to realize that his adversary shared neither his aims nor his methodology. Indeed, Whitgift embarks on his enterprise with much the same fatalism that infects Richard Hooker's magisterial refutation of Puritan ideology.[33] In their gloomy intimations of Anglican failure both Hooker and Whitgift seem to concede that the reasoning of an orthodox apologist, no matter how cogent, not only will fail to alter the convictions of his detractors but will inevitably produce the opposite effect. To enter into a debate with a devout Puritan is to kindle his ardor.[34] Whitgift's recognition that the Admonition controversy was being used by Cartwright to "cast up zeal"—his own and that of his followers—points to the heart of Cartwright's analysis of the soul's afflictions.

Like Bale, Cartwright saw the natural flow of human and individual history as an ever-deepening descent into error and spiritual insensibility. "The Hebrews do derive the name of time of a verb which signifieth to corrupt, because indeed it doth corrupt all; and, as the times are, so are men which live in them; that even very good men carry the note of the infection of the times wherein they live. And the stream of the corruption thereof, being so vehement and forcible, doth not only drive before it light things, but it eateth also and weareth the very hard and stony rocks."[35] Left to his own devices, man invariably prefers the numbing sleep of reprobation to the anxious waking state of the true Christian. Ease and forgetfulness are potent seducers.

As energy yields to enervation, men falter in their search for enlightenment. They grasp at shadows of truth, declare themselves satisfied, and rest in the bogus peace they imagine they have won. But complacency and self-deception prove no refuge. To wall out a hostile world, man must wall himself in. Trapped in a prison with his own corruption as cellmate, man attempts to implicate the exterior world in his crime. His mind becomes a tainted witness "reading" what it expects and wishes to see rather than what it actually sees. "For the bodily eye beholding a man neuer so stedfastly, yet if the minde haue a fore-iudgement that it cannot be he, it cannot be but he must needs seeme otherwise then he is, the perswasion of the minde being stronger manifoldly then the bare sight of the eye."[36] The carnal man is like a lunatic lover: ever more deeply consumed by the subjectivity of his passion, always measuring reality in terms of its capacity to buttress his delusion. By so "framing a prejudice against the truth,"[37] he is doomed to misread those signs that would be obvious to a man unafflicted with his malady. "They are like the foolish hungry Wooers which snap every shadow of look or word that may carry any sound of good liking unto them, passing by the frownes and threats whereby they of modest behaviour, and setled understanding, would take themselues answered."[38]

The Anglican reformation, according to Cartwright and his followers, had failed to address this sinful obstinacy of the human soul. The obvious obstructions to the life of faith had been removed: scripture once more held its rightful place of preeminence; the ungrounded pronouncements of the papacy had been jettisoned; the doctrine of Christ had been restored to its purity. The Church of England had not, however, thoroughly laid low the mountains nor filled the valleys. Vestiges of popish worship (although now cleansed of their false doctrinal associations) were allowed to remain. To men convinced of the soul's infinite capacity for self-deception, such compromised symbols and practices posed a grave and unnecessary threat.[39] The complacent soul seeks no painful severance from its past errors; it is only too pleased to resume the security of its former ways.

Fallen man is by nature a traditionalist. Cartwright is horrified when Whitgift argues for the maintenance of certain devotional modes by reason of a continuous tradition of their use. Augustinian praise of the seemliness of custom is no palliative to the reformer; that which is customary is always to be distrusted.[40] Sin, not purity or goodness, is the commodity most likely to endure. Cartwright, like Bale, delights in tracing the genealogies of false custom, in mapping the myriad ways in which truth becomes obscured by falsehood. Like Bale, he is a born euhemerist, peeling back the accretive layers of myth to uncover the historical facts beneath them. Consider the mystical efficacy of crossing. Cartwright argues that early Christians crossed themselves to witness their fearless worship of the crucified God. In time, a legitimate emblem of nonconformist resistance to persecution became compromised. As Cartwright laments, "superstition is always strengthened and spreadeth itself with the time."[41]

The failure of Anglican worship went deeper than a reluctance to forsake a discredited system of worship. What was lacking was a new religious program—one capable of truly awakening the English soul. Anglican ceremony provided no such alarum; indeed its practices conspired to assist the soul in evading its responsibilities. Cartwright's critique of holy days is characteristic of his assault on Anglican devotion. Whereas Whitgift praises holy days for stabilizing weak minds by means of ordered ceremony,[42] the reformer looks upon their infrequency and irregularity as an inducement to spiritual truancy. Holy days, says Cartwright, cause us to "pull out of our minds, or ever we be aware, the doctrine of the gospel, and causeth us to rest in that near consideration of our duties for the space of a few days, which should be extended to all our life."[43] Paradoxically, Cartwright thus sees the soul as both weaker (i.e., more prone to sin) and stronger (i.e., capable of greater exertion) than does his rival.

The sporadic practice of preaching elicited the same disdain meted out to the institution of holy days. Perhaps even a greater irritant to the reformers, though, was the nature of the Anglican pulpit performance itself. The frequent use of reading either from scripture or from officially prepared and sanctioned homilies struck Cartwright as a travesty of godly preaching. The preacher was charged with providing "a prick to stir up [his auditory's] dulness,"[44] dullness born of either an insufficient comprehension of God's law or a limpness of spirit in embracing it. To arouse his sleeping audience and ready them for the reception of God's grace, the preacher structured his sermon so as to badger their reluctant souls. His performance was to be studied, for doctrine must be grounded in truth, and yet extemporaneous, for response to the shifting moods of the parishioners must be swift and accurate.[45] What results is a game of cat and mouse. The audience, ever prone to sin, anxiously seeks secure hiding places; the preacher, ever vigilant, faithfully routs them out of their false retreats. The key to the preacher's success lies in his ability to wield skillfully the two great weapons of consolation and admonition. Both must be employed to prevent his charges from resting—either in an imagined security or in an unwarranted despair.

> And undoubtedly hereof it cometh that the word of God is no more effectual in this realm than it is, for because it is preached hand over head, without knowledge and understanding the estate of the people. For so oftentimes the promises and glad tidings of the gospel of our Saviour are preached unto those

that, being before secure in their sins, are after the hearing of
the promises rocked into a dead sleep thereof; and they that are
overthrown with the conscience of their sin, and confounded
in themselves, are, by the sharpness of the law and hearing of
the judgment of God, broken into pieces and driven to des-
peration.[46]

The preacher must play the adversary to his auditory, creating the
jolt of contention that shocks the soul into sensibility. "[T]he peace
which is without truth is more execrable than a thousand contentions. For as by striking of two flints together there cometh out fire,
so it may be that sometimes by contention the truth which is hidden
in a dark peace may come to light, which by a peace in naughtiness
and wickedness, being as it were buried under the ground, doth not
appear."[47]

The Puritan preacher, then, worked as did the nonconformist artist, using spiritual strife as an instrument of sharpening understanding and exciting devotion. As a physician, he cured diseases by treating them with their opposites.

> Philosophy, which is nothing else but reason, teacheth that,
> if a man will draw one from vice which is an extreme unto
> virtue which is the mean, that it is the best way to bring him as
> far from that vice as may be, and that it is safer and less harm
> for him to be led somewhat too far than he should be suffered
> to remain within the borders and confines of that vice where-
> with he is infected. As if a man would bring a drunken man to
> sobriety, the best and nearest way is to carry him as far from his
> excess in drink as may be; . . . as we see, to bring a stick which
> is crooked to be straight, we do not only bow it so far until it
> come to be straight, but we bend it so far until we make it so
> crooked of the other side as it was before of the first side, to this
> end that at the last it may stand straight, and as it were in the
> midway between both the crooks.[48]

The end of the preacher's work was to produce a state of spiritual
tension not unlike the Wycliffite "love-drede." His aim was to disrupt
religious stasis without plunging the soul into psychological disor-

der. By playing one extreme off another, the preacher guided his audience toward a spiritual mean partaking of both stability and "unsettledness"—the one to sustain the soul in its present trials, the other to impel it onward to new ones.[49] Clearly, the Puritan saw the concept of the *media via* differently than his Anglican counterpart: its creation and maintenance was to be a product not of sweet and reasonable compromise but of violent contention. The individual, like the nonconformist movement itself, was expected to recreate its personality constantly, seeking new formulations and new balances between the warring impulses in his soul. To do otherwise was to invite the demon of sleepy stagnation.[50]

Neither Anglican reading nor homilies could address the needs of Cartwright's stubborn souls. The naked scriptural text, admirable in itself, ordinarily lacked the power to penetrate that shield of habitual sin raised precisely to ward off the disturbing news of the gospel. The job of the preacher, says Cartwright, is to employ "all those means of setting an edge of the Gospel, that it might pierce and go through. . . . For it is not enough that there be knowledge to enlighten the vnderstanding, but that the affections be moued, and the conscience bee wrought, that men may be with-drawne from euill, & stirred vp to good."[51] "[T]he word, by interpretation [must be] broken and bruised [for then it] carrieth a sweeter savour unto the understanding than when it is by reading given gross and whole."[52] The homily, felt Cartwright, was no better. All-purpose lectures on set topics, the homilies lacked accuracy; their great and general discharges of spiritual shot rarely hit their intended targets.

[W]hence sermons are applied to the present circumstance / which by chaunge of times / budding off new vices / rising of errors / etc. vary almost euery day: this kinde of interpretation (as that which is starke / and annumed cannot poursue them. for where the preacher with his sermon / is able according to the manifold windinges / and turninges of sinne / to winde / and turne in with yt to th end he may stricke it: the homilies are not able to turne / nether off the right hand / nor off the left / but to what quarter soeuer the enemies are retyred / yt must keepe the traine wherin it was set off by the maker.[53]

The ultimate success of Cartwright's ideal minister was as much dependent on his status within the congregation as upon his pastoral cunning. As a diagnostician, probing for the symptoms of spiritual malaise, the minister needed familiarity with his patients. As an adversary, stirring up the parishioners' dullness with the prick of contention, he required "a sufficient wall of partition between [himself] and the people."[54] The Anglican minister was too distant, often alienated from his charges by prelatical appointment or the irregular residence encouraged by pluralism. On the other hand, the minister of a Separatist congregation was insufficiently distinguished from his fellow believers. Elected as an equal among equals, he too often lacked the learning of a university education and the social distinction it conferred.[55]

Between these extremes of alienation and intimacy, Cartwright and his followers sought to establish the Presbyterian mean: ministers tied to their congregations by local election and yet sequestered by their education and by an electorate limited to the householders of the parish. Throughout his career Cartwright monitored the precarious position of his ideal churchman. In his controversy with Whitgift, he laid heavy emphasis on the fraternity between minister and congregation.[56] During his ministry in the Low Countries, he struck a paternal note. Heeding his own prescription of curing by opposites, to these men whose isolation in a foreign country heightened their vulnerability to the Separatist heresy, he preached of the minister's extraordinary status. "And therefore we ought the more to pray for them, that are exalted by the Lord, that by their fals the Gospell of God may not be dishonoured. And as they are placed in higher place, and are indewed with greater guifts, so the more earnestly we ought to pray for them."[57]

The governing concern of Cartwright as disputant, preacher, and counselor is the awakening of the elect, anesthetized, along with the sinful multitude, by a religion of rote responses. As an antidote to the soul's proclivity for rest and idleness, Cartwright, like so many of his Puritan contemporaries, prescribes a regimen of work. Not only must the soul be kept on edge by the watchful prodding of both minister and congregation, the body as well must be forced out of its lethargy. Like Bale before him, Cartwright finds the busy city rather than the placid country more fertile ground for the growth of the gracious soul. Where minds and bodies are driven from private reverie by the noise and movement of the great public crowds, men are less likely to fall victim to the insensibility of a retired existence.[58] The very friction of human contact seems to burn away the impurities of the unclean soul. In his debate with the Catholic translators of the New Testament, Cartwright proves ill at ease with his adversaries' vision of John the Baptist as a hermit withdrawing from society for the cultivation of a private spirituality. He tries, as did Bale, to turn John into an urban soothsayer, a preacher to the crowd rather than a lone voice in the wilderness.[59] Although Cartwright does not share Bale's obsession with the sexual deviancy of the cloister, his endorsement of urban activity testifies to the continuing nonconformist fear of isolation and solipsism. In community and the diligent pursuit of public activity, the dangers of spiritual inertia and the subjectivity of personal vision were to be neutralized.[60]

The use of directed, public activity—religious and commercial—to propitiate the demons of the sleeping mind is nowhere more evident than in the Puritan treatment of the garden. We have already witnessed the deep distrust that the nonconformist harbored for the values of the *hortus conclusus*. The poet of *Pierce the Ploughman's Crede* saw the claustrophobia and stagnation of the Dominican convent through the images and conventions of the walled garden of the dream vision. Spiritual enlightenment was found instead in a field industriously altered for commercial purposes.[61] Cartwright's prose demonstrates little affection for the pastoralism so fashionable among court poets; nostalgia for an agrarian past is perceived as Catholic. The images of the shepherd and his flock, sanctioned by the New Testament, are dutifully invoked by the reformer, but there is no passion in his voice. The images that genuinely fire Cartwright's imagination are almost always industrial or commercial. Urban metalsmiths hammering away at their anvils and merchants wagering their livelihoods on the currents of the sea—these are the true heroes of Cartwright's religious vision.

> And iff in well ordered cities / ther is no man admitted to set vpp in any mysterie / onlesse he haue offered to the Maisters

off the companie / some worke for a masterpeece / and declaration that he hathe skil / in that he will open his shop for: how
muche more in the ministerie off God / owght it to be pro-
uided / that before he be allowed to worke / in the great mis-
terie [craft] off our saluation / and laye hand to the framyng of
the siluer vessels of the church off God: the maisters off the
companie especially (whiche are the Elders off the church) being best able to iudge / owght to haue triall / how he handleth
the goulden hammer off the word off God.[62]

Only in a private letter to Arthur Hildersham does one find the
reformer invoking the garden world, and there his treatment runs
stubbornly counter to the spirit of the day. Advising the young Hildersham on the proper course of divine studies, Cartwright declares
that scripture must be the beginning of all such labors:

[F]or whithersoever you goe out of the paradise of the Holy
Scriptures, you shall in the best grounds meet with thornes and
thistles, of which you are in danger of pricking, if you carry not
the forest bill of the Lords Word wherewith to stubbe them and
crabb them up; neither is there any so free from evill aires,
when you goe from the sweet and wholesome breathes of the
Lords Garden, where you are not in some perill of infection,
unlesse as it were by some Receyt of the Word as it were next
your heart, you stop the passage against it.[63]

Cartwright's garden is no Renaissance world of escapist play and
fantasy. It is a paradise, but one in which work dominates play. The
garden is God's word in which all true believers must labor to understand the meaning of his laws. Immediately outside its safe boundaries lie the sharp thorns of adversity and the infectious air of false
belief. Into this world of suffering the believer must go, gathering
the tools he has labored to acquire in the garden: "the forest bill of
the Lords Word" and "som Receyt" of scripture. Employing the wisdom earned in his study of scripture, he then struggles to restore the
fallen world of nettles in the perfect image of the Bible's *locus amoe-
nus*. The visionary spirit of Cartwright's garden is diluted by the
infiltration of alien notions of duty, labor, and obligation, much as in

Milton's Eden where mankind's parents act as industrious caretakers on the estate of a capitalist God.[64]

Christopher Hill has argued with eloquence that the Puritan obsession with labor and its nemesis, idleness, was the inevitable outgrowth of a system of belief promulgated by the beneficiaries of England's first industrial revolution.[65] The sociological and economic foundations of Puritan industry, however, ought not to obscure its theological basis, which rests upon the core of the nonconformist dilemma. The necessity of protracted activity—strenuous, concrete, and public—as a prelude to and authorization of the private and subjective experience of inspirational vision has been testified to from the earliest phases of nonconformist thought. When Cartwright rehearses this paradigm of radical spirituality, he echoes two hundred years of Lollard and Puritan conviction: "[O]ur stay in the truth standeth not in that the Church knoweth it, or wee by the Church, but in that we our selves know it through perswasion of the spirit by meanes of exercise in the word, most especially by hearing it preached."[66] Furthermore, we have seen that the precarious balance between nonconformity's contradictory impulses toward extremes of reason and inspiration required of the believer a state of continuous vigilance. The pursuit of labor in church, home, and marketplace was the stimulant prescribed. Although by the late sixteenth century many Puritans had shed the bellicosity of John Bale and his Lollard ancestors as well as their zeal for persecution, the ethos of struggle had by no means lost its centrality in the psychology of nonconformity. That the locus of that struggle was gradually shifting from the fires of Smithfield to the fires of the smithy's shop is evidence of changes in the social, political, and economic environment of nonconformity, not of movement within the heart of the nonconformist sensibility itself.

"RAVISHED AND RAPT MEN"

Of necessity the Puritan program of reform to which Thomas Cartwright subscribed was to be broadcast not only to the faithful but to the nation at large. Within the reprobate multitude there still lurked those elect souls untouched by the dull edge of Anglican devotion. Moreover, even those already moved by the spirit were also moved by the ethical climate of the times. The genuine range of Puritan concern remained, however, severely circumscribed. The beneficiaries of their pastoral care were the members of what Patrick Collinson has called "a church within a Church," a small body of true believers set in the midst of a nominally Protestant society.[67] Within this select auditory, most Puritan ministers addressed an even more limited clientele—and Cartwright was no exception. He instinctively gravitated toward the doubting soul, not the naturally zealous one. Presumably the tenor of his own religious experience helped determine his field of expertise. His writings record no personal sense of a great awakening. Unlike a John Cotton or a Richard Sibbes, Cartwright offers no account of the joyous feeling of "wading in grace." In his work as a pastoral minister, he found excess of enthusiasm a rare malady; the more common disease of the faithful was a dearth of affection.[68] As such, the minister's primary task was to stimulate the zeal of his followers (once their understanding had been awakened). "[T]hey must as preists in the battailes of the Israelites / blow continually the syluer trumpet / not onely that they should euery one take himselfe to his armour: but that in the fight through that passioned / and stirring musicke off trumpettes / they might blow vp and whet the courage off the souliders."[69] Should such efforts falter, he was to console the parishioner with the comforting assurance that enlightened understanding was more essential than moving affection. "[B]etter haue no zeal," Cartwright told the merchants of Antwerp "than zeale without knowledge, which is most dangerous, as a wild horse."[70]

If Cartwright lacked a private experience of excessive zeal, he was, nonetheless, cognizant of the threat it might pose to others. Cartwright, we recall, had had ample opportunity for observing the corrosive effects of undisciplined religious feeling in the case of Anne Stubbe. Moreover, a lengthy stay in the Low Countries had placed him in both contact and conflict with two of the foremost advocates of Separatism, Robert Browne and Robert Harrison.[71] In these more radical Protestants, who preached a religion of sequestered holiness, Cartwright discerned parallels to the spiritual distem-

pers of the Catholic orders. Cartwright's deep distrust of both species of such religious behavior are evident in his reevaluation of the
preeminent nonconformist metaphor for bona fide spiritual experience, the examination. For William Thorpe, the quintessential religious moment had been the prelatical examination. Under the pressure of the apposing of his adversaries, the examinate experienced a
rapturous sense of the presence of the Holy Ghost.[72] In the *Confutation*, Cartwright demonstrates that he shares a sense of the primacy
of the ecclesiastical trial as a ritual of nonconformist experience and
as a basis for its art.[73] Arguing that the holiness of the councils of the
early church shone forth not in the logical acumen of bishops but in
the faithful testimonies of simple, godly men, Cartwright recalls an
incident from the Nicene Council:

> Ruffine maketh mention of heathen Philosophers and Logi-
> cians, assembled at the Councell of Nice: Amongst whom when
> one of them through the great skill in the Art of Logicke,
> wound himselfe (Adder-like) out of the arguments of the Bish-
> ops, that they were not able to put him to silence; there rose vp
> in the Councell 'a simple man, that knew nothing but Christ
> and him crucified,' who so amazed the Philosopher with his
> speech, that not onely as a dumbe man, he had not a word to
> reply, but yeelded himselfe to the truth, that the plaine man
> had uttered.[74]

The amazing triumph of the plain man of God shows a Cartwright
attuned to the spirit of nonconformist dissent, yet the context of his
trial scene is significant. Facing Catholic adversaries, Cartwright happily exploits the time-honored scenario.[75] He is also aware, however,
of the altered circumstances of the day. Jesuits persecuted by Protestant authorities are now threatening to appropriate the trial motif for
their own ends. Thus Cartwright, unlike his predecessors, is forced
to consider more rigorously the validity of the personal inspiration
that accompanies prelatical examination. In contrasting the conduct
of the Puritan and his Catholic counterpart under questioning, Cartwright by necessity must emphasize the learning and rational argumentation of the former. Self-possession and rapturous assertion are
hallmarks of the Catholic response.

> This is true of the professours of the Gospell, of the which, from him that cleaueth wood, to her that draweth water, euery one haue answered unto your sophisticall Diuinity, with such dexterity and readinesse, that they astonished you, and euidently shewed forth the truth of this and other promises, wherein it is said, that (for knowledge) "They should all bee as the Lords Priests." As for your silly soules, wherwith I pray you should they confound their aduersaries, I supposing in answering to all questions and arguments wherwith they are urged; that they beleeue as the Church beleeueth, and that the Church beleeueth as they beleeueth: for this is the common circle of their diuinity, wherein, in this one thing they are like unto sheep, that they can sonnd nothing but, bea, bea.[76]

Note how carefully Cartwright demystifies the examination. The godly examinates, "from him that cleaueth wood, to her that draweth water," are industrious laborers true to their calling; they are not vagabond mystics. They have sufficient learning to answer sophistry with "dexterity and readinesse" and to demonstrate truth to other educated men. They are like the Lord's priests not because they utter prophecy, but because they have knowledge. The Catholic examinate, on the other hand, can utter only the formulaic response. "I beleeue as the Church beleeueth."

Cartwright and the more moderate Puritans were being similarly outflanked by extremists within their own camp. Anabaptists and Separatists were increasingly laying claim to the prerogatives of a persecuted minority and indeed were numbering the Puritans among their oppressors.[77] The rapturous element in the nonconformist equation of enlightenment attracted such men, and Cartwright endeavored to refute them. In his debate with Whitgift, Cartwright speaks skeptically of the actions of the simple man who, when questioned as to his belief, breaks into "mistical rhetoric." Referring to Stephen's examination, Cartwright praises the martyr for his harsh reproofs of his tormentors, but is clearly troubled by this apparent precedent for preaching without a calling.[78] Warning prospective martyrs that such conduct is extraordinary, he urges the examinate to trim his rhetoric, restrain his impulse toward prophecy,

and satisfy himself with a cogent response. " 'That he also repre-
hendeth them sharply,' is no other thing, then diuers of the Martyrs
of god haue doen with vs, which, I think he wil not say to haue
preached, by vertue of any ecclesiastical function. althowgh I confess, that that is not to be lightly doen, and withowt some especial
direction, whereof the lord, in such tymes, doeth furnish his: otherwise those that are priuate men owght to content themselues, with a
simple and playn defence of the truth."[79]

Cartwright's retreat from quasi-mystical devotion was in part a response to the proliferation of alternative voices of dissent, a problem
less worrisome to earlier reformers like Bale. At the same time, his
efforts are appropriate to a spokesman for an opposition party hop-
ing to assume authority. The Puritans were no longer lonely champions of reform. In the earl of Leicester and Sir Francis Walsingham
and others they had won strong political allies. As their leaders
groomed themselves for power, the image of themselves as persecuted outcasts became necessarily blurred. John Bale's eclectic tastes
in dissident behavior were no longer suitable for a "loyal opposition
party." It would not do to have every self-proclaimed godly man
playing the Old Testament prophet. The spirit of prophecy, so enthusiastically endorsed by the previous generation of reformers, proved
to be an indulgence Elizabethan Puritans could ill afford. Cartwright
himself worked consistently to tame its unruliness. He carefully distinguishes, for example, between prophecy's miraculous and ordinary manifestations. The former he associates almost exclusively
with the acts of the Old Testament prophets. Their inspired visions
and fiery rhetoric are relegated to a safely distant past. Even in that
faraway time, Cartwright domesticates the soothsayer's calling. Dan-
iel's prophecy is transformed into an act of literary artistry. He speaks
"not from any sight or revelation by vision" but rather "describ[es]
the maiestie of the Iudge by pleasant and elegant metaphors drawn
from his singular, exact, and diuine knowledge of the word."[80] What
remains for the contemporary reformer is ordinary prophecy—"any
publicke instruction off the people in the will of God"[81]—and its
practice is restricted to the ministerial class.

Cartwright's attack on the ungoverned spirituality of the Anabaptists and Separatists, however, was prompted by more than a fear for

Puritan reputation. The emphasis of the radicals on the gifts of the spirit at the expense of the labors of reason threatened to plunge the soul into the same hellfire of subjectivity that awaited those who succumbed to the spiritual lassitude of Anglican worship. Indeed, Cartwright viewed the sins of Anabaptism and Anglicanism as complementary. The latter promoted an unwarranted trust in the collective wisdom of the church; the former made men prone to "flie vnto secret persuasions off the spirit off God / without the voice of the church."[82] Both miscalculated the power and pervasiveness of evil— within the traditions of the established church and within the convictions of the soul illumined by grace.

The failure of the extremists to acknowledge the centrality of sin deeply troubled Cartwright. Sin was not alien to godly existence but essential to its maintenance and promotion. Only by battling the demons within and without the sanctified breast could the saint exercise his God-given grace and come to feel his own election. The tendency among Separatists and Anabaptists to banish evil outside the sacred circle of the gathered congregation and the hearts of its members weakened the Puritan ethos of struggle by wholly externalizing it. This willing cessation of hostilities between the old and new creatures threatened the soul's unsettledness, inviting the stagnation that Cartwright saw as the hallmark of the spiritually dead.

> It is a vile error you seeme to vrge that the spirit of grace / & of delusion may not or can not be in the same man /. For the most regenerat hath his owne euil spirit, in him euen his natural & worldy spirit, striuinge against the spirit of God, which nature is a spirit of delusion. In deed you do well to add this word (yoakfellows). For those two contrarie spirits can not be at agreement in the same men. And therefore the Godlie are sometimes contrarie to them selues, & that both inwardly & outwardlie.[83]

Those who circumvent the ordinary means of enlightenment by ignoring the impurity they conceal within are condemned to dwell in the fantasies of the unsanctified imagination. The church of the Separatists is just such an unholy dream, Cartwright tells Anne Stubbe. If ever realized, it would not be the "attractive creation" they expect.

"That yf yow had yor hearts desire in the things yow seeke after, and should after yor travaill bringe forth, yet would yor byrth (as I am perswaded) haue so small beiuty in yt, as it should drawe fewe eyes to a comfortable beholding of yt. Nay, I doubt not but many of those which dote after yt being nowe hidden in the wombe, would after it should see the soonne, beginne greately to distaste it, and not without some lothsomnesse to looke vpon it."[84]

The creations of the Puritan imagination, on the other hand, were beautiful. The Puritan artist did not confine himself to the gray world of Anglicanism where the brilliant contrast of sin and grace was faded by the solvent of human tradition. Nor did he limit himself to the dazzling white hues of the Protestant extremists in which the darkness of human nature was temporarily obscured by the bright light of an illusory faith. The Puritan artist, claimed Cartwright, is a master of chiaroscuro, using sin to highlight the contours of the figure of grace. He knows that true beauty consists not in an unnatural homogeneity but in a careful deployment of opposites. In so doing, he imitates his own creator. God, too, is an artist of blacks and whites, of stimulating contradictions yielding unexpected harmonies of the highest order.

> For as in a faire image, the black colour if it be well placed serueth for the beautifying of the image: euen so if a man could with learned eyes behold the gouernment of all things, taking the sinners and wicked (as the black) amongst them: he should see it all verie beautifull: notwithstanding that the wicked being considered in themselues are full of deformitie. And as a cunning artificer, will make good worke, although he haue but a sorie toole: euen so the Lord, through his infinite wisdome, working by the wicked, as by vntoward and crabbed instruments, ceaseth not to make vp his worke, with singular commendation of all who haue any light in them.[85]

The Puritan artist must not strive for otherworldly visions of undiluted goodness; he must represent that goodness in the process of defining itself in the context of evil. His portraits must not be static renderings of "ravished and rapt men" frozen in a moment of ectasy nor of plodding logicians transfixed in a moment of thought. The images he draws must suggest continuous, restless change—figures captured in the act of becoming.[86] Thomas Cartwright saw himself as just such a creator when he fashioned his contributions to the Admonition controversy. His long dialogue with Whitgift is an exercise in the art of nonconformity, a calculating study of a saint in the act of testing and asserting his faith in the shadow of evil. His work is both an act of self-regeneration and an exemplary drama for the edification of the faithful.

THE ADMONITION DRAMA

John Whitgift and Thomas Cartwright viewed their participation in the Admonition controversy from widely divergent perspectives. Whitgift saw himself as a guardian of tradition even though the ecclesiology he sought to maintain was less than twenty years old. This is the pose he strikes in his preface to *The Defense of the Aunswere*:

> [I]t behoveth all godly minds that will not be carried away with rash and over-hasty judgment in this controversy, to consider not only that I have before spoken of the truth of doctrine publicly received and confirmed, but also circumspectly to weigh the circumstances of time, place, person, and the whole state of things now in the church and realm of England; the regard whereof, in mine opinion, must needs cause in all discreet heads a stay of judgment, in comparison that the things themselves barely considered would do.[87]

His aim is to protect "the truth of a doctrine publicly received and confirmed." The members of his audience are "discreet heads" not given to "rash and over-hasty judgment." By a cautious weighing of "the circumstances of time, place, person," he hopes to convince them of the necessity of a "stay of judgment."

Cartwright was no such preservationist. His prose rings with the sound of stonemasons and carpenters busily raising new edifices of

Christian belief over the rubble of discarded custom. Having presented the faithful with the blueprint of his word, God entrusts to them the task of erecting his church.

> Yt is enough / nothing falleth from the liberalitie off the Lord / nothing from the truth off this word. no more then he breaketh promis / which vndertaking to furnish an other off all manner of worckmen vntill his howse be finished / after foundations layed / and patron [pattern] left vnto carpenters / and masons / how to proceed in the rest of the building: withdraweth the master builder. for as the lorde abated the number of sortes of builders: so hathe he deminished the varietie off workes / requisite to the building.[88]

True believers are always to be edifying, always building. The controversy between the reformer and Master Doctor Whitgift was to be a stimulus to this act of continuous creation. "The ende off proufes in controuersies off divinitye" is not a reasoned "stay of judgment," but "that faythe maye be engendred in mindes / which onelye can be grounded on the worde off God."[89]

With this purpose behind them, Cartwright's contributions to the debate with Whitgift must be viewed as examples of pastoral as well as controversial theology. That his work is public, disputatious, and propagandistic presents no impediment to such a classification. Nonconformist devotion, with its constant pressure toward the resolution of private dilemma in public confrontation, almost always displays these characteristics. Indeed, in its early phases Puritanism demonstrates an abiding fear of the kind of self-absorbed introspection that has become synonymous with the movement. Cartwright assures his readers that the reformers have not "nourished any night or corner doctrine, which we whispering in th'eeares of certeine woulde not haue had come owt of doores of our priuate houses."[90] To Whitgift's contention that a man's thoughts are more reliably revealed in a letter to an associate than in public utterances, Cartwright objects:

> [A]ll vnderstand / that men be more soudeine in letters to their freindes / then in their bookes: and that they burne more can-

dell / and make the file off their Judgement / and vnderstanding passe oftener vppon those writinges / which they will submit to the Judgement off all men / then to the judgement off
one: vpon those / which they knowe shall come on the racke off
their wrangling ennemies / then which shal finde rest / in the
bosome of an easie and frendly interpretation: vpon those /
which they thincke shall remaine vnto all posteritie / then
which they thincke shall dye / at least with him to whom they
wrote.[91]

Cartwright's argument, with its subtle evocation of prelatical examination, rehearses the salient features of his reading of the soul's afflictions: the need to arouse sleeping souls, first by rigorously exercising the "file off their Judgement and vnderstanding," then by
stimulating their affections "on the racke off their wrangling ennemies"; and the need to circumvent the dangers of an undisciplined
awakening, one which is too "soudeine" and too "easie." To minister
to these contrary impulses toward spiritual lethargy and self-intoxica-
tion is the aim of Cartwright's *Replies*. The task demands a writer
who is both a doctor who teaches and a pastor who affects.[92] He
must be able to speak two languages: the language of reason and the
language of emotion. Both professions are practiced and both
tongues spoken in Cartwright's work.

It is the language of affection that so markedly distinguishes Cartwright's *Replies* from orthodox religious disputation. Whitgift himself
was quick to recognize this foreign element in his adversary's discourse. He mocks Cartwright's unlicensed and unpredictable retreats
into the rhetoric of emotion, dismissing them as a "heat of words"
and a "hot eloquence."[93] Whitgift's criticism eventually focuses on
the use of metaphor and similitude as instruments of religious debate. For Cartwright's language of affection is above all metaphoric.
A typical instance of Cartwright's practice is to be found in the discussion of the government by elders. Cartwright begins his defense
of Presbyterian ecclesiology in a language that is precise and unadorned. He cites the reasons for the superiority of such a church
discipline mustering what scriptural justification he can.[94] When he
comes upon his adversary's dismissal of an elected church govern-

ment—the uneducated members of the congregation being unfit to choose wisely—Cartwright alters his mode of discussion. Gradually he builds toward a metaphoric rhapsody grounded not in scholastic disputation but in biblical declamation:

> And I say, further, where we have an express commandment laid upon us to do a thing, there all disputations must cease, of hardness, of impossibility, of profit, or else of peace. For, first, God hath not commanded any orders in his church which are impossible; and, if they seem hard, it must be remembered that the best and excellentest things are hardest, and that there is nothing so hard which diligence and travail to bring it to pass will not overcome; which thing if it be proved true in worldly affairs, the truth thereof will much more appear in the matters pertaining unto God, considering that, if God with his blessing do surmount all the difficulties in worldly matters, which are otherwise hard to be compassed, he will in his own matters, and matters pertaining to his glory, fill up the valleys although they be never so low, bring down the hills although they be never so high, plane the ways be they never so rough; so that he will make, of a way not passable in the eyes of flesh, a way tracked and easy to go in, and to walk towards that kingdom whereunto he calleth us.[95]

Cartwright's swelling hymn to God's capacity to make clear the way for true religion has its thematic and imagistic roots in the gospel descriptions of John the Baptist, but the biblical image has been inflated and embellished. Not only does this rhetorical fusillade serve as a crescendo and climax to Cartwright's examination of the validity of Presbyterian rule, it provides a metaphor for the debate itself. Cartwright and Whitgift battle for supremacy because "the best and excellentest things are hardest, and . . . there is nothing so hard which diligence and travail to bring it to pass will not overcome." The two contestants wield their weapons fashioned of reason, common sense, and historical precedent, but in the end the conflict is resolved on a plane of mystic assertiveness testifying to the presence of God's intervening hand. Whitgift, of course, wishes to have nothing to do with a form of argumentation that first endorses reason as a pathway to religious enlightenment and then mocks its incapacity to complete the journey. To Cartwright's figurative flight, he can reply only with a contemptuous, "These be but words of course, to no purpose."[96]

For Cartwright, such language is at the heart of godly discourse. Each of his crucial arguments finds its final, transcendent formulation in metaphor. The failure to move beyond the language of Anglicanism, which Cartwright derides as "wandering words and dead things," is to allow the soul to slip back into its natural lethargy. Thus he completes his rejection of Whitgift's attempts to link the dissent of the godly to papist treachery with a vast chain of metaphoric comparisons between Puritan and Anglican responses to the corruption of Rome.

> And judge whether they be more joined with the papists, which . . . separate themselves by three walls, or by one; they that would be parted by the broad sea from them, or which would be divided by narrow water, where they make a bridge to come again, and displace the truth of the gospel, as they have done in times past; they that would not only unhorse the pope, but also take away the stirrups, whereby he should never get into the saddle again; or they that, being content with that that he is unhorsed, leave his ceremonies, and his government especially, as stirrups whereby he may leap up again, when as occasion serveth; they that are content only to have cut the arms and body of the tree of antichristianity, or they which would have stump and root all up.[97]

The reader is snatched up by the author's fiery assertion and rousing images and carried into a conviction of truth that has nothing to do with rational judgment.[98] Cartwright's flaming chariot of rhetoric holds little appeal for his opponent. Whitgift is furious with the reformer's inability to understand the proper domain of such discourse. Similitudes have no place in logical argumentation; they are useful only in making difficult concepts accessible to simple minds. They carry no weight in the proof of a proposition. "[Y]our similitudes fail marvellously in sundry points, which I must admonish you of, because you glory so much in them, and think that you have reasoned strongly, when you have used the weakest kind of argument that can be to prove anything; for, as the logicians say, '*Similitudo rem illustrat, sed non probat*: A similitude maketh a matter plain, but proveth it not.' "[99] That the similitude is a form of speech that belongs properly to the realm of conviction and persuasion and hence emotion is asserted repeatedly by Whitgift.[100]

The use of metaphor and simile is not the only feature that characterizes Cartwright's language of affection. When Cartwright wishes to escape the contingencies of human logic, he instinctively assumes what might be called the prophetic voice. Highly wrought, oracular, and ritualistically repetitive, the prophetic voice of the Puritan disputant self-consciously imitates Old Testament invective.[101] "Wo is vnto that howsholde that hathe such a stewarde / and wo shall be vnto that stewarde that vppon suche a prouision / vndertaketh the stewardshippe of the howse off God. But wo and wo again shall be to him / that not onely himselfe famisheth the howsholde which he hathe / but teacheth others to doo so."[102] Cartwright is not unique in his fondness for imbedding such speech within apparently reasoned discourse. Lollards such as Jack Upland and the author of *The Lanterne of Liʒt* frequently lapsed into the vocabulary and speech patterns of the Hebrew prophet.

As is so often the case in nonconformist prose, such interludes typically begin with the words of an Isaiah or a Jeremiah and then move without apparent break into the words of the author, the seam between the two passages hidden beneath the continuity of style.[103] Perhaps the most zealous advocate of the practice was Anthony Gilby, whose imitations of the oracular voice are so extensive and so neatly grafted onto their scriptural stems that it becomes impossible to separate the human voice from the divine. In his *Answer to the deuillish detection of Stephane Gardiner*, Gilby pushes the prophetic voice to its limits. While discussing the dangers of Roman ceremony, he imagines himself a prophet speaking the words of an angry Jehovah.

> Heare therfore then wicked nacion, and know that he whom thou hast caste awaye: is the corner stone where vpon what so euer buylding is stablisshed, it groweth vp to be a holi temple

vnto the Lord, and who so euer doeth fall vpon this stone, he shalbe shaken in pieces . . . he shal most spedily be broken to powder that the whole world mai at length lerne, how horible a thing it is to fall into the handes of the lyuynge God. . . . You that liue now in the later ende of the worlde, beynge admonished by a thousande oracles and warninges of the prophetes, threateninge battail, famine and pestilence: do not chaunge your wycked purpose. . . . No man renueth his hert, no man chaungeth his maners. Ther is not one that doeth good, no not one.[104]

The interlude, titled "The complaint of God against Idolatours," is set off from the text with the words "Geue eare for God sayth it."

The spinning out of a speech from an original thread of scripture was an activity common to Protestants of all persuasions, the technique being well suited to the teaching of scriptural lessons. The sermon writer, in particular, found it useful first to cite a passage from the Bible and then to rephrase the passage in various ways in order to stimulate the understanding and memory of the audience. The nonconformist, however, uses these scriptural interludes to other ends. Whitgift, reacting to the Puritan habit of surrounding their own words with biblical citations and text, complains: "They have painted the margent of their book with quoting of scriptures, as though all were scripture they write."[105] Although his tone is mocking, Whitgift's assessment is accurate. Cartwright, like Gilby, blends his own prose with scripture neither for pedagogical nor strictly forensic purposes. As he himself explains, the words of the Bible are cited more "for proof of the phrase" than "proof of the matter."[106] The Puritan honeycombed his speech with the divine word in order to make his own words holy, to transform himself through language in the image of God's truth. He sought to dwell in the timeless landscape of the Bible and to recapitulate its meaning in his life and words. The citations of scripture function as aids to a kind of Puritan semantic *compositio*.[107] Unlike the Jesuit (or the dramatist) who mentally transports himself into a physical landscape, the Puritan projects himself into the language of the Bible. When he speaks in the manner of the Hebrew prophet, he translates his spiritual being into a holy tongue. Like the examinate before the prelate, his voice becomes a medium for God's Spirit and his words, as Whitgift taunts, become "as though all were scripture."[108]

The Puritan voice of prophecy is then histrionic. When the dissenter launches into a speech of prophetic fury, he plays a part. As he assumes the mantle of prophecy, he is translated into another level of discourse and existence. The world of contingency, logic, and reason suddenly falls away. Projected by his language into a world of play, he is permitted to be something other than what he once was. Thomas Cartwright, a man embittered by ill health, exile, and obstructed advancement, becomes for a moment another Thomas Cartwright—defender of the faith and heir to a tradition of beleaguered sainthood stretching back to the murdered Abel. As in all nonconformist moments of transcendence, the embrace of otherness is only partial.[109] Cartwright does not cease to be Cartwright: he becomes instead a gracious image of his former self. Self-annihilating ecstasy is as much a taboo for him as it was for the early followers of Wyclif. It is noteworthy that Whitgift himself recognizes the element of play in Cartwright's discursive style. More than once, the Anglican worthy chides Cartwright for his "gibing and jesting eloquence" and mocks his inconsistencies "as though you were not the same man, but played some other part."[110]

The domain of the histrionic imagination was, of course, the world that Cartwright had attacked when he berated the mysticism of the Catholic or the Anabaptist. Presumably Cartwright eased his anxieties of criminal complicity by grounding his metaphoric reveries in scriptural figures. The minister as watchman and shepherd, God as an architect of his temple, the word as a hammer—all of Cartwright's favorite images rely on biblical precedent.[111] Like a child learning to walk, the Puritan polemicist first relied on the steadying hand of his Father's word, but once having gained momentum and balance, he proceeded on his own, often unaware that the guiding hand had ever been removed. But the Puritan excursion into the maze of spiritual transfiguration required more than the "thred of the word of God" to ensure the safety of the journey.[112] To escape to a world of mystical assertion, the saint had first to labor in one of logical demonstration. Thus Cartwright's *Replies* to the work of John Whitgift are spoken not only in the language of affection, but in the language of understanding as well. This latter is the tongue we are accustomed to hearing in a debate between two men over an unresolved issue. Addressed to the intellect rather than the emotions, it is a voice that seeks to discover truth and convince men of that truth by its forensic acumen. However, the presence of this second voice in Cartwright's work ought not deceive the reader into believing that the writer's intentions mirror those of his Anglican opponent. Cartwright, like his nonconformist ancestors, always uses rational discourse as a prelude to and justification of the act of visionary inspiration.

In a revealing image found in the prefatory letter to the *Confutation*, Cartwright depicts the process of spiritual enlightenment as a gradual movement from the flat plains of readily accessible truth to the hillocks of simple mysteries to the high mountain of an inspired awakening. "And as in the most champion and plaine grounds of the books of Scripture, there are some mysteries (as hillockes) higher than the rest of their fellowes; so in the greatest and steepest hill thereof there is footing whereby with labour and trauaile, with much reading, and often prayer wee may come to that heigth of it, wherein wee may see and discouer so far of the land of Canaan, and the kingdome of heauen, as our places and callings, sexes, and ages do require."[113] The rapidly shifting language of the passage reflects the delicate balance between the rational and intuitive elements of nonconformity. The image begins hesitantly with a similitude; the parenthetical expression is a nervous warning that writer and reader are entering a domain of figurative speech. As the passage progresses, the conjunctive element of the simile drops out and the language becomes purely metaphorical. The summit of otherworldly vision reached, Cartwright suddenly pulls back from both his figurative language and its mystical implications. The visionary moment becomes hemmed in by an orderly listing of a series of all too reasonable qualifications. In the language of the Admonition controversy we can feel the same tense balance between reasoned and inspired speech, the latter rousing the spirit to a new degree of alertness and the former disciplining that spirit to prevent it from careening recklessly into the realm of unsanctified sight.

Cartwright was conscious of this play between the languages of intellect and of feeling and sought his precedent in the writings of Paul. In particular, he was drawn to Paul's alternating use of plain-speaking and metaphoric invention, how he ordinarily spoke once in metaphor and once in "plain and flat terms." In *The Rest of the Second Replie*, Cartwright notes it is "the custome of scripture" that the writer "expoundeth in the next vers, . . . that which he spake before, by a metaphore or borowed speach."[114] Cartwright is not simply approving Paul's pedagogical technique; he is interested in the way in which the speech and hence the experience of the visionary can be controlled and made safe by the use of plain-speaking. The act of linguistic transubstantiation, the metaphor, is licensed because its terms are carefully explained, because its mysterious spell is exorcised by a complementary act of ratiocination. Like guilty magicians, nonconformist writers (even those more overtly belletristic in their work than Cartwright) compulsively spoil their own illusions. William Turner, for example, routinely disrupts his allegory by explicating its fictions. "Hunter: It is not the manner that the hunter should go him selfe vnto the wilde beast, but he hathe done hys parte if he hath sent his houndes vnto hym. Dean: What meane ye by that. Hunter: I meane that is enoughe at this time, and in this part of the worlde, to write vnto him, and to tell him his fautes in writing though I come no nearer."[115]

Thus in the Admonition controversy, the mystic, metaphorical reveries of Thomas Cartwright, the prophet, are grounded in the businesslike proceedings of Thomas Cartwright, the polemicist. Only from this perspective can we comprehend Cartwright's embrace of a language of mathematical clarity even as he speaks a language of dark conceits. Although Cartwright flaunts his use of logic throughout the Admonition tracts, his self-congratulations are often curiously accompanied by an open display of distaste for the rigors of logical demonstration: "And, for that you are so hard with other men for their logic, I will desire the reader to pardon me if I pursue these things more narrowlier than some peradventure will like of, or I myself delight in."[116] When confronted by such a passage, the reader may well wonder about the depth of the Puritan devotion to reason and logic. Do Cartwright and his colleagues honestly believe in the capacity of human reason, aided by classical logic, to arrive at truth?

Or is their use of division, definition, and syllogism merely an empty performance meant to conceal from themselves and their foes the subjectivity of their vision? The ambiguity in Cartwright's attitude toward learning is everywhere evident. In the *Replies* Cartwright voices both pain at his brethren's inferior attainments in scholarship and complacency with their superior spiritual achievements— all overlaid by an envy and contempt for the hours of devoted study that Whitgift's preferments have made possible. "But, if you be so greatly learned, and we so unlearned and smally read, then the truth of our cause shall more appear that is maintained with so small learning and reading, against men of such profound knowledge and great reading. And yet I know not why, if we be not too idle, we should not be able to read as much as you, which may have leisure to read a good long writer, or ever you can ride only to see and salute your houses and livings, being so many and so far distant one from another."[117] Clearly Cartwright wants it both ways.

Much the same impression is to be gleaned from the syllogistic orgies of John Penry and William Turner.[118] Turner's use of the syllogism in *The Rescuynge of the Romishe Foxe* (1545) represents a classic instance of a Puritan author transforming an instrument of logic into an instrument of rhetoric.

> Euery strange doctrine is to be shoned of Christen men and to be cast out of the chirche / but euery doctrine is strange which is not conteyned in the holy scripture / ergo all doctrines that ar not conteyned in the scripture ar to be shoned of Christen men / and to be cast out of the chirche / But non of these tradationes ar conteyned in the holy scripture / there fore they are to be shoned of all Christen men and to be casten out of the chirche / . . . All thos preceptes ar to be bannisshed out of the chirche / where to we are forbidden to gyue hede / but vnto the preceptes of men whiche refuse the truthe ar we forbidden to gyue hede / therfore / all preceptes of men which refuse the truthe ar to be bannisshede out of the chirche. But the pope and hys papistes ar fals prophetes and refuse the truthe / ergo all theyr preceptes ceremonies & doctrines are to be bannisshed out of the chirche.[119]

As syllogism echoes syllogism in a crescendo of logical reasoning, language and thought seem to burst the bounds of their narrow containers. As proposition tumbles over proposition, the act of ratiocination is buried under the mounting emotional fervor of the writer. Logical demonstration suddenly yields to mystical affirmation as the *ergo* of Greek reason fades into the *amen* of Hebrew spirituality. And yet the preamble of logic is not really obliterated by the text of feeling. Turner's language is at once scientific and sacramental. The two elements of Puritan thought are inseparable, neither capable of existing without the other.[120] The value accorded learning and skill in reasoning always rests uncomfortably with a streak of anti-intellectualism, an uneasy alliance first struck in the early days of Lollardy.

Thomas Cartwright's deployment of his two languages of reason and feeling is determined as much by the ritualistic shape of nonconformist drama as by the contingencies of Whitgift's argumentation. Cartwright is at all times conscious that he is performing on the Puritan equivalent of the stage, frequently invoking theatrical metaphors to define the nature of the encounter.[121] Whitgift is typically portrayed as a demonic player of the kind that Bale had ridiculed in his plays. His citations of ancient authorities minus their actual words are dumb shows without value. "Here are brought in Justin Martyr, Irenoeus, Tertullian, Cyprian, and councils, as dumb persons on the stage, only to make a shew, and so they go out of the stage without saying anything."[122] Cartwright, in contrast, is a member of that ancient troupe of saintly actors who have performed in the ecclesiastical courts of England and in the pages of the recorded examinations, satires, saints' lives, plays, and polemical pamphlets of the reformers. William Turner speaks for them all when he declares, "I playe in thys tyme of nede, the deuyne warryer, to defend the forsayd city [of God] and endeuoure my selfe to ouercome thenimies of the same."[123] Cartwright's stage is the field of disputation where, as champion of Christ's adopted children, he engages in a battle not with John Whitgift, vice-chancellor of Cambridge and future archbishop of Canterbury, but rather Master Doctor or the A. (i.e., the Answerer), a character out of the pages of nonconformist satire. He is the blood relative of Bale's Catholic bogeyman, Edmund Bonner, and William Turner's gallery of rogues: Mistres Missa and

Doctor Porphyry, the Roman wolf and Master Steward of the Stewes. He is the father of Martin Marprelate's John of Cant. and Dumb John of London.

Cartwright's contributions to the Admonition controversy have the same rhythmic pulse as the plays of John Bale: they present a series of dramatic tableaux depicting the conflict of truth and falsehood yielding to the mystic affirmation of sainthood. Each vignette conforms to the same ritualistic pattern, while minor alterations in the script keep the elect audience in a continuous state of spiritual alertness. Like most Puritan dramas, Cartwright's sacrament of struggle has no real end. For Whitgift, the exercise was terminated as soon as all the arguments, pro and con, had been exhausted. For Cartwright, the absence of new subject matter was of no consequence. The struggle of the saint against his foes is in essence always the same. Identical arguments can be endlessly recycled, requiring only slight variations in content and form to be of use to the saintly contender and his supporters. So Cartwright went on flailing. His victory was evident not only from his godly conduct during the fight but from his eagerness to continue it as well. Whitgift's premature withdrawal from the field was itself testimony to his spiritual impotence. Like Bale's villains, who childishly expect the game to conclude when they have decided to go home, Whitgift shows himself unaware that the real drama, that of Cartwright's representative act of spiritual regeneration, continues without him.

It is, perhaps, disconcerting to speak of anything so dry and flat as the Admonition controversy as a product of the dramatic imagination. Even a brief glance at Whitgift's and Cartwright's labors, such as Donald McGinn provides in his considerably condensed version of the controversy, should explain the willingness of the literary scholar to surrender its documents to the historian. In reaching the texts of this controversy, however, we have not traveled all that far from the more boldly literary creations of the nonconformist mind. At no time during the period under investigation do we find the advocates of nonconformity drawing a distinct line between belletristic and nonbelletristic writing. Jack Upland saw no apparent contradiction in his attempt to debate the great theological issues of his day in the plebeian medium of vituperative satire. What is more, he seems totally at home in a form of popular art that injects large doses of bogus university logic into what is clearly a poetical argument. As we have seen, the strange conjunction of syllogistic reasoning and prophecy proved the ideal container for Upland's convictions.[124]

The blending of logic into rhetoric and rational disputation into dramatic art is perhaps clearest in the varied products of John Bale's prolific pen. Bale appears to have tried his hand at virtually every form of the written word, and yet his writings are all of a piece, not only in terms of their theological content but also in their theatricality. Thora Blatt has said, not without justice, that all of John Bale's plays are versified pamphlets.[125] The problem in this formulation is its failure to recognize that the equation is valid in both directions. John Bale's pamphlets are a form of dramatized prose. That a reader instinctively perceives Bale's *oeuvre* to be inherently more dramatic than Cartwright's is not an indication of two divergent views on the meaning, nature, and use of dramatic discourse but of varied temperaments and circumstances. Just as Jack Upland was less willing than the author *Pierce the Ploughman's Crede* to venture far into the realm of fictive creation, so Cartwright is less prone than Bale or Marprelate to do the same.

Within his own work, we can see how the varied pressures of the times affect Cartwright's artistic daring. In the first *Replye* to Whitgift, the author's use of metaphoric argumentation is both profuse and vivid. His attacks on Whitgift partake of some of the spirit of Bale's lively fictive encounters between saintly reformers and evil prelates. As the stakes in his battle with Whitgift rose, as he began to pine for the security and status to which his learning would ordinarily have entitled him, Cartwright began to retreat from metaphor, satire, and drama. The last of Cartwright's treatises, *The Rest of the Second Replie*, is remarkably barren in style. Cartwright had not lost his ability to write vivid prose: the metaphoric paean to the glories of the Christian warfare (tucked safely away in the preface) is as rich a piece of prose as Cartwright had ever conceived. His prose becomes dry because he instinctively fled the dangers of imaginative vision in the times of his troubles. It is interesting that when Cartwright again took up the gauntlet, this time with the Rhemist translators as his foes, he reverted to the style of the first *Replye*. Indeed, his prose in the *Confutation* surpasses that work in the "irregularity" of its argumentation. Clearly, the Roman party represented a "safe" enemy, one so clearly opposed to the vision of the nonconformists that the full fury of their spirit might be justly unleashed.[126]

From Jack Upland onwards, one can see the adherents of nonconformist theology redefining the nature of religious discourse in practice and theory. Both Upland's and Cartwright's opponents had assumed the existence of a sharp distinction between learned and popular discourse. The former belonged to the university, and its principal tool was the scholastic logic that had its roots in Aristotle. The latter was largely a matter of rhetoric, dressing up arguments to make them more accessible. From the fourteenth century onward, nonconformists had acted to tear down the barriers between the "lerned" and the "lewed." Rhetoric became an instrument of truth-finding as well as of truth-telling, logic a tool of emotional persuasion as well as of rational intellection. They found their place in an anxiety-ridden sphere in which the worlds of rhetoric and logic, drama and disputation, and literature and history intersected.[127] The language they spoke, formed of syllogisms and metaphors, reflected the contradictory impulses of their theology. For a relatively brief period, a new theory of logic and rhetoric gave their longstanding practice a degree of scholarly respectability. Ramist logic and rhetoric were introduced into England in the last quarter of the sixteenth century.[128] Ramism, with its emphasis on the syllogism as the basic unit of argumentation, on the dichotomy as the principal means of classification, and on a logic that was, at its core, deeply rhetorical, was of obvious appeal to nonconformist minds.[129] Peter Ramus's logical apparatus struck many members of Europe's learned community as a miraculous shortcut to truth. His was a system as legitimate as the logic of the schools but unencumbered by tediousness and difficulty. To men whose response to the value of logic and reason was so divided, who had sought since the late Middle Ages a reputation for logical procedure if not always its substance, Ramism indeed seemed a godsend. William Perkins employed its teachings when he wrote his famous handbook of sermonic oratory, *The Art of Prophesying*; John Milton fashioned his own textbook of Ramist logic in the next century. Ramism, however, did not provide nonconformity with a new way of thinking about the nature and purposes of communication; its basic outlook had long been present in the thought and writing of the earliest reformers. Ramism merely provided a systematization of attitudes and practices already extant, imbuing them with an aura of international respectability. The Puritans needed neither Peter Ramus nor Omar Talus to teach them how to assail their adversaries with syllogisms and similitudes.

Martin Marprelate, the unwelcome ally of Thomas Cartwright in the battle against episcopacy, was a Puritan adept at playing syllogistic games. He was both the heir and the chief glory of a tradition of satiric drama that we have traced back to the dialogues of the Lollard propagandists. His work and its curious relationship to Cartwright's Admonition tracts will be explored in the next chapter.

CHAPTER FIVE

Martin Marprelate

SYLLOGISTIC LAUGHTER

Robert Codrington, the seventeenth-century biographer of the earl of Essex, records a now-famous encounter between that aspiring young courtier and his volatile sovereign.[1] Elizabeth, so the story goes, was excoriating the libelous attacks of Martin Marprelate upon her bishops before certain members of the court. Among her audience was Essex. Observing the queen's displeasure with the unknown satirist and reminded of the prohibition against his work, Essex is said to have plucked the offending volume from beneath his robes, exclaiming in mock terror, "Why, then, what will become of me?" The incident, if true, would seem to substantiate the extravagant claims Marprelate himself made for his popularity among the English nobility. "I have been entertained at the Court," he writes in his second satire. "Every man talks of my Worship. Many would gladly receive my books, if they could tell where to find them."[2] The sudden and dramatic appearance of the contraband text from beneath the folds of the earl's cloak also captures something of the surprise that must have greeted the first appearance, in the autumn of 1588, of Martin's peculiar brand of religious disputation. Up to that moment nothing in the battle between Anglican and Puritan had quite prepared court and country for these exercises in calumnious wit.

To their Elizabethan audience, the satires of Martin Marprelate may well have seemed the product of spontaneous generation; to the modern historian blessed with hindsight, Martin's treatises betray a more conventional mode of parentage. In a sense, their appearance can be traced to the unwillingness of more illustrious Puritans to debate the reformation of the English Church beyond the limits dictated by the episcopal establishment. In his dispute with Whitgift, Cartwright had rejected the methodology of Anglican apology; yet he still felt himself bound by decorum to consider theological issues rather than ecclesiastical personalities. In a crucial moment in the Admonition controversy, Whitgift had challenged the right of his foe to criticize the moral and intellectual stature of individual English bishops. Their debate, he insisted, was properly focused on the virtues and deficiencies of the office of bishop, not on the character of the men who occupied it.[3] Cartwright chose not to dispute the claim.

Eleven years after the last of Cartwright's *Replies* had failed to provoke the bishops into continuing a public debate of the issues, Martin Marprelate arrived, shouting defiance at Whitgift's attempt to circumscribe the controversy over church polity.[4] He, Martin, was going to subject his prelatical adversaries to a trial of their moral, intellectual, and spiritual fiber. The result was the seven satires that together compose the Marprelate tracts.[5] Differing in style (and perhaps authorship as well), each nonetheless derives much of its energy and persuasiveness from the gossipy examinations of the lives of the bishops. The adulterous escapades of Mistress Cooper, wife of Thomas, bishop of Winchester, the deforestation of the Fulham estate by John Aylmer, bishop of London[6]—all are fair marks in the game of character assassination. Like John Bale, Marprelate is a counter-historian, subversively chronicling the pageant of sin mounted by the "synagogue of Satan." But not even Bale, that connoisseur of the cloistered impropriety and master of the voyeuristic sneer, can match Martin's joy in exposing the scandals of the episcopal palace. Whereas Bale is earnestly shrill in his accusations, Martin is playfully smug. Here he is exulting over the evidence he has gathered to indict Bishop Aylmer for the theft of a quantity of cloth from three London dyers: "The dyers' names are Baughin, Swan, and Price. They dwell at the Old Swan in Thames-street. I warrant you Martin will be found no liar; he bringeth in nothing without testimony. And therefore I have set down the men's names, and the places of their abode, that you of this Conspiration House may find out this slander of truth against the Lord of good London."[7]

Given Cartwright's reluctance to traffic in keyhole history, the attempt by some church officials to lay the Marprelate tracts at his door seems singularly misguided. However illogical the efforts to associate the stodgy Cartwright with the footloose Martin, the former was compelled to devote considerable energy to refuting the allegation. In his private correspondence with Lord Burghley during his imprisonment in the Fleet and in his public reply to the charges leveled against him by Sutcliffe, Cartwright emphatically denied both his approval of and participation in the publishing of the satires. "For me, I am able to produce witnesses, that the first time that euer I heard of Martin Marprelate, I testified my great misliking & grief, for so naughtie, and so disorderly a course as that was."[8] There is little doubt that the more conservative reformer balked at Martin's irregular proceedings. What is often ignored, though, is the element of self-interest in his denouncing Martin's misconduct. Unlicensed excursions from rigorous demonstration into metaphorical reverie had prompted Whitgift to characterize Cartwright's own efforts as disorderly. By shunting off the burden of Whitgift's accusations onto the activities of one more given to "hot eloquence" than himself, Cartwright might justify his labors not only to his adversaries but to himself as well. While Cartwright found it expedient to disassociate his polemical tracts from the helter-skelter satire of Marprelate, Martin—as will become evident—desperately needed to underscore their compatibility.

A consideration of the complexities behind the curious relationship between the works of Cartwright and Marprelate must be deferred until a later point in this discussion. For now it is sufficient to recognize that on the surface, at least, these nonconformist polemicists offered two readily distinguishable approaches to religious controversial literature. Nowhere is the disparity between their temperaments more manifest than in a comparison of the theatricality of their writings. Cartwright's contributions to the Admonition controversy, it was argued, reveal what might be called the deep structure of the nonconformist drama of self-discovery: an agon between the forces of darkness and light, fought on the field of reason but resolved within the domain of inspiration. While Cartwright's work offers the rudiments of the displaced drama of nonconformity, it offers virtually none of the amenities. There are only the barest traces of fictionalizing; the language has little of the colloquial vigor found in Bale, Gilby, and Turner; and the element of impersonation is largely subliminal. In contrast, the satires of Martin Marprelate come closer to transporting their readers into the world of the theater than any work of the nonconformist imagination encountered thus far.[9]

DRAMATIST WITHOUT A STAGE

The modern devotees of Martin's satire have long recognized the reformer's affinities with the playwrights of his day. Even as they place his work at the forefront of an emerging tradition of prose satire, they acknowledge its inherently dramatic nature. J. Dover Wilson in his seminal article in *The Cambridge History of English Literature* described Martin as "a puritan who had been born a stage clown; he was a disciple both of Calvin and Dick Tarleton. His style is that of a stage monologue."[10] More recently, John S. Coolidge has discerned, in the concept of *decorum personae*, Martin's rationale for a laughter born of "the deliberate interpenetration of religion and theatrical associations."[11] Martin's own contemporaries were swift in recognizing the fraternity between his satires and the stage. Undoubtedly, it was this perception that prompted the bishops to commission stage attacks on the reformer when their more scholarly effort at refutation, Bishop Cooper's *Admonition to the People of England* (1589),[12] proved ineffectual. Even a cursory inspection of Martin's writing explains the readiness of critics old and new to see the satirist as a kind of dramatist in exile. In these satires the dull monotone of pious declamation yields to the lively encounter of opposing voices and personalities.

Martin's jaunty, colloquial manner and his habitual use of direct address add a verbal third dimension to the pages of his work. His adversaries—mocked, cajoled, and reprimanded with an easy familiarity—seem active participants in their own humiliation. "And, Brother Bridges, mark what Martin tells you. You will shortly, I hope, have twenty fists about your ears more than your own. Take heed of writing against the Puritans, while you live!"[13] It is but a small step further for the satirist to give his enemies a voice. In the second of the Marprelate attacks on John Bridges's apology for Anglican episcopacy, Martin's ventriloquism creates a dramatic interlude between the dean and the Puritan gadfly:

> Surely Brother John, I marvel upon what topic-place this reason is grounded; for Scripture is not the foundation, you know, of the established government you defend. 'As though (will Master Bridges say) you are ignorant, Brother Martin, whence I drew this argument. You would make the world believe, that you know not that I reasoned as my Brother London did, in *Harborowe of faithful subjects.'* . . . O! I remember well indeed, Brother Sarum, the place you mean, and I remember that John Aylmer's reason is very like yours.[14]

Although comical, the exchange is generated by the same forces animating all Puritan discourse. As Gordon Stevens Wakefield has noted, "Like St. Paul, the Puritans always imagined an objector at their elbow, and they attempted to answer him faithfully."[15] As for the blatant falsification of Bridges's position, Martin pleads the prerogative of the fool: "Here is *indecorum personae* in this speech, I know; for the Doctor should not give me this warning, but you know my purpose is to play the dunce after his example."[16]

The voices heard in Martin's theater of the mind extend beyond those of the primary antagonists. Members of the audience intervene repeatedly to question, applaud, or reject the propositions urged by the contending spokesmen. Martin's responses to the disruptions occasioned by these novice theologians are by turns patient and indignant. In one such instance, an unruly auditor threatens to waylay the satirist entirely. Speak up, the skeptic urges; Martin obligingly raises his voice (with italics): "Therefore, our Lord Bishops—'*What sayest thou, man?'*—*our Lord Bishops*, I say, as John of Canterbury, Thomas of Winchester, (I will spare John of London for this time; for, it may be, he is at bowls, and it is pity to trouble my good brother, lest he should swear too bad), my reverend prelate of Lichfield, with the rest of that swinish rabble, are petty antichrists, petty popes, proud prelates, intolerable withstanders of Reformation . . ."[17] But to increased volume the onlooker accords no greater authority. He remains unconvinced, vocalizing his dissent from the safety of the satire's marginal sidelines: "Master Marprelate, you put more than the question in the conclusion of your syllogism."[18] Even as Marprelate's angry retort extends the comic interplay between author and imagined audience, so does it mock the Anglican disregard for boundaries—in politics as well as religious discourse. "This is a pretty matter, that standers-by must be so busy in other men's games. Why, sauceboxes, must you be prattling? You are as mannerly as bishops, in meddling with that [with which] you have nothing to do; as they do in taking upon them civil offices."[19]

The sense of an audience's presence is further enhanced by Martin's frequent lapses into the *sotto voce* of the confidant. The dramatic aside, its commentary often in ironic counterpoint to the fully voiced dialogue, draws author and spectator into a conspiracy against the tyranny of the prelates. "For will my Brother Bridges say that the Pope may have a lawful superior authority over his Grace of Canterbury? I'll never believe him, though he say so. Neither will I say that his Grace is an infidel (nor yet swear that he is much better); and therefore Master Dean meaneth not that the Pope should be this High Priest."[20] Although Martin often characterizes his spectators as skeptical and uncommitted, they are almost always seen as sympathetic to reform. They are, in fact, close relatives of the ubiquitous naïfs of the nonconformist disputational pamphlet. Confused and disturbed by the preaching of the nonconformist hero, these figures of spiritual immaturity inquire anxiously into the validity of his convictions. "What an horrible heresy is this, will some say. Why, gentle Martin, is it possible that these words of the French *Confession* should be true? Is it possible that there ought to be an equality between his Grace and the Dean of Sarum, or some other hedge-priest? Martin saith it ought to be so. Why then, Martin, if it should be so, how will the Bishops satisfy the reader on this point? Alas, simple fellow, whatsoever thou art, I perceive thou dost not mark the words of the *Confession*."[21]

Typically, by the end of the lesson, their underlying receptivity to the truth triumphs. Mentor and protégé are united by a mutual participation in the engendering and fortification of grace. So is Turner's naïve parliamentarian converted to the doctrines of the hunter in *The Huntyng of the Romyshe Vuolfe* and Bale's young child to the beliefs of his brother in *A Dialoge or Communycacyon*. Even when the inquiring soul proves recalcitrant, as does Gilby's chaplain of Barwick or Northbrooke's Youth, the reader is often led to anticipate imminent, if not immediate, capitulation.[22] The dynamics that govern the intercourse between the nonconformist hero and his hesitant ally reproduce in dramatic terms the delicate play between antagonism and camaraderie characteristic of the ideal minister's relationship with his congregation.[23]

Martin Marprelate's transformation of the world of Anglican and Puritan disputation into a stage spectacle is often treated as a new phase in the religious controversies of the sixteenth and seventeenth centuries. For Coolidge, Martin's "confounding of the pulpit with the stage" is at once a source of literary delight and of religious foreboding. Does not this confusion of theatrical and spiritual modes of communication threaten to unleash "a laughter that may turn out to be nihilistic?"[24] The amalgamation of pulpit and stage, however, is no new strategy. It is as old as English nonconformity itself. All the expressions of the nonconformist mind explored thus far—including Thomas Cartwright's tedious animadversions—have demonstrated a fundamentally dramatic approach both to the religious life and to the literature illuminating it. The theatrical displays of Martin Marprelate are unmatched in their profusion and in the verve, humor, and subtlety with which they are mounted. Martin's playful elusiveness; his love of the English language for its blunt plain-speaking, its demonic flexibility, and its passionate eloquence; his joyful misbehavior before those whose stature rests on position rather than worth—all these are unique to his personality and art. This iconoclast can titillate even a modern audience whose inability to regard anything with holiness threatens to make irreverence irrelevant; no other satirist of reformation can exert such a hold on our attention. Yet Martin's talents ought not to obscure his place within a tradition of literary dissent.[25] While the skill of his execution is solely his, the dramatic structure and motifs he employs have their roots deep in the nonconformist sensibility.

The metamorphosis of religious debate into a dramatic encounter in dialogue between the author and his fictionalized enemies was seen emerging first in the satires of the Upland series and fully exploited in the pamphlet literature of Bale, Turner, and Gilby.[26] In

Turner's *Examination of the Masse*, the statement and counterstatement of formal disputation blossoms into a full-blown drama—a trial scene replete with judges, defendants, and attorneys, each urging his own vision of religious truth.[27] Martin's creation of a hypothetical audience in the marginal notes has its precedents in Bale's editions of the trials of Thorpe, Oldcastle, and Askew.[28] In both instances, these nonconformist artists are able to produce a safe substitution for the ungoverned commerce between stage world and real world found in conventional theater. The spectator is led toward the enacted drama and yet is confined to and controlled within its peripheries. The use of the dramatic aside as both an instrument of ironic commentary and a conspiratorial link between author and reader is a time-honored convention in nonconformist polemic. Bale and Turner resort to the device in many of their pamphlet dialogues, and William Thorpe makes extensive use of the techinque in recording his examination before Arundel.[29] Martin Marprelate also shares Thorpe's practice of mirroring the primary confrontation of saint and ecclesiastical foe with a series of parallel contests in the manner of the subplots of a stage play.[30]

Nowhere is Marprelate's nonconformist ancestry more evident than in his preoccupation with the examination of the saints as a sacramental rite and as a model of devotional and polemical literature. Nonconformity is always marked by an overriding concern with the shape of the representative life: the life of the saint and the life of the sinner. All of its history constitutes what Bale had called "the image of bothe churches" and its most potent drama the clash of those churches in the experience of prelatical examination. In many ways, Martin is the unlikely heir apparent of the hagiographical tradition of Bale and Foxe. Filling his work with recollections of heresy trials, Martin shares with his fellow reformers a consuming passion for publicizing these events. Only when the examination is rescued from the obscurity of the locked chamber, can a private experience become the basis of a public ritual of communal affirmation. In the *Epistle*, Martin warns the bishops that their failure to fulfill the "Conditions of Peace" he has dictated will force him to become another John Foxe. "You shall not call one honest man before you, but I will get his examination (and you think I shall know nothing of the oppression of your tenants by your bribery, &c.) and publish it, if you deal not according to the former conditions."[31] In *The Just Censure and Reproofe*, Martin's eldest son commends the *Theses* of his father because in them he "hath taught us such a way to reason against these Caiaphases, . . . as will anger all the veins in John Canterbury's heart."[32]

Indeed the familiar ranting tyrant, tainted with the madness of Herod and of the Jewish high priests, appears regularly in Martin's accounts of the trials of the saints, most emphatically in John Penry's appearance before the High Commission.[33] Martin's depiction of the confrontation between Master Madox and John Aylmer, bishop of London, takes a more gamesome turn. This encounter is no matter of life and death but an unpleasant little dispute that rarely rises above the level of name-calling. The climax of the episode is not a moment of spiritual recognition; it is the utterance of the kind of malicious pun that gave rise to the satirist's own *nom de plume*, Marprelate. "The Bishop growing in choler said that Master Madox's name did show what he was; 'for,' saith he, 'thy name is Mad-ox, which declareth thee to be an unruly and mad beast.' Master Madox answered again that the Bishop's name, if it were descanted upon, did most significantly show his qualities. 'For,' said he, 'you are called Elmar; but you may be better called Mar-elm, for you have marred all the elms in Fulham, having cut them all down.' "[34] The ghostly utterance of the prophet is here traded for the inspired jest of the punster.

Even in his more light-hearted renditions of the examinations, Marprelate, like his predecessors, lays claim to historical accuracy. The witnesses are reliable and their testimony firsthand. "I speak not of things by hearsay, as of reports; but I bring my witnesses to prove my matters."[35] Of Penry's troubles, he declares: "[T]his is *true*, for I have seen the notes of their conference."[36] But Marprelate is not Foxe or even Bale. He is an inventor more than a compiler, a creator of fictions more than a gatherer of evidence. Carried on in seven satirical tracts, his own extended battle with the bishops—Whitgift, Aylmer, Cooper, and others—is itself a fabricated, staged examination enacted not only in front of the curtain but behind it as well. Consider Marprelate's brilliant and dangerous exercise in "creative history," his dramatization of Archbishop Whitgift's address to the pursuivants charged with tracking down Martin and his illegal press:

> For I will have him, or else I will no longer be Archbishop of Canterbury. He die at the Groine, as they say? Nay, he'll be hanged ere he'll die there. He is in some corner of England, lurking and doing mischief. I tell you true, I do think him and his brood to be worse than the Jesuits. These Martinists are all of them traitors and enemies unto her Majesty; . . . And therefore, either get him, or we shall never stay their course. And I think I shall go stark mad with you, unless you bring him.[37]

The stylized recording of the examination does not change significantly from Thorpe's day to Marprelate's. Perhaps because the event and its telling were conceived of as religious ritual, the history of the genre is not a story of evolution from simple to complex forms but rather one of continuous and self-conscious preservation, indeed of ossification. Although Marprelate might easily have mastered the rudiments of the form from Thorpe or Bale, he appears to have relied on a more contemporary document—the Puritan Register.[38] The Register was the brainchild of John Field. As unofficial secretary to the Presbyterian movement of the 1570s and 80s, Field had collected various documents connected with the struggle for reform, prominent among them the records of numerous examinations often penned by the examinates themselves.[39] In these documents Marprelate might have found more than the raw material for his attack on the prelates; he might also have discovered a style for that attack. For the Register is a typical nonconformist document, typical in its subversion of an orthodox genre—the diocesan register, with its "cool" accounting of heresy trials—into a "hot" instrument of Puritan polemic and devotion. Typical too is its mixing of tones and modes of discourse: the Register includes forensic treatises, petitions, letters, satirical epistles, dramatic dialogues, and poetry as well as the documentary histories of the "troubles" of persecuted saints.

Marprelate similarly would blend game and earnest, satire and prophecy, fiction and fact, although game, satire, and fiction would predominate as they do not in the Register. Everywhere in the Register, one discerns the voices and intonations that will surface to such brilliant effect in the Marprelate tracts.[40] That curious ability to turn evasion and humility into satiric assertion was not Marprelate's alone. William White possessed it as well:

> Q: White you were released, thinking you would be conform-able, but you are worse than you were. W: Not so, if it please you. L: he woulde haue no lawes. W: If there were no law, I hope I would liue like a Christian. L: Thou art a rebel. W: Not so my Lord, a true subiect. L: yea I sweare by god thou art a very rebell. . . . W: My Lord I thanke god my hart standeth right toward god & my prince. . . . L: Take him away. W: I would speake a word which I am sure will offend, and yet I must speake yt: I heard the name of god taken in vaine: if I had done it, it had bene a greater offence, than that I stande heere for. Q: White, White, you do not behaue your self well. W: I pray your worship shew me wherin, & I will craue pardon, and amend it. L: I may sweare in a matter of charity. W: There is now no such occasion.[41]

And for sheer satiric impudence, Marprelate has a potent rival in John Wilson: "B. [the Bishop of York] Naye, I thought alwayes what a stir we should haue with him. but thou perswadest people to meet-ings & priuate assemblies. W. My L. yow now put me in minde of a dutie that I haue not yet done, but by the grace of god I will remem-ber it thereafter, & will exhort the people of god to meet togeather to comfort & edifie one another in these things which they haue bene taughte & learned. Although I heare that for these thinges one is clapt in closse prison."[42] Martin Marprelate is a artist of unique ability and energy—but he is above all an artist of nonconformity and so shares his subject, his technique, his form, and his style with a host of ancestors and contemporaries.

THE MASKS OF MARTIN MARPRELATE

The theatrical world Martin Marprelate creates in his sat-ires is vibrantly alive with a kaleidoscopic assembly of colorful characters, shifting settings, and varied incidents. At times the roar and bustle of his cockpit threaten to bewilder the reader. Keeping this maddening host of plays and players in check is the master of ceremonies, Martin Marprelate himself. Never in the course of his work does the satirist's persona surrender his claim to the center stage. He is omniscient, presiding over all the festivities with a comic air of self-importance and self-satisfaction: "But you see, my worshipful Priests of this crew, to whom I write, what a perilous fellow Master Marprelate is. He understands all your knavery, and, it may be, keeps a register of them."[43] Whereas Martin's nonconformist predecessors had often donned their literary guises timidly, the author of the Marprelate tracts was not so shy. He worked persistently and boldly to create a substantial persona complete with a bogus family of satirically inclined offspring. Although Martin's stage personality is conceived with more daring than those of his fellow polemicists, it is a figure readily recognizable for its kinship with the nonconformist soothsayers of the past. His dominant mask sports the familiar features of the simple man of truth. Martin, like so many of the nonconformist satirists of both the Middle Ages and the Renaissance, appropriates the blunt speech of the intelligent but unlearned commoner. Parrying the thrusts of his own Puritan allies, unhappy with the crudity of his antiprelatical humor, Martin invokes an ancient defense: "I did think that Martin should not have been blamed of the Puritans for telling the truth openly. For, may I not say that John of Canterbury is a petty pope, seeing he is so? You must then bear with my ingramness [ignorance]. I am plain; I must needs call a spade a spade; a pope a pope."[44] Here, as elsewhere, the satirist promotes himself as a champion of a plain style of speaking and debating.

The call for a language of accessibility had been heard before among the reformers, notably in the work of the early Tudor polemicists. Martin Marprelate's desire to translate the complexities of the controversies between Anglican and Puritan into a language and style comprehensible to the English multitudes must have weighed heavily in his choice of the satiric medium.[45] When Martin Senior praises his younger brother's attempts to speak an ungarnished English, the satirist's desire to establish an unambiguous voice for religious disputation seems straightforward enough: "Neither do I deny, boy, but that thou art Tom Tell-troth, even like thy father, and that thou canst not abide to speak unto thine uncle Cantur. by circumlocutions and paraphrases; but simply and plainly thou breakest thy mind unto him."[46]

Martin's own prose, however, is never as simple as the author claims. Granted, Martin revels in the short, staccato sentence: neither elegant periphrasis nor complex subordination is to his taste. His speech often has the bare simplicity of a stichomythic exchange. An avid partisan of colloquial diction,[47] his distrust of metaphor rivals that of Puritan writers of a far less reckless bent. Even scripturally sanctioned figures are conspicuously absent in his work. Yet Martin's language slips and slides with a fiendish ingenuity. "And what could be more aptly spoken to the purpose, or more fitly prove an archiepiscopal calling? But the reason following proveth it yet more evident, and that is the illsample of Archbishop Titus, whom the Doctor of Divility in this 65th page affirmeth to have been Archbishop of Crete."[48] In the midst of his proclamations of simple ignorance, Martin's words belie his assertions. Protestations of lewedness are quickly followed by ostentatious erudition. Exaggerated postures of rustic simplemindedness warn the reader that Martin's rude mask is only partly genuine.[49]

Martin's acting skills are not confined to impersonations of the saint behind the plow. He is equally adept at playing the righteous man of learning. Boasting of his skill in the schoolman's logic, Martin often interrupts his proofs to call attention to his mastery of "learned discourse." In the *Epitome*, a strutting Martin declares himself sole inventor and practitioner of a new mood of syllogistic reasoning: "But, indeed, I have invented a new mood of mine own (for I have been a great schoolman in my days) which containeth in it a great mystery. The mystery I will expound, it may be, in a book for the purpose."[50] Just as comic exaggeration signaled the element of imposture in Martin's simple man, so here the satirist's bombast casts doubt on his pretense to godly learning. Martin's exasperating shifts between inspired innocent and painful scholar are yet another expression of the fundamentally divided nature of the Puritan and Lollard personalities. Intellect and spirit always coexist in an unresolved tension that produces saints who alternately see themselves as "learned" and "godly." Functionally, the instability of Martin's persona operates much like Thomas Cartwright's twin roles as doctor of reason and pastor of affection.[51] Juggling the voice of intuitive conviction with that of logical inference, both polemicists frustrate the expectations of the audience—promoting confusion among their adversaries and spiritual perspicuity among their allies. As soon as the auditor girds himself to face one mask, the Puritan champion dons the other.

In the last twenty-five years, students of the Marprelate tracts have directed their investigations away from the narrow search for the historical Martin and toward an understanding and appreciation of his literary identity. Critics accustomed to the more fixed and consistent personae of eighteenth-century satire are often struck by what one Marprelate scholar, Raymond Anselment, has aptly called the "transparency" of Martin's persona.[52] As we have seen, rather than raising a single mask, the satirist puts on many. Anselment's explanation for this erratic behavior derives from his characterization of Marprelate as an antirhetorician, that is, a satirist dedicated to ridiculing the very basis of religious disputation. Martin's failure "uniformly [to] project one image" is not a failure at all, argues Anselment, because "Martin's personae are governed by rhetorical intentions in which pragmatism outweighs mimesis."[53] Such an approach can be useful in understanding the rhetorical strategy of the reformer's work but errs in its implication that Marprelate's conception of his satirical calling was ultimately dictated by literary imperatives rather than spiritual ones. Martin belonged to a tradition of antiprelatical satire in which the emphasis had always rested more on the antiprelatical than on the satiric. Although Marprelate's affection for things literary was stronger than that of his predecessors, his final allegiances lay, as did theirs, with the Holy Ghost rather than the Muses. Had his nature been otherwise, the Marprelate tracts would be largely indistinguishable from the prose satire of Thomas Nashe. They would be works of technical and verbal ingenuity, but lacking in religious conviction.

The transparency of Martin Marperlate's fictive self was born of the nonconformist distrust of the unchecked imagination. For generations of radical satirists, the adoption of a fictional identity had been regarded with extreme trepidation. The fear of spiritual disorientation—produced in part by a vision of religious transformation as an act of gracious recreation rather than of willful self-annihilation—had haunted even the earliest reformation artists. Jack Upland had warily cloaked himself in the garb of the innocent uplander, rarely exploiting his adopted personality. Caution similarly diluted William Turner's portrait of the artist as a zealous hunter of the wolves and foxes of Roman ritual. In his early satires, the character of the hunter is barely sketched; in the later works, the author's apparent willingness to exploit the dramatic possibilities of the dialogue never extends to the delineation of his persona. The incapacity to embrace fully the otherness of literary experience afflicting Upland and Turner also prompted men like Bale, Gilby, and Cartwright to stop short of an unbroken imitation of the voice of the prophet.

By inventing a persona whose radical shifts in personality prevented the mistaking of a fictional mask for the actor, Martin circumvented some of the danger inherent in artistic experience. The fact remains, however, that Marprelate ventured further into the labyrinth of play and the imagination than any nonconformist satirist had before him. None proved more amenable to employing his imaginative faculties to give to nonconformist ideas "a local habitation and a name." And hence none was more impelled to ponder the nature of and the justification for his work than he.

AN APOLOGY FOR SATIRE

Martin's Tudor ancestors, Anthony Gilby and William Turner, had both attempted to provide a rationale for their satirical pamphleteering, albeit with less rigorous application than their successor. Gilby's justification for his satirical stance in *A Pleasaunt Dialogue* is virtually indistinguishable from the Wycliffite defense of vituperative speech. "In this Dialogue that I sende vnto you, if I do seeme sometimes pleasaunt, know that it is not without some bitternes of minde, as had the Prophetes, when they had do with halters & neutrals: whose foolishnes being counted great wisdome in the worlde, they did thus deride."[54] The authority for his literary practices is scriptural. While the Lollards habitually invoked Elijah's ridicule of the priests of Baal and Paul's scornful judgment of the Corinthians,[55] Gilby offers neither chapter nor verse; by his time awareness of both citations would be presumed. It is significant that Gilby claims to be justifying "pleasaunt" speech when, in fact, it is virulent ridicule for which he seeks biblical sanction. The tendency to equate scorn with laughter is a trademark of the nonconformist temper. Like the Lollards, the Puritans were inclined to regard true laughter as the exclusive prerogative of the glorified saints in heaven; those still serving their tenure on earth were advised to content themselves with either weeping for mankind's errors or hotly denouncing them. Cartwright was echoing two hundred years of nonconformist sobriety when he responded to Whitgift's portrait of the Puritan as morose and melancholy. "Where he saith we seldom or never laugh, it is not therefore that we think it is not lawful to laugh, but that the considerations of the calamities of other churches and of the ruins of ours, with the heavy judgments of the Lord which hang over us, ought to turn our laughing into weeping; besides that a man may laugh although he shew not his teeth."[56] The guarded laugh coyly condoned here is no laugh at all: it is a sneer.

Gilby's apologia for his art was not of a nature to placate Martin Marprelate's vocational anxieties. Martin is not averse to vitriolic speech, but then he is not inclined to dismiss laughter either. Although his laughter is often diluted by scorn, he comes closer to showing his teeth than any other Puritan jester: "Py, hy, hy, hy! I cannot but laugh, Py, hy, hy, hy, hy!"[57] William Turner, on the other hand, does address some of the problems faced by Martin in the plying of his trade. Turner, like Marprelate, readily acknowledges that his efforts to popularize contemporary religious issues have not met with unqualified approbation even within his own party.[58] In the third of his hunting satires, Turner responds to his critics. There are abroad, he says, a new order of "coullesse Monkes, much more precise and earnester in theyr monkery then the olde Monkes, whyche holde nowe that it is unlawfull for a Christen man to exercyse any kynde of play or pastyme, and therfore vtterly condemne Huntyng [i.e., Turner's satires]."[59]

Turner offers two related excuses for his conduct that will be crucial in Martin's defense of his playful discourse. First, Turner argues that his satire is lawful because it is pursued only as a form of recreation: "I thynke that a gentleman may hunt and hauke, and exercyse suche lyke pastymes, so that he occupy it measurably, and be not hyndered thereby from suche workes of hys vocation, as by the lawe of God he is bounde to exercyse."[60] Satire is play and, so long as it does not interfere with the earnest pursuit of a divinely appointed vocation, it is permissible. Second, he suggests that his own form of recreation differs from the usual holiday sport: "But amonge all kyndes of huntyng me thynke, that is best, whych as it hath measurable pastyme, so is most profytable for the commonwealth."[61] His species of play behavior is not merely pleasant; it also serves the common good. The idea that play can be consciously directed toward utilitarian ends outside itself subverts the concept of play as a form of self-contained and self-justifying activity.[62] When Turner's saintly Hunter and his naïve companion, the Forester, come upon the evil Dean, the two heroes call for some "honeste mirth and merye communication."[63] The two sets of epithets—virtually code words for a satirical dialogue concerning spiritual matters—are typical examples of the self-revealing oxymorons of the reformers. Is mirth or laughter ultimately subject to moral evaluation? That is, can it be honest? Does one ordinarily associate the act of communication (Turner seems deliberately to employ the technical, quasi-scientific term) with merriment? The natural deployment of Turner's words would be "honest communication and merry mirth," but the reformer is attempting to force the disparate realms of earnest and game into an uneasy conjunction. Turner vocationalizes play much as Cartwright and Milton industrialize the garden.

Martin Marprelate appears to have been familiar with Turner's pamphlets: the metaphor of the hunting of the Roman fox surfaces in the first of his own satires.[64] Whether that familiarity extended to Turner's vindication of religious laughter is neither clear nor of great moment. What is important is that Martin was to invoke essentially the same defense offered by Turner; that the argument was made with greater urgency and passion merely underscores the degree to which Martin had outdistanced his progenitors in his artistic daring. The most careful consideration of the lawfulness of what Martin calls "'pistle-making" occurs rather late in the sequence of satires. *Hay Any Worke for Cooper*, the last major tract to appear publicly, was printed in Coventry in the spring of 1589.[65] The tardy appearance of Martin's act of self-examination is not surprising. Although his earlier satires had aroused the disgust of the Puritan worthies, the heady air of success surrounding their printing must have overshadowed any trepidation Martin might have felt over his unorthodox practice. By the printing of *Hay Any Worke*, the unsilenced criticisms of his own allies combined with the increasingly violent persecution of Martin's associates must have led Martin to inquire more closely into his motives.

The fruits of Martin's reassessment of his work appear first in the humorous context of an attack on the card-playing addiction of William Chaderton, the bishop of Chester:

> And I tell you true, our brother Westchester had as lief play twenty nobles in a night at primero on the cards as trouble himself with any pulpit labor; and yet he thinks himself to be a sufficient bishop. . . . And take heed of it, Brother Westchester; it is an unlawful game, if you will believe me. . . . What, would you have men take no recreation? Yea; but it is an old-said saw, Enough is as good as a feast. And recreations must not be made a trade and an occupation, quoth Master Martin Marprelate. I tell you true, Brother mine, though I have as good a gift in 'pistle-making as you have at primero, and far more delight than you can have at your cards, for the love I bear to my brethren; yet I dare not use this sport but as a recreation, not making any trade thereof.[66]

Martin, like Turner, holds that many activities, unlawful if pursued as full-time trades, are often acceptable when sparingly used for recreative purposes. The penning of satire is such an activity for Marprelate; it cannot be a legitimate calling in itself. The bishops have failed not because they play at cards or even because they meddle in civil affairs; they fail because they have allowed their extracurricular pleasures to divert them from their true calling—the preaching of the word.[67]

Martin's defense, as here stated, is finally an accusation: the bishops are inveterate gamesters, while he is but an occasional player. Denouncing in one's adversaries the crimes one fears in oneself is, after all, the most potent nonconformist rite of assurance. Much of Marprelate's energy is therefore directed toward stigmatizing the world of the Anglican episcopacy as one of uninterrupted play and disorder. The Anglican bishops thereby assume the role performed in an earlier age by the religious orders. Martin himself is not unaware of the analogy. "You strive in vain; you are laid open already. Friars and monks were not so bad; they lived in the dark, you shut your eyes, lest you should see the light."[68] The satirist's portrayal of the advocates of episcopacy as contemporary mendicants, men who had voluntarily withdrawn from the healthy mainstream of human experience and chosen instead to dwell in the stagnation of their own fevered imaginations, may have been aided by Elizabeth's often shabby treatment of her bishops. Invested with ultimate responsibility but never ultimate authority, the bishops became a hapless shield raised to deflect criticism of ecclesiastical policy away from the throne.[69]

The heart of Martin's assault on the bishops' elevation of recreation over vocation is an indictment of the language of Anglican apology. In the sixth of the Marprelate tracts, *The Just Censure and Reproofe*, Martin Senior names and defines a species of language first analyzed by his father, Martin the Great. "But to satisfy thy demand, the Bishops' English is to wrest our language in such sort, as they will draw a meaning out of our English words, which the nature of the tongue can by no means bear."[70] The prelatical lords of England, claims Marprelate, can speak only the self-contained jargon of their profession. In doing so, they declare their enmity toward nonconformity's search for a universal medium for religious discourse—and toward its battle against a babel of tongues marked by exclusivity, unintelligibility, and self-interest. The Lollard satirists had derided the emptiness of a devotional program spoken and sung in a tongue foreign to the auditory for whose benefit it had been devised. John Bale, we recall, had dramatized the variance between the demonic voice and its saintly counterpart in the stuttering alliteration of his Vices and the homiletic flatness of his Virtues. Cartwright had pronounced Anglican speech unfit to inculcate truth, because it wandered without the tether of scripture, and incapable of casting up zeal, because it possessed no passionate spirituality. For two hundred years, nonconformists had seen in the language of orthodoxy the speech of lost souls.

Martin's denunciation of the bishops' "cunning and mystical kind of unnatural English" draws upon many of these earlier criticisms. Cartwright's charge of lifelessness is echoed in Martin's assault on the tediousness of John Bridges's long-winded prose. The labyrinthine sentences of the dean, says Marprelate, are able neither to inform the understanding nor to fortify the spirit. His words produce universal assent by exhaustion not conviction. "I was never so afraid in life, that I should not come to an end till I had been windless. Do you not see how I pant?"[71] Weighty argumentation gives way to sheer bulk. "A very portable book: a horse may carry it, if he be not too weak."[72] The foundering of Bridges's tome in the marketplace (Martin, of course, has been entertained at court and spoken of by every man) prompts the satirist to mourn the impending bankruptcy of the dean's printer: "Nay, I think you had more need to gather a benevolence among the clergy to pay Chard toward the printing of your book; or else labour to his Grace to get him another 'protection.' For men will give no money for your book, unless it be to stop mustard-pots as your brother Cosins' *Answer to the Abstract* did."[73] Behind Martin's lightheartedness is a sober recognition of the utility of satire as a vehicle for broadening the audience of England's religious controversies. Martin's exuberant and affective prose defies (as does most Puritan discourse) the boundaries between "lerned" and "lewed." Its audience is all England. Bridges's burdensome prose, in contrast, is for strictly limited consumption.

Marprelate's indictments of the linguistic abuses of the bishops are always readily translatable into denunciations of their moral and religious conduct.[74] An ungodly man, argues Martin, cannot hope to defend his ungodly cause in a godly style: "Presbyter John defended our church government, which is full of corruptions; and therefore the style and the proofs must be of the same nature that the cause is."[75] Since the awakening of dissent at the close of the fourteenth century, reformers had invested the word with all the spiritual potency that in both Anglicanism and Roman Catholicism had been apportioned among ceremonial pageantry, music, visual images, and the splendor and power of the church hierarchy itself. That men so deeply consumed by a devotion to language should fasten on speech as the most accurate gauge of inward disposition is not surprising.[76] Thus the dean of Sarum's verbosity is not merely an unfortunate stylistic aberration but also a sign of his disloyalty to the cause of religious truth. Commenting on a periodic sentence gone astray, Marprelate remarks: "Fleering, jeering, leering—there is at all no sense in this period. From the words 'yet,' 'afterward,' unto the end, Master Doctor's mind was so set upon a bishopric that he brought nothing concerning Crispus to answer the word 'yet.' "[77] Martin lampoons the deadening literalism of the Anglican approach to the master language, scripture, in his tale of a gin-loving priest. Sir Geoffrey Jones, in a rash moment, had forsworn to frequent a certain alehouse. Regretting in time the vow that kept him from his familiar haunt, Geoffrey devised a remedy for his unhappy situation: "And so he hired a man to carry him upon his back to the alehouse. By this means he did not go, but was carried thither, whereunto he made a vow never to go."[78] Martin's satire is double-barreled. He exposes the ill-becoming conduct of an episcopal lackey while satirizing the corruption of language for the sake of preserving the appearance, not the substance, of semantic integrity.

What emerges from Marprelate's racy tales of ill-speaking and ill-living Anglicans is a portrait of a verbal universe folded in upon itself, its life- and truth-giving links to the common speech of man and the inspired word of God utterly severed. The bishops and their supporters are the heirs of Jack Upland's lawless friars, John Bale's repressed monks, and William Turner's compromising priests; they are the aimless wanderers in the nonconformist vision of human history, condemned to expend their spirits in idle play rather than fruitful work. In the end, they can only understand each other and then imperfectly. Martin's assaults on the anarchy of Bishops' English no doubt eased the strictures his conscience had placed on his own use of a language given more to "merry mirth" than "honest communication." Just as Bale had closeted the demons of play into the subplot of the Vices, thereby liberating himself to pursue his own lawful play, so Martin drew a circle about his prelatical gamesters in order to sanction his own holy gaming.

Like all nonconformists, Marprelate was acutely sensitive to the instability of human language, to its capacity to distort meanings it was invented to clarify and to mask truth it was devised to reveal. Unlike his spiritual brethren, however, Martin reveled in that flexibility and ambiguity. He delighted in how the abbreviation of a name, as in John of Cant. for John Whitgift, Lord Archibishop of Canterbury, might transform a verbal miter into a verbal coxcomb.[79] And the disparity between apparent praise and intended scorn was a thing of joy to Martin: "And therefore hath not the learned and prudent Master Dean dealt very valiantly (how wisely let John Cant. cast his cards and consider) in assaulting this fort of our precise brethren; which he hath so shaken with good vincible reasons, very notably out of reason, that it hath not one stone in the foundation more than it had."[80] How could Martin justify such an indulgence in pleasures that were anathema to the nonconformist mind? To suggest, as John Coolidge has done, that Martin authorizes his satire by invoking the principle of *decorum personae*, i.e., "I could not deal with his book commendably, according to order, unless I should be sometimes tediously dunciacal and absurd,"[81] is to confuse the rules of the game with the justification for the game. Martin was all too aware of the tightrope he walked, cognizant of the fact that a misguided step could plunge him into the same verbal chaos he accused the bishops of promulgating. And so he walked with a balance pole in his hand: the element of high seriousness and earnest labor with which he countered the comic and gamesome air of his language and thought.

Even more than William Turner, Martin felt compelled to inject direction, purpose, and duty into his play. His work was to vibrate between comic invention and serious intent. The satirist's definitive formulation of the strategy appears in *Hay Any Worke*. Early in the tract, as we have seen, Martin broaches the topic in a comic vein by comparing his occasional satire with the bishops' addiction to card-playing. In typical Marprelate fashion, matter first deemed appropriate for jesting is later handled seriously:

> I am not disposed to jest in this serious matter. I am called
> Martin Marprelate. There be many that greatly dislike my do-
> ings. I may have my wants I know; for I am a man. But my
> course I know to be ordinary and lawful. I saw the cause of
> Christ's government, and of the Bishops' antichristian dealing
> to be hidden. The most part of men could not be gotten to read
> anything written in the defense of the one, and against the
> other. I bethought me, therefore, of a way whereby men might
> be drawn to do both; perceiving the humours of men in these
> times (especially of those that are in any place) to be given to
> mirth. I took that course. I might lawfully do it. Aye, for jesting
> is lawful by circumstances, even in the greatest matters. The
> circumstances of time, place, and persons urged me thereunto.
> I never profaned the Word in any jest. Other mirth I used as a
> covert, wherein I would bring the truth into light. The Lord
> being the author both of mirth and gravity, is it not lawful in
> itself, for the truth to use either of these ways, when the cir-
> cumstances do make it lawful?[82]

In a passage marked by simplicity, brevity, and perspicuity, the author explains his rationale for his extravagant rhetorical displays. All his efforts at comedy and satire, all his exploitations of the protean nature of human speech, have been an effort to introduce the crucial religious issues of the day in a more congenial form. Cartwright's contribution to that struggle was, I have argued, deeply rhetorical, dramatic, and pastoral. Martin goes further, pushing his work closer and closer to a literature of the dramatic imagination.[83] Martin's abiding religious concerns, however, are never far from his own mind or those of his readers. At times, those concerns are briefly eclipsed by authorial pranks, but more often it is the wit that is shadowed by the earnest declamation.

Martin's continuous attempts to rein in merriment with serious-ness are matched by his endeavors to ground verbal free-play in a language of precision, clarity, and semantic stability. Cartwright found the counterweight to his prophetic voice in plain style and in logic. Martin speaks both of these languages. To them he adds a mastery of the argot of the lawyer's chamber: "You will go about, I know, to prove my Book to be a libel; but I have prevented you of that advantage in law; both by bringing in nothing but matters of fact; which may easily be proved, if you dare deny them; and also, in setting my name to my Book."[84] The profusion of legalisms in Martin's prose has encouraged some critics to discern the shadow of the Inns of Court in Martin's past. Such language, however, need not reflect personal experience; the voice of the court, with its abhorrence of ambiguity, is a perfect antidote to Martin's slippery-tongued ingenuity.[85] It is the language of logical demonstration, nonetheless, that most attracts Martin's attention as a means of controlling and sanctioning his fanciful impulses. The syllogism long formed the backbone of nonconformist proof, having been drafted into the service of reform as early as the fourteenth century. Turner, Penry, and Cartwright all delighted in its potential as both a rhetorical and a logical weapon in religious debate.[86] Martin is not remiss in his own demonstrations of affection for the syllogism. His reasoning seems to fall naturally into the rhythm of major, minor, and conclusion.[87]

If Martin discovers a degree of security in corseting his imagination within the narrow confines of syllogistic propositions, he also brings to them an element of imaginative invention. Tempestuous language alters a medium of dispassionate thought into one of emotional display. The intervention of offstage voices of doubt shatters the self-containment of the syllogism, transforming it into an open-ended, dramatic confrontation between opposing parties.[88] The assignment of personal names to the moods and elements of the syllogism further enhances the theatricality of Martin's school logic. Above all, Martin changes the nature of logical reasoning by deliberately undermining its objectivity with his claims of artistic freedom. In *The Just Censure and Reproofe*, Martin Senior explains to his naïve sibling that it is easier for their father

> . . . to alter his course than for any one writer that I know of,
> because he hath chosen such a method as no man else besides
> hath done. Nay, his syllogisms, axioms, method, and all are of

his own making; he will borrow none of those common school rules, no not so much as the common grammer as it appeareth by that excellent point of poetry, written in Latin by him against Doctor Winken de Word. There thou shalt see such grammar, such art, such wit and conveyance of matter, as for the variety of the learning, and the pleasantness of the style, the like is not elsewhere to be found.[89]

The passage is telling for it shows the extent to which the Puritan was willing to collapse the world of literary play and logical work. Poetry, grammar, rhetoric, and logic are all seen as coexistent. Art and wit are as much at home in Martin's logic as the syllogism is in his buoyant satire.

The nonconformist saw grace as an extraordinary force of God whose intervention within nature and custom offered man an unearned release from his bondage to that world. Grace, in itself, was contrary to all things terrestrial, and its miraculous infusion into the soul signaled the most cataclysmic of spiritual changes. Expectations bred of causality were violated, the rules and laws that governed the life of the unenlightened soul contravened. And yet, as Gilby had noted, such spiritual transformation was "a miracle without misorder."[90] Nature was recreated by grace, but grace manifested itself in essentially natural ways.[91] Just as the nonconformist saw grace as subtly altering the natural order without destroying it, so in his approach to religious discourse, he came to envision the sanctified imagination as suffusing the realm of logical rigor. Imagination liberated logic while logic disciplined imagination. In both the experience and the literature of nonconformity, nature and grace, work and play were to meet in a perfect commerce—a fraternity without fusion.

Martin's participation in this vision of a language and an art conceived as both laborious and playful, natural and yet gracious, is evident in his satirical argumentation. In the *Epistle*, a proud Martin boasts of his logical skill: "But what do you say, if by this lusty syllogism of mine own making I prove them popes once more, for recreation's sake."[92] The sentence veers back and forth, propelled by contrary impulses toward an ordered process of reasoning and a liberated process of imagining. His syllogism is lusty; his acts of proof are for recreation's sake; his demonstrations are objects of art, that is, of his own making. In this curiously artistic logic and logical art, a syllogism may be false in form, but by being so it may contain a higher truth.[93] We can see here the fundamental nonconformist conviction that for all its validity as a prelude to gracious inspiration, logical reasoning must finally yield to the intuitive perception of a truth that transcends the strictures of the human intellect. Cartwright held no love for Martin, yet his sense of reason's impotence in the face of authentic vision does not differ significantly from Martin's own qualifications about the efficacy of ratiocination: "I have been bold to utter that which I think, not doubting also but that the light of truth shall be able to scatter all those mists of reasons which shall go about to darken the clearness thereof."[94]

Martin Marprelate devised a satiric strategy bound to a long tradition of literary dissent. Like his predecessors, he proceeded to confound pulpit and stage in order to create a drama displaced from its theatrical context. His complex creation engendered bewilderment among his adversaries. How might they best counter his syllogistic laughter and his learned proofs masquerading as crude jest? The radical shifts in the episcopacy's response to the Marprelate tracts illuminate the struggle of contrary elements that constitutes the radical poetics of nonconformist literature. The bishops began their attack on Martin by speaking to what the satirist himself had dubbed "this whole learned discourse." Although Thomas Cooper's *Admonition to the People of England* is a well-reasoned defense of the practices and policies of the Anglican bishops, it was doomed from the start. As soon as the bishops turned to the satirist's earnest voice, he countered their weighty defenses with jest and play. The frustrated defenders of the Elizabethan settlement were forced to reconsider their strategy; the result was the commissioning of pamphlets, broadsides, and plays aimed at refuting Martin at his own level. The doggerel verses of Mar-Martine appeared in May 1589, less than two months after the printing of Marprelate's attack on Cooper's book.[95] Throughout the remainder of 1589 and well into 1590, Martin was reviled in print and on stage. Writers such as John Lyly and Thomas Nashe were recruited to the Anglican cause.[96] The problem with this explosion of literary derision was that the works were emphatically not a refutation of Martin at his own level but merely at one of his levels. Even the most accomplished of Martin's foes, Thomas Nashe, could match Martin only on the field of wit, not in the arena of religious conviction. Neither variety of attack launched by the bishops could suffice in itself as a response to Martin Marprelate's Janus-faced art.

FATHERS AND SONS

By making play vocational, Martin eased a conscience troubled by the heterodoxy of his literary project. The imposition of internal safeguards, however, did not seem to silence all his doubts. From the beginning, Martin fortified his uncertain enterprise from without as well as from within. To justify his own world of play, jest, and notoriety, he sought an external repository of work, earnestness, and respectability. For this he turned to Thomas Cartwright. Throughout the Marprelate tracts, the name and works of Cartwright are invoked to sanction Martin's course. Thomas Cartwright was the stable rock upon which Martin hoped to ground his airy flights into imaginative space. As we have seen, Cartwright's own work was less than stable; it was rather an explosive blend of rational disputation and inspired prophecy. To the more volatile Martin Marprelate, Cartwright must have seemed, nevertheless, a very secure anchorage indeed. The first satire is honeycombed with references to Cartwright's triumph over evil as incarnated in John of Cant. himself, at the time of their battle merely John Whitgift.[97] Martin's glowing accounts of Cartwright's victory are unabashed attempts to participate vicariously in the Puritan champion's reputation for godly demeanor and scholarship. Five times the playful Martin conjures up the image of the grave Cartwright in this first work alone.[98]

The negative response of Cartwright to Martin's satire must have come as a rude shock to the rather complacent author of the *Epistle*. By his own testimony, Cartwright was vociferous in his disapproval of the Marprelate tracts from their first appearance; and his "precise brethren" were no less censorious. The Puritan leaders, it will be remembered, were then struggling to attain the esteem and respectability due an opposition party. Having themselves been charged with disorderly proceedings, they were not likely to regard with favor the extravagances of the Marprelate style. Martin's frustration with the disapprobation he encountered among his supposed allies surfaces clearly in his next broadside, the *Epitome*. Even before he has properly begun, the satirist makes light of an assault that could have only aroused deep concern in a reformer whose style was comic but whose aims were serious. Boasting of his popularity at court, Martin notes that the faction most likely to laud his project has abandoned him: "[Y]ou see how I am favoured of all estates (the Puritans only excepted)."[99] Anger and disappointment drive Martin to return again and again to the proffered insult: "I did think that Martin should not have been blamed of the Puritans for telling the truth openly. . . . What! will the Puritans seek to keep out the Pope of Rome, and maintain the Pope at Lambeth?"[100] Have the Puritans acted out of fear of being associated with his unorthodox activities? Then Martin will encourage the bishops to assume just such a connection: "Because you will do this, I will tell the Bishops how they shall deal with you. Let them say that the hottest of you hath made Martin, and that the rest of you were consenting thereunto."[101]

Martin's menacing gesture underscores the awkwardness of his position. He desperately wants the respectability only the Puritan leaders can lend him—so desperate that he is willing to chain himself to them by implicating them in his "crime." At the same time, Martin cannot ignore the genuine breach between himself and his brethren. Their approach to the purification of England's corrupted church is undeniably at odds with his own strategy. The ambivalence behind this first reaction to the rejection of his spiritual campaign, its blend of indignation and sorrow, is evident in the remainder of Martin's satires. Martin is forced to maintain the semblance of an alliance between himself and his precise brethren and simultaneously compelled to demonstrate the distance separating their temperaments. At one moment, Martin will declare his loyalty to his Puritan fathers; at the next, he will underscore his rebellion. "This is the Puritans' craft in procuring me to be confuted, I know. I'll be even with them, too."[102] The Malvolio-like threat seems curiously out of place in the mouth of a Puritan amidst fellow Puritans.

Martin's attitude toward Cartwright remains reverent if rather cool. References to the reformer conspicuously diminish in the second and third tracts: there are but two passing glimpses of Cartwright's career offered.[103] At only one other point in the tracts does Marprelate again fall back on the memory of Cartwright's glory as a restorative in his own struggle with the bishops. The incident occurs in *Hay Any Worke*, the satire in which Martin begins to confront more forthrightly the dangers of his crusade. In this moment of vocational crisis, Marprelate again invokes the image of Cartwright as the bold Christian warrior. He does so in response to Thomas Cooper's having used the initials T. C. as the only acknowledgment of his proprietary role in the assembling of the *Admonition*. Amused by the chance equation of two men whom he regards as spiritual opposites, Martin exploits the contrast between the "holy" T. C. and the "prophane" T. C. "A crafty, whoresons brethren-bishops, did you think because the Puritans' T. C. did set John of Cant. at a *non-plus* and gave him the overthrow, that therefore your T. C., alias Thomas Cooper, Bishop of Winchester, or Thomas Cook, his chaplain, could set me at a *non-plus*? Simple fellows! methinks he should not."[104] Throughout the satire, the enmity between the two T. C.'s is employed by Martin as a means of identifying himself with Cartwright's righteous cause.

Martin's tactic of respectability by association was a familiar strategy among nonconformist satirists. There appears to be more than the expediency of plagiarism at work in Jack Upland's habitual reproduction of large portions of the writings of the early Lollards in his own satire.[105] Upland sought to invest his efforts with an aura of learning and legitimacy and did so by looking back upon university-trained reformers such as Purvey and Repingdon. Those Lollard popularizers could in turn justify their vernacular proselytizing by filching from Wyclif's learned Latin treatises. In the long history of English nonconformity, it is not uncommon to find these chains of spiritual authority being forged. Those adherents of reform who, because of a lack of education, a literary turn of mind, or a desire to rehearse crucial issues in a less erudite voice, sought to convey their beliefs in more popular modes typically looked to the serious labors of other reformers as a justification for their own activities. The interlacing of the words of the earnest reformer (often without citation) with those of the more gamesome satirist was, in some sense, a secular transformation of the scriptural imbedding practiced by all nonconformists. In both cases, authority was perceived as being transferred in the act of one writer "living the language" of another writer, who was in a closer and more stable communion with the divine.

Martin's reliance on the stay of Thomas Cartwright's labors did not endure beyond the writing of *Hay Any Worke*. By the last three Marprelate tracts, the author was seeking to tether his buoyant imagination elsewhere—to the substantial canon of Master William Tyndale, the Henrician evangelist, biblical translator, and martyr.[106] His name first surfaces in the *Theses Martinianae*, a collection of defamatory articles to which the bishops are invited to respond. The fifty-second of Martin's propositions reads: "That the doctrine of the Church of England in the days of King Henry the Eighth was the doctrine which the blessed martyrs of Christ Jesus Master Tyndale, Master Doctor Barnes and Master Fyrth taught them and delivered unto us."[107] Although Tyndale is bracketed with Barnes and Firth (selections from the works of all three men had appeared in a popular text edited by John Foxe), the preeminence of England's first great Pauline theologian is quickly asserted. The fifty-seventh thesis is drawn directly from Tyndale's writings, as are many of the others that follow. Noting that Foxe's volume was published during the reign of King Henry VIII, *cum privilegio*,[108] Martin argues that all doctrine therein is "to be accounted the doctrine of Faith and Sacraments in the Church of England and so is approved by statute." Martin's logical legerdemain thus secures Tyndale's life and views as the state-approved model for godly doctrine and deportment. If the reader has failed to gather the significance of this fact, Martin Junior rehearses the implications of Tyndale's canonization in his epilogue to the *Theses*. However, it is against the Puritans more than the bishops that Martin Junior plays his Tyndale card: "And therefore you Puritans, that mislike of him [Martin], take heed that you be not found amongst posterity to be the betrayers of this doctrine (for your ease and quietness' sake), which you are bound to deliver unto your children, without corruption or mangling, though it cost you your lives a thousand times."[109]

The modern-day Puritans, Martin Junior suggests, are timid and politic men who have squandered their zeal and faith for the paltry price of security and physical well-being. Martin and his sons are the true heirs of Tyndale; they are men who combine wisdom with the martyr's thirst for spiritual warfare.

Martin's choice of Tyndale as his new paternal guardian was shrewdly made. Tyndale had all the necessary prestige, and his self-sacrifice lent him an air of sanctity Martin's Puritan contemporaries necessarily lacked. Perhaps even more important for the satirist's purposes, Tyndale was safely entombed in the past. He could not start up as Cartwright had done and embarrass his disciple. And so in the last satires it is the memory of a martyred evangelist that provides the foundation of Martin's castle of the imagination. Indeed, Martin's farewell jest, near the close of *The Protestatyon*, rests comfortably on the earnest assertions of Master Tyndale: "But whensoever I am married, it would do me good at the heart, to see a dozen of good and honest lord bishops dance at my wedding; saving that, as Master Tyndale hath very well noted, *Practise of Prelates*, page 374, it is not possible, naturally, that there should be any good and honest lord bishop."[110]

THE IDENTITY OF MARTIN MARPRELATE

Scholars and detectives being creatures of like disposition, it is not altogether surprising that so much of the critical energy expended on the Marprelate tracts has been directed toward the unmasking of Martin himself.[111] The contemporary revaluation of Martin Marprelate's literary stock seems only to have furthered this regrettable fixation. It seems to become all the more important to name the man now acknowledged as the foremost prose satirist of Renaissance England and the patriarch of a tradition that includes both Nashe and Swift. For those drawn to the mystery, the matter of Martin's identity inevitably becomes an obsession, thrusting aside all other claims upon our attention. Among the casualties of the long-standing dream of running Martin Marprelate to earth is an appreciation of the issue of spiritual identity that lies at the very center of

Martin's work. It has been the principal contention of this investigation that much of nonconformist writing is, in the deepest sense of the word, dramatic—and, more often than not, self-dramatizing. Each of the works studied thus far documents the invention of identity in a theater of the soul: the elect personality's struggle to enact its ideal self and secure its legitimate spiritual inheritance. The experience culminates in the sense of calm that comes from the acceptance of one's saintly role on a divine stage. What transforms this rite of self-awareness from a private ceremony of complacency into a public celebration of the mystical unity of Christ's body is the nonconformist insistence that the triumph of the individual is the triumph of the community. Because the godly life is uniform in its shape, if not in its particulars, the autobiography of one saint is the biography of all saints. Ritualistic art is by nature repetitive and, as the nonconformists knew, always threatened with a loss of efficacy should the repetition become rote. There are nonconformist dramas in which the trial of truth is a kangaroo court and the act of self-discovery is in fact a self-serving sleight of hand. But more commonly such drama does provide a genuine testing ground for spiritual knowledge and fertile soil for the growth of religious consciousness.

Martin Marprelate's rite of self-discovery is performed with more understanding and feeling than any such work encountered thus far. As a group the satires constitute a sustained exercise in the nonconformist art of self-examination, an exploration of the roots of identity and calling. The first of Martin's productions, the *Epistle*, is alive with a youthful buoyancy and an easy confidence. His defense of jesting is appropriately itself an ingenious jest: "Again, 'May it please you' to give me leave to play the dunce for the nonce, as well as he [Bridges]; otherwise dealing with Master Doctor's book, I cannot keep *decorum personae*."[112] The satirist is similarly breezy in the second satire. If in the opening of the *Epitome* Martin winces at the lash of his precise allies, he quickly regains his former good humor. The period following the heady success of the first two tracts, however, appears to have been one of reappraisal. The uninhibited assaults on Bridges's book may have suited the times, but with the united front of reform splintering and the bishops campaign of terror intensifying, the stakes of Martin's game were rising. The *Minerall and Meta-*

physicall Schoolpoints, printed toward the end of January 1589, was a stopgap measure, giving Martin time to ponder his conscience and the Anglican response. The work is appropriately neutral in style and tone, marked by a waiting-room drabness. Although offering the same blend of doctrine and gossip, the playful satire of the earlier tracts is rigidly docketed within a format of numbered theses.

From this period of reassessment emerges *Hay Any Worke for Cooper*, containing the first closely considered defense of Martin's artistry. Although Martin begins his *apologia pro sua ironia* with the voice of the jester—facetiously conflating Puritan 'pistles and Anglican primero—when he later returns to the task, the jester abruptly exits. Martin's need to reaffirm the serious purposes he had once masked in playful discourse surfaces in a hesitant experiment with the more traditional posture of Puritan dissent—the prophet's voice of impassioned denunciation: "O cursed beasts, that bring this guilt upon our Estate! Repent, caitiffs, while you have time. You shall not have it, I fear, when you will."[113] New strains of high seriousness and confessional earnestness pervade much of the remainder of the satire.[114]

Marprelate is himself aware of the change and, at one point, summons up the 'old' Martin to forestall the emerging monotone. "Wo, wo! But where have I been all this while? Ten to one, among some of these Puritans. Why, Martin? Why, Martin, I say, hast thou forgotten thyself? Where hast'e been? Why man 'cha' been a-seeking for a salmon's nest, and 'cha vownd a whole crew, either of ecclesiastical traitors, or of bishops of the devil . . ."[115] It is as if an old friend had suddenly blown into town. The rhythms of colloquial speech and the masquerade of country ignorance are briefly resurrected. But if the old Martin has returned to stay, he has returned a chastened man. Never again in the Marprelate tracts will the effervescent humor of the first satires be fully recaptured. Martin remains unshaken in his spiritual convictions, yet his sense of his calling is altering. *Hay Any Worke* ends on a note of urgency. The reader can feel the breath of the archbishop's pursuivants hot upon the satirist's neck. The author rehearses a litany of abbreviated complaints as if afraid that he will not be permitted to consider them at leisure.[116] Will the fate of Waldgrave's family, their lives disrupted by the violence of Whitgift's minions, likewise befall the author? Will there be time and place to expose further the evil of the bishops? Will there be time and place for a Martin Marprelate? The work concludes on a valedictory note: "Farewell, farewell, farewell, old Martin! And keep thee out of their hands for all that. For thou art a shrewd fellow; thou wilt one day overthrow them. Amen. And then thou swearest by thy faith, quoth John of London."[117] Martin may reappear, but it may be he will be wearing another disguise.

Marprelate's sense of urgency in previewing the charges to be brought against the bishops in *More Worke for the Cooper* proved prophetic. On August 14, 1589, Whitgift's agents seized the Martinist press and, along with it, the manuscript of *More Worke*; Martin's second barrage against Cooper's *Admonition* was never to be published. The printer, John Hodgkins, along with his assistants, Valentine Simms and Arthur Tomlyn, were arrested, sent to the Tower, and eventually tortured in a feckless attempt to discover Martin's true identity. Between the printing of *Hay Any Worke* and the seizure of press and printers, two further interim tracts were printed: Martin Junior's *Theses Martinianae* and Martin Senior's *Just Censure and Reproofe*. It has been repeatedly argued that these satires are not the work of the original Martin but the effort of collaborators. Martin himself, however, had predicted the appearance of a swarm of young Martinists; and in the *Epitome* he had urged those bishops unversed in Martinist logic to seek enlightenment from one of them, his son Martin Senior.[118] Martin Senior does, in fact, initiate his younger brother into the mysteries of that logic in the *Just Censure*. Had the original Martin plotted and later produced the debut of his two sons? Or had Martin's followers chosen to introduce their own writings under names suggested by their leader? Whatever the circumstances of authorship attending the appearance of these two "secondary tracts," they display a remarkable unity with the psychological, spiritual, and stylistic progress made in the course of the Marprelate canon as a whole.

Martin's concern with the effects of his works, evident in his first attack on Cooper's tract, intensifies in Martin Junior's edition of his father's *Theses*. In a preface marked more by resignation than ire, Martin the Great glances at his two adversaries. The bishops, he observes, are angered by both his cause and his manner of writing.

His once anticipated allies, the Puritans, are well disposed toward his matter, but "the form they cannot brook."[119] They "delight neither in heat nor cold; and so make me as weary in seeking how to fit them, as the Bishops are in labouring to find me."[120] The attempt to rekindle their emotional fervor in retrospect was quixotic; his nostalgic roll call of the Henrician martyrs speaks eloquently of squandered resources. As for the bishops, they are no doubt beyond amendment. Martin may never have thought to reclaim them through his efforts, but now, for the first time, the satirist acknowledges failure. Martin must instead turn inward; he must place his own spiritual house in order as the conclusion of his satiric mission, be it forced or voluntary, approaches. All that is left for him is the task of making yet another public vindication of his method and a public record of the abominations of the Anglican episcopacy.[121] Once beyond the preface, Martin's indictments are again straitened by the controlled and unadventurous form of the numbered aphorism. The search for ligatures of the imagination, for fictional settings, for emotional as well as logical causality, is abandoned.[122] There is precious little space for the free play of mind that marks the satirist's early work.

The *Theses* concludes with an epilogue by Martin's young heir, yet another attempt to loosen the fetters of staid reason with a bygone humor. Martin Junior's inquiries as to the whereabouts of his father sport the rough-and-tumble style of the fool: "Speake then, good nuncles, have you closely murdered the gentleman in some of your prisons? Have you strangled him? Have you given him an Italian fig? Or, what have you done unto him? Have you choked him with a fat prebend or two? What? I trow, my father will swallow down no such pills."[123] The young and carefree Martin Junior reincarnates the attitudes and style that governed the satirist's first works. His jocular manner runs counter to the mounting force of the satirist's earnestness and the confessional quality that has come to supplant comic posturing and braggadocio. Martin Junior's revels are short-lived, however: a second, more punctilious son, Martin Senior, makes his stage entrance in *The Just Censure and Reproofe*, printed within a week of the *Theses*. Adding to the proliferation of voices of restraint in the later satires, Martin Senior vows to chastise "the rash and undiscreet headiness of the foolish youth," his younger brother.[124] Although he finds fault with the disorder of Martin Junior's proceedings, Martin Senior is not without praise for the stripling's heartiness of spirit and his heroic effort to master the intricacies of Martinist logic and the simplicity of Martinist plain style.[125] More learning and less imagination are the remedies Martin Senior prescribes for his brother's feverish state: "I promise thee, I think thou hast a pretty mother-wit of thine own; but, poor boy, thou wantest wisdom, withal, to govern they wit."[126] The dialogue of the two brothers is playful and mischievous. Martin Senior's solemn pronouncements capture perfectly the sanctimonious air of a still young man anxious to project maturity and sagacity. His supercilious reprimands mock with deadly accuracy the quibbling of those precise brethren who had divorced themselves from Martin's work for fear of losing dignity or ease.

Despite their humorous tone, the satires of Martin's children represent a significant shift toward a more painful 'pistle-making. The debate between naïve goodness and tutored wisdom boasts a long and fruitful history in nonconformist discourse: from the agon between the neophyte pilgrim and the mature Pierce in *Pierce the Ploughman's Crede* to the contests between religious novitiates and superiors in William Turner's dialogues.[127] These dialectical encounters not only chart the contours of a typical spiritual education but also examine the necessary interplay between the zeal of youth and the understanding of age. In a sense, what we find in these ancillary debates, embedded within the larger context of the soul's conflict with its enemies, is a struggle within the nonconformist sensibility itself. Although the embodiments of reason, control, experience, and wisdom typically triumph, they do so with a gesture of deference to the energy of the figures of youth. As Martin Senior says to his young sibling: You have wit and enthusiasm; now you must learn to use them with restraint. The overt division of the once integrated satirist of the Marprelate tracts into opposing voices of playful excess and earnest declamation, with an unquestionable bias toward the latter, is an act of retrenchment. Unexpectedly, the jovial manner of the earlier satires is being exposed, not as an illicit strategy but rather as a juvenile one.

The subplot engagement between the champions of two satiric strategies, one associated with Martin's earlier conduct and the other with his developing austerity, ends with the qualified victory of self-restraint over unbridled freedom. It is this emergence of a revalued earnestness that prepares us for the last act of what might be dubbed "The Satirist's Progress."[128] The final effort of the Martinists was *The Protestatyon*, printed in September 1589. This valedictory satire is imbued with an air of grim determination predicated upon the author's growing spiritual resolution in the face of a new, irresistible wave of persecution. It is a work written in blood, composed in the shadow of the Tower. That it is an ultimately cheerful piece is vivid testimony to the author's reanimated spirituality. Only one month prior to the appearance of *The Protestatyon*, the press had been seized and the printers arrested and tortured. With this sobering event in mind, Martin begins his last attempt to justify his course. "These events I confess do strike me and give me just cause to enter more narrowly into myself to see whether I be at peace with God, or no."[129] The confessional tone of these opening lines will be maintained throughout this solemn but never morbid exercise in spiritual self-examination. The fate of his allies prompts Martin to ponder once again the ancient link between nonconformity and martyrdom. In the early satires, Martin jests of the final price to be paid for an unwavering loyalty to the Lord; the rack and the flames are distant thoughts. By the time of *Hay Any Worke*, reminders of pursuit, arrest, and threatened death begin appearing with alarming frequency. The young Martinists are preoccupied with the idea of Christian sacrifice and (appropriate to their youth) with the fear it occasions. Witness their plaintive refrain, "If my father be dead." A more positive view of sacrifice emerges, however, in their homage to the martyrs of the Henrician and Marian periods. In *The Protestatyon*, the martyrdom of the past becomes the martyrdom of the present, and Martin passionately embraces its ideals. Hurling defiance at his tormentors, Martin insists that only by blood can the church grow to maturity, only by persecution can the soul come to fulfillment. "But tell them from me, that we fear not men, that can but kill the body; because we fear that God, who can cast both body and soul into unquenchable fire. And tell them also this. *That the more blood the Church loseth, the more life and blood it gets.*"[130] Martyrdom and the ritual conflict of intellect that precedes it form the true eucharist of nonconformity.

In the light of this moment of self-illumination, Martin looks back on his brief but intense career with a new perspective. His work has all been directed to the greater glory of God; he is not apologetic for either the content or the form of his assault on error. Yet he is aware that his serious joviality has not been the curative he intended. The original purposes of the satire, to convince the bishops of their need to reform and to embolden their opponents, have failed and faded in importance. What his work has achieved is a purpose decreed by God, not planned by himself. His struggle with the demons of misbelief has liberated his soul from its bondage, enabling him to participate in the body of true believers. The community he joins and to which he adds his testament of spiritual courage is one that transcends the labels of Puritan and Anglican: "[T]o be a right Martinist indeed is to be neither Brownist, Cooperist, Lambethist, Schismatic, Papist, Atheist, Traitor, nor yet Lord Bishop; but one that is at defiance with all men, whether he be French, Dutch, Spanish, Catercap, Pope or Popeling—so far forth as he is an enemy to God and her Majesty."[131]

The liberation of the church "from the great tyranny and bondage wherewith these tyrants [the bishops] do oppress the same" is not achieved, but the kind of spiritual liberation that comes with having fought the good fight is granted. And Marprelate's personal victory in publishing his evangelical "acts" is a common victory for saints living, dead, and yet to come. A feeling of peace and tranquillity permeates the cathartic last act of Martin's drama. Tension is not obliterated; it is transformed into a feeling of charged stasis. The new tone of the satirist is perhaps best exemplified by one of the few jests that the new Martin permits himself in *The Protestatyon*. My life, says Martin, is no cause of concern to me: "I have long ago set up my rest; making that account of it, as in standing against the enemies of God, and for the liberty of His Church, it is no value in my sight. My life in this cause shall be a gain to the Church, and no loss to myself, I know right well; and this is all the reckoning which, by the assistance of the Lord, I will make as long as I live, of all the torments they have devised for me."[132] The term to "set up my rest" is drawn from the card game of primero and means "to stake one's all upon an event; to resolve finally, come what will."[133] The quiet conjunction of the solemn resolution with the smiling reference to his former equation of 'pistle-making and gambling is indicative of Martin's transformation from a serious jester to a man whose gravity is delicately leavened by a still vibrant sense of the need for play, jest, and game. Noting that the married man is less secure from the pursuivant than the single man, Martin lays claim to the status of a bachelor: "[T]he very truth is that hitherto I never had wife nor child in all my life."[134] A marriage may be forthcoming, however, and he envisions the nuptials with the same fragile blend of moral seriousness and good humor. He would invite some good lord bishops to dance with him, he says, but as we all know there are no good lord bishops.[135]

Martin's prediction of his wedding day is a revealing moment. It marks his recognition that his satires are ultimately the product of a carefree bachelorhood. Now, after his brief sojourn in a world governed largely by the imagination and dedicated to the free pursuit of play, he is ready to move on. Like Milton's fallen Adam and Eve, he stands expectantly on the brink of a world of work and responsibility. Art has brought him thus far but can bring him no further. His recreation done, he is now ready to pursue his service to God with a new sense of purpose.[136] As if to mark the occasion, Martin begins to shed the multiple masks he had assumed in the previous satires. More and more, this last work moves away from fictionality and toward autobiography. The reader looks upon an actor who has stepped down from his stage. We are invited into the dressing room and are asked to watch the discarding of costume and the removal of makeup. Challenging the bishops to a public debate, Martin offers to appear unmasked: "I, who do now go under the name of Martin Marprelate, do offer personally to appear, and there to make myself known in open disputation, upon the danger, not only of my liberty, but also of my life; to maintain, against all our bishops, or any else whosoever that shall dare in any scholastical manner to take their parts, the cause of the Church government which is now in controversy betwixt me and our prelates."[137] Martin is an inveterate actor (as are all men who see life as a drama of true identity revealed) and so this claim to a naked honesty is, in some way, his final disguise, his last role. Nonetheless, the reader is as close to the man behind the mask as he will ever come within these satires. Beyond this verge lies the real world in which, the author insists, he must continue his struggle for redemption. And so the player exits, inviting his audience to join him at his wedding outside the boundaries of fiction.

Martin Marprelate's satire has long been admired for its technical brilliance. But even those critics who acknowledge the high seriousness that underlies its jests, fail to perceive its passionate rendering of the soul's search for Christian identity amid the noise and confusion of a fallen world. It is this pageant of the soul's awakening that transmutes silver to gold, that turns a glorious satire into a deeply moving exercise in spiritual self-discovery. Not until Milton do we find another such nonconformist mind growing so majestically to spiritual fruition through the medium of the displaced drama.

Epilogue

For the literary scholar of the Renaissance, the nonconformist will always be perceived as an enemy. The reformer's fear of ambiguity and verbal complexity, his distrust of imaginative experience, his anxiety over the easy and affective commerce between art and life—all brand him as the nemesis of those forces that helped create the literature of the English Renaissance. Yet, ironically, given his distaste for polyphony, the nonconformist provided a strong counterpoint to the chorus of English writers singing hosannas to their muses, thereby contributing to the depth and richness of their songs. The alarums raised by the reformers over the dangers of the artistic enterprise in general and the dramatic venture in particular may happily have failed to deter men like Spenser, Shakespeare, and Jonson from practicing their craft, but those warnings did compel them to examine their motives with greater rigor and urgency. To conduct that examination, each positioned within his work representative voices of Puritan dissent. Jonson mocked the Puritan demon into submission in his brilliant caricature of nonconformist hypocrisy, Zeal-of-the-land Busy;[1] Shakespeare likewise humiliated the puritanical Malvolio, but not before allowing him to raise disturbing questions as to the conduct of his tormentors;[2] Spenser, in the end, surrendered his vast imaginative universe to that ravager of art and order, the Blatant Beast.[3] All three poets felt obligated to respond to the charges leveled against their endeavors: their art is the more profound for having confronted the challenge.

As literary practitioners themselves, the nonconformists prove more interesting than fulfilling. For the average reader, the intrusive moral and doctrinal seriousness, accompanied by an imagination more forensic than playful, has a deadening effect. Of all their productions considered in this essay, only the brilliantly corrosive satires of Martin Marprelate justify the sustained interpretative effort traditionally devoted to more canonical works. Martin Marprelate is, no doubt, a worthy last act to any five-act play; he is, nonetheless, upstaged by the epilogue. In surrendering his preeminent place, Martin reminds us of the nonconformist predilection for the inconclusive conclusion, a terminus whose provisional nature beckons to a more satisfying sense of closure beyond. Neither the theory nor the practice of the nonconformist artist ends with Marprelate. In many of the finest Puritan sermons of the later Renaissance and in the allegorical pilgrimage of Bunyan's Christian, the reformers' inward theater of spiritual struggle continued.[4] And the true climax to this tradition occurs well outside the boundaries of the present study—in the life and art of Milton.

It is in Milton's varied creations that nonconformist theatricality finds its most notable expression. Milton's critics have commonly seen their subject's corpus as a belated contribution to the Christian humanism of the High Renaissance. It would be foolhardy to deny Milton's great debt to the central literary currents of the sixteenth and seventeenth centuries but equally misguided, I think, to ignore the less clearly perceived literary and religious obligations felt by the poet. Milton is both the heir and the chief glory of England's tradition of radical poetics, his writings and career mirroring those of his nonconformist ancestors. The affinities between his work and that of John Bale are especially pronounced. Like Bale, Milton exhibits a lifelong fascination with the drama—a fascination testified to in the earliest verse letters.[5] His experimentation with the form of the court masque in the early 1630s shows an artist already moved by the divided spirit of the nonconformist dissidents.

Comus is a drama closely allied to the work of the self-exiled playwrights of nonconformity. Like much of his later output, Milton's masque depicts a confrontation between a naïve saint and an experienced foe, the one an exponent of gracious dependency, the other a champion of demonic self-sufficiency. The centerpiece of the drama is a debate over whose subject, the nature of nature, Bale's characters had similarly contended in *Thre lawes*. The Lady's triumph bears all the earmarks of a nonconformist victory. Her immediate tool is reason, but it is the transcendent argument of faith that proves decisive.

> Thou art not fit to hear thyself convinc't;
> Yet should I try, the uncontrolled worth

> Of this pure cause would kindle my rapt spirits
> To such a flame of sacred vehemence,
> That dumb things would be mov'd to sympathize,
> And the brute Earth would lend her nerves, and shake,
> Till all thy magic structures rear'd so high,
> Were shatter'd into heaps o'er thy false head.[6]

That the final, iconoclastic act of liberation is achieved through divine agency rather than maiden virtue overthrows Comus's fallacious claims to spiritual self-containment; that the vehicle of God's grace is drawn from "the goodly exil'd traine of gods and goddesses" suggests Milton's as yet unbroken loyalty to the cultural imperatives of his youth. The subplot of *Comus*, the search of the two brothers for their lost sister, similarly echoes the motifs and themes of radical Protestant literature. The siblings' debate over man's capacity to extricate himself from evil recalls Bale's *Dialoge or Communycacyon* written for his two sons. As in the conflict between Marprelate's Martin Senior and Martin Junior and Turner's the Hunter and the Forester, the outcome favors the more experienced voice of understanding without dismissing the more youthful voice of zeal.

It is beyond the scope of this epilogue to examine in detail the nonconformist patterns evident in the entire Milton canon. Yet that such an investigation is both possible and desirable is clear. In form and temperament, Milton's prose is deeply indebted to the disputational writings of his Lollard and Puritan forbears. Milton himself contrasted prose, the cool medium of thought, with poetry, its heated counterpart, but, like most nonconformists, he combined them in hybrid modes of discourse. Whereas in his later career he wrote a cool poetry (that is, poetry heavily infused with the rational debate of doctrinal issues), in his earlier days he had preached revolution in a hot prose (that is, prose unexpectedly interrupted by metaphoric argumentation and prophetic declamation). The frequent self-advertisements that punctuate the controversial tracts are often passed over or else pillaged for biographical information. When viewed in the context of radical poetics, they move from the periphery to the center of Milton's disputational art. John Bale, too, had suspended his narratives of England's wars of truth to focus upon the holy faces of himself and his family peering forth from the surrounding gloom. The ritualistic celebration of the self in a work pretending to historical objectivity served a dual purpose. It underscored the conviction that even in the darkest days God continued to gather his chosen, and, of more importance, it authenticated the writer's claim to spiritual authority. Autobiographical testimony to a life lived in analogy to apostolic purity was the surest evidence that an artist practiced divine compilation and not demonic creation.

In the works of Milton's final phase the presence of a nonconformist artistic spirit is increasingly apparent. If the traditional sequence of the author's great triad of poems is accurate, we have a series of works that more and more obviously draw their substance from the dramatic imagination of radical dissent. Although *Paradise Lost* as a whole does not conform to the usual shape of the Puritan drama, many of its individual episodes do, as in the case of Abdiel's verbal duel with Satan in Book V.[7] It is this paradigm of saintly growth through successive temptations that informs the psychology and narrative structures of *Paradise Regained* and *Samson Agonistes*. Christ and Samson both discover their proper calling in a series of intellectual confrontations with their enemies. Satan, Dalila, Harapha of Gath, and even the kindly Manoa are all Miltonic embodiments of the cloistered imagination—men and women who expect to find truth and strength in themselves, not in their Lord. Only by battling their rivals' claims to spiritual authority do Christ and Samson transcend the limits of human reason and begin to play the true parts ordained for them by God. When Samson, "in the hour of his answering," declares to the Chorus, "Be of good courage, I begin to feel / Some rousing motions in me which dispose / To something extraordinary my thoughts,"[8] he is experiencing that cathartic moment of religious self-awareness that three centuries of nonconformist artists had sought to dramatize. With a dramatic formula inherited from his nonconformist ancestors, but an idiosyncratic genius all his own, Milton created in *Samson Agonistes* the most compelling of nonconformity's displaced dramas—a genuine trial of truth seen emerging in the soul's combat with spiritual insensibility.

Notes

1. Barbara K. Lewalski, *Protestant Poetics and the Seventeenth-Century Lyric* (Princeton: Princeton University Press, 1979); John N. King, *English Reformation Literature: The Tudor Origins of the Protestant Tradition* (Princeton: Princeton University Press, 1982); Janel Mueller, *The Native Tongue and the Word: Developments in English Prose Style, 1380–1580* (Chicago: University of Chicago Press, 1984). To these works may also be added Andrew D. Weiner, *Sir Philip Sidney and the Poetics of Protestantism: A Study of Contexts* (Minneapolis: University of Minnesota Press, 1978).

2. See Lewalski, pp. ixff., 13ff., where the author argues for "a consensus overarching the Anglican-Puritan divide" and for the existence of a "classic Protestant paradigm of sin and salvation" that informs all Protestant art. Janel Mueller's reliance in her study on "scripturalism," loosely defined as "a writer's absorption with the text of the Bible and with rendering its meaning in English—an absorption so intense as to mark the writer's own style with the impress of Biblical modes of expression" (p. 40), likewise assumes that the notion of "grounding" a text in scripture held the same connotations for thinkers of differing theological outlooks.

3. Patrick Collinson, *The Elizabethan Puritan Movement* (Berkeley: University of California Press, 1967). Also, by the same author, *The Religion of the Protestants* (Oxford: The Clarendon Press, 1982) and "A Comment: Concerning the Name Puritan," *Journal of Ecclessiastical History*, 31 (Oct. 1980), 483–88.

4. John F. H. New, *Anglican and Puritan: The Basis of Their Opposition, 1558–1640* (Stanford: Stanford University Press, 1964). Diametrically opposed to New's formulations is the equally reductionist vision of the Georges in which the Puritan all but ceases to exist. Charles H. and Katherine George, *The Protestant Mind of the English Reformation* (Princeton: Princeton University Press, 1961).

5. Elbert N. S. Thompson, *The Controversy between the Puritans and the Stage*, Yale Studies in English, No. 20 (New York: Henry Holt and Company, 1903), p. 9.

6. Peter Lake, *Moderate puritans and the Elizabethan Church* (Cambridge: Cambridge University Press, 1982).

7. See Collinson, *Religion of the Protestants*, pp. 189ff., and "A Comment," pp. 484ff. Lake follows Collinson (see pp. 279ff.) as does Weiner (see pp. 3–18).

8. For a good example of a well-informed challenge to traditional assumptions about the sharp division between Anglican and Puritan doctrine in the latter part of the sixteenth century see the forthcoming entry by Darryl J. Gless, "Nature and Grace," in *The Spenser Encyclopedia*, ed. A. C. Hamilton et al. (Toronto: University of Toronto Press, 1986?).

9. Lake, p. 280.

10. Perry Miller, *The New England Mind: The Seventeenth Century* (Boston: Beacon Press, 1961).

11. Thompson, *The Controversy between the Puritans and the Stage.*

12. Lawrence A. Sasek, *The Literary Temper of the English Puritans*, Louisiana State University Studies, Humanities Series, No. 9 (Baton Rouge: Louisiana State University Press, 1961), p. 92.

13. Among the prominent tracts are Clifford Davidson, ed., *A Middle English Treatise on the Playing of Miracles* (Washington, D.C.: University Press of America, Inc., 1981); John Northbrooke, *A Treatise against Dicing, Dancing, Plays, and Interludes*, ed. John P. Collier (London: The Shakespeare Society, 1843); Phillip Stubbes, *The Anatomy of Abuses*, ed. Frederick J. Furnivall (1879; rpt. Millwood, N.Y.: Kraus Reprint Co., 1965); Stephen Gosson, *Playes Confuted in Five Actions*, ed. Arthur Freeman (New York: Garland Publishing, Inc., 1972); John Rainolds, *The Overthrow of Stage-Playes*, 2d ed. (Oxford: Ihon Lichfield, 1629); William Prynne, *Histriomastix, The Players Scovrge or Actors Tragaedie* (London: Printed by E. A. and W. I. for Michael Sparke, 1633). Facsimiles of the complete antitheatrical tracts are now available in fifty volumes in Arthur Freeman, ed., *The English Stage: Attack & Defense, 1577–1730* (New York: Garland Publishing, Inc., 1972–74).

14. Stephen Greenblatt, *Renaissance Self-Fashioning from More to Shakespeare* (Chicago: University of Chicago Press, 1980).

15. William Ringler, "The First Phase of the Elizabethan Attack on the Stage, 1558–1579," *Huntington Library Quarterly*, No. 4 (1942), 391–418.

16. Anne Hudson, ed., *Selections from English Wycliffite Writings* (Cambridge: Cambridge University Press, 1978), pp. 187–89.

17. Davidson, pp. 46–55.

18. Northbrooke, p. xvii.

19. David Leverenz, *The Language of Puritan Feeling: An Exploration in Literature, Psychology, and Social History* (New Brunswick: Rutgers University Press, 1980), p. 32. In *The Antitheatrical Prejudice* (Berkeley: University of California Press, 1981), p. 85, Jonas Barish similarly dismisses the work's theatrical divisions as either a means for ordering the text or a running irony.

20. In considering Tyndale's strategies of self-definition, Greenblatt (pp. 76–79) recognizes that for dissidents the inquisitorial process constitutes a form of theater. He erroneously labels this a "demonic theater," failing to see how nonconformists viewed only the play of their enemies as demonic. Their own participation in such trials became the basis of their contrasting

"holy theater." Barish notes in "Plato's puritanism" the attempt to "aestheticize politics" (p. 14). In his discussion of the Puritans (pp. 165 ff.), he rightly argues that the reformers tended to see the world itself as theater. Behind the observation is the long-standing assertion that the pulpit and the stage constitute two competitive forms of theater.

21. Although nonconformist displaced drama originates in the dynamics of scholastic debate, its development runs directly counter to the pattern Joel B. Altman traces for the emergence of Elizabethan drama. *The Tudor Play of Mind: Rhetorical Inquiry and the Development of Elizabethan Drama* (Berkeley: University of California Press, 1978).

22. Russell Fraser, *The War against Poetry* (Princeton: Princeton University Press, 1970). Richard A. Lanham, *The Motives of Eloquence: Literary Rhetoric in the Renaissance* (New Haven: Yale University Press, 1976).

23. Fraser, p. 46.

24. Perhaps Fraser's curious assertion that the world of the Renaissance playwright is one of "impersonal dedication" and free of monetary considerations while that of the preacher is corrupted by "crasser considerations of mine and thine" (pp. 80, 76) is in itself an attempt to see the academy as a world unfettered and uncontaminated by capital.

25. Cited in n. 19 above.

26. See particularly Christopher Hill, *Society and Puritanism in Pre-Revolutionary England*, 2d ed. (New York: Schocken Books, 1967); Michael Walzer, *The Revolution of the Saints: A Study in the Origins of Radical Politics* (New York: Atheneum, 1969).

27. For a critical view of Foxe's reliability as an historian see John A. F. Thomson, "John Foxe and Some Sources for Lollard History: Notes for a Critical Appraisal," *Studies in Church History*, 2 (1963), 251–57. The influence of Foxe's attempts to minimize distinctions between Lollard and later reformed doctrine can be felt in most nineteenth-century treatments of Wyclif and his followers where the myth of "the morning star of the Reformation" was fostered. The best consideration of the confluence of native medieval reform and imported Lutheran doctrine can be found in the work of A. G. Dickens. See Dickens's *The English Reformation* (New York: Schocken Books, 1964) and *Lollards and Protestants in the Diocese of York, 1509–1558* (London: Oxford University Press, 1959).

28. The strongest argument for seeing Tyndale (and his disciple John Bale) as the direct doctrinal ancestors of the Elizabethan Puritan movement is presented by William A. Clebsch, *England's Earliest Protestants, 1520–1535* (New Haven: Yale University Press, 1964). Clebsch argues that Tyndale late in his career sketched the outlines of Puritan covenant theology. For the classification of Foxe as a moderate Puritan, see Leonard J. Trinterud, *Elizabethan Puritanism* (New York: Oxford University Press, 1971).

CHAPTER ONE

1. K. B. McFarlane, *Lancastrian Kings and Lollard Knights* (Oxford: Clarendon Press, 1972), pp. 90–91, 119. There is some evidence of Swinderby's activities as late as January 1392. For a sample of Swinderby's writings, see John Foxe, *The Acts and Monuments*, ed. Rev. George Townsend (New York: AMS Press, Inc., 1965), III, 107–30. For a Lollard pronouncement on the relative values of exile and martyrdom, see Thomas Arnold, ed., *Select English Works of John Wyclif* (Oxford: Clarendon Press, 1869), I, 207; hereafter cited as "Arnold."

2. McFarlane, *Lancastrian Kings*, pp. 200–206. For Clanvowe's writings, see V. J. Scattergood, ed., *The Works of Sir John Clanvowe* (Totowa, N.J.: D. S. Brewer, Ltd., and Rowman and Littlefield, 1975). Clanvowe's martial exploits would appear to violate the Lollard antipathy to war in general and crusading in particular. For Lollard views on the subject, see F. D. Matthew, ed., *The English Works of Wyclif Hitherto Unprinted*, Early English Text Society, O.S. 74, 2d ed. (1902; rpt. Millwood, N.Y.: Kraus Reprint Co., 1973), p. 91, hereafter cited as "Matthew"; Josiah Forshall, ed., *Remonstrance against Romish Corruptions in the Church* (London: Longman, Brown, Green and Longmans, 1851), pp. 60ff.

3. C. W. Dugmore, *The Mass and the English Reformers* (London: Macmillan & Co., Ltd., 1958), pp. 52–55.

4. The relationship between Wyclif's theology and Lollardy continues to be a matter of controversy. See K. B. MacFarlane, *John Wycliffe and the Beginnings of English Nonconformity* (London: English Universities Press, 1952), pp. 88ff.; Gordon Leff, *Heresy in the Later Middle Ages* (Manchester: Manchester University Press, 1967), II, 559ff. Anne Hudson has argued persuasively from a wealth of documentary evidence for a significant and continuous debt among Lollards to Wyclif's teachings. See Hudson, *Selections*, pp. 8–10; and Hudson, "A Lollard Compilation and the Dissemination of Wycliffite Thought," *Journal of Theological Studies*, N.S., 23 (1972), 65–81.

5. W. A. Pantin, *The English Church in the Fourteenth Century* (Cambridge: Cambridge University Press, 1955), pp. 132–33. For evidence of the Lollard tendency toward egocentricity and anti-intellectualism, see Matthew, pp. 422, 427–28; Arnold, I, 310.

6. For a discussion of the contemporary association of Lollardy and rebellion, see M. E. Aston, "Lollardy and Sedition 1381–1431," *Past and Present*, 17 (1960), 5–7.

7. John A. F. Thomson, *The Later Lollards: 1414–1520* (Oxford: Oxford University Press, 1965), pp. 67ff.

8. Hudson, *Selections*, p. 10. See also Norman P. Tanner, ed., *Heresy Trials in the Diocese of Norwich, 1428–1431*, Camden Fourth Series, No. 20 (London: Royal Historical Society, 1977), p. 30.

9. On the codification of examination questions, see Anne Hudson, "The Examination of Lollards," *Bulletin of the Institute of Historical Research*, 46, No. 114 (1973), 145–59.

10. Reginald Pecock, *The Repressor of Over Much Blaming of the Clergy*, ed. Churchill Babington, 2 vols. (London: Longman, Green, Longman, and Roberts, 1860).

11. The term "known men" became a common synonym for Lollard. See John Fines, "Heresy Trials in the Diocese of Coventry and Lichfield, 1511–1512," *Journal of Ecclesiastical History*, 14 (1963), 166; and Foxe, IV, 214, 218.

12. Hudson, *Selections*, p. 187.

13. Davidson.

14. Margaret Deanesly, *The Lollard Bible* (1920; rpt. Cambridge: Cambridge University Press, 1966), p. 456.

15. Dom Gregory Dix, *The Shape of the Liturgy*, 2d ed. (Westminster: Dacre Press, 1945).

16. For two representative views on the Eucharist, see Hudson, *Selections*, pp. 110–15; Forshall, *Remonstrance*, pp. 115–16. The author of *A Tretise of Miraclis Pleying* is particularly conservative in his views of the sacraments (Davidson, pp. 43ff.).

17. Tanner, pp. 26–29. See Greenblatt, pp. 85–86. The supremacy of the book in self-fashioning precedes the work of Tyndale and his contemporaries.

18. For the place of the Bible in the Middle Ages, see Beryl Smalley, *The Study of the Bible in the Middle Ages* (Oxford : Basil Blackwell, 1952). For the centrality of scripture in Wycliffite theology, see Michael Hurley, S.J., "'Scriptura sola': Wyclif and His Critics," *Traditio*, 16 (1960), 275–352. Beryl Smalley has argued persuasively for the Bible as Wyclif's "refuge against anarchy" in "The Bible and Eternity: John Wyclif's Dilemma," *Journal of the Warburg and Courtauld Institutes*, 27 (1964), 75ff.

19. Anne Hudson, ed., *English Wycliffite Sermons* (Oxford: Clarendon Press, 1983), I, 465; British Library MS Cotton Titus D.V., fol. 15r.

20. Woodburn O. Ross, ed., *Middle English Sermons*, Early English Text Society, O.S. 209 (Oxford: Oxford University Press, 1940), p. 224.

21. "To Sir John Oldcastle," in Frederick J. Furnivall, ed., *Hoccleve's Works: Minor Poems*, Early English Text Society, E.S. 61 (London: Kegan Paul, Trench, Trubner and Co., 1892), p. 13.

22. Furnivall, "To Sir John Oldcastle," p. 13.

23. Margaret Aston, *Lollards and Reformers: Images and Literacy in Late Medieval Religion* (London: The Humbledon Press, 1984), pp. 101–33, 193–217; see also Anne Hudson, "Some Aspects of Lollard Book Production," *Studies in Church History*, 9 (1972), 148.

24. Hudson, *Sermons*, I, 465; see also Hudson, *Selections*, p. 115.

25. Matthew, p. 37.

26. Matthew, p. 38; see also British Library MS Harley 1203, fol. 95v.

27. Matthew, p. 38.

28. Deanesly, p. 456.

29. Arnold, I, 233.

30. Josiah Forshall and Frederic Madden, eds., *The Holy Bible, Made from the Latin Vulgate by John Wycliffe and His Followers* (Oxford: Oxford University Press, 1850), I, 48–49.

31. Lillian M. Swinburn, ed., *The Lanterne of Liȝt*, Early English Text Society, O.S. 151 (London: Kegan Paul, Trench, Trubner and Co., 1917), p. 63. See also Hudson, *Sermons*, I, 466; MS Cotton Titus D.V., fol. 38r. The conviction that scripture is self-authenticating (*autopistos*), generating its own light for interpretation, is central to all nonconformist thought. For a discussion of Renaissance manifestations, see John R. Knott, Jr., *The Sword of the Spirit: Puritan Responses to the Bible* (Chicago: University of Chicago Press, 1980), pp. 32–38.

32. Thomas F. Simmons and Henry E. Nolloth, eds., *The Lay Folks' Catechism*, Early English Text Society, O.S. 118 (1901; rpt. Millwood, N.Y.: Kraus Reprint Co., 1972).

33. G. R. Owst, *Literature and Pulpit in Medieval England* (Cambridge: Cambridge University Press, 1933); John A. Yunck, *The Lineage of Lady Meed*, Publications in Mediaeval Studies, No. 17 (Notre Dame: University of Notre Dame Press, 1963). See also Margaret Aston's discussion of the problem in *Lollards and Reformers*, pp. 187–89.

34. Ross, *Sermons*, p. 281.

35. O. B. Hardison, Jr., *Christian Rite and Christian Drama in the Middle Ages* (Baltimore: The Johns Hopkins Press, 1969), pp. 35–79. For the importance of the priest's role in the Eucharist, see Thomas F. Simmons, ed., *The Lay Folks' Mass Book*, Early English Text Society, O.S. 71 (1879; rpt. London: Oxford University Press, 1968), p. 139.

36. Hawise Moone offers a characteristic Lollard corollary of this assertion: "that he oonly that is moost holy and moost perfit in lyvng in erthe is verry pope, and these singemasses that be cleped prestes ben no prestes, but they be lecherous and covetouse men and fals deceyvours of the puple . . ." Tanner, p. 141.

37. For Lollard views on confession, see Matthew, pp. 327ff.; Hudson, *Sermons*, I, 276–77; Arnold, III, 253ff. For Lollard views on excommunication, see James H. Todd, ed., *An Apology for Lollard Doctrines*, The Camden Society (London: John Bowyer Nichols and Son, 1842), pp. 13–28.

38. Tanner, pp. 12, 20–21.

39. For a discussion of Lollard wills, see McFarlane, *Lancastrian Kings*, pp. 207–20.

40. Lionel Rothkrug has recently argued that the regional divisions between reformation and orthodoxy in Europe may be traced to the absence or

presence respectively of strong local traditions of relic worship. "Religious Practices and Collective Perceptions: Hidden Homologies in the Renaissance and Reformation," *Historical Reflections,* 7 (1980).

41. Matthew, p. 478; see also Arnold, I, 235.

42. Tanner, p. 140. For further evidence of the household as church, see MS Cotton Titus D.V., fols. 32v–33r; Bodleian MS Douce 53, fols. 22v–23r; Fines, pp. 165–66; A. K. McHardy, "Bishop Buckingham and the Lollards of the Lincoln Diocese," *Studies in Church History,* 9 (1972), 141.

43. Matthew, p. 469. See also Arnold, I, 250–51; British Library MS Egerton 2820, fol. 91v.

44. Hudson, *Sermons,* I, 466.

45. Arnold, III, 437.

46. Hudson, *Sermons,* I, 474; see also Hudson, *Sermons,* I, 444–45.

47. Swinburn, p. 86; see also Hudson, *Sermons,* I, 581–82.

48. For a discussion of late medieval views on deathbed confessions, see Thomas N. Tentler, *Sin and Confession on the Eve of the Reformation* (Princeton: Princeton University Press, 1977), pp. 6–10.

49. Ross, *Sermons,* p. 130; see also Owst, *Literature and Pulpit,* p. 168.

50. Ross, *Sermons,* p. 127.

51. Aston, *Lollards and Reformers,* pp. 102–5.

52. Ross, *Sermons,* p. 128.

53. Davidson, p. 36.

54. Hudson, *Sermons,* I, 611–12. See also MS Douce 53, fol. 32r: "Loue and drede ben two ӡatis of lyf . . ."

55. Forshall, *Remonstrance,* pp. 52–53. See also Matthew, p. 82; and Hudson, *Sermons,* I, 471.

56. Matthew, p. 339; see also Matthew, pp. 422ff.

57. Hudson, *Sermons,* I, 459; Arnold, I, 238.

58. For an extreme example, see P. L. Heyworth, ed., *Jack Upland, Friar Daw's Reply and Upland's Rejoinder* (Oxford: Oxford University Press, 1968), p. 106; see also Foxe, III, 282.

59. Hudson, *Sermons,* I, 446. For a consideration of man's search for the miraculous, see Bodleian MS Eng. th. f. 39, fols. 41v–42r; MS Egerton 2820, fol. 18v.

60. Donald Jay Grout, *A History of Western Music,* 2d ed. (New York: W. W. Norton and Company, Inc., 1973), pp. 127–28.

61. Matthew, p. 169.

62. Matthew, p. 191.

63. Matthew, p. 192.

64. Arnold, III, 155.

65. Arnold, III, 482; see also Arnold, II, 73. The Wycliffite version of Richard Rolle's *Commentary on the Psalms* carefully distinguishes between "hiӡ curious syngynge in wis of lypis to stonye [astonish] deuoute mens deuo-

cciouns & delite foolis in vanyte" and the "inward" singing of the apostles who "so acoordyngli all in a tune: songen moost plesingli to god in doinge her office." Bodleian MS 288, fol. 96v.

66. Forshall and Madden, *Holy Bible*, I, 41.

67. Forshall and Madden, *Holy Bible*, I, 43ff.

68. Forshall and Madden, *Holy Bible*, I, 43.

69. Forshall and Madden, *Holy Bible*, I, 44–45.

70. Augustine, *On Christian Doctrine*, trans. D. W. Robertson, Jr., The Library of Liberal Arts (Indianapolis: Bobbs-Merrill Co., Inc., 1958), pp. 88–89.

71. Arnold, I, 207.

72. Forshall and Madden, *Holy Bible*, I, 52.

73. Thomson, *Later Lollards*, pp. 244–45.

74. Deanesly, pp. 451–52. For Wyclif's five requirements for proper study of the Bible, see Hurley, pp. 295–96.

75. For the Bible as a holy object of veneration, see Aston, *Lollards and Reformers*, pp. 108–10; for the Bible as an emanation of God realized in words, see Smalley, "The Bible and Eternity," pp. 83–84.

76. Hudson, *Sermons*, I, 502.

77. Arnold, III, 137.

78. Arnold, III, 437.

79. Heyworth, *Upland*, pp. 76–77.

80. Matthew, p. 56.

81. Arnold, III, 123.

82. Tanner, pp. 18, 57, 58. See also Hudson, *Selections*, pp. 99ff.; and Hurley, p. 289.

83. See Michael Wilks's consideration of the Lollard attempt "to emulate the righteousness of their ideal identities," which he links to the fundamentally Platonic assumptions of Wyclif's politics. "Reformatio Regni: Wyclif and Hus as Leaders of Religious Protest Movements," *Studies in Church History*, 9 (1972), 119ff.

84. Scattergood, *Clanvowe*, p. 70.

85. For a discussion of Wyclif's views on the church, see Leff, pp. 516–44.

86. Swinburn, pp. 6ff.

87. It is not surprising that Janel Mueller—having accepted the purely rational Wycliffite—should speak of "the intellectual and verbal confidence that pervades" Lollard preaching (p. 48).

88. The author of an exposition of Matthew 24 offers three rules by which the Lollard may distinguish the true from the false prophet: by their grounding; by their antipathy to the pope; and by their hostility to the mendicant orders. MS Harley 1203, fol. 101v; see also MS Egerton 2820, fol. 102r.

89. Heyworth, *Upland*, p. 84.

90. Leff, pp. 500–510. See also Wilks's discussion of the Wycliffite "theme of double substances," in his "Reformatio Regni," pp. 112–13.

91. The reformers' response to images has been a major focus for Lollard studies for some time. John Phillips's *The Reformation of Images: Destruction of Art in England, 1535–1660* (Berkeley: University of California Press, 1973) is mainly concerned with later manifestations of iconoclasm but includes a brief survey of Lollard attitudes. In "Lollards and Images: The Defense of Religious Art in Later Medieval England," *Journal of the History of Ideas*, 34 (1973), 27–50, W. R. Jones discusses the Lollards' "persistent confusion of ethics with aesthetics." Margaret Aston's chapter on "Lollards and Images" in her *Lollards and Reformers*, pp. 135–92, is the most useful and comprehensive study of the problem; her distinctions between various strains of Lollard belief concerning images are particularly useful.

92. Hudson, *Sermons*, I, 352. See also MS Cotton Titus D.V., fol. 21r, where the author typically links orthodox views of the sacrament (signs without substance) to orthodox hypocrisy (words without deeds).

93. Malcolm Mackenzie Ross, *Poetry and Dogma: The Transfiguration of Eucharistic Symbols in Seventeenth-Century Poetry* (New Brunswick: Rutgers University Press, 1954). Ross's speculations on the dogmatic roots of rhetorical devices remain useful if his dismissal of Protestant sacramentalism does not.

94. Arnold, III, pp. 273–74.

95. Matthew, p. 183. See also Arnold, II, 103, 109; and Pantin, pp. 82–83.

96. Matthew, pp. 174, 348; Arnold, I, 196; and MS Douce 53, fol. 2v–3r.

97. Forshall and Madden, *Holy Bible*, I, 35.

98. Forshall and Madden, *Holy Bible*, I, 35.

99. Matthew, p. 302; see also Matthew, p. 315. See MS Eng. th. f. 39, fol. 2r, for a similar account of God's concern with fixed symbols and the idolatry they encourage.

100. The Lollard insistence that the poor priests avoid permanent office is another example of the reformer's fear of the fixed and immutable; see Matthew, p. 252.

101. Arnold, III, 173.

102. For an example of a Lollard "metaphor chain," see Matthew, p. 307.

103. Hudson, *Selections*, p. 83.

104. Peggy Ann Knapp, *The Style of John Wyclif's English Sermons* (The Hague: Mouton, 1977), p. 93.

105. J. W. H. Atkins, *English Literary Criticism: The Medieval Phase* (London: Methuen and Co., Ltd., 1952), pp. 147–51.

106. See Greenblatt (pp. 9ff.) for a discussion of the need to either discover or invent a hostile other as an element in Renaissance self-fashioning. Greenblatt (pp. 65–66) sees the process as extending to both Catholic and Protestants. I contend that the process exerts a stronger attraction on the nonconformist, whose often violent rejection of traditional authority heightened his anxiety about the ultimate sources of authentic vision.

107. McFarlane, *John Wyclif*, p. 83; Leff, p. 527. Both authors link Wycliffite

beliefs to those of the Spiritual Franciscans. For evidence of Lollard ambivalence toward the mendicants, see "The Rule and Testament of St. Francis" in Matthew, pp. 40–51.

108. Aston, "Lollardy and Sedition," pp. 13–14.

109. Tanner, p. 48. Foxe's translation reads: "Unto whom Margery answered, that she had talked with the said friar, rebuking him because he did beg, saying, that it was no alms to give him any good thing, except he would leave his habit, and go to the plough, and so he should please God more, than following the life of some of those friars." Foxe, III, 595.

110. The two poems appear in Rossell Hope Robbins, ed., *Historical Poems of the Fourteenth and Fifteenth Centuries* (New York: Columbia University Press, 1959), pp. 166–68.

111. See Anne Hudson's description of four currently unpublished debates in dialogue: "A Lollard Quaternion," *The Review of English Studies*, 22 (1971), 435–42. Ms. Hudson notes (pp. 437–38): "None of the texts printed so far are in this form, though some, with their regular alternation of the views of the orthodox church followed by the objections of 'true men,' resemble the type."

112. MS Egerton 2820, fol. 102v.

113. MS Egerton 2820, fol. 116r.

114. MS Egerton 2820, fol. 116v.

115. Arnold, III, 426; see also the discussion of examinations in MS Cotton Titus D.V., fols. 29r–30r.

116. Arnold, III, 427.

117. MS Cotton Titus D.V., fols. 29r–30r. The customary disclaimers by Lollard preachers of definitive readings of scriptural passages are similiar in content, tone, and purpose. See MS Harley 1203, fol. 91r; see also Walter Brute's disclaimer in Foxe, III, 136.

118. Hudson, *Selections*, p. 20.

119. Tentler has argued (pp. 349ff.) that having destroyed orthodox confession, the Reformation never reached a consensus on a substitute form of discipline and consolation. It is my belief that radical Protestants found their substitute in the examination.

120. Bodleian MS Rawlinson C. 208, fol. 6v. A modern, but often inaccurate, version of Thorpe's work is available: "The Examination of William Thorpe," in Alfred W. Pollard, ed., *Fifteenth-Century Prose and Verse* (New York: E. P. Dutton and Co., 1903), p. 106. Future references to Thorpe's examination will include both manuscript and text ("Pollard") citations. Although often confused with "oppose," "appose" maintains its distinct meaning—to interrogate, examine, or pose hard questions—into the seventeenth century.

121. The distinction is made in MS Eng. th. f. 39, fols. 10v–11r.

122. Walter Brute in his responses to the inquiries of the bishop of Hereford recorded distrust of miracles as a hallmark of the servants of Christ. Foxe, III, 157–58.

123. MS Eng. th. f. 39, fols. 11r-v; for further evidence of the Lollard tendency to rationalize the miraculous, see British Library MS Additional 24.202, fol. 21v.

124. MS Cotton Titus D.V., fols. 57r-v.

CHAPTER TWO

1. Anne Hudson (*Selections*, pp. 187–88) has argued that "the subject of miracle plays is not one that seems to have attracted much attention from the Lollards"; both the *Floretum* and the *Rosarium* contain only brief antitheatrical entries under "histrio." The most interesting commentaries on the *Tretise* include Rosemary Woolf, *The English Mystery Plays* (London: Routledge and Kegan Paul, 1972), pp. 77–101; Davidson, pp. 1–21; and V. A. Kolve, *The Play Called Corpus Christi* (Stanford: Stanford University Press, 1966), pp. 124–49.

2. Some Lollards appear to have regarded the guilds (responsible for the mounting of the popular cycle plays) as a secular version of the religious orders. In *þe Grete Sentence of Curs Expouned* members of the guilds are likened to both mendicants and possessioners: conspirators "aȝenst þe comyn fraternyte of Crist, þat alle Cristene men token in here cristendom, and aȝenst comyn charite and comyn profit of Cristene men." Arnold, III, 333.

3. Pantin, pp. 253ff.

4. Dix, pp. 594ff.; see also Hardison, pp. 77ff.

5. The links between vernacular drama and the church liturgy have long occupied the attention of medieval scholars beginning with Karl Young, *The Drama of the Medieval Church*, 2 vols. (Oxford: Clarendon Press, 1933). Other documents in the controversy include Hardison; Clifford C. Flanigan, "The Roman Rite and the Origins of the Liturgical Drama," *University of Toronto Quarterly*, 42 (1974), 263–84; Kolve, *The Play Called Corpus Christi*; and Stanley J. Kahrl, *Traditions of Medieval English Drama* (London: Hutchinson University Library, 1974).

6. On the intimate connections between the medieval pulpit and stage, see Owst, *Literature and Pulpit*, pp. 473–544. Expositors are most prominent in the Ludus Coventriae or N-town cycle but may also be found in more "realistic" works such as the Brome *Abraham and Isaac*.

7. R. M. Lumiansky and David Mills, eds., *The Chester Mystery Cycle*, Early English Text Society, S.S. 3 (London: Oxford University Press, 1974), p. 142.

8. Throughout Lollard writing one encounters the fear of mingling, as in the discussion of "þis mengid lawe" (the collapse of the distinction between spiritual and temporal lordship) in MS Egerton 2820, fol. 45v.

9. Robbins, p. 163.

10. Davidson, pp. 12–14.

11. Davidson, p. 42. See Greenblatt's argument (p. 27) concerning the way in which theater demystifies by exposing as illusion the reality to which it pays tribute.

12. Matthew, p. 206

13. Kolve, *The Play Called Corpus Christi*, pp. 13–21.

14. See Clifford Davidson's argument (pp. 14–15) for the particular Lollard animosity toward heightened verisimilitude which he associates with both nominalism and Franciscanism.

15. Davidson, p. 40.

16. Deanesly, p. 456.

17. Hudson, *Sermons*, I, 426.

18. Hudson, *Selections*, p. 20.

19. For a Lollard's own account of his examination, see MS Rawlinson C. 208.

20. Thomson, *Later Lollards*, p. 229; see also Hudson, "Examination," pp. 147ff.

21. Swinburn, p. 78.

22. "On the Council of London" in Thomas Wright, ed., *Political Poems and Songs Relating to English History* (London: Longman, Green, Longman, and Roberts, 1859), I, 253–63.

23. "Hic amici facti sunt Herodes et Pilatus." "On the Council of London," p. 259. For a similar comparison, see MS Egerton 2820, fols. 30v–31v.

24. "Omnibus impatiens, et nimis elatus." "On the Council of London," p. 261.

25. See Matt. 26:65; Mark 14:63. For examples of mad tyrants from the mystery cycles, see Richard Beadle, ed., *The York Plays* (London: Edward Arnold, 1982), pp. 270–71; A. C. Cawley, ed., *The Wakefield Pageants in the Towneley Cycle* (Manchester: Manchester University Press, 1958), pp. 81ff.; K. S. Block, ed., *Ludus Coventriae or The Plaie called Corpus Christi*, Early English Text Society, E.S. 120 (1922; rpt. London: Oxford University Press, 1974), p. 276.

26. McFarlane, *John Wyclif*, p. 59; McFarlane, *Lancastrian Kings*, p. 222. See also Joseph Dahmus, *William Courtenay: Archbishop of Canterbury, 1381–1396* (University Park: Pennsylvania State University Press, 1966), pp. 31–106; and Margaret Aston, *Thomas Arundel: A Study of Church Life in the Reign of Richard II* (Oxford: Clarendon Press, 1967), pp. 320–35.

27. For Foxe's apology for these "but newly-trained soldiers in God's field," see Foxe, III, 588. For an assessment of Foxe's reliability as a historian of

Lollardy, see Thomson, "John Foxe and Some Sources for Lollard History."

28. The commonly held view that Philip Repingdon became an avid persecutor of Lollard heretics has been disputed by Hudson, *Selections*, p. 158.

29. For a brief discussion of Thorpe's career, see McFarlane, *John Wyclif*, pp. 137ff. For a history of the manuscripts and printed texts of Thorpe's work, see Hudson, *Selections*, pp. 155–56.

30. Foxe, IV, 235, 238, 259, 683, 685. The work was grouped among a series of Lutheran texts prohibited by royal proclamation under Henry VIII (IV, 676–79); two other traditionally suspect texts were *Wyclif's Wicket* and another work attributed to Thorpe, *The ABC against the pride of the Clergy*. Foxe claims that he found the *"ABC"* attributed to Thorpe in an "old register" (III, 249).

31. Henry Christmas, ed., *Select Works of John Bale*, The Parker Society (Cambridge: Cambridge University Press, 1849), p. 241. Greenblatt (pp. 76–78) similarly argues that the dissidents regarded "the inquisitorial process as theater."

32. Arundel is named "þe grettist enimy þat crist haþ in yngland" in MS Cotton Titus D.V., fol. 13v.

33. For an example of the tyrant-minion relationship, see Cawley, pp. 78–90.

34. MS Rawlinson C. 208, fol. 89r; Pollard, p. 165.

35. MS Rawlinson C. 208, fols. 65r-v; Pollard, p. 147.

36. MS Rawlinson C. 208, fol. 82r; Pollard, p. 160.

37. MS Rawlinson C. 208, fols. 84r-v; Pollard, p. 162.

38. MS Rawlinson C. 208, fols. 18r-v, 19r; Pollard, pp. 4–15. It is emblematic of the nonconformist devotion to the book that so often the intervention of the Holy Spirit in heresy trials is occasioned by a problem of textual interpretation and witnessed by a hermeneutic miracle.

39. MS Rawlinson C. 208, fols. 70v–71r; Pollard, pp. 151–52. In the devil's party view, of course, Thorpe's "progress" is seen as regressive: "[S]ere þe lengir þat ȝe appose him, þe more weyward he is." MS Rawlinson C. 208, fol. 67v; Pollard, p. 149.

40. MS Rawlinson C. 208, fol. 6v; Pollard, pp. 105–106.

41. It is instructive that Foxe in advertising the utility of studying Thorpe's *Examination* envisions a mirrored response from the reader. Just as Thorpe's enlightenment proceeds from ratiocination and inspiration, so the reader will be enlightened: first learning then marveling, first hearing then beholding. "[T]hou shalt have, good reader, both *to learn and to marvel*: to learn, in that thou shalt *hear truth discoursed and discussed, with the contrary reasons of the adversary dissolved*; to marvel, for thou shalt *behold here in this man, the marvellous force and strength of the Lord's might, spirit, and grace*, working and fighting in his soldiers, and also speaking in their mouths, according to the word of his promise, Luke xxi." (Emphasis added.) Foxe, III, 249.

42. MS Rawlinson C. 208, fols. 90r-v; Pollard, p. 166.

43. MS Rawlinson C. 208, fols. 90v–91r; Pollard, p. 167.

44. Tanner, p. 44; Foxe translates: ". . . saying, moreover, in English: 'Lewd wrights of stocks hew and form such crosses and images, and, after that, lewd painters gleer them with colours. And if you desire so much to see the true cross of Christ, I will show it you at home in your own house.' Which this deponent being desirous to see, the said Margery, stretching out her arms abroad, said to this deponent: 'This is the true cross of Christ, and this cross thou oughtest and mayest every day behold and worship in thine own house; and therefore it is but vain to run to the church, to worship dead crosses and images.'" Foxe, III, 594. See also MS 288, fol. 96v, where men are said to please God most by "acros puttynge hem silf ouertwert [athwart] to þe world: & þe world to hem."

45. MS Rawlinson C. 208, fol. 91r; Pollard, p. 167. Thorpe discusses the benefits of recording his examination in his prologue. MS Rawlinson C. 208, fols. 2v–3r; Pollard, pp. 102–3.

46. In his *Shakespearean Iconoclasm* (Berkeley: University of California Press, 1985), pp. 1–75, James R. Siemon provides an especially useful discussion of iconoclasm and its implications for theatrical representation. In suggesting that historicity is the inevitable concomitant of iconoclasm (pp. 66–72), however, he fails to recognize the paradox at the heart of dissident thinking. Although it is true that nonconformists routinely declare their loyalty to the historical, it is also true that their pursuit of the typical led them to a high valuation of the figural. Beryl Smalley ("The Bible and Eternity," pp. 75ff.) argues persuasively that it is possible to view the early nonconformists as being essentially ahistorical. Hence it is that even the most extreme reformers found themselves marginally drawn to the creation of "images, similes, emblems, allegories, and dramas" (Siemon, p. 57).

47. For one view on the historical accuracy of Thorpe's work, see Hudson, *Selections*, pp. 155–56.

48. MS Rawlinson C. 208, fols. 40r–v; Pollard, p. 130. The preference for hearing over sight is a hallmark of Puritan as well as Lollard thought; see Aston, *Lollards and Reformers*, pp. 183–84.

49. See Altman's useful discussion (pp. 43–45 especially) of the emergence of complex Elizabeth drama from a reversal of the nonconformist pattern, i.e., from universal to particular, from thesis to hypothesis.

50. MS Rawlinson C. 208, fol. 28v; Pollard, p. 121.

51. Hardison provides a helpful summary of the long-standing debate over the constitutive elements of the drama. His recapitulation has specific reference to the "drama of the mass" but is readily applicable to the issues raised here. See in particular his treatment of identification or impersonation in drama (pp. 32ff.). Greenblatt argues erroneously that Thorpe's quest for refuge in the authority of Christ resembles More's in its "simultaneous affir-

mation and effacement of personal identity" (p. 77). The nonconformist seeks congruity not convergence.

52. MS Rawlinson C. 208, fols. 53r–54r; Pollard, pp. 138–39. A similar discussion of the use of the saint's life as modeled on the life of Christ and the apostles may be found in William Tyndale, *An Answer to Sir Thomas More's Dialogue*, ed. Henry Walter, The Parker Society (Cambridge: Cambridge University Press, 1850), p. 59.

53. MS Egerton 2820, fols. 75v–76r.

54. Yunck, p. 111. For general histories of medieval satire, see Samuel Marion Tucker, *Verse-Satire in England before the Renaissance* (New York: Columbia University Press, 1908); John Peter, *Complaint and Satire in Early English Literature* (Oxford: Clarendon Press, 1956); and A. R. Heiserman, *Skelton and Satire* (Chicago: University of Chicago Press, 1961).

55. For two attacks on Lollardy's "newfangledness," see Furnivall, "To Sir John Oldcastle," p. 13; Heyworth, *Friar Daw's Reply*, ll. 23–26, 71–74, 893ff.

56. For Bale's and Foxe's roles as Protestant hagiographers, see Leslie P. Fairfield, *John Bale: Mythmaker for the English Reformation* (West Lafayette: Purdue University Press, 1976) and William Haller, *The Elect Nation: The Meaning and Relevance of Foxe's Book of Martyrs* (New York: Harper and Row, 1963).

57. Matthew, pp. 374, 376–79; Heyworth, *Jack Upland*, ll. 101–6.

58. For a general study of poetry and religion in the fifteenth century, see V. J. Scattergood, *Politics and Poetry in the Fifteenth Century* (New York: Barnes and Noble, 1972), pp. 218–63.

59. In the absence of a well-defined opposition against which it might play out the dilemma of its internal contradictions, nonconformity tended to break down into its constituent elements, producing arminianism and antinomianism. Such would be the case in the New World and, ironically, in an England made unsafe by Cromwell's victories. For discussions of the development of extremist factions within the nonconformist camp in the New World and in England, see David D. Hall, *The Antinomian Controversy, 1636–1638* (Middletown: Wesleyan University Press, 1968), and Christopher Hill, *The World Turned Upside Down* (New York: The Viking Press, 1972).

60. Heyworth, *Jack Upland*, ll. 101ff.

61. Heyworth, *Jack Upland*, ll. 180–81, 298–306.

62. Heyworth, *Jack Upland*, ll. 177–79.

63. W. W. Skeat, ed., *Pierce the Ploughman's Crede*, Early English Text Society (London: N. Trubner and Company, 1873), ll. 744–53.

64. The Lollards, as we have witnessed, were criticized for their desire to learn to read and write. Margaret Aston has pointed out that that desire was itself a challenge to an orthodox establishment "geared to a world in which literacy was a preserve of the minority, and the minority were churchmen"

(*Lollards and Reformers*, p. 105). Thus, in the passage quoted from the *Crede*, the Lollard author arraigns that friar who rises by learning of books and becoming a writer on the same charges for which he himself might be indicted.

65. For the tradition of the rude satirist, see Alvin Kernan, *The Cankered Muse: Satire of the English Renaissance*, Yale Studies in English, No. 142 (New Haven: Yale University Press, 1959), pp. 14–30. For Langland's reputation as a radical during the Edwardian Reformation, see King, pp. 323ff. Foxe (IV, 248ff.) attributed *The Plowman's Tale* to Chaucer, insisting that Chaucer was himself a Lollard. Although Chaucer presumably did not embrace Lollard principles, he has been connected by McFarlane with the Lollard knights of Richard's court. For a discussion of this courtly circle, see McFarlane, *Lancastrian Kings*, pp. 182–85.

66. Heyworth, *Friar Daw's Reply*, ll. 40–45.

67. Ross, *Sermons*, p. 307.

68. Hudson, *Sermons*, I, 402. See 1 Kings 18:27; 2 Cor. 12:13.

69. Robbins, "The Layman's Complaint" and "The Friar's Answer," pp. 166–68.

70. "The Friar's Answer," ll. 1–4.

71. "The Friar's Answer," ll. 21–28.

72. "The Layman's Complaint," ll. 1–6. See Pantin's discussion of "the rise of a new and cantankerous type of educated or half-educated laity" (p. 161).

73. "The Friar's Answer," ll. 33–36.

74. *Crede*, ll. 35–38.

75. See Aston's argument that the conning of such orthodox materials in English could precipitate dissent (*Lollards and Reformers*, pp. 144–45).

76. For a conventional Lollard view of pilgrimage, see Swinburn, pp. 84–87. See also MS Rawlinson C. 208, fols. 38v–39v; Pollard, p. 129.

77. *Crede*, ll.34–36.

78. For a Lollard view on the competition between the mendicant orders, see MS Egerton 2820, fols. 30r-v.

79. *Crede*, ll. 64–66.

80. For a Lollard assault on the self-destructing language of orthodoxy, see British Library MS Additional 24.202, fol. 1v.

81. Swinburn, pp. 133–34.

82. *Crede*, ll. 123–27.

83. *Crede*, ll. 146–51.

84. *Crede*, ll. 153–54.

85. *Crede*, ll. 173–78.

86. *Crede*, l. 156.

87. On the distractions of church architecture as well as church music, see MS Egerton 2820, fol. 91v; see also Swinburn, pp. 37–41.

88. *Crede*, ll. 169–70.

89. See *Crede*, ll. 189–90, 197–98, 215–17.

90. *Crede*, ll. 219–20.

91. *Crede*, ll. 280–81.

92. *Crede*, l. 430. On the tradition of the saintly plowman in medieval satire, see Heiserman, pp. 190ff.

93. Tanner, pp. 115–16. Such declarations often include insulting puns on the names of popular shrines. "Also that no pilgrimage shuld be do to the Lefdy of Falsyngham, the Lefdy of Foulpette [Woolpit] and to Thomme of Cankerbury, ne to noon other seyntes ne ymages" (p. 148). The same kind of malicious punning marks nonconformist satire through Martin Marprelate. See also Jones, pp. 35–37.

94. *Crede*, ll. 440–41.

95. Arnold, I, 409. For a discussion of late medieval attitudes toward laughter, see Kolve, *Play Called Corpus Christi*, pp. 124–44.

96. *Crede*, ll. 474–75; 675–77.

97. *Crede*, ll. 560–64.

98. *Crede*, ll. 523–28.

99. *Crede*, ll. 538–47. Heiserman (pp. 221–22) mistakenly argues that Lollard satires are not "philosophical quests" but rather simple revelations of the sins of the clergy. He fails to see that that revelation is part of a larger process of ideological self-fashioning.

100. W. W. Skeat, ed., *The Plowman's Tale*, in *The Complete Works of Geoffrey Chaucer* (Oxford: Clarendon Press, 1897), VII, ll. 1065–68. Heiserman (pp. 224–28) provides an extended discussion of the poem's place in the tradition of medieval satire.

101. Heyworth, *Jack Upland*, pp. 6–19.

102. *Plowman's Tale*, ll. 1373–80.

103. *Plowman's Tale*, ll. 1234–36.

104. *Plowman's Tale*, ll. 1269, 1271, 1274–75.

105. Hudson, *Selections*, pp. 84–87.

106. *Plowman's Tale*, ll. 909–16.

107. Heyworth, *Jack Upland*, p.53.

108. Owst, *Literature and Pulpit*, pp. 210–470.

109. Heyworth, *Jack Upland*, l. 61.

110. Heyworth, *Jack Upland*, ll. 47, 43–44.

111. Heyworth, *Jack Upland*, ll. 83–89.

112. Heyworth, *Jack Upland*, ll. 101–6.

113. Heyworth, *Jack Upland*, ll. 134–36.

114. Heyworth, *Jack Upland*, ll. 408–11.

115. Heyworth, *Friar Daw's Reply*, ll. 1–4; see Jeremiah 9:1.

116. Heyworth, *Friar Daw's Reply*, ll. 210–15.

117. Heyworth, *Friar Daw's Reply*, ll. 278–81.

118. MS Cotton Titus D.V., fol. 67v. As Heiserman notes, the mingling of

discursive modes and levels of diction characterizes the bulk of medieval and early Renaissance satire (p. 213). He sees the blending of incantatory prophecy and scholarly disputation as part of a "methodical confusion" that gives structural voice to the poem's attack on disorder. In Skelton, he further argues that aureate and plain styles are mingled to address a wider audience (pp. 178–85, 241, 285.) Neither explanation, I think, accounts for the Lollard practice. As has been argued, the presence of convention does not automatically suggest its conventional use.

119. Heyworth, *Upland's Rejoinder*, ll. 130–63.

120. *Crede*, ll. 421–25.

121. F. N. Robinson, *The Works of Geoffrey Chaucer*, 2d ed. (Boston: Houghton Mifflin, 1961), p. 573, ll. 839–41.

122. Altman, pp. 34–62.

CHAPTER THREE

1. John Bale, *The true hystorie of the Christen departynge of the reuerende man, D. Martyne Luther* (Marburgh? 1546?). John Bale, *A brefe Chronycle concernynge the examinacion and death of syr Johan Oldecastell*, in Henry Christmas, ed., *Select Works of John Bale*, The Parker Society (Cambridge: Cambridge University Press, 1849), pp. 1–59; hereafter cited as *Syr Johan Oldecastell* and *Works* respectively.

2. For a discussion of the nature and date of Bale's conversion, see Fairfield, pp. 31–49. Further biography is available in Honor McCusker, *John Bale: Dramatist and Antiquary* (Bryn Mawr, Pa.: N.p., 1942). Bale's own accounts of his life are to be found in John Bale, *The vocacyon of Iohan Bale to the bishoprick of Ossorie in Irelande*, in *The Harleian Miscellany* (London: Robert Dutton, 1808), I, 328–64, and scattered through many of his other works.

3. For a bibliography and chronology of Bale's plays, lost and extant, see W. T. Davies, "A Bibliography of John Bale," *Oxford Bibliographical Society: Proceedings and Papers* (Oxford: Oxford University Press, 1940), V, 201–80. For Cromwell's role in the Reformation, see Dickens, *The English Reformation*, pp. 109ff.

4. Dickens (*Lollards and Protestants*, p. 169) has sought to qualify "the popular view that Yorkshire was a hotbed of Catholic sedition throughout the Tudor period."

5. John Bale, *The Image of bothe churches*, in *Works*, p. 254.

6. For a discussion of the political and theological leanings of the Marian exiles, see Christina H. Garrett, *The Marian Exiles: A Study in the Origins of Elizabethan Puritanism* (1938; rpt. Cambridge: Cambridge University Press, 1966).

7. William Whittingham, *A brieff discours off the troubles begonne at Franck-*

ford, ed. Edward Arber (London: N.p., 1908); M. M. Knappen, *Tudor Puritanism: A Chapter in the History of Idealism* (Chicago: University of Chicago Press, 1939), p. 129. Although Bale, unlike his younger companion John Foxe, sided with the moderates, he offers high praise for Geneva as "the wonderfull miracle of the whole worlde." It is "a spiritual and Christian congregation: vsing one order, one cloyster, and like ceremonies." John Bale, *The Pageant of Popes,* Englished with sondrye additions by I.S. [Iohn Studley] (London: Thomas Marshe, 1574), sig. D4v.

8. *Image of bothe churches,* p. 365.

9. For a discussion of Bale's career as a Carmelite hagiographer, see Fairfield, pp. 22–27. Some of his early saints' lives are contained in Bodleian MS Selden supra 41, fols. 197r–220v, and Bodleian MS 73, fols. 140–55.

10. John Bale, *The first two partes of the Actes or vnchaste examples of the Englyshe Votaryes* (London: John Tysdale, 1560).

11. For a discussion of Bale's attitude toward Wyclif, see Vaclav Mudroch, *The Wyclif Tradition,* ed. Albert Compton Reeves (Athens: Ohio University Press, 1979), pp. 9–12. See also King, pp. 70–71.

12. See Leverenz's penetrating discussion of the Puritan tendency to relieve inward conflict by splitting the confusion of ambivalence into the clarity of external opposites (pp. 108ff.).

13. The sources of Bale's historiography are Augustine and, more immediately, John Wyclif and William Tyndale. See Tyndale's description of the necessary conflict of the churches of faith and of works in *An Answer to Sir Thomas More's Dialogue* (pp. 107–10). Much of Bale's fascination with the Byzantine workings of the Roman see has its roots in Tyndale's detailed accounts of papal intervention in national and international affairs. *The Practice of Prelates,* ancestor to Bale's *Pageant of Popes* and *Actes of the Englyshe Votaryes,* may well be the earliest use of history as an instrument of religious disputation according to C. H. Williams, *William Tyndale* (London: Thomas Nelson and Sons, Ltd., 1969), p. 96. Tyndale like Bale sees history as a devotional tool as well. "[R]ight meditation or contemplation," he argues, ". . . is nothing else save the calling to mind, and a repeating in the heart" of the lives of the saints and their foes. William Tyndale, *Doctrinal Treatises and Introductions to Different Portions of the Holy Scriptures,* ed. Henry Walter, The Parker Society (Cambridge: Cambridge University Press, 1848), p. 441.

14. John Bale, *An Expostulation or complaynte agaynste the blasphemyes of a franticke papyst of Hampshyre* (London: Ihon Daye, 1550), sig. A5r.

15. John Bale, *Yet a course at the Romyshe foxe* (Zurich: 1543), fol. 16r.

16. Quoted by McCusker, p. 9. The same contradictory impulses of attraction and repulsion evident among the Lollards are manifested among the early Protestants. John Foxe called himself a preaching friar, and Robert Barnes like Bale was recruited from the mendicant ranks. The most thorough treatment of the similarities between friar and reformer is Irvonwy Morgan,

The Godly Preachers of the Elizabethan Church (London: Epworth Press, 1965). This lucid study rightly proclaims the Puritans to be heirs of the mendicant preachers but fails to account for the virulent hostility with which the children assailed the cloister of their fathers. So essential was that loathing to the Puritan sense of identity that their attacks on the monastery continued long after the orders might be construed as either threat or rival. See John Milton on "monkish . . . sophistry" and "cloistered virtue." Merritt Y. Hughes, ed., *John Milton: Complete Poems and Major Prose*, (Indianapolis: The Odyssey Press, 1957), pp. 686, 728.

17. See Greenblatt (p. 9) on the internalization of authority and false authority. For a seventeenth-century formulation of the struggle between the old and new creatures, see Alexander Grosart, ed., *The Works of Richard Sibbes*, Nichol's Series of Standard Divines: Puritan Period (Edinburgh: James Nichol, 1864), IV, 320–21.

18. John Bale, *King Johan*, ed. Barry B. Adams (San Marino: The Huntington Library, 1969), p. 148n; all citations to the text of *King Johan* refer to this edition.

19. For a discussion of the relationship between the thought of Bale and that of Foxe, see Haller, pp. 48–81, as well as J. F. Mozley, *John Foxe and His Book* (London: Society for Promoting Christian Knowledge, 1940), pp. 29 passim. More recent studies, among them V. Norskov Olsen, *John Foxe and the Elizabethan Church* (Berkeley: University of California Press, 1973), pp. 36ff., have contested Haller's concept of the elect nation. While it is true that both Foxe and Bale demonstrate an abiding concern for the universal church, it is also evident that they accord the English Church a special status within God's larger scheme. The pervasive sense of the link between England and Israel found in the Calvinist Geneva Bible has been discussed by Knott, *Sword of the Spirit*, p. 29.

20. For a discussion of the Puritan fascination with the idea of the undefiled island, see Christopher Hill, *Puritanism and Revolution* (New York: Schocken Books, 1964), pp. 50–122. See also Fairfield on Bale's "myth of the beleaguered isle" (p. 94).

21. *Actes of the Englyshe Votaryes*, Pt. I, fols. 27v–29r.

22. Bale speaks equivocally of his complicity in the crimes of the orders in the dedicatory epistle to *The Pageant of Popes*, sig. C4r.: "[I] do not declare things heard or redde only, but things knowen by experience, who lived 24. yeares in that secte, and was present among them being no small souldiour of the Pope: where what is it that I haue not seene, what that I haue heard, which is unworthy of Christ, Christians, monkes, and also of men, from whose superstitions at that time I was not free, but vtterly abhorred their filthiness and mischiefe."

23. John Bale, *The Apology of Johan Bale againste a ranke Papyst* (London: Ihon Day, 1550?), fol. 4r.

24. *Image of bothe churches*, p. 484. Tyndale (*Doctrinal Treatises*, p. 314) describes the malady in similar terms: "For the person that burneth cannot quietly serve God, inasmuch as his mind is drawn away, and the thoughts of his heart occupied with wonderful and monstrous imaginations. He can neither see, nor hear, nor read, but that his wits are rapt, and he clean from himself."

25. *Apology*, fol. 24v.

26. *Yet a course*, fol. 10r. See Hill, *Society and Puritanism*, pp. 57–58, 97, 191. See also Christopher Hill, "Puritans and 'The Dark Corners of the Land,'" *Transactions of the Royal Historical Society*, 5th ser., 13 (1963), 77–102.

27. Marguerite d'Angoulême, *A Godly Medytacyon of the christen sowle*, trans. Elyzabeth doughter to Kynge Henri the viii (Wesel: Dirik van der Straten, 1548), fol. 41v. For Bale's treatment of the wavering multitude, see the following: John Bale, *A Mysterye of Inyquyte contayned within the heretycall Genealogye of Ponce Pantolabus* (Geneva: Mychael Woode, 1545), fol. 33r; *Image of bothe churches*, pp. 418, 484, 494, 582; *Actes of the Englyshe Votaryes*, Pt. 2, fol. 55r-v.

28. *Apology*, fol. 8r. See Tyndale, *Doctrinal Treatises*, 414–21, in which he examines the "childishness" of the Jews whose ceremonies are an ABC of religion. "[H]e which hath the Spirit of Christ is now [however] no more a child."

29. John Bale, *A Comedy concernynge thre lawes*, in John S. Farmer, ed., *The Dramatic Writings of John Bale* (New York: Barnes & Noble, Inc., 1966), pp. 11–12; hereafter cited as *Thre lawes* and *Dramatic Writings*.

30. *Mysterye of Inyquyte*, fol. 40r.

31. *Mysterye of Inyquyte*, fol. 37r.

32. *Mysterye of Inyquyte*, fol. 5r. For a discussion of demonic language in the plays, particularly the alliterative style of the Vices, see Thora Balslev Blatt, *The Plays of John Bale: A Study of Ideas, Technique, and Style* (Copenhagen: G. E. C. Gad, 1968), pp. 201–5.

33. *Image of bothe churches*, pp. 259–60. Leverenz sees "unstructured, unranked, interchangeable lists" as a characteristically Puritan way of providing rhetorical analogues for "the 'play' of sinful emotions" (p. 27).

34. *Image of bothe churches*, p. 417.

35. *Mysterye of Inyquyte*, fol. 60v.

36. John Bale, *The Epistle exhortatorye of an Englyshe Christyane unto his derelye beloued contreye of Englande* (Basel, 1544), fol. 24r. See also *Image of bothe churches*, p. 458.

37. *Image of bothe churches*, p. 604. Bale goes on to list some thirty-five biblical figures drawn from the workaday world.

38. See Gilby's discussion of satirical language in Anthony Gilby, *A Pleasaunt Dialogue, Betweene a Souldior of Barwicke, and an English Chaplaine* (1581), sig. A7r.

39. *Apology*, fol. 45v.

40. *Syr Johan Oldecastell*, p. 54. See David Norbrook, *Poetry and Politics in the English Renaissance* (London: Routledge and Kegan Paul, 1984), p. 42. The antiquarian John Leyland found in the plain style of the early reformers the cause of their obscurity. Bale, however, in his commentary on Leyland's work, defended the Lollards claiming that "authoryte it woulde adde vnto them, to apere fyrst of all in their owne symplycyte or natiue colours without bewtie of speche." John Bale, *The Laboryouse Journey and serche of John Leylande*, ed. W. A. Copinger (Manchester: Priory Press, 1895), pp. 41–42. On the status of Lollard and pseudo-Lollard literature among other Edwardians, see also King, pp. 37, 51.

41. See *Thre lawes*, p. 6. Fairfield (p. 93) discusses the pattern of purity, decline, and renewal in Bale's work. See also Beryl Smalley's illuminating discussion of the link between cyclical views of history and the embrace of a realist metaphysic ("The Bible and Eternity," pp. 85ff.). Although Smalley is chiefly concerned with Wyclif, her views may be applied to later radical adherents of the Platonic perspective.

42. *Thre lawes*, pp. 4–5.

43. Quoted by McCusker, p. 7.

44. *Thre lawes*, pp. 10–11.

45. *Thre lawes*, p. 12.

46. *Thre lawes*, p. 16.

47. *Thre lawes*, p. 17. The devil in monk's clothing is a stock figure in nonconformist dramatic writing. He appears earlier in Lollard and other medieval satire. Theodore Beza's Satan addresses his cowl, confessing that the disguise has the power to soil even him. Theodore Beza, *A Tragedie of Abrahams Sacrifice*, trans. Arthur Golding, ed. Malcolm W. Wallace (Toronto: University of Toronto Library, 1906), p. 210.

48. *Thre lawes*, p. 17. The fear of sexual misidentity among the nonconformists would appear to precede the controversy over transvestism in the professional theater. Both Bale and Foxe seem particularly fascinated with the transvestism of Joan of Mentz. See *Pageant of Popes*, fols. 55r–56v, and Foxe, V, 455; VIII, 236. David Leverenz offers a compelling Freudian explanation for such horror (pp. 32–35).

49. *Thre lawes*, p. 20. Foxe prints a verse satire, apparently commissioned by Cromwell, that contains a like stanza. "The Fantassie of Idolatrie" in Foxe, V, 406. A. G. Dickens (*Lollards and Protestants*, pp. 124–25) describes yet another piece of Cromwellian propaganda by Wilfrid Holme, "The Fall and Evill Success of Rebellion." It too employs the satiric list of saintly cure-alls.

50. See Hill, *Society and Puritanism*, pp. 124ff., for his discussion of the "industrious sort of people."

51. *Thre lawes*, p. 16.

52. *Thre lawes*, p. 25.

53. *Godly Medytacyon*, fol. 39v. Leverenz sees repetition as a hallmark of the Puritan "obsessive style," and "as a way of mastering a threatening new world that lacked both outward and inward clarity" (p. 116).

54. *Thre lawes*, p. 29.

55. *Thre lawes*, p. 43.

56. *Thre lawes*, p. 58.

57. *Thre lawes*, p. 61.

58. *Thre lawes*, p. 67. Villains in nonconformist art are often so deluded. The inquisitors in Foxe's account of the Oxford disputations of Ridley and Latimer (significantly likened to an "interlude" or "pageant") declare such a premature end to the action, "triumphing before the victory." Foxe, VI, 520.

59. *Thre lawes*, p. 53.

60. Although it is clear here that Bale intends to distinguish between Iniquity's tragedy and his own comedy, in general his use of the terms is problematical. For a discussion of the issue, see McCusker, p. 77.

61. For a discussion of the continued popularity of the cycles, see Harold C. Gardiner, *Mysteries' End: An Investigation of the Last Days of the Medieval Religious Stage* (New Haven: Yale University Press, 1946).

62. Comic realism is traditionally associated with evil in medieval drama. See Murray Roston, *Biblical Drama in England from the Middle Ages to the Present Day* (Evanston: Northwestern University Press, 1968), pp. 24ff. Nevertheless, there are a number of virtuous figures similarly treated, among them Noah, Joseph, and the Shepherds. In nonconformist drama, on the other hand, comic realism and the good are incompatible.

63. *Thre lawes*, p. 35.

64. Beza urges a similar process of self-discovery in the prologue to *Abrahams Sacrifice*, p. 4. God's wonders are most manifest in Moses, Abraham, and David, he writes, "in the liues of whome if men would nowe a dayes looke uppon them selues, they should knowe them selues better than they doe." See Jonas Barish's penetrating analysis of Ben Jonson's attempts "to detheatricalize the theater" by substituting rhetoric for spectacle. Barish's characterization of Jonson's ambivalence toward the stage is a more accurate portrait of Puritan responses to the stage than the pure rejectionist stance he argues for elsewhere (pp. 135–50).

65. The moralities appear to have their sources in the less negatively regarded traditions of penitential literature and pulpit oratory. See Owst, *Literature and Pulpit*, and Robert Potter, *The English Morality Play* (London: Routledge and Kegan Paul, 1975), pp. 6–29.

66. For a discussion of other radical Protestant moralities, see David Bevington, *Tudor Drama and Politics* (Cambridge: Harvard University Press, 1968), pp. 24–35, 106ff.

67. U. Milo Kaufmann has argued that the emergence of "heavenly meditation" in the latter part of the seventeenth century made possible Bunyan's special brand of allegory, filled not with flat emblems but "palpable abstractions": "real individuals who do not incarnate but exemplify a particular quality." The practice Kaufmann describes, however, may easily be traced through the whole corpus of nonconformist literature back to the embryonic allegories of the Lollards. *The Pilgrim's Progress and Traditions in Puritan Meditation* (New Haven: Yale University Press, 1966), pp. 90–103.

68. W. T. Davies, p. 241. See also Ruth H. Blackburn, *Biblical Drama under the Tudors* (The Hague: Mouton, 1971), pp. 37–38.

69. For a discussion of Perkins and the doctrine of calling, see Hill, *Puritanism and Revolution*, pp. 215–38.

70. John Bale, *Johan Baptystes preachynge in the wyldernesse*, in Farmer, *Dramatic Writings*, p. 136. Bale himself had similarly maintained his old calling, hagiography. Only now his task was done in the Spirit.

71. *Johan Baptystes*, p. 149.

72. *Johan Baptystes*, p. 137.

73. *Johan Baptystes*, p. 146.

74. For Bale's discussion of Satan's "unclarkelye" reading of scripture, see *Mysterye of Inyquyte*, fol. 7v.

75. Blatt, p. 123. For a discussion of Bale's debt to Thomas Kirchmayer's *Pammachius*, a play Bale claims to have translated into English, see Charles H. Herford, *Studies in the Literary Relations of England and Germany in the Sixteenth Century* (Cambridge: Cambridge University Press, 1886), pp. 131–37.

76. *Image of bothe churches*, p. 253. On Bale's near conflation of sacred and secular history (both literary and political), see Norbrook, pp. 39ff.

77. *Apology*, fol. 79r.

78. *King Johan*, ll. 48–49.

79. *King Johan*, l. 60

80. *King Johan*, ll. 304–5.

81. *King Johan*, ll. 365–66.

82. *King Johan*, ll. 194–210.

83. Tyndale, in contrasting the operations of faith and imagination, describes the Pope as selling ladders to heaven: "His fatherhood sendeth them to heaven with *Scala coeli*; that is, with a ladder to scale the walls: for by the door, Christ, will they not let them come in. That door have they stopped up; and that because ye should buy ladders of them." In the same work, scripture faithfully read is compared to a rope cast down from heaven to draw men up. "Thou must . . . go along by the scripture as by a line, until thou come at Christ, which is the way's end and resting-place" (*Doctrinal Treatises*, pp. 244, 317).

84. All four extant, printed plays are described as being "compyled by

Iohan Bale." John King provides an illuminating analysis of Bale's view of his authorial vocation and his use of the term "compiler" (pp. 69–71). See also Norbrook, p. 38. Foxe left open the end of *Christus Triumphans*, anticipating that its final act, the marriage of Christ and Ecclesiae, would be written by God.

85. In Foxe's *Christus Triumphans*, Satan enters in the fifth act bearing costumes so that his acting troupe of villains may alter their roles. John Hazel Smith, ed. and trans., *Two Latin Comedies by John Foxe the Martyrologist*, Renaissance Society of America (Ithaca: Cornell University Press, 1973) p. 337.

86. *King Johan*, ll. 792–97.

87. John Bale, *A Tragedye or enterlude manyfestyng the chefe promyses of God unto man*, in Farmer, *Dramatic Writings*, pp. 85–86.

88. *King Johan*, l. 829.

89. Dissimulation first appears in the disguise of Raymundus. The shifting roles of the Vices underscore their instability. Foxe's villains in *Christus Triumphans* also play a multiplicity of roles, historical and allegorical; the Virtues remain fixed. See Smith, *Two Latin Comedies*, pp. 329, 335. Tyndale (*Doctrinal Treatises*, p. 42) describes Antichrist in the same way: "But his nature is (when he is uttered, and overcome with the word of God) to go out of the play for a season, and to disguise himself, and then to come in again with a new name and new raiment."

90. *King Johan*, ll. 1215–22.

91. Interestingly, the papal legate denounces the king as a "loller" although the word does not acquire its theological meaning until two hundred years after the events dramatized.

92. *King Johan*, ll. 2127–35. See Gordon Stevens Wakefield's useful distinction between Puritan and Catholic conceptions of sainthood, *Puritan Devotion* (London: Epworth Press, 1957), p. 145.

93. *King Johan*, ll. 1283–89.

94. *Actes of the Englyshe Votaryes*, Pt. 2, fols. 106v–107r. Significantly, Bale describes the persecution of himself and his wife in terms of a Caiaphas play: "Ther did they worshyp it in their scarlet gownes with cappe in hand, and here they improued it with scornes and with mockes, grennying vpon her lyke termegauntes in a playe. But let them no more loke to be forgotten of their posteryte, than were Judas and Pylate whome the worlde yet speaketh of." In his autobiography (see n. 2 above) Bale discerns similar parallels, largely with Paul's life. King views "Bale's tendency to dramatize and fictionalize his own experience" as "the definitive feature of his polemical art" (p. 65). The pattern is endemic to nonconformity. Murray Roston has coined the useful term "post-figuration" to describe the Protestant's practice of "reenacting . . . in his life leading incidents from the lives of scriptural heroes" (see pp. 69ff.). He rightly links this habit of mind with Protestants of more radical temperament. See also Lewalski, p. 128, where she associates Calvin-

ists with the act of seeing themselves as the antitype fulfilling the biblical type.

95. *King Johan*, ll. 2191–92.

96. *King Johan*, l. 2465.

97. *King Johan*, l. 1119.

98. The recasting of the end of *King Johan* to make it suitable for presentation during the reign of Elizabeth suggests Bale's continuing interest in the drama as well. See also Fairfield, pp. 146ff.

99. *Vocacyon*, p. 345.

100. *Expostulation or complaynte*, C3r-v.

101. Anne Askew was burned at the stake in 1546 at Smithfield. She was a student of John Lascells whose theology was largely Lollard with some evidence of the influence of German ideas. Dickens, *Lollards and Protestants*, p. 34. See also King, pp. 72ff., where he argues that "the encounter between accuser and accused is implicitly dramatic in its use of dialogue."

102. For a discussion of Bale's use of his sources in fashioning his version of the examination of Oldcastle, see Fairfield, pp. 124–29; see also W. T. Waugh, "Sir John Oldcastle," *English Historical Review*, 20 (1905), 451–55.

103. *Syr Johan Oldecastell*, p. 35.

104. John Bale, *The first examinacyon of Anne Askewe*, in *Works*, p. 177.

105. *Anne Askewe*, p. 224. See also p. 241, where Bale compares the court officers to "tormentors in a play."

106. *Anne Askewe*, p. 139. See also Tyndale's similar conception of the miraculous (*Doctrinal Treatises*, p. 411). In *A Pathway into Holy Scripture* he uses the simile of the trial with its arraignment, examination, judgment, and release to describe the onset of grace in the individual (*Doctrinal Treatises*, pp. 16–17).

107. For discussions of Protestant and radical Protestant attitudes toward the sacraments, see Dugmore; Wakefield, pp. 29–36; Stephen Mayor, *The Lord's Supper in Early English Dissent* (London: Epworth Press, 1972), pp. 1–46.

108. Foxe, V, 646; VI, 611; VI, 621.

109. Foxe, VI, 616–17. See Greenblatt's description of More's conception of his theatrical role as martyr, a role that More insists must be assumed timorously and hesitantly (pp. 71–72). Nonconformist martyrdom is almost always marked by increasing certainty and assertiveness.

110. Hardison, pp. 35–79.

111. Foxe, VII, 422.

112. William Tyndale, *Expositions and Notes on Sundry Portions of the Holy Scriptures Together with the Practice of Prelates*, ed. Henry Walter, The Parker Society (Cambridge: Cambridge University Press, 1849), p. 251.

113. Foxe, VI, 607.

114. Foxe, VI, 607. Other such instances in which the examinate enacts a

biblical role are common. Stephen Gratwick likens himself to Christ tempted by Satan (Foxe, VIII, 320); and William Wood imagines himself a new Paul freed by the conflict of new Pharisees and Sadducees (Foxe, VIII, 568).

115. Foxe, V, 455. Each of John Philpot's examinations are referred to as parts or acts of a tragedy (Foxe, VII, 605ff.). Bale also appears to use the term "pageant" when describing the dramatic antics of Antichrist and company. See *Pageant of Popes* (the translator's title), fols. B4v, 158r, 185v–186r; *Actes of the Englyshe Votaryes*, fols. 41r-v, 80r-v.

116. Foxe, V, 455–61.

117. Bale, *The Christen departynge of Martyne Luther*. Leverenz (p. 27) notes that Richard Baxter had urged the penning of exemplary lives over the writing of plays.

118. For Turner's "fox" satires, see William P. Holden, *Anti-Puritan Satire* (New Haven: Yale University Press, 1954), p. 2. Bonner is again savaged by Bale in *A declaration of Edmonde Bonners articles* (London: Ihon Tysdall for Frauncys Coldocke, 1561).

119. It has been noted above, in Chapter Two, that it is a common feature of the examination to signal the emerging triumph of the examinate with a reversal in the direction of the questioning.

120. *Yet a course*, fol. 13r. Herford (pp. 29ff., 57ff.) argues that the polemical dialogue, developed on the Continent and adopted by exiled English reformers, constitutes a species of drama: what he calls a "drama of debate." The preponderance of courtroom exchanges leads him to isolate a so-called "trial-motive." Although it is clear that men like Bale and William Turner learned much from their foreign hosts, the existence of a long-standing English tradition of ecclesiastical courtroom drama is indisputable.

121. Bale similarly urges the readers of his autobiography to gather strength by perceiving the analogy between their own afflictions and his exemplary suffering for Christ. *Vocacyon*, p. 359.

122. *Yet a course*, fol. 44v.

123. *Yet a course*, fol. 52r-v.

124. *Apology*, fol. 8r. In his second attack on Bonner, Bale again contrasts godly and demonic play. Bonner is the grand Vice who presides over "that prodigiouse apes play of antichrist," the Eucharist. He is a "naturall proteus," and like Sedition must be bound by the word of God before he will speak truly. "Plaies or christen Comedyes hee abhorreth aboue all, because they haue opened so playnely the knaueries of his Romish secte." Bale, *A declaration of Edmonde Bonners articles*, sig. *4r.

125. John Bale, *An Answere to a papystycall exhortacyon* (1548?).

126. John Bale, *A Dialoge or Communycacyon to be had at a table betwene two chyldren* (London: 1549).

127. "The fyckle promyse of a wanton boye, not grounded in Gods knowledge is here preferred to all other kinds of vowyng." *Apology*, fol. 24v.

128. Norbrook (p. 36) speculates that radical dialogues such as Luke Shepherd's *Jon Bon and Mast Person* may have been performed. Although its origins lie elsewhere, nonconformist displaced drama necessarily bears a marked resemblance to other varieties of "closet drama," such as the plays of Seneca.

CHAPTER FOUR

1. For representative works, see William Turner, *The Huntyng of the Romyshe Vuolfe* (Basel? 1554?); Anthony Gilby, *An answer to the deuillish detection of Stephane Gardiner* (London: J. Day, 1547); Rev. John Udall, *The State of the Church of England*, ed. Edward Arber (London: The English Scholar's Library, 1879). Also known as *Diotrephes*, *The State of the Church of England* first appeared in 1588 and was later printed in *A parte of a register* (1593). Although usually ascribed to Udall, the tract has recently been attributed to Job Throckmorton; see Leland H. Carlson, *Martin Marprelate, Gentleman: Master Job Throckmorton Laid Open in His Colors* (San Marino: Huntington Library, 1981), pp. 332–38. For a discussion of some of the satirical pamphlets of the early Reformation, see M. M. Knappen, *Tudor Puritanism: A Chapter in the History of Idealism* (Chicago: University of Chicago Press, 1939), pp. 21ff.; for a discussion of the religious satire of the period, see Holden, *Anti-Puritan Satire*.

2. Gilby, *A Pleasaunt Dialogue*, sig. D7r.

3. See King's discussion of Bale's canonization of the Lollard artist (pp. 70–71).

4. Knappen, pp. 283–302.

5. See William Perkins, "A Dialogue of the State of a Christian Man," *The Work of William Perkins*, ed. Ian Breward (Appleford: Courtenay Press, 1970); see also Collinson, *Elizabethan Puritan Movement*, pp. 423ff. The use of dialogue and allegory in later Puritan preaching recalls the dramatic patterns of the late medieval sermon as documented by Owst in *Literature and Pulpit*.

6. Quoted by Samuel Clarke, *The Lives of Thirty-Two English Divines*, 3d ed. (London: Printed for William Birch, 1677), p. 18.

7. Clarke, p. 17.

8. Thomas Cartwright, *A Commentary upon the Epistle of Saint Paule written to the Colossians* (London: Nicholas Okes, 1612), p. 201; hereafter cited as *Colossians*.

9. John Ayre, ed., *The Works of John Whitgift*, The Parker Society (Cambridge: Cambridge University Press, 1851), I, 514; hereafter cited as Ayre.

10. The series of letters between Cartwright and Anne Stubbe are reprinted in Albert Peel and Leland H. Carlson, eds., *Cartwrightiana* (London:

George Allen and Unwin, Ltd., 1951), pp. 58–75; hereafter cited as *Cartwrightiana*.

11. *Cartwrightiana*, p. 69.

12. This and other letters to Burghley are reprinted in the appendix to A. F. Scott Pearson, *Thomas Cartwright and Elizabethan Puritanism, 1535–1603* (Gloucester: Peter Smith, 1966), p. 457.

13. Walter Travers, *A Full and Plaine Declaration of Ecclesiastical Discipline out of the word of God* (1617), sig. A3v; the work is a translation of *Ecclesiasticae Disciplinae, et Anglicanae Ecclesiae Ab Illa Aberrationis* (1574).

14. Thomas Cartwright, *A Confutation of the Rhemists Translation, Glosses and Annotations on the New Testament* (1618), pp. 395–96; hereafter cited as *Confutation*.

15. Col. 2:1; *Colossians*, p. 107; for Paul's metaphor of the foot race see 1 Cor. 9:24–6 and Heb. 12:1. Also see Thomas Cartwright, *The Second Replie of Thomas Cartwright* (1575), pp. 174–75; hereafter cited as *Second Replie*.

16. *Second Replie*, pp. 243–44.

17. Pearson, pp. 149ff. See also Dr. Williams's Library MS Morrice A (OLP), fols. 49–50r, 135, 176–77r, and MS Morrice B (II), fols. 131–34r, 204–5r, for a series of letters between a hesitant Cartwright and a group of zealous brethren.

18. Thomas Cartwright, *A briefe Apologie of Thomas Cartwright against all such slanderous accusations as it pleaseth Mr Sutcliffe in his severall pamphlettes most iniuriously to loade him with* (1596); hereafter cited as *Apologie*.

19. *Apologie*, sig. A2r. Note that these Caiaphases are blasted in "their penne," signaling the translation of the Puritan drama of examination from the prelatical hall to the pamphlet.

20. Pearson, pp. 365–70.

21. Despite Marprelate's praises, Cartwright had only unkind words for the satirist; see *Apologie*, sig. C2v; also Pearson, p. 451.

22. The Vestiarian controversy of the previous decade provided both parties with a warm-up exercise. See Knappen, pp. 72–102. The following are the texts that comprise the Admonition controversy: *An Admonition to the Parliament* and *A Second Admonition to the Parliament*, in W. H. Frere and C. E. Douglas, eds., *Puritan Manifestoes: A Study of the Origin of the Puritan Revolt* (London: Church Historical Society, 1954); hereafter cited as *Manifestoes*. John Whitgift, *An Answere to a certen Libel*, in Ayre. Thomas Cartwright, *A Replye to an answere*, in Ayre. John Whitgift, *The Defense of the Aunswere*, in Ayre. Thomas Cartwright, *The Second Replie of Thomas Cartwright*. Thomas Cartwright, *The Rest of the Second Replie of Thomas Cartwright* (1577); hereafter cited as *Rest of Second Replie*.

23. *Second Replie*, p. 139.

24. Donald McGinn, *The Admonition Controversy* (New Brunswick: Rutgers

University Press, 1949), pp. 25ff. Although technically addressed to England's legislature, the printing of the pamphlet near the close of the 1572 session suggests that a wider audience was being sought.

25. *Manifestoes*, p. 16. "Discipline" is a difficult term to define. Typically it is taken to comprehend both the Puritans' insistence on a ministry called "by common consent of the whole church" and their vision of that church as an institution devised to instruct and punish, to coax and compel its members to live in strict accordance with the spirit and letter of God's law. See Hill, *Society and Puritanism*, pp. 219–58.

26. For an excellent discussion of the differences between the Anglican and Puritan conceptions of compliance with scripture, see John S. Coolidge, *The Pauline Renaissance in England: Puritanism and the Bible* (Oxford: Clarendon Press, 1970), pp. 4–11. See also Knott, who speaks of the Puritan conception of scripture as "a field of force" (*Sword of the Spirit*, pp. 32–38).

27. William Pierce, ed., *The Marprelate Tracts: 1588–1589* (London: James Clarke and Co., 1911), p. 21; hereafter cited as *Tracts*. For Whitgift's response, see Thomas Cooper, *An Admonition to the People of England*, Puritan Discipline Tracts (London: John Petheram, 1847), pp. 28ff.

28. McGinn, *Admonition Controversy*, pp. 86, 113, 109, 90.

29. Ayre, I, 510; see also Ayre, I, 522.

30. Collinson, *Elizabethan Puritan Movement*, pp. 51, 260. For another Puritan's view of his audience see Axton's examination in MS Morrice A (OLP), fol. 7r.

31. John Bale, *A Tragedy or enterlude manyfestyng the chefe promyses of God unto man*, in Farmer, *Dramatic Writings*, pp. 85–86.

32. Ayre, I, 91.

33. Richard Hooker, *Of the Laws of Ecclesiastical Polity*, ed. Christopher Morris (London: J. M. Dent and Sons, Ltd., 1969), I, 77ff. During an examination conducted in 1583, the examinate's aping of Cartwright's arguments causes Whitgift to reflect on his past battles with Cartwright. He laments the controversy which he sees as having driven men to popery; but he insists he does not "repent me of my workes against mr. Carwrighte." MS Morrice B, fol. 44v.

34. On the Puritan need for adversaries, see both Whitgift's and Cartwright's formulations, Ayre, II, 234; *Second Replie*, p. 23.

35. Ayre, II, 223.

36. *Confutation*, p. 160.

37. Ayre, I, 17.

38. *Confutation*, p. 660.

39. See Barish, pp. 95ff. Barish insists on seeing the typical Puritan as unaware of the human capacity for self-deception when, in fact, the assumption of the existence of that capacity lies at the heart of Puritan pastoral art.

See Collinson, *Elizabethan Puritan Movement*, p. 43.

40. *Manifestoes*, p. 76: "It is not true to say, it is old, therefore it is good."

41. Ayre, III, 126. His argument resurfaces in the testimonies of a number of Puritan examinates; see MS Morrice A (OLP), fol. 12v. The Lollards as well appear to have been fascinated with "the evolution of error." For an example, see Bodleian MS Eng. th. f., fols. 6r-v, where the origins of image worship are discussed in a passage based on Wisdom of Solomon 13:11–19.

42. Ayre, II, 569.

43. Ayre, II, 567. For a similar Lollard argument that every day should be a holy day, see British Library MS Additional 24.202, fol. 21v. The call for continuous "holyday" suggests the persistent nonconformist tendency to dilute and domesticate the miraculous.

44. Ayre, I, 520.

45. The debate over set forms of prayer involved similar issues. Many key Puritans, Cartwright among them, wavered on the matter, generally favoring set prayer but anxious to leave open the possibility of free prayer. For two conflicting views on the range of Puritan opinion, see Horton Davies, *The Worship of the English Puritans* (Westminster: Dacre Press, 1948), pp. 98–127; and Collinson, *Elizabethan Puritan Movement*, pp. 356–60.

46. Ayre, I, 514.

47. Ayre, II, 238. At times the adversarial relationship slipped into open warfare. The Puritan register is filled with accounts of the hostilities occasioned by the placement of a hot gospeler amid a lukewarm congregation. See MS Morrice B (II), fols. 82v–4v.

48. Ayre, II, 442–43.

49. For a fine discussion of Calvinist "unsettledness," see Michael Walzer, *The Revolution of the Saints: A Study in the Origins of Radical Politics* (New York: Atheneum, 1969), pp. 133ff.

50. In his attack on Prynne's style of argumentation in *Histriomastix*, Barish notes that both visually and verbally the polemicist's text "conspire[s] to chivvy and harass the reader so that he cannot reach a point of rest, to keep up a perpetual din that blocks him from the sound of his own thought" (p. 87). I believe that Prynne is simply demonstrating his mastery of Puritan discourse, be it polemical or pastoral. He acts systematically, as does Cartwright, to unsettle his audience, thereby preventing the intellectual stagnation that leads to error. Barish is similarly in error, I believe, in arguing that Milton alone requires stasis through endless change (p. 96). Virtually all nonconformists, medieval and Renaissance, so structure their lives and art.

51. *Colossians*, p. 100.

52. Ayre, III, 34.

53. *Second Replie*, p. 395.

54. *Confutation*, p. 19.

55. Writing to Anne Stubbe, Cartwright rejects her church because no one in its egalitarian membership is learned in the language of scripture. *Cartwrightiana*, p. 62.

56. Ayre, I, 475–76, 520.

57. *Colossians*, p. 36; see also *Colossians*, pp. 11, 24, 237.

58. See Chapter Three, p. 97.

59. See Chapter Three, pp. 112–14. Of Hilarian's retreat from the human community, Cartwright wonders, "Why should not hee being but one man, rather go to the citie to see a thousand, then that a thousand should come out of the Citie to see him?" *Confutation*, p. 50.

60. *Second Replie*, p. 578.

61. *Crede*, pp. 16ff.

62. *Second Replie*, p. 151.

63. *Cartwrightiana*, p. 110.

64. Hughes, pp. 292–93 (Book IV, ll. 610–33). The Lollards, like the Puritans, tend to introduce the concepts of labor into the world of play until these two aspects of human behavior become almost indistinguishable. See MS Additional 24.202, fol. 22r.

65. Hill, *Society and Puritanism*, pp. 124–44.

66. *Confutation*, p. 216.

67. Collinson, *Elizabethan Puritan Movement*, p. 375.

68. *Rest of Second Replie*, pp. 207–8.

69. *Second Replie*, p. 340. For a discussion of the image of warfare in Puritan writing, see Walzer, pp. 268–99.

70. *Colossians*, p. 121. To the Rhemists, he notes, while both understanding and affection are necessary to lawful praying, "the understanding may be perfect and full, without the affection and devotion, whereas the affection roveth and wandereth uncertainely when it hath not the light of understanding carried before it." *Confutation*, p. 424.

71. For Cartwright's debate with Harrison, see *Cartwrightiana*, pp. 48–58.

72. See Chapter Two, pp. 59–61. For an example of the continuing attraction of this rite of Puritan theatricality, see Robert Johnson's examination in *A parte of a register, contayninge sundrie memorable matters written by diuers godly and learned in our time* (Amsterdam and New York: Theatrum Orbis Terrarum, Ltd., and DeCapo Press, 1973), p. 109.

73. In his consideration of the oath *ex officio*, Cartwright speculates, nevertheless, that prelatical interrogation may foster disunity rather than community among the Puritans; see *Cartwrightiana*, pp. 30ff.

74. *Confutation*, p. 295.

75. For Cartwright's familiarity with the tradition of the examination with special reference to Thorpe and Oldcastle, see *Cartwrightiana*, pp. 41–42.

76. *Confutation*, p. 48.

77. *Tracts*, p. 215n. On the dilemma of Cartwright and other moderates,

see Lake, pp. 77–92. See also the epistolary debate between White and an Anabaptist in MS Morrice B (I), fols. 546–80, in which the Anabaptist expropriates the traditional voice of dissent, leaving White in the unhappy role of the mad tyrant.

78. Acts 6, 7. Stephen is described as a deacon not a minister.

79. *Rest of Second Replie*, p. 106.

80. *Confutation*, p. 305.

81. *Rest of Second Replie*, p. 326.

82. *Second Replie*, p. 334

83. *Cartwrightiana*, p. 259.

84. *Cartwrightiana*, p. 74.

85. *Confutation*, p. 31. For a similar argument, see Gilby, *An answer to the deuillish detection*, fol. 170r.

86. Ayre, III, 468.

87. Ayre, I, 4.

88. *Second Replie*, p. 325. For another example of the Puritan fondness for metaphors of carpentry and building, see MS Morrice B (I), fol. 414.

89. *Second Replie*, pp. 18–19.

90. *Second Replie*, pp. 7–8.

91. *Second Replie*, p. 92; see also Wilcox's preference for public over private prayer in MS Morrice B (II), fol. 184v. Greenblatt correctly notes that intense self-scrutiny is not a hallmark of the early reformers. He mistakenly concludes, however, that autobiography is therefore an uncharacteristic mode of reformed discourse (p. 85). As we have seen, the ritual reporting of the life crisis is at the center of nonconformist art.

92. *Second Replie*, p. 295.

93. Ayre, II, 168, 305.

94. As usual these citations tend to cluster about the crucial verse "Tell it to the church," upon which Elizabethan Puritans based their demand for a congregational role in exercising discipline and choosing leaders. Ayre, III, 168ff. See Matt. 18:17.

95. Ayre, III, 186.

96. Ayre, III, 186.

97. Ayre, I, 120. For further examples, see also Ayre, I, 475–76, and *Second Replie*, p. 363.

98. Gilby claims that Christ spoke figuratively "to rauishe the myndes of his disciples." Gilby, *An answer to the deuillish detection*, fol. 96r.

99. Ayre, I, 476–77.

100. Ayre, III, 342.

101. Horton Davies, p. 65. Janel Mueller's recent study provides the most rigorous analysis of the prophetic voice of "scripturalism" (pp. 34–39).

102. *Second Replie*, p. 363.

103. For an example of such speech, see Swinburn, pp. 71–72. John Bale

was no stranger to the practice. His commentary on Revelation deftly weaves his own warnings against the papacy with the prognostications of John. *Image of bothe churches*, p. 639.

104. Gilby, *An answer to the deuillish detection*, fols. 145v–146r.

105. Ayre, I, 142; see also Ayre, III, 233.

106. Ayre, I, 58. The Bible, says Cartwright, is beyond the realm of human logic (Ayre, I, 176).

107. For a discussion of *compositio*, see Louis L. Martz, *The Poetry of Meditation: A Study in English Religious Literature of the Seventeenth Century* (New Haven: Yale University Press, 1962), pp. 25–32. For a discussion of specifically Puritan meditation, see Kaufmann, *The Pilgrim's Progress and Traditions in Puritan Meditation*.

108. The nonconformist belief that the words of the preacher constitute a species of scripture dates back to the Lollard movement: "And not onli þis manheede is cristis mouþe, but also alle trewe prestis and prophetis of þe olde lawe & newe lawe. And oþer trewe feiþful men þat speken goddis lawe to his glorie and edificatioun of his chosen." MS Cotton Titus D.V., fols. 25v–26r. Cartwright himself declares that sermons "being duely made, . . . may be termed the word of God, so farre forth as backed and grounded out of Scripture, they are accompanied with the power of the Spirit, either to the regeneration of the elect, or iust conviction of the reprobate." *Confutation*, p. 514. See also Travers's distinctions among kinds of inspiration in MS Morrice B (I), fol. 370.

109. Wakefield, p. 102. See Greenblatt's suggestive discussion of Tyndale in which he detects an effort to translate interior being into a mere voice (p. 111). Again he fails to recognize, however, how prophetic utterance does not seek a total immersion of the self in an authenticating other.

110. Ayre, I, 215; III, 387.

111. In those rare instances when he employs a nonbiblical image, he warns, "This similitude is warily to be used." *Colossians*, p. 60. For a Lollard formulation of the need to ground human discourse in the word, see MS Cotton Titus D.V., fol. 19v, where the preacher declares that "of þo holi bokis we drawyn þe begynnyng of our speche" and "þat [we] sett fast þe bilding of [our] speche in þat."

112. *Rest of Second Replie*, p. 247.

113. *Confutation*, sig. B4r.

114. Ayre, III, 229; *Rest of Second Replie*, pp. 81–82.

115. Turner, *Romyshe Vuolfe*, sig. B2v; see also *A parte of a register*, p. 339. Leverenz provides a lucid discussion of the Puritan compulsion to "show their scaffolding" (p. 146).

116. Ayre, I, 281; see also Ayre, II, 17.

117. Ayre, II, 191.

118. For an example of Penry's use of the rhetorical syllogism, see *An ex-*

hortation vnto the gouernours, and people of hir Maiesties countrie of Wales, in John Penry, *Three Treatises concerning Wales,* ed. David Williams (Cardiff: University of Wales Press, 1960), pp. 90–96.

119. William Turner, *The Rescuynge of the Romishe Fox* (1545), sigs. D4v–D5r. For a similar Lollard "misuse" of syllogism, see British Library MS Harley 1203, fol. 112v.

120. Barish assails Prynne for a similar habit of placing "question-begging terms" in "logical slots as if they were dispassionate, neutral data on which reasonable conclusions might be reared" (pp. 85–86). Given that such practice is pervasive even among university-trained nonconformists, accusations of faulty reasoning would seem only to obscure the deeper roots of the rhetorical logic of the dissenters.

121. For examples of the stage metaphor, see Ayre, I, 59; *Second Replie,* p. 494.

122. Ayre, I, 213.

123. William Turner, *A newe dialogue where in is conteyned the examination of the masse* (London: Ihon Day and William Seres, 1548?), sig. A2v. See Barish's argument for the Puritan need to shift the drama of salvation from "an outer to an inner and invisible stage" (p. 159).

124. For the interpenetration of the language of logic and the language of inspiration, see MS Cotton Titus D.V., fol. 67v.

125. Blatt, p. 10.

126. Greenblatt argues that for Sir Thomas More, "when the *consensus fidelium* is threatened, the possibility of playful, subversive fantasy . . . is virtually lost" (p. 63). The same pattern of retreat may be observed in Cartwright's later career.

127. Barish argues brilliantly that in Plato the battle between poetic responsiveness and poetic austerity leads to an attempt "to aestheticize politics" (p. 14). I would argue that the same ambivalence leads to a similar aestheticizing of Puritan discourse.

128. For a discussion of the introduction of Ramist logic and rhetoric into England, see William Samuel Howell, *Logic and Rhetoric in England, 1500–1700* (New York: Russell and Russell, Inc., 1961), pp. 140–230.

129. Walter J. Ong, *Ramus, Method, and the Decay of Dialogue* (Cambridge: Harvard University Press, 1958). Ong's characterization of Ramism as a rhetorical logic extends through the whole of his work, but the following pages may be consulted: 35, 49, 100, 125, 290.

CHAPTER FIVE

1. Robert Codrington, "The Life and Death of the Illustrious Robert, Earl of Essex," in *The Harleian Miscellany,* ed. William Oldys and Thomas Park

(London: Printed for John White, John Murray, and John Harding, 1808), I, 219.

2. *Tracts*, p. 118. For a discussion of Marprelate's popularity among the nobility, see William Pierce, *An Historical Introduction to the Marprelate Tracts* (London: Archibald Constable and Co., Ltd., 1908), pp. 159–60n. See also Giles Wigginton's testimony before Archbishop Whitgift: "I vnderstand by hearesay (yt wch I suppose you know well enough) yt many lordes & ladies & other great & wealthy personages of all estates haue read it, & so they will ioyne wth me in mine hauing & reading of it, if I haue done eyther of both." MS 31 Morrice A (OLP) fol. 29v.

3. Ayre, II, 321, 393–94. John Field, in defending the first *Admonition*, justifies the use of satirical invective but significantly stops short of targeting persons as opposed to places. See MS Morrice B, II, fols. 185v–186r.

4. *Tracts*, p. 29. Leland Carlson has recently argued for Job Throckmorton's authorship of the Marprelate tracts. He attributes their appearance to Throckmorton's increasing frustration with the absence of ordinary forums for theological debate. See Carlson, *Martin Marprelate*, p. 309.

5. The seven tracts are *The Epistle* (printed at East Molesey by Robert Waldegrave, October 15–20, 1588); *The Epitome* (printed at Fawsley House by Waldegrave, November 25–29, 1588); *Certaine Minerall and Metaphisicall Schoolpoints* (printed at the White Friars by Waldegrave, January 26–28, 1589); *Hay Any Worke for Cooper* (printed at the White Friars by Waldegrave, March 20–27, 1589); *Theses Martinanae* or *Martin Junior* (printed at the Priory by John Hodgkins, July 22, 1589); *The Just Censure and Reproofe* or *Martin Senior* (printed at the Priory by John Hodgkins, July 29, 1589); *The Protestatyon* (printed at the Priory, September 20–30, 1589).

6. *Tracts*, pp. 216, 234–35; *Tracts*, pp. 49–50.

7. *Tracts*, pp. 29–30.

8. Cartwright, *Apologie*, sig. C2v. See Pearson, pp. 277–89, 451, 455.

9. The only possible exceptions are John Bale's rather flat exercises in Tudor stagecraft.

10. J. Dover Wilson, "The Marprelate Controversy," in *The Cambridge History of English Literature*, ed. A. W. Ward and A. R. Waller (Cambridge: Cambridge University Press, 1909), III, 383–84.

11. John S. Coolidge, "Martin Marprelate, Marvell, and *Decorum Personae* as a Satirical Theme," *PMLA*, 74 (1959), 527. See also Bacon's disdain for "matters of religion . . . handled in the style of the stage." Francis Bacon, "An Advertisement Touching the Controversies of the Church of England," in *The Works of Francis Bacon*, ed. Basil Montague (London: William Pickering, 1827), VII, 32.

12. For a discussion of the popular assaults on Martin, see Carlson, *Martin Marprelate*, pp. 61–74.

13. *Tracts*, p. 18.

14. *Tracts*, pp. 132–33.

15. Wakefield, p. 23.

16. *Tracts*, p. 146.

17. *Tracts*, p. 24.

18. *Tracts*, p. 24. Behind the obvious jest is a serious preoccupation with consistency. Marprelate may mockingly assert that he has sacrificed consistency in Bridges's characterization in order to be true to his imitation of the dean's foolish style, but his real concern is with the faithful adherence to one's religious convictions. John Aylmer's *Harborowe of faithful subjects* had become for the Puritans an emblem of Anglican hypocrisy. Aylmer's sympathy to church reform, expressed in that work, was evidently discarded upon his elevation to the London see. For a typically satiric treatment of the subject, see [Job Throckmorton?], *A Dialogue Wherin is Plainly Laide Open, the tyrannical dealing of L. Bishopps against Gods children* (printed at Rochelle by Robert Waldegrave, 1589), sig. Br-v.

19. *Tracts*, p. 24.

20. *Tracts*, p. 40.

21. *Tracts*, p. 27.

22. The same pattern occurs in *The State of the Church of England*. Printed in April of 1588, copies of the book were seized at Waldegrave's shop before they might be distributed. The dialogue later appeared in *A Parte of a Register* published in the spring of 1593. Though the book has traditionally been attributed to John Udall, Carlson now argues for Throckmorton/Marprelate as the author (*Martin Marprelate*, pp. 332–38). Regardless of who the writer might be, the work is one of the richer dramatic satires in the nonconformist canon. Interestingly, the paths of two doubters are traced: Demetrius the usurer eventually embraces the preacher of dissent, while Pandochus the innkeeper rejects his call to faith. Udall, pp. 30–31.

23. See Chapter Four, pp. 146–47.

24. Coolidge, "Martin Marprelate," p. 528.

25. See Joy Lee Belknap King, "A Critical Edition of *A Dialogue Wherin Is Plainly Laide Open, the Tyrannicall Dealing of L. Bishopps against Gods Children*." Diss. Rutgers University, 1968.

26. For Upland, see Chapter Two, pp. 84–85; for Bale, see Chapter Three, p. 130; for Turner and Gilby, see Chapter Four, pp. 132–33.

27. Turner, *Examination of the Masse*, A7-A8.

28. See Chapter Three, p. 123. Ben Jonson similarly shows his fear of the ungoverned interaction between play and audience by placing fictional spectators on his stage.

29. See Chapter Two, pp. 59–61.

30. See Chapter Two, pp. 63–64. For another example of nonconformist subplotting, see Turner, *The Rescuynge of the Romishe Fox*, sigs. H3v–H4r.

31. *Tracts*, p. 82.

32. *Tracts*, p. 364.

33. Whitgift predictably plays the enraged autocrat deriding the saintly Penry as "boy," "knave," "varlet," and "lewd slanderer." Penry, of course, suffers his torments with typical aplomb. For a penetrating study of ecclesiastical justice in Tudor England, see Hill, *Society and Puritanism*, pp. 344–53.

34. *Tracts*, p. 49. Martin apparently draws the line at jesting at Biblical names. He upbraids Bishop Cooper for playing with John's name in a sermon; see *Tracts*, p. 90.

35. *Tracts*, p. 59.

36. *Tracts*, p. 65.

37. *Tracts*, p. 359. The speech resembles medieval stage renditions of Herod's appeal to his knights on the eve of the slaughter of the innocents.

38. Although a portion of these collected papers were published in 1593 under the title *A Parte of a Register*, the bulk remained in manuscript. Now in Dr. Williams's Library, the Morrice MSS consist of three volumes: A (Old and New Loose Papers); B (Seconde Parte of a Register); and C (Transcript). A detailed description of the manuscripts and their contents was prepared by Peel. See Albert Peel, ed. *The Seconde Parte of a Register. Being a Calendar of Manuscripts under That Title Intended for Publication by the Puritans about 1593, and Now in Dr. Williams's Library, London*, 2 vols. (Cambridge: University Press, 1915).

39. The same value Foxe assigned to the direct testimony of the examinates whose "troubles" he documented is found in the Register. Whenever the account is autobiographical that fact is prominently advertised. Examinates often stress their attempts to recall events accurately; some apparently took extraordinary measures to achieve that accuracy. See John Wilson's account, MS Morrice B, II, fol. 60v. "Now if yow mervaile how I should thus stricktly observe ye worde both of my answere, & the articles, as also of my sermon & other thinges in this reporte you must vnderstande that for the 2. first I haue a copy out of their owne recorde. for the third I did pen it at large verbatim, immediatly after it was preched beinge then fressh in my memorye, because I . . . suspected it would be called into question . . ." The quasi-scriptural status accorded to the "acts" of these latter-day apostles is once again underscored. The life and the words that accurately describe it are almost one: "[L]et the fayth and profession of a Christian be rightly scanned after the line of God's word." I. G., *M. Some laid open in his coulers*, p. 111.

40. For an analogue to the Marprelate habit of willful fabrication followed by a confession that disarms criticism without erasing the effect of the misreading, see MS Morrice B, II, fol. 52r.

41. MS Morrice B, I, fols. 583–84.

42. MS Morrice B, II, fol. 56r.

43. *Tracts*, p. 79.

44. *Tracts*, p. 118.

45. Raymond A. Anselment, *'Betwixt Jest and Earnest': Marprelate, Milton, Marvell, Swift and the Decorum of Religious Ridicule* (Toronto: University of Toronto Press, 1979), p. 34.

46. *Tracts*, p. 363.

47. For examples, see *Tracts*, pp. 23, 40, 215.

48. *Tracts*, p. 164.

49. *Tracts*, p. 272.

50. *Tracts*, p. 159. Marprelate is a Puritan artist who only threatens to produce a text in logic; it is Milton who eventually assumes and completes the task. See Howell, pp. 210–16.

51. Marprelate speaks of this typically Puritan division of preaching labor in *Hay Any Worke for Cooper*: "he that teacheth which is the Doctor: he that exhorteth which is the Pastor." *Tracts*, p. 235.

52. Raymond A. Anselment, "Rhetoric and the Dramatic Satire of Martin Marprelate," *Studies in English Literature: 1500–1900*, 10 (1970), 111.

53. Anselment, "Rhetoric," p. 111.

54. Gilby, *A Pleasaunt Dialogue*, sig. A7v.

55. See Chapter Two, p. 71.

56. Ayre, III, 523. See Anselment (*'Betwixt Jest and Earnest'*, pp. 10–28) for a useful discussion of later Puritan views of laughter. For the outlook of one of Martin's contemporaries, see Thomas Carew's letter to John Aylmer (MS Morrice B II, fol. 64v), where he contrasts "the monstrous enimies laughinge & clapping their handes" with "the godly generally mourninge & holdinge downe their heades."

57. *Tracts*, p. 217.

58. Martin complains, "The Puritans are angry with me; I mean the Puritan preachers. And why? Because I am too open; because I jest." *Tracts*, p. 118.

59. Turner, *Romyshe Vuolfe*, sig. A1v.

60. Turner, *Romyshe Vuolfe*, sigs. A1v–A2r.

61. Turner, *Romyshe Vuolfe*, sig. A2r.

62. Johan Huizinga, *Homo Ludens: A Study of the Play Element in Culture* (Boston: Beacon Press, 1955), pp. 8ff. I am indebted to Huizinga's suggestive discussion of play throughout this chapter. The nonconformist concept of vocational play no doubt draws upon Horace's insistence that poetry both instruct and delight. The emphasis among the reformers, however, is overwhelmingly didactic.

63. Turner, *Romyshe Vuolfe*, sig. A6r.

64. *Tracts*, pp. 43–44. See also Martin's reference to Turner's notorious prelate-baiting dog (*Tracts*, p. 86).

65. Its successor, *More Worke for the Cooper*, was destroyed when the Marprelate press was seized en route to Manchester. On the seizure of the press, see Pierce, *Historical Introduction*, pp. 190ff. "'Pistle-making" is Marprelate's

term for the business of the reform-minded satirist. An allusion to Paul's epistolary activities is apparently intended—not unexpected in a Puritan convinced that the words of an inspired preacher might be regarded as a form of scripture.

66. *Tracts*, pp. 217–18.

67. If Carlson is correct in identifying Throckmorton as Martin, these strictures on playing versus working take on added significance. Throckmorton was a country squire and a Member of Parliament. In his situation, 'pistlemaking might indeed be construed as recreative activity. For a comical example of the Anglican penchant for play over work, see Martin's tale of a starstruck priest from Essex. Having ascended the pulpit to deliver one of his infrequent oratorical exercises, Good Glibbery of Halstead is immediately distracted by a young boy's speedy exit from the church. A play, he learns, is about to be performed—perhaps the adventures of Robin Hood. Memories of his former glories as a thespian prove too potent for the cleric: "Good Glibbery, though he were in the pulpit, yet had a mind to his old companions abroad (a company of merry grigs, you must think them to be, as merry as a Vice on a stage), seeing the boy going out, finished his matter presently, with John of London's Amen; saying, 'Ha, ye faith, boy! Are they there? Then, ha' with thee.' And so, came down, and among them he goes." *Tracts*, pp. 226–27.

68. *Tracts*, p. 121.

69. Whitgift recognized that the bishops were forced to rely on magistrates who were unwilling to support the disciplinary action of the episcopacy; see Ayre, I, 122.

70. *Tracts*, p. 373.

71. *Tracts*, p. 138.

72. *Tracts*, p. 122.

73. *Tracts*, pp. 32–33.

74. The conjunction of linguistic and moral indecorum is made manifest in the ludicrous spectacle of John Young, bishop of Rochester, presenting a benefice under his control to himself: " 'I John of Rochester, present John Young.' " *Tracts*, p. 36.

75. *Tracts*, pp. 124–25.

76. In "The defense of the mynisters of Kent," the Answerer chides the Accuser for his awkward "couplement" of an indictment and its illustration; the stylistic indecorum is viewed as an emblem of moral indecorum. MS Morrice B, I, fol. 407. This formulation may be found in orthodox literature as well. See Cooper, *Admonition*, p. 27.

77. *Tracts*, p. 35.

78. *Tracts*, p. 84.

79. Giles Wigginton mocks his adversaries by alternately omitting or abbreviating their titles. See MS Morrice B, II, fols. 26v, 31r, 33v.

80. *Tracts*, p. 123.

81. *Tracts*, p. 17. See Coolidge, "Martin Marprelate," p. 526.

82. *Tracts*, pp. 238–39.

83. Martin's project may be viewed as an effort to rewrite the works of the Admonition controversy.

84. *Tracts*, p. 81.

85. See Carlson's attempt to link Marprelate to the legal profession (*Martin Marprelate*, p. 101). Turner was also fond of legal language. See Turner, *Examination of the masse*.

86. Donald McGinn, in arguing for John Penry's authorship of the Marprelate tracts, has pointed to Martin's and Penry's shared affection for the syllogism. As we have seen, such an affection was a hallmark of nonconformist writing since the Middle Ages. See Donald McGinn, *John Penry and the Marprelate Controversy* (New Brunswick: Rutgers University Press, 1966), pp. 57ff. See also Carlson's contrast of syllogistic reasoning in the work of Penry and Marprelate (*Martin Marprelate*, pp. 259ff).

87. *Tracts*, p. 23.

88. *Tracts*, p. 24.

89. *Tracts*, pp. 362–63. See a similar claim to the artist's prerogative in logical discourse in I. G., *M. Some laid open in his coulers*, p. 108. The tract has been assigned by Carlson to Marprelate (*Martin Marprelate*, pp. 138–57).

90. Gilby, *An answer to the deuillish detection*, fol. 20r.

91. This view of grace is the common inheritance of all Calvinists including the defenders of the episcopacy. See the forthcoming article by Darryl J. Gless, "Nature and Grace," in *The Spenser Encyclopedia*, ed. A. C. Hamilton et al. (Toronto: Toronto University Press, 1986?), which provides a useful corrective to New's overly simplistic division between Anglican and Puritan attitudes (pp. 6–28).

92. *Tracts*, p. 28.

93. Lifting an unsound syllogism from Dean Bridges's *Defence*, Martin places Puritan truth in this false Anglican rack. "You may see what harm you have done by dealing so loosely. I know what I shall say to these Puritan reasons. They must needs be good, if yours be sound. Admit, their syllogisms offended in form as yours doth; yet the common people . . . will find an unhappy truth in many of these conclusions, when, as yours is, most false." *Tracts*, p. 98.

94. Ayre, II, 494.

95. For a discussion of the satire of Martin's opponents, see Holden, pp. 45ff. It is interesting to note that these popularized versions of more rigorous theological debate inevitably mimic the numbing, accretive quality of tract titles. *The Second Replie of Thomas Cartwright agaynst Master Doctor Witgiftes second answer touching the Churche Discipline* is transformed into *Marre Mar-Martin: or Marre-Martins Medling, in a Manner Misliked*.

96. A number of anti-Martinist satires have been attributed to the two authors. Lyly is often credited with having written *Pappe with an Hatchet*, and Nashe with *The Return of Pasquill, First Parte of Pasquills Apologie*, and *An Almond for a Parrat*.

97. *Tracts*, p. 43.

98. For references to the work and life of Cartwright, see *Tracts*, pp. 18, 19, 43, 63, 163, 216, 376–77.

99. *Tracts*, p. 118.

100. *Tracts*, p. 118–19.

101. *Tracts*, pp. 119.

102. *Tracts*, p. 215.

103. *Tracts*, p. 163, 376–77.

104. *Tracts*, pp. 215–16.

105. For a discussion of Upland's borrowings from the work of the Lollard popularizers, see Heyworth, *Jack Upland*, pp. 35–37.

106. Bale had relied heavily upon the work of Tyndale in much the same way. See Fairfield, pp. 51, 85, 94, 125.

107. *Tracts*, p. 314.

108. *Tracts*, p. 315.

109. *Tracts*, p. 326.

110. *Tracts*, p. 406.

111. Perhaps the most unhappy of the Marprelate detectives has been Donald McGinn, who insisted, in the teeth of contrary evidence and common sense, that dour Penry was responsible for these effervescent tracts. See Carlson's lengthy refutation in *Martin Marprelate*, pp. 271–307. Carlson's own arguments for Throckmorton are persuasive; less convincing is his attempt to attribute virtually every satiric piece from the 1570s through the 1590s to that same hand. As I have attempted to demonstrate, Martin's literary practice partakes of a nonconformist tradition of composition available to other writers of like temperament and conviction. For other discussions of the authorship of the tracts, see Edward Arber, *An Introductory Sketch to the Martin Marprelate Controversy, (1588–1590)*, The English Scholar's Library (London: 1879), p. 196; Leland H. Carlson, "Martin Marprelate: His Identity and His Satire," in *English Satire*, ed. Leland H. Carlson and Ronald Paulson (Los Angeles: William Andrews Clark Memorial Library, 1972), pp. 3–53; William Pierce, *Historical Introduction*, pp. 274ff.; John Dover Wilson, *Martin Marprelate and Shakespeare's Fluellen: A New Theory of the Authorship of the Marprelate Tracts* (London: A. Moring, Ltd., 1912); Ronald B. McKerrow, "Did Sir Roger Williams Write the Marprelate Tracts?" *The Library*, 3, (Oct. 1912), 364–74.

112. *Tracts*, p. 17.

113. *Tracts*, p. 241.

114. *Tracts*, pp. 250ff. At times, the presence of Cartwright's more disciplined prose is readily visible beneath the surface of Martin's writing; the

satirist's discussion of the tripartite nature of Presbyterian government is a page torn from the Admonition controversy. Compare *Tracts*, pp. 252–53, with Ayre, I, 389–90. For a discussion of Marprelate's changing tone, see Anselment, *'Betwixt Jest and Earnest'*, pp. 48ff.

115. *Tracts*, p. 257.

116. *Tracts*, pp. 277ff.

117. *Tracts*, p. 283.

118. *Tracts*, pp. 82, 159.

119. *Tracts*, p. 304.

120. *Tracts*, p. 304.

121. *Tracts*, pp. 304–5.

122. Earlier in the satires Martin had urged the bishops to confine their argumentation to syllogisms in order to control their unruly prose. See *Tracts*, p. 100. Martin now appears to be taking his own advice.

123. *Tracts*, p. 323.

124. *Tracts*, p. 347.

125. *Tracts*, p. 363.

126. *Tracts*, p. 363. See Throckmorton's similiar criticism of the extemporaneous prayers of the fanatical Copinger: "But, if I shall tell you simplie and plainlie what I thinke, this prayer of Maister Copingers (though it were full of outwarde zeale and feruentnesse, if not too feruent, because he vsed many of these othes, loude sighes and groninges, when as I conceiued the matter in weight, did nothing answere those patheticall outcries) was not, me thought, squared after the rule of knowledge, neither in methode, matter nor manner, nor yet savouring of that humilitie and discretion, as were to bee wished in so zealous a professour as he made shewe of." Job Throckmorton, *The Defence of Iob Throckmorton, against the slaunders of Maister Sutcliffe* (Middleburg: Richard Schilders, 1594), sig. A3r.

127. See the pairings of the Hunter and the Forester in Turner, *Romyshe Vuolfe*, and of Knowledge and Fremouth in Turner, *Examination of the Masse*.

128. The reader should be reminded that it is not necessary to insist upon a single artist as being responsible for this work; we may well be dealing, particularly in the satires of Martin Junior and Senior, with a committee of authors. Nonetheless, the remarkable coherence of the whole Marprelate series suggests that even if different hands participated in its creation, there was a marked unity of purpose and method in their work. There is a dramatic shape and an emotional consistency that transcend the individual satires of the canon. If it is true that more than one author was involved, it is simply testimony to the strength of the original author's invention and imagination that all subsequent writers fell so easily into the hypnotic rhythms of Martin's words and worlds. It is testimony as well to the persistent nonconformist need to create heroes whose utility rests more with their representative than their individual qualities.

129. *Tracts*, p. 397.

130. *Tracts*, p. 398. This view may be contrasted with Cartwright's doubts about the efficacy of persecution and the value of martyrdom. See Chapter Four, pp. 135–36.

131. *Tracts*, p. 411.

132. *Tracts*, p. 405. The language of reckoning and accounts recalls the parable of talents with its emphasis on the final judgment of the human soul at death. See V. A. Kolve's discussion of the parable with reference to the medieval *Everyman*. "*Everyman* and the Parable of Talents," in *Medieval English Drama*, ed. Jerome Taylor and Alan H. Nelson (Chicago: University of Chicago Press, 1972), pp. 316–40.

133. *Tracts*, p. 405n.

134. *Tracts*, p. 405.

135. *Tracts*, p. 406.

136. Donald McGinn (*John Penry*, pp. 125ff.) sees Martin's new seriousness as a sign of his movement toward an endorsement of Separatism. If true this would lend support to his contention that John Penry, a convert to Separatism, was the author of the Marprelate tracts. The fact remains, however, that Martin continued to denounce the Separatists to the end of his career as a satirist. See *Tracts*, pp. 98–99, 252, 414.

137. *Tracts*, p. 401.

EPILOGUE

1. The quarrel between Jonson and the Puritans needs to be reassessed. As Jonas Barish has so incisively shown in his chapter "Jonson and the Loathed Stage" in *The Antitheatrical Prejudice*, Jonson held ambivalent feelings toward the stage, lamenting the playwright-artist's lack of full control over his materials and audience. As Barish fails to see, the pattern of Jonson's thought and the shape of his literary career bear a remarkable similarity to those of the typical nonconformist artist.

2. Malvolio's less than disinterested reading of the forged letter would appear to be a satire on the Puritan misuse of scripture and in particular the Puritan habit of turning randomly to a text and "crushing" it to yield assurances of election (i.e., favor in his master's eyes). Siemon, in *Shakespearean Iconoclasm*, has recently argued with considerable skill for a far more pervasive dissident influence on Shakespeare's art. Siemon contends that the English tradition of iconoclasm helps determine Shakespeare's approach to the nature and reliability of the dramatist's stage icons.

3. Jonson is the source of the speculation that the Blatant Beast was intended as an allegory of Puritan backbiting. "That in that paper S. W. Raughly had of the Allegories of his Fayrie Queen, by the Blating Beast the

Puritans were understood, by the false Duessa the Q. of Scots." R. F. Patterson, ed., *Ben Jonson's Conversations with William Drummond of Hawthornden* (London: Blackie and Son, Ltd., 1924), p. 17.

4. On *Pilgrim's Progress*'s typically Puritan movement from the triumph of the individual to the consolidation of Christian community, see John R. Knott, Jr., "Bunyan and the Holy Community," *Studies in Philology*, 80 (Spring, 1983).

5. Hughes, pp. 8–9.

6. Hughes, p. 108.

7. Similarities with Bale's work are again evident. The contrary depictions of Satan's Pandemonium and God's heavenly court constitute yet another nonconformist attempt to present "the image of bothe churches." The activity in Book III describes, in fact, a Puritan service, filled with words (preaching) and music (the singing of psalms and hymns), while the Hell of Books I and II invokes images of the debased visual devotion of the unregenerate church, "the synagogue of Satan."

8. Hughes, p. 584.

Bibliography

MANUSCRIPTS

Bodleian Library
  MS 73.
  MS 288.
  MS Douce 53.
  MS Eng. th. f. 39.
  MS Rawlinson C. 208.
  MS Selden supra 41.

British Library
  MS Additional 24.202.
  MS Cotton Titus D.V.
  MS Egerton 2820.
  MS Harley 1203.

Dr. Williams's Library
  MSS Morrice A, B, C.

PRINTED PRIMARY SOURCES

A parte of a register, contayninge sundrie memorable matters written by diuers godly and learned in our time. Amsterdam and New York: Theatrum Orbis Terrarum, Ltd., and DeCapo Press, 1973.

Arnold, Thomas, ed. *Select English Works of John Wyclif.* 3 vols. Oxford: Clarendon Press, 1869.

Augustine. *On Christian Doctrine.* Trans. D. W. Robertson, Jr. The Library of Liberal Arts. Indianapolis: Bobbs-Merrill Co., Inc., 1958.

Ayre, John, ed. *The Works of John Whitgift.* The Parker Society. 3 vols. Cambridge: Cambridge University Press, 1851.

Bacon, Francis. "An Advertisement Touching the Controversies of the Church of England." In *The Works of Francis Bacon.* Ed. Basil Montague. Vol. VII. London: William Pickering, 1827.

Bale, John. *An Answere to a papystycall exhortacyon.* [1548?].

————. *The Apology of Johan Bale againste a ranke Papyst.* London: Ihon Day, [1550?].

————. *A Breue Cronycle of the Bysshope of Romes blessynge.* London: John Daye, [1549?].

————. *A declaration of Edmonde Bonners articles.* London: Ihon Tysdall for Frauncys Coldocke, 1561.

————. *A Dialoge or Communycacyon to be had at a table betwene two chyldren.* London, 1549.

————. *The Epistle exhortatorye of an Englyshe Christyane unto his derelye beloued contreye of Englande.* Basel, 1544.

_____. *An Expostulation or complaynte agaynste the blasphemyes of a franticke papyst of Hampshyre*. London: Ihon Daye, 1550.

_____. *The first two partes of the Actes or vnchaste examples of the Englyshe Votaryes*. London: John Tysdale, 1560.

_____. *King Johan*. Ed. Barry B. Adams. San Marino: Huntington Library, 1969.

_____. *The Laboryouse Journey and serche of John Leylande*. Ed. W. A. Copinger. Manchester: Priory Press, 1895.

_____. *A Mysterye of Inyquyte contayned within the heretycall Genealogye of Ponce Pantolabus*. Geneva: Mychael Woode, 1545.

_____. *The Pageant of Popes*. Englished with sondrye additions by I. S. [Iohn Studley]. London: Thomas Marshe, 1574.

_____. *The true hystorie of the Christen departynge of the reuerende man, D. Martyne Luther*. [Marburgh?], [1546?].

_____. *The vocacyon of Iohan Bale to the bishoprick of Ossorie in Irelande*. In *The Harleian Miscellany*. Vol. I. London: Robert Dutton, 1808.

_____. *Yet a course at the Romyshe foxe*. Zurich, 1543.

_____, ed. *A Treatyse Made by Johan Lambert*. 1538.

Beadle, Richard, ed. *The York Plays*. London: Edward Arnold, 1982.

Beza, Theodore. *A Tragedie of Abrahams Sacrifice*. Trans. Arthur Golding. Ed. Malcolm W. Wallace. Toronto: University of Toronto Library, 1906.

Block, K. S., ed. *Ludus Coventriae or The Plaie called Corpus Christi*. The Early English Text Society, E.S. 120. 1922; rpt. London: Oxford University Press, 1974.

Cartwright, Thomas. *A briefe Apologie of Thomas Cartwright against all such slanderous accusations as it pleaseth Mr Sutcliffe in his severall pamphlettes most iniuriously to loade him with*. 1596.

_____. *A Commentary upon the Epistle of Saint Paule written to the Colossians*. London: Nicholas Okes, 1612.

_____. *A Confutation of the Rhemists Translation, Glosses and Annotations on The New Testament*. 1618.

_____. *The Rest of the Second Replie of Thomas Cartwright*. 1577.

_____. *The Second Replie of Thomas Cartwright*. 1575.

Cawley, A. C., ed. *The Wakefield Pageants in the Towneley Cycle*. Manchester: Manchester University Press, 1958.

Christmas, Henry, ed. *Select Works of John Bale*. The Parker Society. Cambridge: Cambridge University Press, 1849.

Clarke, Samuel. *The Lives of Thirty-Two English Divines*. 3d ed. London: Printed for William Birche, 1677.

Codrington, Robert. "The Life and Death of the Illustrious Robert, Earl of Essex." In *The Harleian Miscellany*. Ed. William Oldys and Thomas Park. Vol I. London: Printed for John White, John Murray, and John Harding, 1808.

Cooper, Thomas. *An Admonition to the People of England*. Puritan Discipline Tracts. London: John Petheram, 1847.

d'Angoulême, Marguerite. *A Godly Medytacyon of the christen sowle*. Trans. Elyzabeth doughter to Kynge Henri the viii. Wesel: Dirik van der Straten, 1548.

Davidson, Clifford, ed. *A Middle English Treatise on the Playing of Miracles*. Washington, D.C.: University Press of America, Inc., 1981.

Farmer, John S., ed. *The Dramatic Writings of John Bale*. 1907; rpt. New York: Barnes and Noble, Inc., 1966.

Forshall, Josiah, ed. *Remonstrance against Romish Corruptions in the Church*. London: Longman, Brown, Green, and Longmans, 1851.

Forshall, Josiah, and Frederic Madden, eds. *The Holy Bible, Made from the Latin Vulgate by John Wycliffe and His Followers*. Vol. I. Oxford: Oxford University Press, 1850.

Foxe, John. *The Acts and Monuments of John Foxe*. Ed. Rev. George Townsend. 8 vols. New York: AMS Press, Inc., 1965.

Freeman, Arthur, ed. *The English Stage: Attack and Defense, 1577–1730*. New York: Garland Publishing, Inc., 1972–74.

Frere, W. H., and C. E. Douglas, eds. *Puritan Manifestoes: A Study of the Origin of the Puritan Revolt*. London: Church Historical Society, 1954.

Furnivall, Frederick J., ed. *Hoccleve's Works: Minor Poems*. The Early English Text Society, E.S. 61. London: Kegan Paul, Trench, Trubner and Co., 1892.

Gilby, Anthony. *An answer to the deuillish detection of Stephane Gardiner*. London: J. Day, 1547.

――――. *A Briefe Treatice of Election and Reprobation*. London: David Moptid and Iohn Mather, [1575?].

――――. *A Commentarye upon the Prophet Mycha*. London: Ihon Daye, 1551.

――――. *A Pleasaunt Dialogue, Betweene a Souldior of Barwicke, and an English Chaplaine*. 1581.

Gosson, Stephen. *Playes Confuted in Five Actions*. Ed. Arthur Freeman. New York: Garland Publishing, Inc., 1972.

Grosart, Alexander, ed. *The Works of Richard Sibbes*. Nichol's Series of Standard Divines: Puritan Period. 7 vols. Edinburgh: James Nichol, 1864.

Heyworth, P. L., ed. *Jack Upland, Friar Daw's Reply and Upland's Rejoinder*. Oxford: Oxford University Press, 1968.

Hooker, Richard. *Of the Laws of Ecclesiastical Polity*. Ed. Christopher Morris. 2 vols. London: J. M. Dent and Sons, Ltd., 1969.

Hudson, Anne, ed. *English Wycliffite Sermons*. Vol. I. Oxford: Clarendon Press, 1983.

――――, ed. *Selections from English Wycliffite Writings*. Cambridge: Cambridge University Press, 1978.

Hughes, Merritt Y., ed. *John Milton: Complete Poems and Major Prose*. Indianapolis: Bobbs-Merrill Company, Inc., 1957.

I. G. M. *Some laid open in his coulers.*

Lumiansky, R. M., and David Mills, eds. *The Chester Mystery Cycle.* The Early English Text Society, S.S. 3. London: Oxford University Press, 1974.

Matthew, F. D., ed. *The English Works of Wyclif Hitherto Unprinted.* The Early English Text Society, O.S. 74. 2d ed. 1902; rpt. Millwood, N.Y.: Kraus Reprint Co., 1973.

Northbrooke, John. *A Treatise against Dicing, Dancing, Plays, and Interludes.* Ed. John P. Collier. London: The Shakespeare Society, 1843.

Patterson, R. F., ed. *Ben Jonson's Conversations with William Drummond of Hawthornden.* London: Blackie and Son, Ltd., 1924.

Pecock, Reginald. *The Repressor of Over Much Blaming of the Clergy.* Ed. Churchill Babington. 2 vols. London: Longman, Green, Longman, and Roberts, 1860.

Peel, Albert, ed. *The Notebook of John Penry.* The Camden Society, No. 67. London: Royal Historical Society, 1944.

_____, ed. *The Seconde Parte of a Register. Being a Calendar of Manuscripts under That Title Intended for Publication by the Puritans about 1593, and Now in Dr. Williams's Library, London.* 2 vols. Cambridge: Cambridge University Press, 1915.

Peel, Albert, and Leland H. Carlson, eds. *Cartwrightiana.* London: George Allen and Unwin, Ltd., 1951.

Penry, John. *Th' Appellation of Iohn Penri unto the Highe court of Parliament.* 1589.

_____. *A Briefe Discovery of the Untruthes and Slanders.*

_____. *The Historie of Corah, Datham, and Abiram.* 1609.

_____. *An Humble Motion with Submission.* 1590.

_____. *I Ihon Penry.* London, 1593.

_____. *Three Treatises concerning Wales.* Ed. David Williams. Cardiff: University of Wales Press, 1960.

_____. *To My Beloved Wife Helener Penry.* London, 1593.

_____. *A Treatise Wherein is Manifestlie Proved.* 1590.

Perkins, William. *The Work of William Perkins.* Ed. Ian Breward. Appleford: Courtenay Press, 1970.

Pierce, William, ed. *The Marprelate Tracts: 1588–1589.* London: James Clarke and Co., 1911.

Pollard, Alfred W., ed. *Fifteenth-Century Prose and Verse.* New York: E.P. Dutton and Co., 1903.

Prynne, William. *Histriomastix, The Players Scovrge or Actors Tragaedie.* London: Printed by E. A. and W. I. for Michael Sparke, 1633.

Rainolds, John. *The Overthrow of Stage-Playes.* 2d ed. Oxford: Ihon Lichfield, 1629.

Robbins, Rossell Hope, ed. *Historical Poems of the Fourteenth and Fifteenth Centuries.* New York: Columbia University Press, 1959.

Robinson, F. N., ed. *The Works of Geoffrey Chaucer*. 2d ed. Boston: Houghton Mifflin Company, 1961.

Ross, Woodburn O., ed. *Middle English Sermons*. Early English Text Society, O.S. 209. Oxford: Oxford University Press, 1940.

Scattergood, V. J., ed. *The Works of Sir John Clanvowe*. Totowa, N.J.: D. S. Brewer, Ltd., and Rowman and Littlefield, 1975.

Simmons, Thomas F., ed. *The Lay Folks' Mass Book*. Early English Text Society, O.S. 71. 1879; rpt. London: Oxford University Press, 1968.

Simmons, Thomas Frederick, and Henry Edward Nolloth, eds. *The Lay Folks' Catechism*. The Early English Text Society, O.S. 118. 1901; rpt. Millwood, N.Y.: Kraus Reprint Co., 1972.

Skeat, Walter W., ed. *Pierce the Ploughman's Crede*. The Early English Text Society. London: N. Trubner and Co., 1873.

————, ed. *The Plowman's Tale*. In *The Complete Works of Geoffrey Chaucer*. Vol. VII. Oxford: Clarendon Press, 1897.

Smith, John Hazel, ed. and trans. *Two Latin Comedies by John Foxe the Martyrologist*. Renaissance Society of America. Ithaca: Cornell University Press, 1973.

Stubbes, Phillip. *The Anatomy of Abuses*. Ed. Frederick J. Furnivall. 1879; rpt. Millwood, N.Y.: Kraus Reprint Co., 1965.

Swinburn, Lillian M., ed. *The Lanterne of Liȝt*. Early English Text Society, O.S. 151. London: Kegan Paul, Trench, Trubner and Co., 1917.

Tanner, Norman P., ed. *Heresy Trials in the Diocese of Norwich, 1428–31*. Camden Fourth Series, No. 20. London: Royal Historical Society, 1977.

Throckmorton, Job. *The Defence of Iob Throckmorton, against the slaunders of Maister Sutcliffe*. Middleburg: Richard Schilders, 1594.

[Throckmorton, Job?]. *A Dialogue Wherin is Plainly Laide Open, the tyrannical dealing of L. Bishopps against Gods children*. Printed at Rochelle by Robert Waldegrave, 1589.

Todd, James H., ed. *An Apology for Lollard Doctrines*. The Camden Society. London: John Bowyer Nichols and Son, 1842.

Travers, Walter. *A Full and Plaine Declaration of Ecclesiastical Discipline out of the word of God*. 1617.

Turner, William. *The huntyng and fyndyng out of the Romishe fox*. Basel, 1543.

————. *The Huntyng of the Romyshe Vuolfe*. [Basel?], [1554?].

————. *A newe dialogue where in is conteyned the examination of the masse*. London: Ihon Day and William Seres, [1548?].

————. *The Olde Learnyng and the new*. London: Robert Stoughton, 1548.

————. *A preseruatiue, or triacle, agaynst the poyson of Pelagius*. London: Hester, 1551.

————. *The Rescuynge of the Romishe Fox*. 1545.

Tyndale, William. *An Answer to Sir Thomas More's Dialogue*. Ed. Henry Walter. The Parker Society. Cambridge: Cambridge University Press, 1850.

_____. *Doctrinal Treatises and Introductions to Different Portions of the Holy Scriptures*. Ed. Henry Walter. The Parker Society. Cambridge: Cambridge University Press, 1848.

_____. *Expositions and Notes on Sundry Portions of the Holy Scriptures Together with the Practice of Prelates*. Ed. Henry Walter. The Parker Society. Cambridge: Cambridge University Press, 1849.

Udall, John. *The State of the Church of England*. Ed. Edward Arber. London: The English Scholar's Library, 1879.

Whittingham, William. *A brieff discours off the troubles begonne at Franckford*. Ed. Edward Arber. London: N.p., 1908.

Wright, Thomas, ed. *Political Poems and Songs Relating to English History*. 2 vols. London: Longman, Green, Longman, and Roberts, 1859.

_____, ed. *The Vision and Creed of Piers Ploughman*. Vol II. London: John Russell Smith, 1856.

Young, Karl. *The Drama of the Medieval Church*. 2 vols. Oxford: Clarendon Press, 1933.

SECONDARY SOURCES

Altman, Joel B. *The Tudor Play of Mind: Rhetorical Inquiry and the Development of Elizabethan Drama*. Berkeley: University of California Press, 1978.

Anselment, Raymond A. *'Betwixt Jest and Earnest': Marprelate, Milton, Marvell, Swift and the Decorum of Religious Ridicule*. Toronto: University of Toronto Press, 1979.

_____. "Rhetoric and the Dramatic Satire of Martin Marprelate." *Studies in English Literature: 1500–1900*, 10 (1970), 103–19.

Arber, Edward. *An Introductory Sketch to the Martin Marprelate Controversy (1588–1590)*. London: The English Scholar's Library, 1879.

Aston, Margaret. *Lollards and Reformers: Images and Literacy in Late Medieval Religion*. London: The Humbledon Press, 1984.

_____. "Lollardy and Sedition, 1381–1431." *Past and Present*, 17 (1960), 1–44.

_____. *Thomas Arundel: A Study of Church Life in the Reign of Richard II*. Oxford: Clarendon Press, 1967.

Atkins, J. W. H. *English Literary Criticism: The Medieval Phase*. London: Methuen and Co., Ltd., 1952.

Barish, Jonas. *The Antitheatrical Prejudice*. Berkeley: University of California Press, 1981.

Bevington, David. *Tudor Drama and Politics*. Cambridge: Harvard University Press, 1968.

Blackburn, Ruth H. *Biblical Drama under the Tudors*. The Hague: Mouton, 1971.

Blatt, Thora Balslev. *The Plays of John Bale: A Study of Ideas, Technique, and Style*. Copenhagen: G. E. C. Gad, 1968.

Campbell, Lily B. *Divine Poetry and Drama in Sixteenth-Century England*. Cambridge: Cambridge University Press, 1959.

Carlson, Leland H. *Martin Marprelate, Gentleman: Master Job Throckmorton Laid Open in His Colors*. San Marino: Huntington Library, 1981.

———. "Martin Marprelate: His Identity and His Satire." In *English Satire*. Ed. Leland H. Carlson and Ronald Paulson. Los Angeles: William Andrews Clark Memorial Library, 1972.

Clebsch, William A. *England's Earliest Protestants, 1520–1535*. New Haven: Yale University Press, 1964.

Collinson, Patrick. "A Comment: Concerning the Name Puritan." *Journal of Ecclesiastical History*, 31, No. 4 (1980), 483–88.

———. *The Elizabethan Puritan Movement*. Berkeley: University of California Press, 1967.

———. *The Religion of the Protestants*. Oxford: The Clarendon Press, 1982.

Coolidge, John S. "Martin Marprelate, Marvell, and *Decorum Personae* as a Satirical Theme." *PMLA*, 74 (1959), 526–32.

———. *The Pauline Renaissance in England: Puritanism and the Bible*. Oxford: Clarendon Press, 1970.

Craig, Hardin. *English Religious Drama of the Middle Ages*. Oxford: Clarendon Press, 1955.

Cruttwell, Patrick. *The Shakespearean Moment and Its Place in the Poetry of the 17th Century*. New York: Vintage Books, 1960.

Dahmus, Joseph. *William Courtenay: Archbishop of Canterbury, 1381–1396*. University Park: Pennsylvania State University Press, 1966.

Davies, Horton. *The Worship of the English Puritans*. Westminster: Dacre Press, 1948.

Davies, W. T. "A Bibliography of John Bale." In *Oxford Bibliographical Society: Proceedings and Papers*. Vol. V. Oxford: Oxford University Press, 1940.

Deanesly, Margaret. *The Lollard Bible*. 1920; rpt. Cambridge: Cambridge University Press, 1966.

Dickens, A. G. *The English Reformation*. New York: Schocken Books, 1964.

———. *Lollards and Protestants in the Diocese of York, 1509–1558*. London: Oxford University Press, 1959.

Dix, Dom Gregory. *The Shape of the Liturgy*. 2d ed. Westminster: Dacre Press, 1945.

Dugmore, C. W. *The Mass and the English Reformers*. London: Macmillan & Co., Ltd., 1958.

Fairfield, Leslie P. *John Bale: Mythmaker for the English Reformation*. West Lafayette: Purdue University Press, 1976.

Fines, John. "Heresy Trials in the Diocese of Coventry and Lichfield, 1511–

1512." *Journal of Ecclesiastical History*, 14 (1963), 160–74.

Flanigan, Clifford. "The Roman Rite and the Origins of the Liturgical Drama." *University of Toronto Quarterly*, 42 (1974), 263–84.

Fraser, Russell. *The War against Poetry*. Princeton: Princeton University Press, 1970.

Gardiner, Harold C. *Mysteries' End: An Investigation of the Last Days of the Medieval Religious Stage*. New Haven: Yale University Press, 1946.

Garrett, Christina H. *The Marian Exiles: A Study in the Origins of Elizabethan Puritanism*. 1938; rpt. Cambridge: Cambridge University Press, 1966.

George, Charles H., and Katherine George. *The Protestant Mind of the English Reformation*. Princeton: Princeton University Press, 1961.

Gless, Darryl J. "Nature and Grace." *The Spenser Encyclopedia*. Ed. A. C. Hamilton et al. Toronto: University of Toronto Press, [1986?].

Greenblatt, Stephen. *Renaissance Self-Fashioning from More to Shakespeare*. Chicago: University of Chicago Press, 1980.

Grout, Donald Jay. *A History of Western Music*. 2d ed. New York: W. W. Norton and Company, Inc., 1973.

Hall, David D. *The Antinomian Controversy, 1636–1638*. Middletown: Wesleyan University Press, 1968.

Haller, William. *The Elect Nation: The Meaning and Relevance of Foxe's Book of Martyrs*. New York: Harper and Row, 1963.

Hardison, O. B., Jr. *Christian Rite and Christian Drama in the Middle Ages*. Baltimore: The Johns Hopkins Press, 1969.

Harris, Jesse W. *John Bale: A Study in the Minor Literature of the Reformation*. University of Illinois Studies in Language and Literature, vol. 25. Urbana: University of Illinois Press, 1940.

Heiserman, A. R. *Skelton and Satire*. Chicago: University of Chicago Press, 1961.

Herford, Charles H. *Studies in the Literary Relations of England and Germany in the Sixteenth Century*. Cambridge: Cambridge University Press, 1886.

Hill, Christopher. *Milton and the English Revolution*. New York: Penguin Books, 1979.

––––––. *Puritanism and Revolution: Studies in Interpretation of the English Revolution of the 17th Century*. New York: Schocken Books, 1964.

––––––. "Puritans and 'The Dark Corners of the Land.'" *Transactions of the Royal Historical Society*, 5th Ser., 13 (1963), 77–102.

––––––. *Society and Puritanism in Pre-Revolutionary England*. 2d ed. New York: Schocken Books, 1967.

––––––. *The World Turned Upside Down: Radical Ideas During the English Revolution*. New York: The Viking Press, 1973.

Holden, William P. *Anti-Puritan Satire*. New Haven: Yale University Press, 1954.

Howell, Wilbur Samuel. *Logic and Rhetoric in England, 1500–1700.* New York: Russell and Russell, Inc., 1961.

Hudson, Anne. "The Examination of Lollards." *Bulletin of the Institute of Historical Research*, 46, No. 114 (1973), 145–59.

———. "A Lollard Compilation and the Dissemination of Wycliffite Thought." *Journal of Theological Studies*, N.S., 23 (1972), 65–81.

———. "A Lollard Quaternion." *The Review of English Studies*, 22 (1971), 435–42.

———. "A Lollard Sermon-Cycle and Its Implications." *Medium Aevum*, 40 (1971), 142–56.

———. "Some Aspects of Lollard Book Production." *Studies in Church History*, 9 (1972), 147–57.

Huizinga, Johan. *Homo Ludens: A Study of the Play Element in Culture.* Boston: Beacon Press, 1955.

Hurley, Michael, S.J. " 'Scriptura sola': Wyclif and His Critics." *Traditio*, 16 (1960), 275–352.

Jones, W. R. "Lollards and Images: The Defense of Religious Art in Later Medieval England." *Journal of the History of Ideas*, 34 (1973), 27–50.

Kahrl, Stanley J. *Traditions of Medieval English Drama.* London: Hutchinson University Library, 1974.

Kaufmann, U. Milo. *The Pilgrim's Progress and Traditions in Puritan Meditation.* New Haven: Yale University Press, 1966.

Kernan, Alvin. *The Cankered Muse: Satire of the English Renaissance.* Yale Studies in English, No. 142. New Haven: Yale University Press, 1959.

King, John N. *English Reformation Literature: The Tudor Origins of the Protestant Tradition.* Princeton: Princeton University Press, 1982.

King, Joy Lee Belknap. "A Critical Edition of *A Dialogue Wherin Is Plainly Laide Open, the Tyrannicall Dealing of L. Bishopps against Gods Children.*" Diss. Rutgers University, 1968.

Knapp, Peggy Ann. *The Style of John Wyclif's English Sermons.* The Hague: Mouton, 1977.

Knappen, M. M. *Tudor Puritanism: A Chapter in the History of Idealism.* Chicago: University of Chicago Press, 1939.

Knott, John R., Jr. "Bunyan and the Holy Community." *Studies in Philology*, 80 (Spring, 1983), 200–25.

———. *The Sword of the Spirit: Puritan Responses to the Bible.* Chicago: University of Chicago Press, 1980.

Kolve, V. A. "Everyman and the Parable of Talents." In *Medieval English Drama.* Ed. Jerome Taylor and Alan H. Nelson. Chicago: University of Chicago Press, 1972.

———. *The Play Called Corpus Christi.* Stanford: Stanford University Press, 1966.

Lake, Peter. *Moderate puritans and the Elizabethan Church*. Cambridge: Cambridge University Press, 1982.

Lanham, Richard A. *The Motives of Eloquence: Literary Rhetoric in the Renaissance*. New Haven: Yale University Press, 1976.

Leff, Gordon. *Heresy in the Later Middle Ages*. Vol. II. Manchester: Manchester University Press, 1967.

Leverenz, David. *The Language of Puritan Feeling: An Exploration in Literature, Psychology, and Social History*. New Brunswick: Rutgers University Press, 1980.

Lewalski, Barbara K. *Protestant Poetics and the Seventeenth-Century Lyric*. Princeton: Princeton University Press, 1979.

McCusker, Honor. *John Bale: Dramatist and Antiquary*. Bryn Mawr, Pa.: N.p., 1942.

McFarlane, K. B. *John Wycliffe and the Beginnings of English Nonconformity*. London: English Universities Press, 1952.

————. *Lancastrian Kings and Lollard Knights*. Oxford: Clarendon Press, 1972.

McGinn, Donald J. *The Admonition Controversy*. New Brunswick: Rutgers University Press, 1949.

————. *John Penry and the Marprelate Controversy*. New Brunswick: Rutgers University Press, 1966.

McHardy, A. K. "Bishop Buckingham and the Lollards of the Lincoln Diocese." *Studies in Church History*, 9 (1972), 131–45.

McKerrow, Ronald B. "Did Sir Roger Williams Write the Marprelate Tracts?" *The Library*, 3 (Oct., 1912), 364–74.

Martz, Louis. *The Poetry of Meditation: A Study in English Religious Literature of the Seventeenth Century*. New Haven: Yale University Press, 1962.

Mayor, Stephen. *The Lord's Supper in Early English Dissent*. London: Epworth Press, 1972.

Miller, Perry. *The New England Mind: The Seventeenth Century*. Boston: Beacon Press, 1961.

Milward, Peter. *Religious Controversies of the Elizabethan Age: A Survey of Printed Sources*. London: The Scolar Press, 1978.

Morgan, Irvonwy. *The Godly Preachers of the Elizabethan Church*. London: Epworth Press, 1965.

Mozley, T. F. *John Foxe and His Book*. London: Society for Promoting Christian Knowledge, 1940.

Mudroch, Vaclav. *The Wyclif Tradition*. Ed. Albert Compton Reeves. Athens: Ohio University Press, 1979.

Mueller, Janel. *The Native Tongue and the Word: Developments in English Prose Style, 1380–1580*. Chicago: University of Chicago Press, 1984.

New, John F. H. *Anglican and Puritan: The Basis of Their Opposition, 1558–1640*. Stanford: Stanford University Press, 1964.

Norbrook, David. *Poetry and Politics in the English Renaissance.* London: Routledge and Kegan Paul, 1984.

Nuttal, Geoffrey F. *The Puritan Spirit.* London: Epworth Press, 1967.

Olsen, V. Norskov. *John Foxe and the Elizabethan Church.* Berkeley: University of California Press, 1973.

Ong, Walter J. *Ramus, Method, and the Decay of Dialogue.* Cambridge: Harvard University Press, 1958.

Owst, G. R. *Literature and Pulpit in Medieval England.* Cambridge: Cambridge University Press, 1933.

————. *Preaching in Medieval England: An Introduction to Sermon Manuscripts of the Period c. 1350–1450.* Cambridge: Cambridge University Press, 1926.

Pantin, W. A. *The English Church in the Fourteenth Century.* Cambridge: Cambridge University Press, 1955.

Pearson, A. F. Scott. *Thomas Cartwright and Elizabethan Puritanism, 1535–1603.* Gloucester, Mass.: Peter Smith, 1966.

Peter, John. *Complaint and Satire in Early English Literature.* Oxford: Clarendon Press, 1956.

Phillips, John. *The Reformation of Images: Destruction of Art in England, 1535–1660.* Berkeley: University of California Press, 1973.

Pierce, William. *An Historical Introduction to the Marprelate Tracts.* London: Archibald Constable and Co., Ltd., 1908.

————. *John Penry: His Life, Times, and Writings.* London: Hodder and Stoughton, 1923.

Porter, Harry Culverwell. *Reformation and Reaction in Tudor Cambridge.* Cambridge: Cambridge University Press, 1958.

Potter, Robert. *The English Morality Play.* London: Routledge and Kegan Paul, 1975.

Ringler, William. "The First Phase of the Elizabethan Attack on the Stage, 1558–1579." *Huntington Library Quarterly,* No. 4 (1942), 391–418.

Ross, Malcolm MacKenzie. *Poetry and Dogma: The Transfiguration of Eucharistic Symbols in Seventeenth-Century English Poetry.* New Brunswick: Rutgers University Press, 1954.

Roston, Murray. *Biblical Drama in England from the Middle Ages to the Present Day.* Evanston: Northwestern University Press, 1968.

Rothkrug, Lionel. "Religious Practices and Collective Perceptions: Hidden Homologies in the Renaissance and Reformation." *Historical Reflections,* 7 (1980).

Sasek, Lawrence A. *The Literary Temper of the English Puritans.* Louisiana State University Studies, Humanities Series, No. 9. Baton Rouge: Louisiana State University Press, 1961.

Scattergood, V. J. *Politics and Poetry in the Fifteenth Century.* New York: Barnes and Noble, 1972.

Siemon, James R. *Shakespearean Iconoclasm*. Berkeley: University of California Press, 1985.

Smalley, Beryl. "The Bible and Eternity: John Wyclif's Dilemma." *Journal of the Warburg and Courtauld Institutes*, 27 (1964), 73–89.

———. *The Study of the Bible in the Middle Ages*. Oxford: Basil Blackwell, 1952.

Tentler, Thomas N. *Sin and Confession on the Eve of the Reformation*. Princeton: Princeton University Press, 1977.

Thompson, Elbert N. S. *The Controversy between the Puritans and the Stage*. Yale Studies in English, No. 20. New York: Henry Holt and Company, 1903.

Thomson, John A. F. "John Foxe and Some Sources for Lollard History: Notes for a Critical Appraisal." *Studies in Church History*, 2 (1963), 251–57.

———. *The Later Lollards: 1414–1520*. Oxford: Oxford University Press, 1965.

Trinterud, Leonard J. *Elizabethan Puritanism*. New York: Oxford University Press, 1971.

Tucker, Samuel Marion. *Verse-Satire in England Before the Renaissance*. New York: Columbia University Press, 1908.

Wakefield, Gordon Stevens. *Puritan Devotion*. London: Epworth Press, 1957.

Walzer, Michael. *The Revolution of the Saints: A Study in the Origins of Radical Politics*. New York: Atheneum, 1969.

Waugh, W.T. "Sir John Oldcastle." *English Historical Review*, 20 (1905), 434–56, 637–58.

Weiner, Andrew D. *Sir Philip Sidney and the Poetics of Protestantism: A Study of Contexts*. Minneapolis: University of Minnesota Press, 1978.

Wilks, Michael. "Reformatio Regni: Wyclif and Hus as Leaders of Religious Protest Movements." *Studies in Church History*, 9 (1972), 109–30.

Williams, C. H. *William Tyndale*. London: Thomas Nelson and Sons, Ltd., 1969.

Wilson, J. Dover. "The Marprelate Controversy." In *The Cambridge History of English Literature*. Ed. A. W. Ward and A. R. Waller. Vol. III. Cambridge: Cambridge University Press, 1909.

———. *Martin Marprelate and Shakespeare's Fluellen: A New Theory of the Authorship of the Marprelate Tracts*. London: A. Moring, Ltd., 1912.

Woolf, Rosemary. *The English Mystery Plays*. London: Routledge and Kegan Paul, 1972.

Wright, Louis B. *Middle-Class Culture in Elizabethan England*. Chapel Hill: University of North Carolina Press, 1935.

Yunck, John A. *The Lineage of Lady Meed*. Publications in Mediaeval Studies, No. 17. Notre Dame: University of Notre Dame Press, 1963.

Index

Admonition controversy, 137–42, 153–54, 157, 174, 257; as drama, 140–41, 157–72, 245

Admonition to the Parliament, 137–38, 246, 252

Allegory, 127, 166, 230, 244; Bale, John: use of, 115–16; Lollardy: use of, 38–41, 80, 127, 240

Alnwick, William (bishop of Norwich), 43

Altman, Joel B., 88–89, 219, 230

Anabaptism, 153–57, 164, 249

Anglicanism, 141–42, 143–47, 151, 155, 156, 173; among critics, 139–41; "Troubles at Frankfort," 91; vs. Puritanism, 3–5, 217, 218, on argumentative method, 139–42, 157–65, 169, on ecclesiology, 137–38, 147, 157, 159–60, on scripture, 137–38, 146, 162–64, 246, 257

Anselment, Raymond A., 186, 255, 259

Antichrist, 4, 24, 35, 54, 67–68, 78, 93

Aristotle, 9, 171

Ars nova, 28–29

Arundel, Thomas (archbishop of Canterbury), 22, 47, 58–67, 73, 77, 113, 141, 180, 229

Askew, Anne, 58, 123–24, 125, 126, 180, 242

Aston, Margaret, 225, 231–32, 232

Augustine, 30, 32, 94, 115, 143, 235

Aylmer, John (bishop of London), 174, 177, 181, 253, 255

Bacon, Sir Francis, 252

Bale, John, 5, 12, 89, 132, 135, 140, 143, 147–48, 150, 154, 168–69, 170, 174, 176, 178, 179–82, 187, 191, 193–94, 252, 258; *Actes of the Englyshe Votaryes*, 92, 121, 235, 241; allegory: use of, 115–16; *Answere to a papystycall exhortacyon*, 130; *Apology against a ranke Papyst*, 96, 129–30; biography: centrality of, 90, 92, 106, 120–21, 124, 128; bishop of Ossory, 91; Carmelites: relation to, 90, 92, 94, 235; categorizing: difficulty of, 90–92, 219; celibacy: attack on, 95–97, 243; debate: importance of, 103, 111–12, 130–31; *Declaration of Edmonde Bonners articles*, 243; *Dialoge or Communycacyon*, 130–31, 179, 215; dramatic works: 90, 95, 96–97, 101–22, "compiled" vs. written, 108–9, 117–18, 119, 126, 240–41, fear of drama in, 101–2, 109–11, 117–18, 131, formulaic structure, 101, 106–7, 116, 128–29, influence of examination, 107–8, 114, influence of morality plays, 104, 111–12, 118, 239, influence of mystery plays, 101, 104, 109, 111, 112–14, tragedy vs. comedy, 108–9, 239, Vices in, 97–98, 102–10, 116–20, 129, 237, 238, 239, 241, Virtues in, 102–3, 106–10, 113, 120, 122, 129; elect nation: England as, 94–95, 236; examination: prelatical, 123–24, 128–29, 241; exile, 90–92, 115, 130; *Expostulation or complaynte*, 130; Foxe, John: relation to, 12, 58, 67, 94, 124–28, 180, 231, 236, 238, 241, 243; friars: relation to, 94, 95–97, 235–36; Geneva: view of, 91, 235; *God's Promises*, 122; hagiographer, 58–59, 67, 90, 117–18, 123–24, 235, 240; historian, 92–93, 101, 106–7, 114–16, 119–20, 121, 142, 235; iconoclasm, 97, 102–3, 104–5, 119–20; *Image of bothe churches*, 93, 249–50; imagination: cloistered, 95–99, 103, 109, 118, 131; infantilism: of orthodoxy, 96–99, 130–31, 243; *Johan Baptystes preachynge*, 112–14, 122; *King Johan*, 94, 114–22, 129, 131, 242; *Laboryouse Journey and serche of John Leylande*, 238; language: biblical, 99–100, 129, 237, caustic, 99–100, orthodox abuse of, 97–99, 103–4, 117, 129, plain style, 98–100, 238, prophetic, 99–100, 249–50; life of, 90–92; Lollardy: relation to, 93–94, 95–96, 100, 105, 108, 118, 120, 235, 238, 244; Milton, John: links to, 114, 214, 216, 261; *Mysterye of Inyquyte*, 98, 130; *Pageant of Popes*, 235, 236; pamphleteer, 128–31, 132, 170; persecution: centrality of, 93; play: demonic vs. holy, 108–11, 118–19, 121–22, 129–30, 131, 237, 243, game or jest (vs. earnest), 97–99, 101, 116–19; preaching: importance of, 112; Puritanism: relation to, 12, 91, 94; repression: dangers of, 94–99; scripture: centrality of, 114, 122, 130, and history, 115–16; *Temptacyon of our lorde*, 112, 114, 122, 130; *Thre lawes*, 101–12, 113, 123, 214; *True hystorie of the Christen departynge*, 90; Tyndale, William: relation to, 12, 58, 96, 126, 219, 235, 237, 240, 241, 242, 258; unity of his

thought, 92–101; *Vocacyon of Iohan Bale*, 243; vocation or calling, 112–14, 124; vows: attack on, 95–97, 115, 130; *Yet a course*, 128–29

Barish, Jonas, 9–10, 50, 218, 219, 239, 246, 247, 251, 260
Baxter, Margery, 43–44, 45, 61–62, 230
Baxter, Richard, 134, 243
Beza, Theodore, 133, 238, 239; *Abrahams Sacrifice*, 238, 239
Bible, Wycliffite translation of, 29–31, 39–40. *See also* Scripture
Biography, centrality in nonconformity, 16, 21, 34–35, 58, 62–64, 65–67, 67, 90, 92, 106, 117–18, 120–21, 124, 128, 156–57, 169, 174, 180–81, 182, 215–16, 231, 243, 249, 254. *See also* Hagiography
Bishops: as Caiaphases, 57–58, 59–61, 123–24, 181; Lollards: relations with, 15–16, 46–47, 57–58; Marprelate, Martin: enemy of, 173, 174, 177–78, 180–83, 190–95, 202, 206–7
Blatt, Thora Balslev, 170
Bonner, Edmund (bishop of London), 128–29, 140, 168, 243
Book of Common Prayer, Edwardian, 91
Bridges, John (dean of Sarum), 176–77, 178, 192–93, 257, 258
Browne, Robert, 151–52
Brute, Walter, 227
Bunyan, John, 73, 214; *Pilgrim's Progress*, 25, 261
Burghley. *See* Cecil, Sir William

Calvin, John, 91, 133, 138, 176
Carew, Thomas, 255
Carlson, Leland H., 244, 252, 253, 256, 258
Cartwright, Thomas, 12–13, 68; Admonition controversy, 137–41, 153–54, 157, 245, as drama, 140–

41, 157–72; Anglicanism: assault on, 143–47, 151, 155, 156; argumentation: logical vs. metaphoric, 140–42, 159–72, 175; *Briefe Apologie*, 136–37; *Commentary upon Colossians*, 133, 135; *Confutation of the Rhemists Translation*, 152–53, 165, 170–71, 248; displaced drama, 140–41, 157–71; *Ecclesiasticae Disciplinae*, 134, 245; ecclesiology, 137–38, 159–60, 246, 258–59; epistemology, 140–41, 150, 152–53, 159, 160–61, 165; examination: prelatical, 152–54, 159, 164, 248; exile, 136, 138–39; habitual or traditional: distrust of, 142–47, 155, 156–57; history, 142, 143; holy days, 144, 247; imagery: biblical, 164, industrial, 157–58, 249, medicinal, 134, mercantile, 133, 148–49, pastoral, 148–50, sportive vs. combative, 135, 245; imagination: dangers of, 155–56, 170–71, sanctified, 155–57; industry vs. idleness, 147–50, 248; inspiration, 150, 160–61, 165, limits of, 152–54, in preaching, 250; introspection: fear of, 158–59, 249; language: biblical, 160–64, 250, plain style, 166, prophetic, 159–64, rational vs. affective, 159–72, 199; logic: appeals to, 166–67, 170–71, 250, vs. rhetoric, 166–72, 251; Lollardy: relation to, 150, 247, 248, 249–50, 250, 251; Marprelate, Martin: relation to, 169, 170, 172, 174–76, 179, 187, 188, 189, 191–92, 195–96, 198, 199–202, 245, 258, 258–59, 260; metaphor, 154, 159–62, 164, 166; minister: ideal, 134, 147, 179; ministry in Low Countries, 133, 147, 151, at Warwick hospital, 136; persecution: benefits of, 135–36, 143;

polemic as ritual, 140–41; preaching, 133–34, 144–46, 250, as scripture, 163–64, 250, sermons vs. homilies, 146–47; prophecy: limitations of, 154; religious affections, 140, 151; *Replye to an answere*, 134, 138, 141, 170; reputation, 133–41, 245, 246; *Rest of the Second Replie*, 139, 166, 170; Roman church: hostility toward, 143, 148, 151–53, 161, 164, 171; scripture: centrality of, 146, 149, 158, 165–66; *Second Replie*, 137, 139; Separatism: relation to, 134, 147, 151–52, 153–57, 244–45, 248–49; set prayer, 247; simile, 159, 161–62, 165; sin: obstinacy of, 142–46, 155–56; struggle: ethos of, 135, 144–46, 150, 155, 158–59, 160–61, 169, 246; syllogism, 167–68, 171–72; "unsettledness," 145–46, 155; vocation, 153–54; Whitgift, John: rivalry with, 137–39; zeal: dangers of, 151–57, 248

Castle of Perseverance, 38

Cecil, Sir William, Lord Burghley, 134, 175, 245

Chaderton, William (bishop of Chester), 190

Chaucer, Geoffrey, 14, 26, 31, 70, 76, 81, 232

Christian warfare: Bale, John: importance to, 100, 111, 112, 130; Lollardy: centrality in, 19–20, 28–29, 41–49, ritual of self-definition in, 42–43, 56, 68, 73, 74, 80, 84–85; Puritanism: centrality in, 135, 145–46, 246, 248

Clanvowe, Sir John, 14, 34–35, 220

Clarke, Samuel, 133

Clebsch, William A., 219

Codrington, Robert, 173

Collinson, Patrick, 3–4, 5–6, 151, 247

"Compiling" vs. writing, 108–9, 117–18, 119, 126, 240–41

Coolidge, John S., 176, 179, 194, 246

Cooper, Thomas (bishop of Winchester), 174, 177, 181, 198, 201, 206, 254; *Admonition*, 176, 198, 201, 206

Cotton, John, 151

Courtenay, William (archbishop of Canterbury), 15

Cromwell, Oliver, 231

Cromwell, Thomas, 90, 101, 122, 131, 234, 238

d'Angoulême, Marguerite (queen of Navarre), 107

"Dark corners," 97, 105, 158

Davidson, Clifford, 228

Davies, Horton, 247

Davies, W. T., 112

Debate: in Lollardy, 30, 44–49, 67, 72–73, 77, 80, 169, 226; in nonconformity, 12, 26, 103, 111, 112, 130–31, 169, 208–9, 219; in Puritanism, 138–39, 140, 141–42, 173–74, 211, 214

De Blasphema, Contra Fratres, 46–47

Devereux, Robert, second earl of Essex, 173

Dialogue, 8, 59–60, 63–64, 67, 126, 128–31, 132, 177–80, 187, 189, 208, 226, 242, 244. *See also* Debate; Satiric dialogue

Dickens, A. G., 234, 238, 242

Displaced drama, 56, 58–59, 61, 64–67, 73, 74, 83, 87–89, 114, 123–31, 140–41, 157–71, 175, 176–83, 198, 214–16, 219, 244

Drama: competition with pulpit, 50–51, 179, 218–19, 227; emotional identification in, 51, 110–11, 239; impersonation in, 65, 176, 230; liturgical influences, 50–51, 111, 227; Lollard attitudes toward, 16, 29, 75, 89, 227; nonconformist ambivalence toward, 8, 50, 62, 118; Puritan attack on, 6–10, 239; transvestism in, 104, 238; Tudor dissenters: practice among, 90, 95, 96–97, 101–22; verisimilitude: dangers of, 109–11, 115–16, 228, 239. *See also* Displaced drama; Dramatic satire

Dramatic satire, 8, 67, 71, 71–89, 73, 132–33, 176–87, 253. *See also* Satiric dialogue

Dream vision, medieval, 76–77, 88, 148

Dudley, Robert, earl of Leicester, 154

Edward VII, 91

Elect nation, England as, 94–95, 236

Elizabeth I, 90–91, 107, 132, 173, 191, 242

Episcopacy, defense of, 137–41, 157, 176–77, 191. *See also* Anglicanism; Whitgift, John

Eucharist, 25–26, 242, 243; displacement of among Lollards, 16–23, 31–33, 48–49, 50–51, 55–56, 63–64; drama: relation to, 50–52, 54; examination: replaced by, 46–49, 125–27, 209; lay participation, 50–51; Lollard views on, 21–22, 32, 37, 46, 221, 225; priest's role in, 21, 222; Wyclif's views on, 15

Examination, prelatical, 8, 16, 46–49, 56–58, 58–67, 84, 107–8, 114, 123–28, 128–29, 136, 159, 180–83, 221, 226, 241, 242, 243, 245, 246, 254; affinities to tyrant play, 57, 58–59, 59–61, 78–79, 81, 123–24, 181, 241, 254; apposing and answering, 60, 67, 71–73, 84, 152, 226; inspiration experienced in, 60–61, 125–26, 152–54, 164, 229;

sacramental rite, 46–49, 55–58, 125–27, 152, 169, 180, 182, 229, 242–43, 254; theatricality of, 57–58, 125–28, 229, 243, 248; training of examinates, 46–47, 56, 125–26, 153–54

Fairfield, Leslie P., 238, 242
Field, John, 137–38, 182, 252
Foxe, John, 5, 11, 12, 58, 67, 94, 124–28, 135, 180–81, 202, 219, 228–29, 235–36, 239, 242–43; *Acts and Monuments*, 124–28; Bale, John: relation to, 12, 58, 67, 94, 124–25, 126, 231, 235, 236, 238, 241, 243; *Christus Triumphans*, 241; examination as sacrament, 125–27, 242–43, 254, as theater, 125–28, 243; historian, 11, 124–25, 219, 228–29. *See also* Hagiography
Franciscans, Spiritual, 43, 225–26
Fraser, Russell, 9–10, 50, 219
Friar Daw's Reply, 85–87
Friars, 191, 232; Bale, John: relation to, 94, 95–97, 235–36; Lollardy: antipathy toward, 30–31, 36, 40, 69–70, 72–80, 84–87, 227, need for, 42–44, 50, 73, 225–26; Puritanism: relation to, 191, 235–36
"Friar's Answer," 44, 71–73. *See also* "Layman's Complaint"

Gardiner, Harold C., 239
Gardiner, Stephen (bishop of Winchester), 126, 127
George, Charles H. and Katherine, 217
Gilby, Anthony, 132, 162–63, 176, 179, 187–88, 197, 237, 249; *Answer to the deuillish detection*, 162–63, 244; *Pleasaunt Dialogue*, 132, 179, 187–88
Gosson, Stephen, 7

Grace, 20, 24, 33, 47–49, 60–61, 93–94, 113–14, 144, 155, 156, 197, 257
Gratwick, Stephen, 243
Greenblatt, Stephen, 7, 218–19, 221, 225, 228, 229, 230–31, 236, 242, 249, 250
Gregory, Pope, 93, 94
Grete Sentence of Curs Expouned, 38, 227
Grindal, Edmund (archbishop of Canterbury), 137

Hagiography, 26, 58, 65–67, 67–68, 118–19, 123–28, 134, 169, 180–81, 204, 231, 240, 241
Haller, William, 236
Harrison, Robert, 151–52
Heiserman, A. R., 233, 233–34
Henry VII, 90
Henry VIII, 90, 106, 116, 121, 202, 229
Herbert, George, 134
Hereford, Nicholas, 57
Herford, Charles H., 243
Heyworth, P. L., 83
Hildersham, Arthur, 149
Hill, Christopher, 10–11, 150, 238
Hoccleve, Thomas, 18, 43
Hodgkins, John, 206
Holi prophete Dauid seith, 16–17, 31–32
Hooker, Richard, 141–42
Hudson, Anne, 7, 12, 15–16, 56, 220, 226, 227
Huizinga, Johan, 255

Iconoclasm, of nonconformity, 50, 61–62, 76–77, 79, 97, 102, 119, 143, 225, 230, 247, 260
Illiteracy, problem of, 18–19, 20, 23, 231–32
Imagination: fear of, 8, 27–29, 31, 40, 53–55, 64, 75, 85, 87–89, 95–

97, 103, 109, 117–18, 127, 131, 155–56, 170–71, 186–87, 213, 216; sanctified, 33–34, 36, 60–61, 65–67, 155–57, 197–98
Innocent III, Pope, 68, 114
Inspiration, 164, 250; in epistemology of Lollardy, 31–36, 61, 86, of Puritanism, 140–41, 150, 152–53, 160–61, 165, 197–98, 214–15; examinate's experience of, 47–48, 60–61, 112, 126, 152–53, 181

Jack Upland, 69–71, 83–89, 140, 162, 169–71, 179, 187, 193, 258
Jack Upland's Rejoinder, 87
Jones, W. R., 225
Jonson, Ben, 213, 239, 253, 260–61

Kaufmann, U. Milo, 240
King, John N., 3, 238, 241, 242
Kirby, Thomas, 91
Kirchmayer, Thomas, 240
Knapp, Peggy Ann, 41
Knott, John R., Jr., 222, 236, 246, 260
Kolve, V. A., 54, 260

Lake, Peter, 4
Langland, William, 70, 73
Language: affective, 159–64, 168; biblical, 160–64, 185, 237; caustic or satiric, 71, 78, 84–85, 99–100, 162, 169, 187–88, 237, 252; colloquial, 175–76, 185, 205; obsessive, 239; orthodox abuse of, 60, 97–99, 103–4, 117, 129, 161, 191–94, 232, 256; plain style, 41, 86–87, 98–100, 166, 179, 184–85, 233–34, 238; prophetic, 86–87, 99, 129, 162–64, 187–88, 205, 233–34, 249–50; rational, 159, 164–68
Lanham, Richard A., 9–10
Lanterne of Li3t, 25, 75, 162

Lascells, John, 242
Latimer, Hugh (bishop of Worcester), 126, 239
Laughter: Lollard views of, 78, 188, 233; Puritan views of, 176, 179, 188–89, 198, 255
"Layman's Complaint," 44, 71–74. *See also* "Friar's Answer"
Lay piety, 50–51
Leff, Gordon, 35, 225–26
Legenda Aurea, 25
Leverenz, David, 8, 10, 235, 237, 238, 239, 243, 250
Lewalski, Barbara K., 3, 217, 241–42
Leyland, John, 238
Logic: Lollard appeals to, 86–87, 169–70; Puritan appeals to, 112, 185–86, 196–98, 250, 255; vs. rhetoric, 166–72, 196–99, 251, 257
Lollardy, 5, 11–12; allegory: embryonic or nascent, 38–41, 80, 127, 240; anti-intellectualism, 26, 70, 168, 220; biography, 16, 21, 34–35, 58, 62–64, 65–67, 67; Christian warfare, 41–49, as ritual of self-definition, 42–49, 56, 68, 73, 74, 80, 84–85; churches: attitude toward, 22–23, 35, 223, 224; confession: views on, 222, 223; conventicles, 15, 22–23, 223; debate: fondness for, 26, 30, 44, 67, 72–73, 77, 80, 81–82, natural mode of discourse, 44–49, 226; difficulty of identifying, 13–16; displaced drama, 56, 58–59, 61, 64–67, 73, 74, 83, 87–89; drama: attitude toward, 16, 29, 52–55, 73, 75, 89, 227; election: lack of assurance of, 26, 35, 68; epistemology, 20, 23–25, 31–33, 36–37, 46–49, 55, 56, 60–61, 70, 229; Eucharist: attitudes toward, 17, 21–22, 32, 37, 46, 50–51, 221, 222, 225; examination, 8,

16, 78–79, 81, 221, 226, 229, affinities to tyrant plays, 57–59, 59–61, 81, 84, central rite of, 46–49, 56–58, 58–67; friars: antipathy toward, 20, 30–31, 36, 40, 53, 69–70, 72–80, 84–87, 227, 232, need for, 42–44, 50, 73, 225–26; grounding, 24, 27–28, 34, 42, 77, 87, 217, 250; hagiography, 26, 58, 65–67, 231; iconoclasm, 61–62, 76–77, 79, 225, 230, 247; iconography, 41, 61–62, 230; illiteracy, 18–19, 20, 23, 231–32; imagination: dangers of, 27–29, 31, 40, 53–55, 60, 64, 75, 85, 87–89; inspiration, 31–36, 47–48, 60–61, 70, 86, 229, 250; knights: appeal to, 34–35, 39; "known men," 16, 58, 221; language: caustic or satiric, 71, 78, plain vs. prophetic, 86–87, 233–34, 249; laughter, 78, 188, 233; learning, 23–25, 26, 28, 31, 43, 232; logic: appeals to, 86–87; "love-drede," 26–27, 55, 145–46, 223; martyrdom, 14, 220; mediation: loss of, 21–23; metaphor: distrust of, 37–38, 40–41, 62, 225; miracles, 23, 26, 31, 48–49, 65, 223, 227; music: attitude toward, 28–29, 78, 223–24, 232; persecution: thirst for, 42–44, 57, 81; pilgrimage: attitude toward, 24–25, 41, 49, 65–66, 73–80, 82, 232; play vs. earnest, 54, 65, 85; polemic: conventionality of, 20–21, 83; preaching, 45, 50–51, preferred to sacraments, 63–64, as scripture, 250; priesthood: of all believers, 27, 34; devaluation of, 21, 51–52, 222, 225; prophetic stance, 31–36, 70–71, 224; Puritanism: links to, 11, 12, 20, 21, 26, 34, 67, 68, 148, 150, 162, 168, 169–72, 185–86, 187–88, 191, 201–2, 208, 215, 247, 248, 250, 251; sacramental worship, 48–49, 55–56, 62; satiric dialogue, 67–68, 71–89; saving remnant, 33, 34; scripture: *autopistos*, 222, centrality of, 17–23, 23–24, 28–29, 43, 55–56, 72, 221, 224, interpretation of, 29–31, 31–33, 226, levels of meaning, 29–31, preferred to drama, 54–55, ritual dimension, 32–33, 55–56, symbolic language of, 39–40; simile vs. metaphor, 37–38, 230; symbolism, 36–41, 77, 79, 225, 230; wills, 22, 222; wonder: attitude toward, 26–28, 33–34, 55, 76–77; Wyclif: relation to, 11–12, 14–15, 19, 27, 35, 37, 220

Luke Shepherd, 244

Luther, Martin, 90, 96, 219, 229

Lyly, John, 198–99, 258

McFarlane, K. B., 58, 225–26, 232

McGinn, Donald J., 139–41, 169, 257, 258, 260

Marian exile, 91, 132, 234

Marprelate, Martin, 12–13, 67, 71, 99–100, 132–33, 137, 139, 141, 213–14; audience, 171, 177–78, 200, 252; authorship, 174, 206, 252, 256, 257, 258, 259, 260; bishops: attack on, 173, 174, 177–78, 180–83, 190–95, 202, 206–7, 209–11; Cartwright, Thomas: relation to, 169, 170, 172, 174–76, 179, 187, 188, 189, 195–96, 198, 199–202, 245, 258, 258–59, 260; dialogue, 177–80, 187, 189, 196; *Epistle*, 197–98, 199, 204; *Epitome*, 185, 199, 204, 206; examination, 180–83, 254; friars, 191; game vs. earnest, 182, 187, 189–99, 199–212; hagiography, 180–81; *Hay Any Worke*, 190, 194–95, 201, 202, 205–6, 209,

255; high seriousness, 194–99, 205, 212; history, 174, 180–82; identity, 186, 203–12; *Just Censure and Reproofe*, 181, 191, 196–97, 206–9; language: biblical, 185, colloquial, 176, 185, 205, instability of, 194–95, 196, legal, 196, 257, orthodox abuse of, 191–94, 256, plain style, 99–100, 179, 184–85, 208, prophetic, 187–88, 205; laughter, 176, 179, 188–89, 198, 255; literary ancestry, 178, 179–83, 184–89, 192, 196, 201–2, 208, 233; logic: appeals to, 185–86, 196–98, 208, 257; Martin Junior, 202–3, 206–9, 215, 259; Martin Senior, 181, 184–85, 191, 206–9, 215, 259; martyrdom, 202, 207, 209–12, 260; *Minerall and Metaphysicall Schoolpoints*, 204–5; *More Worke for the Cooper*, 206, 255; origins of controversy, 172–76; persona, 183–87; popular attacks on, 198–99, 252, 257–58; *Protestatyon*, 203, 209–12; Puritans: conflict with, 184, 190, 199–203, 207, 255; satire: apology for, 187–99, 205–11, 252, techniques of, 176–83; syllogism, 177–78, 185, 196–98, 257, 259; theatricality, 175–83, 195, 196, 210–12; *Theses Martinanae*, 181, 202, 206–9; Tyndale, William: relation to, 202–3; vocation, 189–91, 203–12
Martyrdom, 120–21, 124–25, 242; among Lollards, 14, 58, 220, 228–29; among Puritans, 134, 135–36, 202, 207, 209–12
Mary I, 91, 122
Meditation, 32, 240, 250; linguistic *compositio* in, 163–64, 201–2
Metaphor, attitudes toward: among Lollards, 37–38, 40–41, 62, 225; among Puritans, 127, 159–62, 164, 166, 185, 250
Miller, Perry, 6
Milton, John, 22, 23, 43, 149–50, 171, 189, 211, 212, 236, 247, 255; Bale, John: links to, 114, 214–16, 261; *Comus*, 214; *Paradise Lost*, 216, 261; *Paradise Regained*, 216; *Samson Agonistes*, 216
Miracles: nonconformist attitudes toward, 23, 26, 48–49, 64, 112, 124, 223, 227, 247; orthodox fondness for, 25
Miracles of the Host, 25–26
Moone, Hawisa, 23, 222
Morality plays, 104, 111–12, 118, 239; Vices in, 97–98, 102–10, 116–20, 129, 237, 238, 239, 241
Morgan, Irvonwy, 235–36
M. Some laid open in his coulers, 254, 257
Mueller, Janel, 3, 217, 224, 249
Mystery plays, 51–55, 101, 104, 109, 111, 112–14, 131, 227, 228, 239; as analogue to Eucharist, 51–52; heroes of, 52; image of holy life, 51–52; Lollard assault on, 52–55, 73. *See also* Examination, prelatical

Nashe, Thomas, 186, 198–99, 203, 258
New, John F. H., 3–4, 257
Nicene Council, 152–53
Nonconformity: artistic community among, 132–33; belletristic vs. nonbelletristic, 169–72; debate: importance of, 12, 26, 30, 103, 111, 112, 130–31, 208–9, 219; drama: ambivalence toward, 7–8, 50, 62, 89, 100–101, 127, 131, 132, 179–80, 214–16; hagiography, 67–68, 90–91, 101, 169, 231; nomen-

clature, 5–6; scripture: centrality of, 16–23, 250; self-definition, 6, 43, 68, 92–93, 175, 191, 218–19, 225, 230–31, 231; self-dramatization, 8–9, 204; stage: opposition to, 6–9, 101–2; struggle: ethos of, 19–20, 28, 46, 100, 134–35, 146, 150, 246; theatricality, 8, 16, 50, 100–101, 140–41, 179–80, 204, 214; tradition: attack on, 100, 247. *See also* Bale, John; Cartwright, Thomas; Lollardy; Marprelate, Martin; Puritanism

Norbrook, David, 240, 241, 244

Northbrooke, John, 6–7, 179

Oldcastle, Sir John, 15, 90, 100, 123–24, 180, 242, 248

Olsen, V. Norskov, 236

Ong, Walter J., 251

"On the Council of London," 57

"On the Minorites," 53, 69

Owst, G. R., 20, 227, 244

Pamphlet, disputational, 23, 128–31, 132–33, 137–38, 170, 178, 187–90, 243, 245

Pantin, W. A., 220, 232

Parte of a register, 132, 182–83, 244, 248, 253, 254. See also *Seconde Parte of a Register*

Pecock, Reginald (bishop of Chichester), 16

Penry, John, 167, 181, 196, 250–51, 254, 257, 260

Perkins, William, 113, 133, 171, 240, 244

Persecution: Bale, John: centrality for, 93; Cartwright, Thomas: ambivalence toward, 135–36; Lollard thirst for, 42–44, 57, 81; Puritan views on, 135–37, 150

Phillips, John, 225

Philpot, John, 243

Pierce the Ploughman's Crede, 25, 69–70, 73–80, 87–88, 111, 148, 170, 208

Pilgrimage, 24–25, 41, 49, 65–66, 73–80, 82, 232, 261

Plato, 9, 50, 219, 224, 238, 251

Play: demonic vs. holy, 108–11, 118–19, 121–22, 127–28, 129–30, 131, 168–69, 218–19, 237, 243; game or jest (vs. earnest), 54, 65, 73, 85, 97–99, 101, 116–19, 149–50, 164, 187, 189–99, 199–212, 213, 248, 251, 255, 256

Plowman's Tale, 70, 80–83, 232

Post-figuration, 241

Preaching: among Lollards, 45, 50–51; among Puritans, 133–34, 190, 244, 256; as scripture, 163–64, 250, 256

Presbyterianism, 133, 134, 137, 147, 159–60, 182, 259. *See also* Cartwright, Thomas; Puritanism

Prophet, Old Testament: Lollard imitation of, 34, 70–71, 224; Puritan imitation of, 187–88, 205

Protestantism, 151, 152, 163, 225, 226, 242; consensus among, 3–5, 217; devotion to scripture, 3, 222; poetics, 3–5. *See also* Anglicanism; Puritanism

Prynne, William, 6–7, 8, 247, 251

Puritanism, 9–10, 21, 50, 185–86, 219; argumentation: logical vs. metaphoric, 159–72; Arminianism vs. antinomianism, 231; artistic community among, 132; among critics, 9–10; debate, 138–39, 140, 141–42, 211, 214; dialogue, 132–33, 157; discipline, 137–38, 246, 249; displaced drama, 140–41,

157–71; ecclesiology, 137–38, 159–60, 249, 258–59; election, 4, 26, 128, 140; epistemology, 140–41, 150, 152–53, 159, 160–61, 165, 198, 214–15; examination, 136, 152–54, 164, 245–46, 248; friars: relation to, 191, 235–36; garden: industry in, 148–50; industry vs. idleness, 147–59, 248; introspection: fear of, 158–59, 249; language of, 159–72, biblical, 160–64, prophetic, 162–64, 205; logic vs. rhetoric, 166–72, 196–99, 251, 255, 257; Lollardy: links to, 11, 20, 21, 26, 34, 50, 67, 68, 127, 145–46, 148, 150, 152, 162, 168, 169–72, 185–86, 187–88, 191, 201–2, 208, 215, 247, 248, 250, 251; martyrdom, 135, 153–54, 202, 207, 209–12; meditation, 163–64, 201–2, 240, 250; metaphor, 154, 159–62, 164, 166, 250; pamphlet drama, 128–31, 132–33, 137–38, 170, 178, 245; persecution: benefits of, 135–36, 150, 154; polemic as ritual, 140–41; preaching, 133–34, 144–46, 244, 250, 256; religious affections, 134, 140, 141, 151, 159–66, 248; satire, 132–33; scripture: centrality of, 137–38, 146, 149, 158, 246, 256; sin: obstinacy of, 142–46, 155–56; stage: opposition to, 6–10, 239; struggle: ethos of, 135, 145–46, 150, 155, 158–59, 160–61, 169, 186, 246, 248; syllogism, 167–68, 171–72, 250–51, 257, 259; terminology, 3–6; theatricality, 7–9, 132–33, 140–41, 164, 168, 179, 219; "Troubles at Frankfort," 91; "Unsettledness," 145–46, 155, 247; vs. Anglicanism, 3–6, 217, 218, on argumentative method, 139–42, 157–65, 169, on ecclesiology, 137–38, 147, 157, 159–60, on scripture,

137–38, 146, 162–64, 246, 257; vocation, 153–54, 189–91, 203–12, 240. *See also* Cartwright, Thomas; Marprelate, Martin
Purvey, John, 201

Ramus, Peter, 171–72, 251
Repingdon, Philip, 57–58, 201, 229
Ridley, Nicholas (bishop of Rochester and London), 125–26, 239
Ringler, William, 7
Rogers, John, 127
Romance of the Rose, 88
Ross, Malcolm MacKenzie, 225
Roston, Murray, 239, 241
Rothkrug, Lionel, 222–23

Saints' lives. *See* Biography; Hagiography
Sasek, Lawrence A., 6
Satire: justification of, 71, 187–99; Lollardy: appeal to, 67–71, practice of, 72–89; Puritanism: appeal to, 132–33
Satiric dialogue, 172, 189; Lollard use of, 67–68, 71–89, 172. *See also* Dialogue; Dramatic satire; Satire
Sawles Warde, 38
Scripturalism, 19, 217, 249
Scripture: accessibility, 20, 146; Anglicans vs. Puritans on, 137–38, 146, 162–64, 246; *Autopistos*, 222; centrality: for Bale, 114, 122, 130, 131, among Lollards, 16–23, 23–24, 28–29, 55–56, 72, 221, 224, among Puritans, 137–38, 149, 158 240; consistency, 19; history: relationship to, 115–16; interpretation 29–31, 31–33, 226; levels of meaning, 29–31; linguistic *compositio*, 163–64, 201–2; orthodox fear of, 18; preaching as, 163–64, 250, 25(ritual dimension, 32–33, 55–56;

sufficiency, 19–20; symbolic language in, 39–40
Second Admonition to the Parliament, 138
Seconde Parte of a Register, 132, 182–83, 247, 249, 252, 254, 255, 256. See also *Parte of a Register*
Seneca, 244
Separatism, 134, 147, 151–52, 153–57, 244–45, 248, 260
Shakespeare, William, 213, 260
Sibbes, Richard, 151, 236
Siemon, James R., 230, 260
Simile, 127, 159, 161–62, 165, 230, 250; Lollard preference for, 37–38; Puritan preference for, 172. *See also* Metaphor
Simms, Valentine, 206
Sixteen Points, 47–48
Smalley, Beryl, 221, 230, 238
Spenser, Edmund, 213, 260–61
State of the Church of England, or *Diotrephes*, 244, 253
Stokesley, John (bishop of London), 102
Stubbe, Anne, 134, 151, 155–56, 244–45, 248
Stubbes, Phillip, 7
Sutcliffe, Matthew, 175
Swinderby, William, 14, 220
Syllogism, 167–68, 171–72, 177–78, 185, 196–98, 250–51, 251, 257, 259. *See also* Logic
Sylvester I, Pope, 68
Symbolism, 119, 122, 143; Lollard attitudes toward, 36–41, 77, 79, 225

Talus, Omar, 172
Tentler, Thomas N., 226
Thompson, Elbert N. S., 6
Thomson, John A. F., 56
Thoresby, John (archbishop of York), 20

Thorpe, William, 47, 58–67, 71, 73, 75, 77, 113, 120, 123–24, 126, 141, 152, 180, 182, 229–31, 248
Throckmorton, Job, 136, 244, 252, 253, 256, 258, 259; *Defence of Iob Throckmorton*, 259; *Dialogue Wherin is Plainly Laide Open*, 253
Tolwyn, William, 128–29
Tomlyn, Arthur, 206
Travers, Walter, 245
Tretise of Miraclis Pleyinge, 6–7, 16, 50, 53–54, 63, 221, 227
Turner, William, 132, 166–69, 176, 178, 179–80, 187–89, 193, 194, 196, 208, 215, 243, 253, 257, 259; *Examination of the masse*, 180, 259; *Huntyng of the Romishe fox*, 178; *Rescuynge of the Romishe Fox*, 167; *Romyshe Vuolfe*, 188–89, 244, 259
Tyndale, William, 12, 58, 96, 126, 202–3, 218–19, 219, 231, 235, 237, 240, 241, 242, 250, 258; *Answer to Sir Thomas More's Dialogue*, 231, 235; *Pathway into Holy Scripture*, 242; *Practice of Prelates*, 203, 235

Udall, John, 244, 253

Vestiarian controversy, 245
Vocation, or calling, 28–29, 63, 112–14, 124, 189–91, 203–12, 240

Wakefield, Gordon Stevens, 177, 241
Waldegrave, Robert, 205
Walsingham, Sir Francis, 154
Walzer, Michael, 11, 247
Whiche ben trew myraclis & whiche ben false, 48
White, William, 183
Whitgift, John (archbishop of Canterbury), 133, 137–42, 143, 144, 153, 157, 158–70, 246, 252, 256; *Answere to a certen Libel*, 138; *De-*

fense of the Aunswere, 138, 157;
Marprelate, Martin: attacked by,
174–75, 177, 178, 181–82, 188, 194,
199, 205–6, 254
Wigginton, Giles, 252, 256
Wilcox, Thomas, 137–38
Wilks, Michael, 224
Williams, C. H., 235
Wilson, J. Dover, 176
Wilson, John, 183, 254
Wood, William, 243
Wyclif, John, 11, 14–15, 79, 92, 95,
201, 219, 235; diplomatic career,
15; Eucharist: views on, 15, 37; ex-
treme realism: consequences, 37,
238; friars: relations with, 42–43;
Lollardy: relation to, 11–12, 14–15,
220, 224; scripture: views on, 19,
221; visible vs. real church, 35,
224

Young, John (bishop of Rochester),
256
Young, Karl, 227
Yunck, John A., 20, 67